CABAL!

ALSO BY MARK EDWARD LENDER

Citizen Soldier: The Revolutionary War Journal of Joseph Bloomfield, 2nd ed., with James Kirby Martin

Fatal Sunday: George Washington, the Monmouth Campaign, and the Politics of Battle, with Garry Wheeler Stone

The War for American Independence

"A Respectable Army": The Military Origins of the Republic, 1763-1783, 3rd ed., with James Kirby Martin

"This Honorable Court": The United States District Court for the District of New Jersey, 1789-2000

McCarter & English: A Sesquicentennial History, with Paul A. Stellhorn and Charles Cummings

Middlesex Water Company: A Business History

One State in Arms: A Short Military History of New Jersey

Dictionary of American Temperance Biography: From Temperance Reform to Alcohol Research, the 1600s to the 1980s

Drinking in America: A History, 2nd ed., with James Kirby Martin

CABAL!

THE PLOT AGAINST GENERAL WASHINGTON

MARK EDWARD LENDER

WESTHOLME
Yardley

Westholme Publishing, LLC
904 Edgewood Road
Yardley, Pennsylvania 19067
Visit our Web site at www.westholmepublishing.com

ISBN: 978-1-59416-326-5
Also available as an eBook

Printed in the United States of America.

~For the five guys~

Jace, Kai, Ryder, Von & Nick

CONTENTS

PREFACE

LATE MAY 1778 found General George Washington at his Valley Forge headquarters, the brutal winter behind him and his battered Continental regiments healing. He was cautiously watching for the rumored British withdrawal from Philadelphia, and he had the luxury of some precious spare minutes to write an old friend. This was Landon Carter of Richmond County, Virginia, a man Washington had known for decades and with whom he had occasionally exchanged correspondence since the early days of the war. Carter was a man of substance: a wealthy and extensive planter, a major force in Virginia politics and society, a prolific author, and a steadfast supporter of American independence.[1] The planter and the general stood at the apex of Virginia society and they shared a long-standing friendship; thus Washington trusted Carter as a peer and confidant. The rebel commander's missive of May 30 reflected as much. Washington had not received a note from Carter since the previous March, and his reply was a lengthy "catch-up" letter, full of candid news of the war, families, personalities, and politics. Part of what the patriot general wrote was painful: "To paint the distresses, & perilous situation of this army in the course of last Winter for want of Cloaths, Provisions, and almost every other necessary, essential to the well being (I may say existence) of an Army, would require more time, and an abler pen than mine," he assured Carter. "Providence," the general observed, certainly had a hand in seeing the rebel army through the Valley Forge ordeal.[2] These were not the sort of things one would write to a casual acquaintance.

And there was something else in the letter, something the general clearly found unsettling but felt he could share with an intimate friend. Washington turned to a matter of which he knew Carter had heard, a matter that had troubled his friend. It concerned a rumored "disposition in the Northern Officers to see me superceeded in my Command." While Washington assured Carter he remained secure in his command and that he retained the loyalty of the officer corps, he left no question of his conviction that a plot had existed to remove or discredit him. "That there was a scheme of this sort on foot last fall admits of no doubt," he wrote. Washington named no names, but he clearly saw Major General Horatio Gates, the victor at Saratoga in 1777, and Major Generals Thomas Mifflin and Thomas Conway at the heart of a wider intrigue against him. His contempt for all three men was palpable. But he assured his fellow Virginian that all was well, at least for the time being. When their supposed conspiracy came to light, the plotters "slunk back—disavowed the measure, & professed themselves my warmest admirers. thus stands the matter at present."[3] He told Carter that as far as he knew he still enjoyed the confidence of Congress, but the implication of the letter was that the matter was not entirely settled.

Washington's letter to Carter was as candid a statement as the general ever made (that we know about) of his belief in an episode historians have called the "Conway Cabal." Had it succeeded—had Washington resigned or been relieved—the Revolution easily could have taken a very different course. Like Washington, most historians have pointed chiefly to Gates, Mifflin, and Conway—the "usual suspects"—as the individuals most anxious to replace Washington with Gates. In late 1777 and early 1778 Washington's accumulated defeats in Pennsylvania stood in stark contrast to Gates's success in the North, and there is no question many patriots had grave doubts about Washington's ability to win the war. But did these doubts actually pose a threat to his command? Many contemporaries thought so, including the commander in chief and his "military family"—his inner circle of young aides and other loyal officers. They firmly believed that the threat was real, and over the years they never saw a reason to change their minds.

Most early historians of the Revolution believed the same. Mercy Otis Warren, who published her history of the Revolution in 1805, and who frequently wrote sympathetically of some individuals identified with the Cabal, also believed "some members of congress . . . were intriguing for his [Washington's] removal." The Franco-Italian writer Carlo Botta, who in 1809 wrote perhaps the first genuinely scholarly history of the War for Independence, was equally sure; he argued that Washington's opponents had engineered a series of "disgusts"—deliberate insults and obstacles—to force the general's resignation. It was future chief justice John Marshall, however, a Continental veteran and a near-worshipful biographer of Washington, who painted the darkest picture of the Cabal. In his multi-volume biography of the general and first president (1804–07), Marshall depicted the Cabal literally as an act of treachery by designing plotters against a noble commander in chief. He did not use the word "evil" in describing those in the Cabal, but the implication was there. Marshall accused Gates, Mifflin, and Conway and thought their scheme had political support. A "party in congress which was disposed to change their general," he wrote, "was far from being contemptible in point of numbers." George Bancroft was even more astringent in discussing the alleged Cabal. In his magisterial *History of the United States* (1850–74) he portrayed the ostensible conspirators as scheming to undermine the commander in chief at every turn, certainly hoping to induce his resignation to make way for Gates.[4] In reading these early histories one sees Washington beset by plotters at almost every turn.

The only notable exception in this early historiography was the historian and Harvard president Jared Sparks. Sparks edited the first published edition of Washington's writings, and although some of his editorial decisions drew criticism he actually was a fine scholar.[5] He spent many years in the early nineteenth century collecting documents on the Cabal, and he tried to track down any surviving members of the revolutionary generation with memories of the events of the day. As late as 1832 he tried unsuccessfully to contact Charles Carroll of Carrollton, the last living Signer of the Declaration, who Sparks knew to have defended Washington during the Cabal episode. He hoped Carroll could shed light on who any conspirators actually were.[6] But try as he might, he finally concluded he could not definitively prove the existence of a conspiracy against the American commander in chief.[7] However, even with his doubts, Sparks, like the other early historians, saw the Cabal through Washington's eyes with scant reference to the motives of the general's critics; the perspective was fully one of "good guys *versus* bad guys"—and Washington's critics were *not* the "good guys."

So matters stood among most historians until 1941. After a century and a half of writings overwhelmingly complimentary to Washington, much of which was actually hagiography, Bernhard Knollenberg published a rigorously critical reappraisal of Washington's leadership. Knollenberg, a successful lawyer, was director of the Yale University Library when he wrote his volume on Washington. He was a fine scholar and his book was an abrupt break with the past: He challenged the received wisdom of the Cabal and dismissed the idea of any organized plot. He even had some nice things to say about Horatio Gates and Thomas Conway. Not everyone fully accepted Knollenberg's conclusions, but his case was compelling enough to cast real doubt on the existence of any serious threat to Washington's command.[8] To various degrees most scholars have maintained this skeptical view of the Cabal ever since. Indeed, two biographies of Horatio Gates, most notably Paul David Nelson's *General Horatio Gates* (1976), have not only agreed with Knollenberg's findings but have argued a very positive view of Gates's contributions to the revolutionary cause. Kenneth R. Rossman has done the same for Thomas Mifflin, another supposed arch-conspirator.[9] The old view of the Cabal has never disappeared, especially in the popular narrative of the War for Independence;[10] but the prevailing scholarly wisdom generally holds that the Cabal never existed as a serious threat to Washington's command.

Rather, this post-Knollenberg view of the various events of late 1777 and early 1778 gathered under the name of "Cabal" were the often understandable concerns, some quite vocal, of Americans frustrated by and worried about the state of the patriot war effort. But such concerns and questions seldom resulted in calls for the relief of the commander in chief, much less an orchestrated stratagem to replace him.[11] Over the almost eight decades since Knollenberg's book appeared the historiography of the so-called "Conway Cabal" has seemingly reversed itself, the plot replaced by a largely ineffectual, if annoying, gang of carping critics who posed no real danger to the commander in chief—no matter what Washington and his partisans thought.

Yet this dismissal of the Cabal may have gone too far. Critics of the Cabal from Knollenberg on have generally staked their case on the lack of any "smoking gun." That is, they have found no documentary record of an orchestrated effort, much less an actual conspiracy, to topple the commander in chief in favor of another officer. But what did they expect to find? Conspirators taking notes? Perhaps minutes of meetings? To reject the Cabal on that basis is unrealistic at best and perhaps even naïve. Good conspirators cover their tracks, and even bad ones try. And there are some tantalizing hints that some of Washington's critics *did* try. As the Cabal controversy first surfaced Major General Thomas Mifflin—for a time the army's quartermaster general, a Pennsylvania politico, and an astringent critic of the commander in chief—warned Horatio Gates, Mifflin's favored general, to guard his correspondence from prying eyes. After the war, Benjamin Rush, whose pen had lashed Washington in the harshest of terms, evidently sanitized his papers or at least tried to guide the early historians of the Revolution away from his role as a Washington critic. He was clearly embarrassed when some of those historians brought his wildly disparaging sentiments on Washington to light.[12] These facts, scanty as they are, hardly accord with a "no smoking gun" theory.

Besides, there *is* a documentary case for the Cabal's existence, although making that case will depend on how we define the Cabal and how we connect the threads of evidence in long-familiar sources with clues found in newer documents. These especially include the more recent and extensive "papers" projects, which allow a better appreciation of the personalities and political maneuverings of those involved in the Cabal. Along with some intriguing newer scholarship, these materials suggest the Cabal has lain unexamined for too long. In fact, there is renewed interest in the controversies that plagued Washington over the winter of 1777–1778. A number of writers, not necessarily sharing identical interpretations of events, are again taking the threats to Washington's command seriously.[13] I am one of them, and in the book that follows I will argue that the challenge to Washington's leadership of the Continental Army was broader, deeper, and more serious than most scholarship since 1941 has allowed. Indeed, it is past time for a new exploration of the "Conway Cabal."

In retelling the Cabal story I will pursue a number of interwoven threads. First, my intention is to move beyond the established account of what we may call the "Classic Cabal"—the machinations (whatever they may have been) of Gates, Mifflin, and Conway as they revolved around a letter from Conway to Gates. Conway's epistle disparaged Washington's leadership, and political fireworks followed when Washington found out about it. As far as most historical accounts have told it, the fallout from "the Letter"—as Henry Laurens, president of Congress during the incident, called it—and Washington's adroit handling of the matter essentially blew the whistle on the Cabal and sent the general's critics running for cover. Matter closed. But were the events connected to "the Letter" the *real* threat to the commander in chief? True, there is more to say about Gates, Mifflin, and Conway, and they will claim considerable attention. But what if these "classic cabalists" had acted with the acquiescence of other senior patriots and often with significant support in Congress? Here was the real danger to Washington's command. Over the Valley Forge winter at least a dozen congressional delegates (or former delegates), as well as other prominent patriots outside of Congress, expressed doubts about Washington's ability to win the war. At first glance twelve or so delegates may not seem like a significant number, but in the context of a Congress that struggled to keep even twenty delegates on the floor at any given time, even a handful of voices could influence the debate on almost any issue. No one was more aware of this than the rebel commander in chief.

This leads to my second concern. If we are to understand the full nature and extent of the challenge to Washington's leadership, we need to account for the various motives and actions of these individuals. No previous account has done so in any comprehensive fashion, but probing this area will require attention to *perspective*—the perspective of late 1777 and early 1778, *not* the view from well over two centuries later. That is, I'll ask what the war, and thus Washington's leadership, looked like when the outcome of the revolutionary struggle was anything but clear, much less with ultimate victory assured. We know a good deal about the "view from headquarters"—the perspective of Washington and his allies—but less about the perceptions of the general's military and civilian critics. What were they? Beyond the fact that much of the patriot war effort seemingly had stalled under Washington's leadership (and perhaps that was enough to rouse critical voices), what *were* the briefs against the commander in chief?

My third point is central to this last question: If Washington was losing the war, assessing reactions to this apparent reality requires an exploration of contemporary expectations of senior officers. What were the fates of senior commanders who failed to deliver satisfactory military or political results? How did Washington compare? Why, in this context, did Horatio Gates seem a logical alternative, even to patriots who thought well of Washington on a personal basis? And further, how did those who believed a change in commanders necessary attempt to bring about the change? It is a story only partially told in previous studies, and I hope to bring clarity to the matter.

Another central question concerns the driving forces behind the Cabal. Who were these men? It is one thing to speculate about "parties," "factions," "juntos," and "cabals"—and contemporaries used all of these terms—but quite another to name actual names. In fact, I am convinced that Washington's allies had it right when they called out Mifflin, Conway, and Gates. The general and his political and military friends had correctly fingered (to quote Claude Rains) "the usual suspects" in the Cabal narrative. These three men had friends in and outside of Congress, but at a particular time—from roughly November 1777 through March 1778—for reasons I hope to make clear, they were able to exercise considerable influence over events. And while they did so for reasons they thought good and proper (at least Gates and

Mifflin did; Conway, as we shall see, was another story), their actions were undoubtedly and knowingly inimical to the authority of the commander in chief.

Finally, as I believe this book will bear out, the Cabal tested Washington as few other things did during the war. I also think his responses to efforts, as he saw them, to undermine his authority revealed a leadership style that would see him safely through the conflict, the Newburgh crisis, and into his presidency. The general could be blunt. We will see as much in recounting his interactions with Gates, Conway, and others; but usually he was nonconfrontational and subtle, disarming or deflecting adversaries with a tactful but steady and determined leadership. As in the field, he was patient in politics, carefully choosing his moments to respond to critics and making effective use of civilian and military allies. It was leadership that defined the difference between a mere general and a commander in chief. If we accept that Washington was essential to the success of the Revolution, then a fuller understanding of his success under the heavy political fire of the Cabal is essential to understanding the success of the Revolution as well.

Cabal! is a book in three parts. The first comprises three chapters in which I'll examine "Preliminaries to Cabal." I'll look at the impact of Washington's performance in early 1777, mostly in New Jersey, when he won the admiration of patriots and raised expectations of victory over the British to new heights. This is important because, ironically, for the general this stellar spring campaign proved a mixed blessing. With patriot hopes so high, Washington's defeats later in the year belied patriot expectations. The war effort had seemed on a winning track and well on the way to victory. What had derailed it? The bright hopes of the spring turned to gloom, and the narrative will trace the consequent rise of questions about Washington's fitness to command. As the final chapter of part 1 will explain, those questions were not just about winning or losing in combat; and my account will be less a military narrative than an exploration of the varied motives of Washington's critics as well as the contexts in which those motives operated.

That said, Washington's record in battle *was* critical to the debates over his role as commander in chief. The subsequent chapters in parts 2 and 3 will turn to the actual course and nature of those debates. I will be looking at the specific flash points that brought tensions between Washington and his critics to dangerous levels. What were the issues at stake? How did such antagonists (and I will insist they *were* antagonists) as Washington, Gates, Mifflin, and others allied with and critical of the commander in chief deal with one another? And critically, was there an actual Cabal—or at least a real desire among a significant number of patriots either to replace General Washington or at least to diminish his role as commander in chief?

Of course this last question is at the center of this book. It is nothing new to note that by late 1777 the commander in chief and his staff—his military "family"—certainly believed an organized plot was afoot, but we need a more careful look at why they thought so. These were intelligent men; in addition to Washington himself we can include Nathanael Greene, Alexander Hamilton, Robert Morris, Benjamin Harrison, Patrick Henry, John Laurens (son of congressional president Henry Laurens), Lafayette, and other officers and patriots of genuine talent. And if, as Knollenberg and other historians have assumed, there was no plot—no Cabal—then we need to ask how some of the brightest minds and best-placed individuals of the revolutionary generation could have been so wrong. What did they see when they surveyed the tide of criticisms directed at their chief? Can we really believe they were in the grip of some mass paranoia? Or did they see a dangerous pattern of events pointing toward an effort to undermine the general? Or even some definite indication of an organized attempt? And if the answer to *any* of these questions is "yes," then perforce a major question follows: Were Washington's critics less innocent—or in their eyes, did they feel a greater necessity to mount a challenge to Washington's authority—than historians since Knollenberg have assumed? There was a *great* deal of smoke here, and I'm going to argue that there was *considerable* fire.

Washington indeed was blessed with a talented staff, but we have to concede the talents and intelligence of many of the general's critics as well. The men chiefly identified with what I have called the "Classic Cabal"—Horatio Gates, Thomas Mifflin, and Thomas Conway—were not fools, and there were reasons many patriots thought well of them. We can safely say the same of certain members of Congress and other patriots who shared a skeptical view of the commander in chief. This being the case, I will suggest an alternative interpretation of the Cabal. Rather than a plot to force the issue with Washington more-or-less quickly, I will pursue the Cabal as a drawn-out affair, which makes sense considering its months-long timeframe. Murmurs of discontent surfaced in October 1777 and became serious in November. Matters were intense from December through March 1778—the period in which Washington faced his gravest challenges—with residual swipes at the general coming later. (And not incidentally, "plot" or "conspiracy" are actually poor descriptions of the Cabal. They imply illegality, and if Congress chose to dispense with Washington's services it had every legal right to recall him—a matter addressed in Chapter 3.)

If Washington had stepped aside in the face of a request for his relief, or for any other reason, the likes of Gates and Mifflin would have been delighted. But was Washington's replacement really at the heart of the matter? Chapters 5 and 6 will argue the real objective of the Cabal may not have aimed at removing Washington *per se*. Rather, the goal was more complex—*much* more complex. The chief threat to Washington's command lay in the Board of War. Established by Congress in 1776 to provide bureaucratic support for the army and to handle mundane military matters for Congress—routine correspondence and record-keeping, among other chores—the board reorganized in late 1777 under the leadership of Mifflin, with Gates assuming the board presidency in January 1778. Without firm congressional oversight, but sometimes with specific congressional approval, the board then expanded its mission in a classic case of what today we would call "mission creep." It strayed from its original purpose as a support organization and moved to take control of the American war effort. The Mifflin-Gates agenda was ambitious: They sought control of setting military policy and strategic goals; determining vital training, organizational, personnel, and logistical functions; and even the assignment of theater commanders. Had Washington lost control of these areas his title of commander in chief would have been utterly hollow. Even if he remained with the army he would have been just another general, in charge of the troops in his immediate theater, but little or nothing more. This was the direction the Cabal was taking. In effect the Cabal was less an organized plot than it was a gradual attempt at an administrative-political takeover of the war effort. We can properly call the "Real Cabal," as I have chosen to term it, an attempted "administrative coup"—aboveboard and legal, but nevertheless a very real threat to Washington's authority as commander in chief. Had it succeeded, Gates and Mifflin would have been the determining actors in American military affairs.

So why didn't it work? That is the business of part 3, in which two chapters and an epilogue delve into Washington's efforts to fight off the Board of War's initiatives and maintain his prerogatives as commander in chief—and then to inflict a measure of payback on his (as he saw them) tormentors. Here the various threads followed in *Cabal!* will come together and offer an assessment of Washington's navigation of the political challenges of those fateful seven or so troubling months. It is enough now to say it was a virtuoso performance, certainly one of the best of his career. Over the months of controversy he met and defeated every attempt to curtail his authority. In the end Washington kept his job because he had the political savvy to convince most of his countrymen he could do it better than anyone else. It was the same reason his countrymen chose him as their first president.

A NOTE ON TERMINOLOGY and organization is in order. As I have in other publications, I have used the word "patriots" or "patriot," with a small "p," as something of a pronoun. It denotes individuals who favored the cause of independence as well as the forces that fought against Great Britain. Depending upon its context, the term includes any American involved with the rebel cause, especially members of Congress and any of the Continental, militia, or other rebel combatant forces. "Patriot" comes in handy when "rebel" or "irregular" or "militia" has appeared repeatedly in a sentence or paragraph; it is a stylistic usage. I use "Whig," a contemporary term for those opposed to Britain and arbitrary power, in the same fashion. In this book it usually refers to those patriots most zealously attached to the independence movement. As such, "patriot" and "Whig" carry no moral connotation. Indeed, in fighting for George III and the empire, plenty of American loyalists fully believed *they* were patriots—that the other "patriots" were traitors and rebels. So, in the same vein, "loyalist," with a small "l," and "tory," with a small "t," simply denote Americans standing with the King (who rates a capital "K"). And while I know loyalists were as American as patriots, I use "Americans" to identify those supporting the Revolution for the same reason I use "patriots."

Then there is "Cabal"; it's a tricky word. A generation ago historian Don Higginbotham (who did not believe in the Cabal), quoting Samuel Johnson, pointed out the term was an eighteenth-century usage for virtually any faction, party, or group "united in some common design." It did not imply any mass following or specific organization in pursuit of a common objective—a small body was enough to be a "cabal."[14] The 1787 edition of *Entick's New Spelling Dictionary* lists "cabal" as a noun and a verb: the former "a private junto of men, an intrigue"; the latter "to intrigue privately, plot, unite, join."[15] It was a familiar term and patriots allied to Washington used cabal, faction, party, junto, and other terms to describe their adversaries; and with particular vitriol Hamilton once called Conway a "calumniator" (a wonderful word). But during the Revolution no one *ever* used the term "Conway Cabal." That was a nineteenth-century invention. I use "cabal" with a lowercase "c" in reference to general parties, factions, "calumniators," and so forth. But "Cabal" with a capitol "C" is *the* Cabal—the effort (or supposed effort) to replace General Washington or the very real effort to undermine his authority as commanding general.

While the various congressional resolutions, proceedings of the Board of War, and acts of individuals can trace the advent and progress of the Cabal on a timeline, *Cabal!* does not employ an exclusively chronological narrative. Part 1 is generally chronological, but chapters dealing with the chief initiatives of the board—which comprised the heart of the Cabal—describe actions and incidents that often occurred in parallel. To better understand them I have elected (with some exceptions) to follow them to their conclusions, which results in chapters that are topical. This approach spares the reader from trying to keep track of who was doing what in a series of confusing events.

Mark Edward Lender
Kean University, Emeritus
2019

PART 1

PRELIMINARIES TO CABAL

~wherein, to the joy of patriots, General Washington frustrates the British in New Jersey, raising his personal popularity and American expectations of victory to new heights, and

~wherein the defeats of 1777 turn patriot optimism to gloom and plunge confidence in Washington to new lows, and

~wherein the fates of losing generals are explored and patriots who doubt Washington can win the war are explained.

ONE

THE SEASON OF HOPE

Early 1777 and Visions of Victory

> I flatter myself, that by the Spring, Things will open favorably for the *Americans*, as there is already an Appearance of their doing so.
>
> —Samuel Mather to Samuel Adams, January 27, 1777[1]

SAMUEL MATHER AND SAMUEL ADAMS were no men to take lightly. Mather was the scion of the celebrated line of New England divines, the son of the Reverend Cotton Mather, perhaps the most eminent of them all. In January 1777, in his seventy-first year, Samuel was pastor of the Bennett Street Church in Boston; an ardent patriot, he had "deliberately and conscientiously embarked in the *American* cause at the beginning of the conflict with *Britain*, as the cause of truth and righteousness and of just liberty."[2] Mather confidently predicted inevitable victory as long as Americans remained on the paths of righteousness, and as 1777 dawned that victory seemed on the near horizon. This was the import of his letter (the source of our chapter epigraph) to his old friend Samuel Adams. Adams, born to old Puritan stock himself, lacked Mather's more distinguished family pedigree, but he had made a name in his own right as one of America's most fiery and prominent revolutionaries. In January he was a Massachusetts delegate to the Continental Congress, and while he shared Mather's conviction that America fought in a righteous cause, he knew the Almighty would need the assistance of rebel victories in the field.[3] Nevertheless, like Mather, Adams believed patriots were on course for success in the coming year. With any luck 1777 would see the Revolution on the way to triumph—if not triumphant. Such were the opinions of two eminent and well-informed patriots.

Mather and Adams were not alone in their bright assessments of the rebel war effort; in early 1777 patriots across the thirteen colonies fairly gushed with similar sentiments. For American rebels the early months of the year were a "season of hope." At least through the late summer, and even beyond, public and private communications reflected a general confidence in Whig arms and military leadership. It was in many ways a curious phenomenon, for in fact these optimistic expectations ran considerably ahead of any military realities. True, Washington had stunned the British at Trenton and Princeton, but imperial forces were anything but defeated, and the Continental Army was still young and struggling to reorganize and replenish its ranks. The American regulars were untested in any major engagement. If we may borrow a term from former Federal Reserve chairman Alan Greenspan, we can reasonably ask if patriots were not in the grip of some military equivalent of "irrational exuberance."[4] This was dangerous. Defeat is always bitter, but it is harsher still when completely unexpected—when high hopes suddenly collide with grim realities and give way to despair and desperation. Desperate people are then open to desperate measures. Thus the nature of this early sense of optimism deserves our attention, for its collapse later in the year led directly to the crisis in the Continental command known since as the "Conway Cabal."

THE DRAMATIC BATTLES OF Trenton and Princeton indeed had ignited patriot morale. Washington's victories had eased much of the sting of the defeats of 1776 and had thrown the British on the defensive for the winter. While General William Howe, royal commander in chief, wintered in New York City, his army commanded only a narrow strip of New Jersey between Perth Amboy and New Brunswick. The state, seemingly all but pacified in mid-December, had erupted in a full-blown insurgency; the New Jersey militia had revived, and British troops ventured out of their garrisons for foraging or intelligence operations only in strength. The fighting was low-intensity, but there was plenty of it.[5] It was this turn of events that had buoyed the observations of Samuel Mather and Samuel Adams, and others looked on from afar with similar optimism. Near Boston, Hannah Winthrop, another Massachusetts blue-blood and wife of Harvard professor and astronomer

John Winthrop, wrote her friend Mercy Otis Warren in mid-January: The "New Year presents a bright view" after "our late successes," she noted, referring to the engagements at Trenton and Princeton. She regretted the capture of Continental major general Charles Lee in December 1776 but left no doubt of the confident state of public morale.[6]

Had Winthrop known the real state of the patriot military she may have been a bit more muted in her hopes for the coming year. In fact, all was not well. While the New Jersey militia was skirmishing gamely, rebel authorities close to the action had no illusions of any decisive militia victory over the redcoats. No one knew this better than New Jersey governor William Livingston, who warned state forces could not stop a major British drive and lamented the legislature's reluctance to reform militia laws to compel greater numbers of men to serve. For the time being, however, militia willing to serve carried the war effort, for in January 1777 the Continental Army was little help. Encamped outside of Morristown, New Jersey, Washington's army numbered mostly militia, many of whom were poorly equipped and supplied and anxious to head home. "The Severity of the Season has made our Troops, especially the Militia, extremely impatient," the general reported to Congress, "and has reduced the number very considerably. Every day more or less leave us."[7] It was an army in name only.

That was soon to change, thanks in large measure to Washington's opponent. The British commander in chief *Sir* William Howe—his victory at Long Island the year before had won him a knighthood—never attacked Morristown. Still gun-shy of the New Jersey interior, Howe's troops clung to their strip of territory in central New Jersey and chose not to confront the main rebel army when, in reality, it was terribly vulnerable. Howe would have to stir eventually, and everyone expected as much; but his winter hiatus ("lethargy" is a better word) was a gift of time for Washington, who used it wisely. In one of his most impressive—if underappreciated—achievements of the war, the rebel commander in chief recruited, organized, and equipped a virtually new Continental Army. It was an accomplishment of the first order, and it showed Washington at his administrative best.

The new Continentals would be different from the regiments of 1776. In September 1776 the general had convinced Congress the Revolution likely faced a protracted war, a war that called for a regular American army to face British and Hessian regulars. This meant troops enlisted for long-term service (earlier Continentals had served only a year) that were well disciplined, adequately equipped, and properly trained. Militia, he explained—poorly trained, ill disciplined, and serving limited tours of duty—simply could not win the war. Yet militia were the darlings of republican ideology; and many in Congress, leery of regular armies, agreed to Washington's "new modeled" army only reluctantly. But the gravity of the military situation was such that most delegates did agree, and Congress voted an army of some seventy-five thousand men. Troops would enlist for three years or "for the war," that is, for the duration of the war. Three-year recruits would receive a clothing issue and bounties of twenty dollars; "for the war" men also would receive a hundred acres of land after the war.[8] The army never came close to meeting recruiting objectives, and Continental regiments were typically understrength. Yet the fact remains that the commander in chief would be able to shape—or try to shape—the troops he could muster into "a respectable army" able to face the enemy on equal terms.

The work was well advanced by March. Despite doubts some patriots expressed over the ability to recruit long-term soldiers, the ranks gradually filled, bolstered by a corps of veterans from 1776. As Congress decamped to Baltimore the previous December, the delegates had granted Washington sweeping administrative powers. The authority was temporary, but for the time being Washington, in effect, *was* the rebel government; and Morristown was more the *de facto* capital of the Revolution than far-away Baltimore. The general used his authority with a light touch, always dealing diplomatically with Whig authorities at all levels; whatever his touch, however, he got results. Recruits, stores, and equipment converged on the encampment; and in the late winter the general felt strong enough to feed small units south where they joined militia in harassing British foraging parties. From Morristown, Samuel Shaw, a Massachusetts artillery lieutenant, described the tempo of operations in early March: "We have had, and still continue to have, more or less skirmishing every two or three days with the enemy's foraging parties, in which, for the most part, we get the better; so that they do not pretend to come out now under twelve or fifteen hundred strong."[9]

Shaw's account was as accurate as it was optimistic; in fact, he was describing a period now known as the "forage war." Washington found that "by keeping four or five hundred Men far advanced, we not only oblige them to forage with parties of 1,500 and 2,000 to cover, but every now and then, give them a Smart Brush."[10] There were plenty of "brushes" and, as Shaw related, over the late winter and early spring most days saw some fighting; there were at least sixty-three actions between February and April.[11] Most of these engagements were skirmishes with few or no casualties, but some clashes were serious. On February 8, Charles Lord Cornwallis led some three thousand men (and five other generals!) to forage near Quibbletown (in modern Piscataway), several miles from New Brunswick. The British got their forage but not before losing some thirty killed and as many wounded in a stiff fight with three hundred Americans under Colonel Charles Scott.[12] Tired of patriot harassment, in mid-April Lord Cornwallis led four thousand men in a surprise assault on five hundred rebels under Major General Benjamin Lincoln at Bound Brook, not far from New Brunswick. Most of Lincoln's men got away, but the incident demonstrated the British could be dangerous when aroused.[13] But patriot troops shook off the occasional bloody nose. The frequent low-intensity actions provided invaluable combat experience, taught the Continentals to work with militia, and kept the harried British constantly on edge.

For the time being this was the war Washington wanted—in fact, the only war he would risk. His instincts were offensive, but major offensive operations were out of the question. His men were still inexperienced and he knew facing European professionals in a major contest would have been suicidal. As early as September 1776 the commander in chief had informed Congress of his policy: "on our side the War should be defensive, It has been even called a War of posts, that we should on all occasions avoid a general Action or put anything to the risque unless compelled by a necessity into which we ought never to be drawn."[14] The Continentals would stay close enough to Howe's troops to exploit an opportunity, skirmishing frequently, while avoiding major combat except on their own terms. Some contemporaries styled Washington's operations "Fabian"—a term the general himself never used—after Roman general Quintus Fabius Maximus Verrucosus, who waged a similar war against Hannibal's superior Carthaginians. Thus, at least for the moment, Washington became the "American Fabius."[15]

In the short run these tactics, born of necessity, proved effective. Fabian operations would not win the war—Fabius did not defeat Hannibal, either—but they bought vital time as Washington expanded his ranks and his troops gained in confidence. In late May Continental rosters listed over 7,300 men fit for duty,[16] with more joining, and Washington judged the situation favorable enough to move closer to the enemy. Breaking camp at Morristown, the commander in chief marched his regiments to defensible positions in the Watchung Mountains above Middlebrook, only a dozen miles north of British-occupied New Brunswick. The army still needed men and it continued to train even as it deployed to Middlebrook, but unit orderly books recorded Washington's conclusion that the "Army is now on a permanent & honble [honorable] footing" and ready for greater things. Some British agreed. In London the *Annual Register* for 1777 conceded spring had seen the rebels virtually overrun New Jersey; the fighting also had served to "inure" the "Americans to military service."[17] The empire was facing a dangerous opponent. It was all quite something for a rebel army that had barely existed in January.

By June the mood among patriots was positively buoyant. Letters of the period leave no doubt many Americans eagerly anticipated the coming campaign, convinced victory was within their grasp. Patriots took heart and these upbeat assessments were nowhere more evident than in Congress. Back in Philadelphia after their sojourn in Baltimore, the delegates caught up on the status of the army and liked what they saw and heard. In Congress, Massachusetts delegate Elbridge Gerry expressed the opinion of many when he wrote: "Mr. Howe is maneuvering in the Jersies, but our Army is on so respectable a Footing, that he has not yet ventured to attack them."[18] John Adams, also representing Massachusetts, was overjoyed to learn of reports of enemy troops supposedly deserting and of American regulars "rapidly increasing" in "Discipline, order, subordination, Cleanliness, Health and Spirits." "All depends on this," he told Major General John Sullivan. "This will surely conduct us to Honour, Glory, and Tryumph"; anything else would lead only to "Disgrace and Ruin." The same day (June 8) Francis Lightfoot Lee wrote fellow Virginian Landon Carter that "it is now reduced to a certainty G.B. [Great Britain] cannot conquer America with her own forces or what forces she can procure in Europe." Thomas Burke of North Carolina, worried earlier about the success of Continental recruiting and the capabilities of the army's new officers, now felt "the Campaign has an Auspicious dawning, and I hope will set with a great and happy Lustre."[19] The New York delegates assured the state Council of Safety that the New Jersey militia had thoroughly "intimidated" Howe, and with the Continentals shaping up "Every thing wears a smiling aspect" in the military sphere.[20] Such unanimity of opinion was a rare thing in Congress.

James Lovell of Massachusetts took a slightly longer view of the struggle, believing the war might last more than one more campaign. Still, he was very much an optimist, and inasmuch as he would number among Washington's most virulent critics by the end of 1777, his outlook in June is especially interesting. Lovell's confidence in the commander in chief and the rebel army was unbounded. He "ventured to assert," he wrote Continental commissary Joseph Trumbull:

> Genl. Howe would never be able to beat Genl. Washington in 20 years. . . . I imagine now the British General finds he cannot for the soul of him beat our army, he will only ravage the Colonies one after another; and leave our military to guard our independence. I have heard some Gentlemen of the Army say our troops will probably be nicely disciplined by the Fall. This will open a fine prospect for us another year, if the enemy should not be able to get any reinforcements next spring, and should be very sickly in the winter and if our militia should turn out with spirit next summer, and we should catch the British troops then a good way from the sea, without any Rivers upon their right, left or rear. How we shall maul them![21]

Lovell's summer euphoria was not unique among Washington's eventual skeptics. Of these, three men are worth noting. Abraham Clark of New Jersey, an ardent republican always wary of military power, confidently anticipated an active campaign. Of course there would be bloodshed, he noted, but the times called for it. William Duer of New York, whose later antagonism toward Washington puzzled many of his fellow delegates, was of a similar frame of mind; he foresaw Howe in store for a "very Severe Drubbing."[22] Benjamin Rush, a young Pennsylvania physician, former member of Congress, and Signer of the Declaration, was an ardent republican radical whose eventual disdain for Washington would rival or surpass Lovell's. But he was jubilant in the early summer. He wrote Brigadier General Anthony Wayne, a fellow Pennsylvanian then with Washington in New Jersey, that the accounts "we receive daily of the strength discipline—and spirit of our army give us great pleasure." Full of spirit himself, Rush asked Wayne not to let Virginia, and, one safely supposes, other states "bear away from *us* [that is, Pennsylvania] the palms of military glory. I am sure our men are made of good stuff for soldiers and officers as any on the continent."[23]

To the extent anyone was actually critical of Washington's conduct in June, it was the strident Whig Samuel Adams—and he groused only at the pace of operations. Adams wanted "decisive" action. "I am apt to be displeased," he wrote to Virginia congressional delegate Richard Henry Lee, "when I think our Progress in War and Politicks is Slow. I wish to see more of an enterprising Spirit in the Senate and the Field."[24] Continuing in this vein, he told another friend he was not "over well pleased, with what is called the Fabian War in America." Americans were not fighting Carthaginians, and Adams fretted about what he saw as a leisurely war. Yet he assured his wife the skirmishing in New Jersey favored patriot arms and that Howe would never get to Philadelphia. The Massachusetts patriot would have some disparaging things to say about Washington's conduct later in the war, but for the time being he admitted he had "no Judgment in Military Matters" and would leave the fighting to "those who are Masters of it"—which clearly, in his opinion, still included the commander in chief.[25]

At this juncture the worst anyone could imagine was a British campaign that somehow might take Philadelphia, although that seemed unlikely. And if the city should fall—so what? John Adams, following developments in New Jersey, felt no apprehensions on that score; the British army might as well have been "in the Crimea," and "Our Fabius" would stop Howe in any case. But if the British took the City of Brotherly Love, it would be "a Millstone about their Necks," and the loss would mean little for the American war effort. John's cousin Samuel agreed. Unless Howe destroyed the rebel army, the capture of Philadelphia would mean nothing.[26] In fact, later in the year the loss of the de facto capital would be the source of tremendous consternation and would put Washington under considerable political pressure. But in the early summer patriots could scarcely credit any such scenario.

As the "forage war" continued in New Jersey, the British pondered their situation. The unexpected reversals at Trenton and Princeton, as well as the wearying combat in New Jersey, clearly indicated the rebels had no interest in quitting. The crown was well aware of resurgent American morale. Only a bold new offensive would knock the rebels out of the war, and Lord George Germain, secretary of state for America and the minister largely in charge of the war effort, believed he had such a grand design. An imperial army would march from Canada to Albany, New York, down the familiar Lake Champlain-Hudson River Valley avenue. British forces already in New York City would control the Lower Hudson and, if the Canadian army needed help, would advance upriver in support. The armies would meet at Albany. A third British column would move east up the Mohawk Valley, also aiming for Albany, forcing the rebels to divert troops to yet another front. The converging British forces would destroy any patriot units that got in the way. The objective of the entire operation was to isolate New England, which London considered the most troublesome of the colonies. At the very least, controlling the Hudson would complicate American efforts to move resources between theaters and, with any luck, might encourage loyalist risings in colonies south of the Hudson. At best, with New England cut off, the British would strangle the Revolution piecemeal. Properly executed, the plan had promise.

Proper execution, however, was problematic from the beginning. Lieutenant General John Burgoyne, who would command the advance from Canada, expected Howe to move up the Hudson in force to support him. Yet Howe, Burgoyne, and Germain never fully clarified who was going to do what. *Support* did *not* necessarily mean direct cooperation with an allied force; the term allowed for independent operations preventing an enemy from concentrating against an allied unit. In fact, this was how Sir William chose to interpret his orders, and he set his sights on Philadelphia. He reasoned such an operation would prevent Washington from sending troops to oppose Burgoyne and—even better—force the patriot chief to meet him in a showdown battle. Howe was convinced Washington would fight to defend Philadelphia, and he wanted nothing more than to smash the Virginian in a general engagement. Realistically such a campaign would leave little time to cooperate directly with the northern army, meaning Burgoyne, unknowingly (he learned only in August Howe would not be coming north), would be on his own.[27]

As patriots in Philadelphia prophesied victory in 1777—and even as many of their effusive letters were in transit—the royal commander considered his options. Attacking the rebel city would not be easy. Howe's advance post in New Jersey was New Brunswick, about sixty-five miles from Philadelphia along fairly good roads. A march to the Delaware would take only four or five days. Yet the general hesitated. The rebels had been aggressive all spring and Sir William was nervous. As he moved toward Philadelphia, could the Americans surprise his rear or strike while his army was crossing the Delaware? Could Washington turn on lightly defended New York City? The risks seemed too real, and Howe decided he had to deal with Washington before marching west.

But how to get at Washington? Sir William wanted nothing to do with an attack on Continental positions above Middlebrook. He had commanded at Bunker Hill, and one such bloodletting was enough in a career. Instead, in June Howe ventured from New Brunswick, pushing deeper into central New Jersey; he hoped the patriot general would leave the hills and follow. Washington refused to take the bait. Finally, Howe feigned an evacuation of New Jersey, loading men and matériel aboard navy transports at Perth Amboy. Sharp-eyed patriots reported Howe's best regiments and artillery were still ashore, but Washington cautiously sent detachments forward. Then, on June 26, Howe turned and struck. In a running action—variously called the Battle of Westfield, Metuchen Meetinghouse, Flat Hills, or Short Hills—Continentals and militia avoided entrapment and regained the heights above Middlebrook. Often overlooked, Westfield was a bigger fight than Trenton or Princeton; and as in other actions, the battle again demonstrated the rebels' ability to move out of harm's way rather than fight on unfavorable terms. It also convinced Howe that Washington would not risk a general engagement in New Jersey, and on June 30 the Royal army quit the state. Sir William would assail Philadelphia, but his army would journey by sea.

Rebels had every reason to be pleased: In their eyes they had won the forage war, and they *had* regained war-torn New Jersey. While senior military leaders understood the young Continental Line was anything but a precision instrument, in popular eyes the regulars seemed in fighting trim and ready to take on bigger tasks. Moreover, Washington basked in popular acclaim in the early days of summer, although, in character, he would hardly reveal as much publicly. Still, he must have been pleased. His achievements at Morristown and in frustrating Howe had delighted patriots across the colonies. In Congress, James Lovell, Robert Morris, John Penn, and others sang his praises; Thomas Burke was only typical when he announced Washington was "very justly admired by all the world."[28] Lieutenant Shaw crowed that the British now had to "acknowledge the genius of a Washington." And some British *did*. Even the *Annual Register* conceded Washington's reputation had soared in America and in Europe.[29] If Washington was not yet the demigod—the iconic figurehead of the Revolution—people admired later in the war, by the end of June his stock nevertheless was riding as high as it ever had.

This was significant, as early in the war the commander in chief's reputation was anything but sacred. His performance through 1776—at least before Trenton—invited few accolades, and not all who met the man found him especially remarkable.[30] Indeed, not all patriots saw Washington as indispensible. In May 1776 an American envoy in Paris, Arthur Lee—of the famous Virginia family and an individual well known to Washington—broadly hinted America might benefit from installing a prominent French general as the rebel commander in chief.[31] We don't know if Washington knew of Lee's thinking, but after the rebel defeats of 1776 he became painfully aware of what some of his key subordinates thought. Major General Charles Lee, the army's second-ranking officer, was his chief critic. Disillusioned with Washington's judgment after the Continental disaster at Fort Washington (November 16), Lee had shared his misgivings with Adjutant General Joseph Reed—in a letter the commander in chief inadvertently saw. To Washington's distress, the message revealed Reed, a man the commander in chief had trusted implicitly, was sympathetic to Lee. In another communication that Washington did *not* see, Lee famously wrote Major General Horatio Gates: "*Entre nous*, a certain great man is most damnably deficient."[32] (And of course in these pages we will hear again from Charles Lee and Horatio Gates.) Given the gravity of the times, no doubt other patriots shared qualms about their commander as well, if not with the bluntness of Lee.[33] Washington, of course, survived these early doubts, but they remind us of how radically the general's fortunes had changed for the better by mid-1777 when it seemed he could do no wrong.

Almost no wrong, that is, for there were a few misgivings about the general's growing popularity. These were the trepidations of republicans worried about the power, or potential power, of any single individual, especially if that individual wore a uniform. In early 1777 the two patriots most concerned on this score were John Adams and Benjamin Rush. According to Rush, Adams lectured Congress on the foolishness of hero worship. One can almost see Adams wagging a finger as he acidly told his fellow delegates: "I have been distressed to see some of our members disposed to idolize an image which their own hands have molten. I speak of the superstitious veneration which is paid to Genl. Washington. Altho' I honor him for his good qualities, yet in this house I feel myself his superior. In private life I shall always acknowledge that he is mine."[34] Rush had noted the New Englander's comments approvingly; indeed, the Pennsylvanian could not have agreed more, and he had much less confidence in the general. In his view Washington lacked the will to properly discipline a winning army; worse, he thought the commander in chief would not "Close the present war" precisely "Because he is idolized by the people of America, and is tho't to be absolutely necessary for us to carry on the war."[35] As in this case, Rush's reasoning was often difficult to follow—why should Washington's popularity hurt the war effort?—but with these sentiments Rush had labeled himself a man to watch as our narrative of the Cabal unfolds. In this instance Rush wrote privately, but he would have more, *much* more, to say quite publicly about the general later in the year. Such ideological objections to Washington's prominence, however, were, if somewhat perversely, yet another confirmation of the popular confidence he enjoyed.

THE SEASON OF HOPE also encouraged confidence in army leadership generally. Indeed, the fighting around Westfield, just before Howe quit New Jersey, put two other officers in the limelight. They were in the thick of the action, and given their future roles in our story, they deserve an introduction here.

The first was New Jersey magnate William Alexander, or, as he preferred, Lord Stirling. Stirling (1726-1783) had holdings in land, iron, and trade; and he enjoyed considerable social and political influence. He was brother-in-law to William Livingston, the state's revolutionary governor. The New Jersey "lord" was claimant to a lapsed Scottish earldom, a claim recognized in Scotland but not in Parliament's House of Lords. The snub soured Stirling on the mother country and helped drive him into the rebel camp, and patriots never begrudged the man his title. Stirling was a *bon vivant* who enjoyed the good life on his estate in Basking Ridge, where he entertained in grand style. If hospitable, he was also impecunious and chronically in debt. His modern biographer, Paul David Nelson, thinks Stirling may have greeted the coming of the Revolution as a diversion from his money problems. In any event, when the imperial crisis came to a head Stirling never hesitated to pitch in with the rebel cause, and he never looked back.[36]

The rebel earl played active political and military roles as New Jersey broke with the empire. He was a critical actor in preparing the state militia for war and then moved to the Continental establishment as colonel of the 1st New Jersey Regiment. In March 1776 Congress appointed him one of New Jersey's two brigadier generals (the other was William Maxwell). The brigadier fought hard at Long Island (where he was captured and subsequently exchanged) and then joined the retreat across New Jersey and the counterattack at Trenton. Stirling soldiered on despite failing health, but he made no complaints on that score. On February 19, 1777, Congress promoted him to major general and he became one of Washington's division commanders. On June 26, during Howe's strike near Westfield, Stirling confronted a numerically superior British column under Cornwallis and escaped only after some stiff fighting and the loss of his artillery.[37] But Washington was pleased with the day's action, and for the rest of the war he looked to Stirling as a trusted confidant. Never a brilliant soldier, Stirling was competent and brave, and Washington appreciated his loyalty.

In fact, the patriot lord would stand by the commander in chief through the darkest days of the war—and before the end of the year he would ignite a genuine crisis in the Continental high command, an incident that brought the Cabal graphically before the public.

Our second character was one of Stirling's subordinates at Westfield. This was an Irish-born colonel in the French army. His family had moved to France when he was a child, and he grew up fluent in English and French;

he had been a soldier since youth, was an able junior officer, and rose steadily to the rank of colonel. Like many other officers of the Bourbon monarchy, he had come to America expecting to burnish his reputation and bolster his chances for promotion upon a return to France. On April 20, 1777, he had arrived aboard the French ship *Amphitrite* in Portsmouth, New Hampshire, glowingly recommended by Silas Deane, one of the American diplomats in Paris. Congress obligingly had appointed him a brigadier general. It was just what he wanted. "I depend upon my military promotion in rank for to increase my fortune and that of my family," he candidly told Continental major general John Sullivan. "I freely own to you it was partly with a view of obtaining the rank of Brigadier in the French army that I have joined this."[38] His name was Thomas Conway.

Conway (1735–c. 1800) made a fine initial impression. Unlike many French officers in America, he spoke English and seemed amiable. John Adams was impressed. Soon after Conway's arrival the Massachusetts delegate met with him several times and was "much pleased with him," finding him "sensible and polite" with "every Air and manner of A Soldier."[39] There was substance behind the "Air and manner." When Washington assigned Conway a brigade in Stirling's division, the Frenchman proved good with troops; he was an excellent disciplinarian who took seriously the training and welfare of his command. Conway's first real test in the field came at Westfield—a fight big enough to gain the attention of Congress—where he performed well as Stirling's men pulled away from Cornwallis. His was the first brigade the advancing Cornwallis struck, Conway later recalled, and he "stopped the enemy, and made my retreat without running, and without losing a single prisoner."[40] A British intelligence report would rate Conway "clever."[41]

Conway would prove "clever" indeed, perhaps too clever by half (as the British cliché goes). It gives little away—and foreshadows much—to note the brigadier would, to his ultimate distress, lend his name to the "Conway Cabal."

On July 23, having lost two vital months of the campaign season fencing with Washington in New Jersey, Howe finally cleared New York Harbor for Philadelphia. The fleet of 260 ships carried some 17,000 troops and 5,000 camp followers, as well as the army's animals and tons of forage, artillery, munitions, and supplies. Scouting reports, highly inaccurate as it turned out, telling of supposedly dangerous rebel defensive preparations discouraged a landing along Delaware Bay, which offered the most direct water route to the city. Thus the British commander ordered the fleet to Chesapeake Bay. On August 25, after thirty-four sweltering days afloat, the exhausted troops began staggering ashore near Head of Elk (modern Elkton), Maryland, some fifty miles from Philadelphia. Mercifully no rebels contested the landing, but Howe had lost another month.

With Howe at sea Washington could only guess his opponent's mission. He considered Philadelphia a likely target, but common sense warned him otherwise. Howe "certainly ought now in good policy," Washington wrote of his rival, "to endeavor to Cooperate with Genl Burgoyne."[42] Had Howe shared Washington's thinking the Royal army would have headed up the Hudson. Accordingly, and initially unsure of where to position his Continentals, Washington sent strong detachments to the Hudson Highlands and, eventually, to Horatio Gates commanding the Northern Army confronting Burgoyne. When he confirmed Howe's objective was indeed Philadelphia, the rebel chief led the balance of his army—about sixteen thousand men—southwest. The American Fabius, previously so averse to a general action, now had Congress urging him to defend their seat. He was more than willing: Washington would fight to hold Philadelphia.

As Washington marched, patriot morale remained unshaken. The rebels who had forced Howe to abandon New Jersey, Whigs were sure, would whip him decisively in Pennsylvania. "Providence," John Adams assured Abigail, had arranged for the summer's campaign to conclude around Philadelphia. Even if Howe took the city it would work to the revolutionaries' advantage. Howe would have to use all of his men just to hold the city, essentially leaving the rest of the country alone. Besides, a British occupation would "purge away" the "Impurities" of a town Adams saw as teeming with loyalists and half-hearted patriots. But this was just speculation in a private letter; in reality he expected Washington to deal effectively with Howe.[43] So did others. Richard Henry Lee notified Thomas Jefferson of the looming campaign, noting congressional calls for the militia of Pennsylvania, Delaware, Maryland, and northern Virginia to reinforce Washington. "Should Gen. Howe venture to enter the Country against this force, I think his ruin will be sure." Samuel Chase of Maryland agreed, predicting Howe was marching to total ruin, while an elated Thomas Burke envisioned a coming "severe blow to British arms" and "an end of the war, much sooner than has hitherto appeared possible."[44] As Howe's army approached, "irrational exuberance" remained in style—and Washington had a lot of patriot expectations to satisfy.

The general did his best to rally popular enthusiasm. As he marched toward Howe, expecting to meet him somewhere south of Philadelphia in Delaware or southeastern Pennsylvania, on August 24 he staged a marvelous piece of military theater. He led the army through Philadelphia in a grand parade of five or six hours that thrilled the populace. John Adams loved it. Washington's gesture reassured everyone of his intension to fight; and to Adams' political joy, the sight of the patriot army in a line miles long made a "good Impression upon the Minds of the timourous Whiggs for their Confirmation, upon the cunning Quakers for their Restraint and upon the rascally Tories for their Confusion." (Ever the complainer, however, Adams grumbled about the troops not marching smartly enough.)[45] Howe, of course, was still at Head of Elk on the twenty-fourth, but he likely heard about Washington's spectacle soon enough. If the march-past was a morale builder for patriots it probably was also an intelligence coup for Sir William. No doubt some of those "rascally Tories" took a long and detailed look at what the rebel general had under his command and got word to General Howe as quickly as possible. Keenly security-conscious himself, Washington must have been aware of this risk, but a brave front evidently seemed more important. As soon as his army cleared the city Washington made for Wilmington, Delaware. From there he would move to counter the imperial forces when Howe moved from Head of Elk.

THE TEST OF ALL THE American commander in chief had accomplished since Trenton and Princeton was imminent. His impressive record—the revival of the Continental Army, the successful spring campaign in New Jersey, the general's hard-earned personal prestige, and patriot faith in his army's ability to win the war—all hung in the balance of what appeared to be a looming showdown with a British army that had beaten him badly a year earlier. It was still very much a "season of hope"—but seasons change. As this chapter's epigraph from Samuel Mather suggested, the season indeed had opened "favorably for the Americans." But how would it close?

TWO

A GENERAL UNDER FIRE

The Chorus of Critics

Things look gloomy here below. We want a General; thousands of Lives & Millions of Property are yearly sacrificed to the Insufficiency of our Commander in Chief.

—Jonathan Dickinson Sergeant to James Lovell, November 20, 1777[1]

On September 10, 1777, John Hancock, the Massachusetts delegate then sitting as president of the Continental Congress, sent a brief letter to General Washington. Hancock was aware the British and American armies were in close proximity south of Philadelphia and that a major engagement was possible, but he felt he had to get in touch with the commander in chief. Tension was building, and Congress was anxious to know what was happening as the rival forces seemed about to close. Hancock reminded the general of a congressional resolution asking to be kept informed of military developments "twice a day or oftner, if necessary." That said, he sent Washington "warmest Wishes" and hopes "that Victory and Success may attend you, and that the Campaign may terminate in such a Manner as to encrease your Fame and Glory."[2] Washington was too busy to respond to Hancock—in fact, he was preparing for battle—but his military secretary, Robert Hanson Harrison, promptly replied. At the moment there was nothing dramatic to report, but Harrison advised Hancock, in effect, to stay tuned: "Some interesting event may take place to morrow."[3] Harrison was right: September 10 was the day before the Battle of Brandywine.

Unknown to anyone at the time, September 11 marked the end of the "season of hope." Given the results at Brandywine, a bitterly contested engagement that raged for most of the day, the eleventh was also the day many Americans began a painful reassessment of Washington's fitness to command. It was the day the "season of hope" gave way to months of anxiety, frustration, intrigue, anger, and fear—the day events began moving toward the "Conway Cabal" and one of the true crises of the War for Independence.

MID-SEPTEMBER FOUND the British and American armies warily facing one another across Chadd's Ford on Brandywine Creek in Pennsylvania. Sir William Howe had led his troops from Head of Elk, Maryland; brushed aside American skirmishers at Cooch's Bridge, Delaware; and followed Washington's careful retrograde into Pennsylvania. The Continental general wanted to fight, but he pulled back several times to prevent Howe from turning his flank. Behind Chadd's Ford, however, Washington finally found ground he considered favorable for a defensive stand. If the British chose to engage, this would be the place. In fact, Washington was itching for a fight as he awaited Howe's next move.[4]

Rebels throughout the region waited as well. Morale and expectations remained high, and confidence in Washington and his army was steady in the face of the British advance. The army seemed eager to fight, and to patriots all portents appeared favorable.[5] John Adams continued his familiar refrains in letters to Abigail, praising Washington's patriotism and once again pooh-poohing the importance of Philadelphia if Howe somehow should manage to take it. Indeed, Adams returned to the theme so frequently one wonders if, unconsciously, he *was* genuinely afraid the city might fall.[6] If so, he was prescient, for on September 11 Howe turned Washington's flank, surprised the division on the American right, and soundly defeated the rebel army at the Battle of Brandywine.[7]

It took some time for patriots to sort out the implications of Brandywine. As often happened in an age without news in "real-time," initial reports of the action were contradictory—even wildly inaccurate. "A thousand various Accounts are circulating," Maryland's Samuel Chase reported from Philadelphia.[8] Although Howe claimed the field, Americans soon learned Howe had not followed up his victory by pursuing the defeated rebels and that Continental forces remained intact. There had not been a complete disaster. Indeed, in the few days after the battle patriot morale did not suffer appreciably.

This is not to say Howe's victory failed to cause some initial "Consternation," as Connecticut's Eliphalet Dyer put it.[9] By late morning on the eleventh, while the battle still raged, the first inconclusive reports of the action filtered into Philadelphia; and by the afternoon the signs looked increasingly ominous. A plainly alarmed woman reported "a Man at this very instant [3:00 P.M.] is parading through the City ringing a Bell and ordering all Houses to be immediately shut up, alarming the inhabitants that General Howe is advancing and that every man who can carry a Gun must appear on the Commons." The city was astir with carts, wagons, animals, and artillery clogging the streets.[10] It appeared the British were coming.

Yet the British did not come, and an uneasy, if hopeful, calm returned to the rebel capital. Patriots got a grip on themselves and, to its credit, there were no signs of panic in Congress. Some delegates even refused to see Brandywine as a major setback. Dyer (erroneously) understood Howe's losses were double Washington's and that in the ranks rebel spirits remained high. Supposedly reinforcements were flocking to the Continental Army, and the troops were anxious to reengage. Samuel Adams thought Howe had suffered another "Bunkers Hill" and gained only a "Patch of Ground" at Brandywine, and Richard Henry Lee's conclusion was every bit as dismissive. "Gen. Howe may say with Pyrrhus," he wrote Patrick Henry, "such another victory will ruin me."[11] There were elements of truth in all of these speculations, and it was certainly the case that Washington's army remained operational and willing to fight. But this time patriot optimism was misplaced, and in fact the situation was dangerous. Reinforcements were not rallying to Washington in appreciable numbers, and Dyer's guess on casualty figures was poorly informed. He had the numbers almost reversed: The British counted just under 600 in killed, wounded, and missing, while rebel losses tallied some 1,300.[12] For Sir William, Brandywine had been no Bunker Hill, and within days patriots began to realize as much.

It is difficult to date precisely when the cracks in the façade of rebel confidence appeared, but by September 16, less than a week after the battle, the fissures were plain to see. A new sense of alarm, even a specter of pessimism, was impossible to miss. John Adams was a bellwether of the changing mood. The Massachusetts patriot, who earlier had looked forward to the campaign with such enthusiasm and who repeatedly had discounted the importance of losing Philadelphia, now had grave second thoughts. In his diary—*not,* this time, in a letter to wife Abigail—he privately admitted "the Prospect is chilling, on every Side. Gloomy, dark, melancholly, and dispiriting," and at this point Adams ran out of adjectives. But he went on: "From whence is our Deliverance to come? Or is it not to come? Is Philadelphia to be lost? If lost, is the Cause lost? No—the Cause is not lost—but it may be hurt."[13] Days later, as Howe's army maneuvered closer to Philadelphia, Adams abandoned his approving posture toward Washington. Losing faith in the general, he called for divine intervention: "Oh, Heaven! grant Us one great Soul! One leading Mind would extricate the best Cause, from that Ruin which seems to await it, for the Want of it. . . . One active masterly Capacity would bring order out of this Confusion and save this Country."[14] This from the man who had proposed Washington as commander in chief in 1775; so much for Adams's bright hopes of the previous spring and summer.

There was a no more committed patriot than John Adams, so if the stewing in the privacy of his diary reflected a sinking confidence in rebel arms it should not surprise us to find other patriots similarly concerned. For other patriots were. Indeed, only a day later (September 17) apprehensions accelerated among delegates. Elbridge Gerry of Massachusetts still hoped for the best, but he advised it was now "necessary to form moderate Expectations." The expectations of Pennsylvania's Robert Morris were rather less moderate: He thought the threat to Philadelphia all too real, so he was packing up his papers and sending them to safety out of the city.[15] And in the letters of still other congressmen we find the first expressions of doubt about the leadership of the commander in chief.

These initial criticisms of the general were quite practical: The rebels had lost the Battle of Brandywine, and after buoyant expectations of the "season of hope" some patriots were asking *why*. And those questions led directly to questions about Continental leadership. One of the most pointed strictures came from delegate Thomas Burke of North Carolina. He saw Brandywine firsthand, the only member of Congress to join the troops of his state during the action. The North Carolinians saw some grim fighting, and Burke was incensed that Howe was able to get around Washington's right flank. For this the congressman blamed Major General John Sullivan of New Hampshire in particular. (Sullivan's division was on the American right and bore the initial brunt of the British attack.) But Burke also came away from Brandywine convinced too many other rebel generals did not know their business. He retained confidence in Washington's judgment, but he expressed "the Melancholy Conviction that his principle Officers are Incompetent, and I fear it is an Evil that cannot be remedied."[16] It was hardly an endorsement of the commander in chief's personnel decisions. Or, inasmuch as Congress had commissioned Washington's subordinates, Burke evidently had just as little faith in his colleagues' ability to pick generals.

James Lovell—the same James Lovell who had prophesied Howe couldn't defeat Washington in twenty years—was not mincing words either. He did not like "the great Burck" (the Massachusetts Whig had a knack for waspish sarcasm), but he shared the North Carolinian's qualms about Continental generals. Lovell was impressed with the performance of Major General Horatio Gates, then confronting Burgoyne in the opening rounds of the Battle of Saratoga, but he thought little of Continental leadership to the south. He wondered if bad luck—"fortune"—alone could explain the defeat at Brandywine. What about the army's commanders? Like Burke, he thought Sullivan ought to share some of the blame, and perhaps even "the Chief."[17] Again, this was on the seventeenth, and it was the first time Lovell had leveled a criticism at Washington, however oblique. It would not be the last.

By the end of September doubts had crept into the officer corps as well, although at this point they were the stuff of private communications. Bavarian-born Johann Kalb was a seasoned professional in the French army (which had German regiments). He had served with distinction in the War of Austrian Succession and the Seven Years' War, and he was ennobled a baron in 1763. Kalb had visited America in 1768, scouting the colonial political atmosphere for the French government, and he came back with Lafayette in 1777. He and the young marquis became close friends. Congress named Kalb a major general on September 5; and although he would be loyal to Washington until his death at the Battle of Camden in 1780, he was candid in his observations after Brandywine. Washington, he wrote, "is the most amiable, kind-hearted and upright man; but as a general he is too slow, too indolent, and far too weak; besides," the baron continued, "he has a tinge of vanity in his composition and overestimates himself. In my opinion whatever success he may have will be owing to good luck and to the blunders of his adversaries, rather than to his abilities. I may even say that he does not know how to improve upon the grossest blunders of the enemy."[18] Kalb was judging Washington by European standards; but he was no one's fool, and it is difficult to imagine other officers not harboring questions about the army's leadership as well. It is equally hard to imagine *anyone* harboring such reservations *prior* to Brandywine.

Washington's life got no easier after Brandywine. Five days later he squared off with Howe again near Malvern, Pennsylvania, willing to try reversing the fortunes of war; but a torrential storm dampened everyone's powder and mercifully there was no fighting that day. But there was on the night of September 20. After dark a British bayonet assault caught Brigadier General Anthony Wayne's Pennsylvania Continentals by surprise at Paoli. Major General Charles Grey had ordered his redcoats to remove the flints from their muskets, and the British bore in with bayonets and cold steel. The redcoats inflicted over 270 rebel casualties at little cost to themselves; it was a stinging and bloody defeat that did no credit to patriot arms. Thereafter, General Grey was "No Flint Grey." Then on the twenty-sixth, after a series of maneuvers that edged Washington out of position, the British marched into an undefended Philadelphia to the tune of "God Save the King." Congress and the Pennsylvania government had evacuated in time to escape capture—the Pennsylvanians to Lancaster and Congress, after a brief stop in Lancaster, to rustic York, over a hundred miles west of Philadelphia. What had been almost unthinkable only two months ago was now a reality—the seat of the rebel government had fallen and Congress, in effect, was in exile.[19]

In the long run the predictions of John Adams would prove correct: The loss of the city did not prove a strategic disaster. Howe indeed lacked the resources to do much more than hold the city and forage in the region. The British proved unable to use Philadelphia to reestablish political control over territory they could not actually garrison in strength. In Paris, upon learning the news of Howe's victory, Benjamin Franklin supposedly quipped that Sir William had not captured the city; rather, Philadelphia had captured him.[20] True enough—*eventually*. In the meantime the city's fall was a body blow to patriot morale. It was also a challenge to Washington. What would he do about it? Could he reclaim the city? He felt he had to try.

The patriot chief certainly understood his credibility was on the line. His opponent had out-generaled him for the past month, and the loss of the *de facto* capital had placed an exclamation point after the fact. Washington also knew that, in the north, Gates was in the process of bringing John Burgoyne to grief. He knew as well that events in the north were giving rise to unflattering (for him) comparisons between his performance and that of Gates. Under the circumstances there is little doubt the general thought he had to act. In what he hoped would be a much larger reprise of Trenton, he targeted the major British position at Germantown, just northwest of Philadelphia proper. With the attack scheduled for October 4, on the third he issued general orders explaining what was at stake in the coming battle—orders that also hinted at what was at stake for himself. The orders reported successes of rebel arms on other fronts: The frigate *Randolph* had defeated a small British flotilla, and at Saratoga the Northern Army under Gates had whipped a British attack John Burgoyne supposedly had led personally (he had not). The northern troops had behaved "with the highest spirit and bravery." Their example, Washington told his army, "surely must animate every man, under the General's [Washington's] immediate command." And now was the time to remind everyone who was still commander in chief: "This army—*the main American army* [my emphasis]—will certainly not suffer itself to be out done by their northern brethren—they will never endure such disgrace; but with an ambition becoming freemen, contending in the most righteous cause, rival the heroic spirit" of the Northern Army. "*Covet!* my Countrymen, and fellow soldiers! Covet! a share of the glory due to heroic deeds!" Washington went on, urging his troops to fight for all they held dear and for their honor and glory. There were no choices "but *Conquest or Death*."[21] Had this pep talk—for that is what it was—been oratory instead of words on paper, Washington would have sounded like an eighteenth-century George Patton.

The counterattack at Germantown failed. Bad luck, bad weather, poor tactical decisions, and heroic British resistance defeated Washington yet again. Congress applauded Washington's effort and, as after Brandywine, some patriots tried to put on a brave front, hoping the Continentals would try again.[22] But those voices were few. Lovell's reaction to Germantown—and Lovell now was clearly the voice of congressional pessimism—was more *a propos*. He hoped Washington's men, "stimulated by the conduct of the brave northern forces," might still manage something significant around Philadelphia; but he grumbled that Germantown was a lost opportunity, a wasted "day of Salvation offered by Heaven to us" unlikely to recur "in 10 campaigns." [23] This was clearly a criticism of army leadership, and there was similar carping. Benjamin Rush, querulous as ever, complained to John Adams "that the event of the battle of Germantown . . . was full of proofs of the truths I formerly communicated to you. We lost a city—a Victory—a campaign by that want of discipline and System which pervades every part of the army." Only Thomas Conway performed well in command, Rush claimed, and concluded "our army is no better than it was two years ago."[24] This was the same Rush, we should recall, who was so happy with "the strength[,] discipline—and spirit of our army" the previous June.[25]

Despite these groans of despair, Henry Laurens, delegate from South Carolina and destined to become president of Congress in December, retained his faith in the commander in chief. Yet it was impossible for him to miss the mood in Congress. He found all sorts of "loose Tongues" among his colleagues. Laurens didn't name names, but he jotted down some of their "buz!" in a note to his son John, a young lieutenant colonel on Washington's staff (who kept his father abreast of army developments and the concerns of Washington's inner circle of officers). "I would if I had been Comm^{r} of that Army with such powers have procured all the necessaries which are said to be wanted without such whining Complaints." From another: "I would . . . have prevented the amazing desertions which have happened[.] [I]t only wants proper attentions at fountain head"—a clear reference to the commander in chief.[26] This was grousing from armchair generals, and there were no calls for Washington's relief; but such grousing *did* reflect an eroding base of faith in the general's leadership. And then as now, such "buz!" had a way of spreading; it always does, and it was no longer private.

Six days after Germantown Benjamin Rush had dinner with Washington and his staff. No longer in Congress but serving as a senior army doctor, Benjamin Rush was a peevish guest. He was furious at the horrible conditions in American army hospitals, which he blamed on army mismanagement.[27] After dinner, which Rush thought was a dreary affair—"no wine—only grog"—he noted where the problems lay in the entire war effort:

> 1. The commander-in-chief at this time the idol of America—governed by Genl Greene—Gen. Knox and Col. Hamilton, one of his aids. A young man of 21 years of age.
> 2. 4 Major Generals,—Greene, Sullivan, Stirling & Stevens. The 1st a sycophant to the general, timid, speculative, without enterprise; the 2nd, weak, vain, without dignity, fond of scribbling, in the field a madman. The 3rd, a proud, vain, lazy, ignorant drunkard. The 4th, a sordid, boasting cowardly sot.[28]

Rush, as the next chapter will explain, was a military naïf, but there was no questioning the sincerity of his feelings. It is also true he had increasingly lost respect for the commander in chief and the army, and in the aftermath of Germantown he gave his spleen full rein.

There were still hopes the army could retake Philadelphia. Patriot defenses below the city commanded the Delaware River, preventing the Royal Navy from supplying Sir William's occupation. If these defenses could hold out until the river froze—as it did in those days—Howe faced the real possibility of starving in place. At best he would be immobilized on short rations in the city; at worst he would have to somehow get out or surrender.

In any event, rebels knew Howe's grip on Philadelphia was tenuous if their river defenses held.[29] And the American river defenses were formidable. On opposite sides of the Delaware the guns of Fort Mercer in New Jersey and Fort Mifflin in Pennsylvania threatened any shipping coming within range. A barrier of *chevaux-de-frise*, pointed obstructions capable of goring the hulls of enemy vessels, lay on the river bottom; and above the *chevaux-de-frise* patrolled the small but effective gunboats of the Pennsylvania navy. Royal Navy cannon pounded Fort Mifflin relentlessly over October and into November; but Mifflin and Mercer gave as good as they got, and the British could not breach the *chevaux-de-frise*. They lost two men-of-war trying, and on October 22 the Continental garrison decimated a Hessian attempt to storm Fort Mercer. This was a story of genuine gallantry, and patriots watched hopefully as the Continentals and Pennsylvania sailors grimly held out.[30]

While the fighting continued on the Delaware, Washington considered his options. The army was rested, if ragged, after Germantown, and he was aware of patriot hopes that he could still defeat Howe. Indeed, Congress was pressing him to confiscate any supplies he needed from regional loyalists to keep the army operational. Lovell, now showing little faith in the commander in chief, thought the Philadelphia theater could benefit from an infusion of new leadership. With Gates busy northward, Lovell had in mind Israel Putnam, then in the Hudson Highlands: "He is a brave man and will not rest long without Enterprise."[31] Fortunately, no one else that we know of expressed a similar interest in the crotchety and problematic Putnam. It was in this atmosphere of patriot concern that Washington convened a council of war on November 8. He asked his generals if, in the event Howe weakened his Philadelphia lines to attack the river forts, the Continental Army should attempt to storm the city. The answer, as he fully expected, was "in the Negative unanimously."[32] Washington was willing to fight, but an attack on a strongly placed enemy would have played directly into Sir William's hands.

A week later the question became moot. After enduring a blistering naval and land bombardment, the rebel garrison evacuated the all-but-destroyed Fort Mifflin on November 15. Five days later hopes that Fort Mercer could fight on collapsed.[33] With Cornwallis closing in with some two thousand men, Mercer's garrison wisely pulled out rather than mount a suicidal last stand. Finally unobstructed by rebel cannon fire, the Royal Navy cleared the *chevaux-de-frise* and chased away the rebel gunboats; the Delaware was open and Howe's army would not starve. Patriots accepted events glumly,

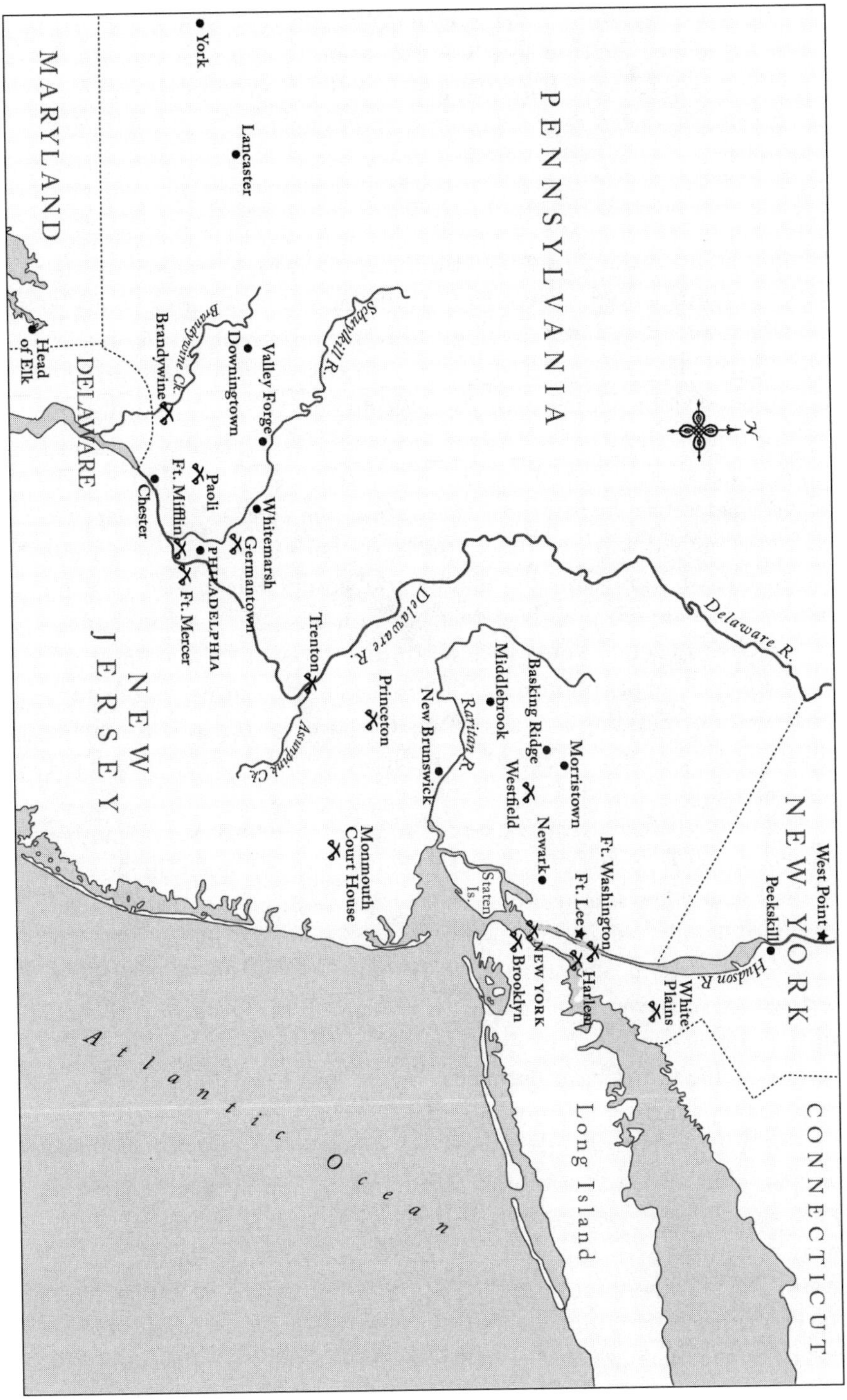
N
PENNSYLVANIA
MARYLAND
DELAWARE
NEW JERSEY
NEW YORK
CONNECTICUT
Long Island
Atlantic Ocean
York
Lancaster
Schuylkill R.
Valley Forge
Downingtown
Brandywine Ck.
Brandywine
Head of Elk
Paoli
Chester
Ft. Mifflin
Whitemarsh
Germantown
PHILADELPHIA
Ft. Mercer
Delaware R.
Trenton
Assunpink Ck.
Princeton
Raritan R.
New Brunswick
Middlebrook
Basking Ridge
Morristown
Westfield
Newark
Monmouth Court House
Staten Is.
Ft. Washington
Ft. Lee
Harlem
NEW YORK
Brooklyn
White Plains
Hudson R.
Peekskill
West Point
Delaware R.

realizing there was little the Continental Army could do in response.[34] For many the loss of the river forts was a blow heavier than Brandywine or Germantown. Defeat on the Delaware was a clear signal the American war effort generally—and thus the cause of independence—was in a state of acute crisis.

Elbridge Gerry, once so satisfied with the American war effort, reacted with utter dismay to the fall of Forts Mifflin and Mercer. Perhaps "fury" is a better word. He pointed the finger of blame directly at patriot military leadership. He complained that the Pennsylvania naval commander, Commodore John Hazelwood, "behaved like a Poltroon" (actually, the commodore had done well under the circumstances), while the Continental Army dithered as the British closed in on the forts. "Delays in the Councils of War" had lost a river that should have been "impregnable" and "Congress are exceedingly dissatisfied." Gerry had little faith in Washington's army, and he wished "most earnestly" that the rival armies were in New England rather than Pennsylvania. Had that been the case, he was sure Yankee "Militia like a Cloud" would have swarmed to "overwhelm the Enemy."[35] This was no vote of confidence either in Washington or in Washington's preference for building a regular American army as opposed to relying chiefly on the part-time citizen soldiers (and we will say more on this subject in Chapter 3).

If Gerry was furious, adjectives fail to capture the feelings of another prominent rebel. This was Thomas Mifflin, who figures centrally in the story of the Cabal. He was a man of genuine note. Born in 1744 to a Quaker mercantile family with important political connections, Mifflin was well educated, well traveled, and urbane. In 1765 he formed his own trading house and became independently wealthy. He broke with the Quakers as he took an early and active role in the patriot cause, and he played a distinguished part in leading Pennsylvania into rebellion. Energetic on Whig committees before independence, Mifflin was a delegate to both Continental Congresses. With no prior military experience he organized a volunteer militia unit and then served in significant quartermaster and field commands in 1775 and 1776. He was close to Washington as an aide and served as the army's quartermaster general. He fought well on Long Island, covering Washington's withdrawal from Brooklyn Heights, and he had rallied volunteer reinforcements for Washington in the darkest days of late 1776. No one had done more to round up militia in preparation for the Trenton operation. Promoted to major general in February 1777, his dedication to the cause was beyond question.[36]

However, Mifflin's relationship with Washington soured as the patriot war effort faltered. The Pennsylvania general looked on with dismay at Washington's successive defeats. In late 1776 Mifflin had opposed Washington's decision—based in part on the very poor advice of Major General Nathanael Greene—to hold Fort Washington, then isolated on upper Manhattan Island on the banks of the Hudson River. On November 16 a British attack overran the fort; patriots lost tons of vital supplies, all of the fort's artillery and munitions, and some three thousand men killed, wounded, or captured. The disaster had appalled the Pennsylvanian, and the later setbacks around Philadelphia—his home territory—left Mifflin infuriated. His faith in the commander in chief simply evaporated.

The motives for his subsequent actions, however, became increasingly personal. Mifflin nursed a growing resentment of Greene, and his agenda against the Rhode Islander was lengthy. Mifflin coveted his own role as an influential aide to the commander in chief, and he took umbrage as Washington turned increasingly to Greene. Alexander Graydon, a former Continental captain reading for the bar in 1777, knew Mifflin well and vividly recalled his hatred of Greene, whom he (Mifflin) disparaged as "neither the most wise, the most brave nor patriotic" of Washington's lieutenants.[37] Mifflin indirectly (and later directly) castigated the commander in chief for listening to Greene. In addition, and unpardonably in Mifflin's eyes, Greene had supported Washington's decision not to rush to Philadelphia in the spring of 1777 after Howe had abandoned New Jersey. Washington, unsure of Howe's intentions, remained close to the Hudson River, thinking the British might move north, while Mifflin insisted (correctly, as it turned out) that Howe would strike for Philadelphia. That Washington arrived in Pennsylvania in plenty of time to confront Howe did nothing to mitigate Mifflin's ire. By then Mifflin and Greene loathed one another, and as Kenneth Rossman, Mifflin's principal biographer, succinctly put it, "enemies of Greene could scarcely be the friends of Washington."[38] At some point, Graydon recorded, Mifflin concluded that Gates, whose "superior talents" had shown brilliantly at Saratoga, "was the man who should, of right, have the station so incompetently sustained by Washington."[39]

It is too much to attribute Mifflin's posture completely to personal pique—he came honestly by his critique of Washington's generalship—but his jealousy of Greene and anger at Washington certainly were intertwined.[40] Greene wrote off Mifflin's pique as wounded vanity, the reactions of a man who failed to receive "such mighty deference" as he thought "himself entitled to."[41] But Mifflin's fall from favor at headquarters had deeper roots. The Pennsylvanian's performance as quartermaster general had been problematic, and Washington was almost constantly fretting over all manner of supply shortages as he confronted Howe. Given the perilous state of Continental finances and the inexperience of most patriot logistics personnel, much of the situation was beyond Mifflin's control. There was a general feeling in the army, however, that Mifflin had not been up to the job; and Washington properly held Mifflin responsible for his department's performance. The commander in chief also found disturbing rumors that Mifflin continued to trade privately while serving as quartermaster. Thus, with or without Mifflin's distaste for Greene, relations between Washington and Mifflin were strained; and when in early November 1777 Mifflin resigned pleading ill health and left the quartermaster department leaderless, the breach between the men was virtually complete.[42]

Whatever his personal relationship with Washington, by mid-November Mifflin had seen enough of the Virginian as commander in chief; and he could not help comparing Washington's losing record to the success of Horatio Gates with the Northern Army. Evidently he saw the fall of Fort Mifflin—a post named after him—on the fifteenth as an emotional final straw. In a November 17 letter to Gates, Mifflin abandoned all forbearance. He had seen enough, and his letter, which merits sober consideration, reflected as much. "You have savd our Northern Hemisphere," he told Gates, "and in Spite of our consummate & repeated Blundering you have changd the Constitution of the Southern Campaign on the part of the Enemy from Offensive to Defensive." If Gates had remained with the main army, Mifflin averred, the major general could have sorted out the jealousies, "Arrogance," and "System of Favoritism" that plagued Washington's command. These failures were driving out officers "who would not worship the Image"—clearly meaning the commander in chief—"& pay an undeserved Tribute of Praise & Flattery to the great & powerful." "The List of our disgusted patriots is long and formidable—their Resentments keen against the reigning Cabal and their powers of Opposition not despicable. The Campaign here must soon close. If no brilliant Action takes Place before it ends," Mifflin was sure, the army would have to find winter quarters in the Pennsylvania interior. Popular protest would be swift. "Great & very general will be the Murmur—so great & so general that nothing inferior to a Commander in Chief will be able to resist the mighty Torrent of public Clamour & public Vengeance."

Mifflin was only warming up. "We have had a noble Army melted down by illjudgd Marches—Marches that disgrace their Authors & Directors—& which have occasiond the severest & most just Sarcasm & Contempt of our Enemies." His exasperation was at full tilt as he asked Gates, "How much are you to be envied my dear General? How different your Conduct & your Fortune!" Mifflin insisted the list of officers resigning in disgust was long and included some of the army's best, and he claimed that the loss of the Delaware forts would make matters worse. "You must know the Consequence," he told Gates: "Loss of the River, Boats, Gallies, Ships of War &c.—good winter Quarters to the Enemy & a general Retreat or illjudgd blind Attempt on our part to save a gone Character"—again, another swipe at Washington. Mifflin ended with a plea. "In Short this Army will be totally lost unless you come down & collect the virtuous Band, who wish to fight under your Banner, & with their Aid save the southern Hemisphere. Prepare yourself for a Jaunt to this Place. Congress must send for you. I have ten thousand things to tell."[43]

By any measure this letter was a bombshell—or it would have been if its contents had become public. There were exaggerations to be sure; not all of the resignations Mifflin claimed had occurred. Yet he accurately related the restiveness with Washington's leadership now stirring among some officers, and he certainly captured the growing public alarm over the state of the patriot military. And, of central importance, *Mifflin's letter was the first unambiguous call for Gates to take charge of the rebel war effort.* His missive to Gates begs no other interpretation.[44]

In the early winter of 1778—at the height of the Cabal controversy—Mifflin would repeatedly and indignantly deny any ill will toward the commander in chief. Indeed, he professed to be wounded by accusations and "jealousies entertained of him, at camp and elsewhere, that he was or had been, aiming to remove General Washington, a thing [he] solemnly disavows."[45] This was nonsense. Such "solemn disavowals" came only after a storm of criticism broke over Washington's detractors; and as we will see, Mifflin's continued inimical actions toward the general would speak louder than any words. In the meantime we must give Mifflin his due for a blunt and sincere assessment (as he saw it) of the American war effort and of his conviction that Washington was not up to his job—and that it was time to trade Washington for Gates.

Mifflin was not alone in his rage. The rebel evacuation of Fort Mercer on November 20 coincided with another cogent (and equally astringent) critique of Washington; and it is not too much to speculate that the loss of the Delaware forts also motivated it. From the pen of New Jersey delegate Jonathan Dickinson Sergeant it was, like Mifflin's letter to Gates, a full-blown indictment of the commander in chief's generalship. Sergeant was no lightweight among patriots. He loathed the British. Before New Jersey sent him to Congress he had been an energetic revolutionary, serving on local Whig committees and sitting in the Provincial Congress. In December 1776 he paid the price for his radical allegiance: The British burned his Princeton home, prompting him to transplant to Philadelphia. On November 1, 1777, Pennsylvania appointed him state attorney general, but he remained in Congress until New Jersey sent a replacement.[46] By then Sergeant joined those who had seen enough of Washington's leadership, and he vented his considerable spleen in a letter to James Lovell—by now every bit a kindred spirit when it came to the subject of the commander in chief:

> Things look gloomy here below. We want a General; thousands of Lives & Millions of Property are yearly sacrificed to the Insufficiency of our Commander in Chief. Two battles [Brandywine and Germantown] he has lost for us by two such Blunders as might have disgraced a Soldier of three Months Standing; and yet we are so attached to this Man that I fear we shall rather sink with him than throw him off our Shoulders. And sink we must under his Management. Such Feebleness & Want of Authority, such Confusion & Want of Discipline, such Waste, such Destruction will exhaust the Wealth of both the Indies & annihilate the Armies of all of Europe and Asia. Twenty Thousand Recruits annually would be absolutely necessary to maintain an Army of forty thousand. I believe this is the most moderate Calculation. In the mean Time People are so disaffected to the Service that no more Recruits can be got. In short, I am quite a Convert to Abraham Clarkes [delegate Abraham Clark of New Jersey] Opinion; that we may talk of the Enemy's Cruelty as we will, but we have no greater Cruelty to complain of than the Management of our Army.

Sergeant was an intelligent man and a committed patriot, but his voice was one of utter frustration and despair. He trusted Lovell as "a Man of prudence" as to whether or not to share the letter with others, and it appears Lovell did. He sent it on to Samuel Adams—who by this time was in no mood to differ with Lovell's dim view of Washington.[47]

Lovell was writing as well, and his mood was no better than Sergeant's or Mifflin's. The next day (November 21) he cracked off a missive to his friend Joseph Whipple of New Hampshire deploring the loss of the river forts. He blamed the fiasco on a lack of "proper Exertions on Shore"—that is, from Washington's army. There was simply nothing "agreeable" happening in the Pennsylvania theater, he told Whipple, and Washington's army was virtually inert. "I should deceive you greatly if I lead you to look for any thing favorable from the *main* army." Gates was sending reinforcements to Washington from the north, but Lovell despaired of Washington putting them to good use, especially after the defeat at Germantown.[48]

A week later Lovell was still fulminating over the fates of "the brave fellows at Fort Mifflin and Red Bank [Fort Mercer]." This time, however, his correspondent was more significant to our story: It was Major General Horatio Gates. Lovell and Gates already were well acquainted and had corresponded earlier in the war, with Lovell making no secret of his admiration for the victor at Saratoga. Now he also made no secret of his opinion that the patriot cause needed Gates in Pennsylvania—and fast. "We want you in different places," he flattered, "but most of all . . . . We want you most near Germantown [not overly far from the Whitemarsh encampment]. Good God! what a Situation are we in! how different from what might have been justly expected! You will be astonished when you come to know accurately what numbers have at one time and another been collected near Philada. to wear out stockings, shoes and breeches. Depend upon it for every ten Soldiers placed under the Command of our Fabius 5 Recruits will be wanted annually during the war."[49] Only Thomas Mifflin (just ten days earlier) had come this close to an open hope Gates would replace Washington in the top Continental command. And it *was* close. Indeed, coupled with Mifflin's letter, Gates could be excused for thinking at least some eminent revolutionaries were virtually inviting him to vie for Washington's job. At the very least Gates, who, as we will soon learn, was about to cross figurative swords with the commander in chief anyway, would have been pleased to know his stock was so high with a ranking member of Congress and another major general.

Thus the chorus of Washington's critics was growing, and the officer corps was not immune to the increasing doubts. A young major (and future president) James Monroe groused that "Every table thro' the line is the Theatre of calumny" as officers argued over favored commanders.[50] From camp at Whitemarsh Joseph Ward, a colonel in the Continental commissary department, wrote two letters expressing his concerns to Samuel Adams and Lovell; and if his tone was less belligerent than Sergeant's or Lovell's, there was no mistaking his frustration. Ward had been in touch with Lovell earlier, and he now agreed with Lovell that the campaign had done nothing for the "honor of the *grand* Army"—that is, the main force under Washington. That honor would "remain disputable months yet to come." In so many words he laid the blame at Washington's feet: "In my humble opinion we made a slip in generalship at the opening of the campaign with the Enemy soon after their landing at Elk, and thereby lost advantages which we cannot now regain." It was now too late to recapture Philadelphia, he wrote, and there was no choice but to go into winter quarters. The only bright spot of the day lay with the "honor and fame" of the Northern Army under Gates.[51] Here was an army officer clearly implying an unflattering comparison between Washington and Gates in letters to two senior and sympathetic revolutionaries.

Other officers were little happier than Ward. In late December Kalb, who still liked Washington personally, questioned the general's judgment and thought his closest advisors (he did not name names) were "certainly gross ignoramouses."[52] Also from Whitemarsh, Lieutenant Samuel Hay of the Pennsylvania Line wrote Colonel William Irvine hoping for the arrival of Gates: "God speed the Brave old fellow and send him safe back to us, for I fear we cannot do much without him." Hay even lamented Conway's absence.[53] Brigadier General Anthony Wayne, who always preferred active operations, grew tired of losing battles under the commander in chief. Like Kalb, Wayne thought Washington was listening to the wrong people. Wayne had not lost hope in the cause, but he told Gates (*another* letter to Gates!) that Washington needed to make more decisions himself rather than relying on councils of war (even though Congress had insisted Washington consult with his generals). Like the general's other critics, Wayne wanted to see more decisive leadership; and he also called attention to the success of Gates's army. "The eyes of all America are fixed on you," he wrote Washington after a council of war, "[and] the Junction of the Northern Army—which Obliged Genl Burgoyne to lay down his arms, gives the Country and Congress some expectation, that a vigorous Effort will be made to Dislodge the Enemy [from Philadelphia]. . . . It's not in our Power to Command success—but it is in our Power to produce a Conviction in the World that we Deserve it."[54] Colonel Daniel Brodhead, another Pennsylvanian—and brother-in-law of Thomas Mifflin—was also a man in whom the commander in chief later would place considerable trust. By early November, however, Brodhead no longer trusted the commander in chief. He wrote Gates that since his (Gates's) departure for the North the main army had "suffered greatly and chiefly by the conduct of Genl W___n. Most of the officers are unhappy under his command."[55] Brodhead was exaggerating, but there was no mistaking the uneasy atmosphere within the Continental officer corps.

Perhaps the most astonishing of these November letters to Gates came from the pen of Major General Arthur St. Clair. Gates must have been surprised, for only months before Congress had relieved St. Clair, as well as his commanding officer Major General Philip Schuyler, in favor of Gates in the aftermath of the debacle at Fort Ticonderoga. Indeed, St. Clair was awaiting court-martial for his role in the action. Washington held St. Clair in some esteem, a fact certainly known to Gates. Yet on November 21 St. Clair wrote Gates a chatty note on the outcome of the Battle of Germantown. He told Gates he (St. Clair) had no hand in the defeat. It had "happened in my absence," he assured the victor of Saratoga; but there was "strange mismanagement in the affair," he confided, and "infinite courts-martial" would surely result. Worse, the battle seemed to confirm the "superiority of the British troops." St. Clair looked forward to the arrival of Gates's "victorious troops," without which Washington's army could do little.[56] The entire epistle was no compliment to Washington, who had no reason to suspect St. Clair was anything but thoroughly loyal to him. Why did St. Clair write such a letter? It seems clear he saw Gates's star ascending and that he was hedging his bets on who might emerge as commander in chief—in which case he was also hedging his bets on his own future. As historian Joseph Lee Boyle has so prosaically put it, St. Clair was "sucking up" to Gates.[57]

How many of these letters were there? There must have been others that never survived to land in any archive. The existing record is enough, however, to reveal a growing and profound alarm over the state of Continental Army leadership; and the same record indicates some senior patriots saw Horatio Gates as the coming man. Indeed, another November letter to Gates—one that has not survived (that we know of) but made the rounds among a circle of patriots—would lead to open conflict within the Continental command and a public airing of the dispute between Washington's critics and allies. Its author was Thomas Conway, and of *that* letter we will learn *much* more.

The Philadelphia Campaign all but concluded with the British victories on the Delaware. While his critics fumed, in early November Washington took post at Whitemarsh, Pennsylvania, safely beyond Germantown. Temporarily out of harm's way on good defensive ground, he and his officers debated next steps. He found the Continental officer corps all but unanimous that waging a winter campaign was impossible. When Washington polled his generals on November 24, only five of the fifteen officers considered any attack on Philadelphia feasible. Another council of war confirmed the decision in early December.[58]

It was not what many Americans wanted to hear. They wanted the army to protect the countryside around Philadelphia from British patrols and raids and, if possible, they also wanted to recapture the *de facto* capital. That is, they wanted Washington to *fight.* Pennsylvania state authorities sent a blunt "remonstrance" to Congress protesting Washington's plans to go into winter quarters; the Pennsylvanians were especially disturbed at rumors the army might encamp west of the Schuylkill River, perhaps as far away as Wilmington. This, they complained, would leave key parts of the region open to the British, would encourage the tories, and would destroy the "Credit of the Continental Currency through out this State."[59] Washington did not see the remonstrance right away (when Congress showed it to him later he was insulted), but Congress had Pennsylvania's concerns very much in mind when it considered the military situation. Delegates were tired of suffering "ourselves to be Attacked instead of attacking." Gerry wrote John Adams that Congress was unanimous in its insistence on a winter offensive. When Washington demurred, on November 28, Congress appointed a Committee at Headquarters comprised of Gerry, Robert Morris (Pennsylvania), and Joseph Jones (Virginia) to meet with the commander in chief to press the point.[60] What they found was an army without the numbers and supplies to open a new campaign; an officer corps upset over matters of rank, late pay, and congressional resistance to granting post-war pensions; and a pervasive sentiment in camp opposed to any venture against Philadelphia.[61]

Certainly Washington had lost the fighting mood of September, and he was tired of being asked to do the impossible. The army, he explained to Congress in excruciating detail, was simply in no condition to mount a major offensive; he lacked numbers, and faltering commissary and quartermaster functions had left the Continentals and attached militia without the necessary sinews of war. Abandoning his usual tact, he drove home the point to Henry Laurens, now president of Congress: "It would give me infinite pleasure to afford protection to every individual and to every Spot of Ground in the whole of the United States," he lectured. "Nothing is more my wish. But this is not possible with our present force."[62] Nothing occurred before the spring of 1778 to make him change his mind. There was no winter campaign.

While the commander in chief fended off demands to keep fighting, a final act in the Philadelphia Campaign played out over the first week of December. Before the weather halted operations, Howe decided on one more effort to bring Washington to battle. On December 5, he marched from Philadelphia and advanced on Whitemarsh. His men skirmished with the rebels through the eighth, but Howe found Washington strongly positioned and reluctant to offer a general engagement. At this, a somewhat disappointed Sir William marched back to Philadelphia to spend a relatively comfortable winter.[63] His departure brought little joy to some patriots. Indeed the Whitemarsh skirmishing left North Carolina's Cornelius Harnett dejected. He had come to expect the worst, and he saw it again at Whitemarsh: Howe had sortied from Philadelphia, he wrote, and "Out general'd us, as usual." Gerry, who was with the congressional committee at Whitemarsh, was perplexed at Washington's reluctance to attack, fretting that "until such an enterprising Spirit prevails . . . the Enemy will Manoeuvre to Advantage." Lovell, now willing to find fault at every turn, was no happier: Howe gave the army "4 days of opportunity," he moaned, but "our Army was not inclined to fight."[64]

Indeed, at this point Benjamin Rush was ready to blame virtually all of the Revolution's military ills on the commander in chief, and he became downright reckless in his accusations. On January 12, 1778, Rush wrote anonymously to Virginia governor Patrick Henry. Why Rush did so has never been explained satisfactorily. He later (after the war) claimed Gates had mentioned to him that Henry did not think much of Washington as a general, and thus Rush may have felt Henry shared the circulating doubts about the commander in chief.[65] Whatever his reasons for contacting Henry, he began by praising the governor's patriotism and "eloquence upon the opinions of this country"; then he launched into a scorching attack on Washington's military reputation, reprising the incendiary arguments of Mifflin and others. He denigrated the main army under Washington: America's "army—what is it? A major genl belonging to it [almost certainly Thomas Conway] called it a few days ago in my hearing a *Mob*." But all was not lost. "A Gates—a [Charles] Lee, or a Conway would, in a few weeks render them an irresistable body of men." The letter fulsomely praised Gates, whose Northern Army "has shewn us what Americans are capable of doing with a *General* at their head."[66] No one ever accused Benjamin Rush of subtlety, and in this case his meaning was unmistakable—if the American cause was to triumph, Washington had to go.

Rush failed to sign the missive, but he hinted that his handwriting might give up his identity and he did not seem to care. He told Henry the letter ought to be burned but its central points circulated. However, if Rush thought he was writing to a kindred spirit in Henry he was badly mistaken. The governor took umbrage, although he failed to burn the letter. Instead, in a manner of speaking he did circulate it—by promptly sending it to Washington. The general, although more than aware of the activity of his critics, learned of Rush's authorship of the letter only in 1784. He was furious and never forgot the incident.[67] The letter *was* a nasty piece of work—Washington justly saw it as a virulent personal attack.

In Virginia the Rush letter left Governor Henry rather puzzled. He wrote Washington "anxious to hear something" of any other news reflecting a wider problem facing the general. From what he had learned from a recent visitor he surmised there was trouble brewing; and he expressed genuine "surprise" at learning "sundry particulars concerning Genl Mifflin," a man Henry had thought a friend of the cause. "'Tis very hard to trace the Schemes and windings of the Enemys to America," he mused in a clear reference to Washington's detractors.[68] Others were equally concerned with Mifflin's conduct, but for the moment that is getting ahead of our story.

As the new year approached, Virginia delegate Francis Lightfoot Lee added a painful benediction to 1777. While he hoped for better things in 1778, he sadly concluded there was little to cheer at present. In fact, he bewailed the recent military situation: "the campaign in this quarter has to be sure been very disgraceful." Lee's New England friend Samuel Adams felt the same. Just over a week later Adams wrote to Francis Lightfoot's brother, Richard Henry, that while Washington's army had suffered no "shameful Defeats," the "promising [1777] Campaign has however ended ingloriously." The problem, Adams believed, was "a miserable Set of General Officers" no one had the courage to weed out. "Is our Army," he asked, "perpetually to be an unanimated one[?]"[69] And if his generals were not up to the challenge wouldn't "our Commander in Chief . . . one day suffer in his own Character by Means of these worthless Creatures?" Had anyone but Richard Henry Lee seen Adams's letter, the reader might have asked how the writer could excoriate Washington's senior officers without blaming Washington for keeping them. In fact, the Adams epistle was surely a jibe at the general. In Lancaster, where he kept his finger on the public pulse, diarist Christopher Marshall sensed the grim temper of the times. He knew all about the arguments over a winter campaign and the frustration among Pennsylvanians at the end of the fighting. He was also aware of "a general murmur in the people . . . against the weak conduct of Gen. Washington." Marshall wondered what the British were thinking. Were they mocking us, he asked: "O Americans, where is your virtue? O Washington, where is your courage?"[70] Thus the campaign of 1777 ended with a whimper in the field, a veritable growl of disappointment in Congress, and a lament from an alarmed citizen. And there was much to lament.

FOR MANY PATRIOTS the defeats in Pennsylvania—serious enough by themselves—seemed to be part of a much broader malaise, something fundamentally wrong with the rebel war effort. The disappointments were not confined to the Philadelphia theater. In July, in the face of Burgoyne's advance from Canada, Major General Arthur St. Clair had evacuated Fort Ticonderoga without a fight. Ticonderoga had enjoyed a reputation as something of a Gibraltar of the North, the key to the defense of the vital Lake Champlain-Hudson River corridor; and its loss, especially without a struggle, shocked patriots. We will say more about this in the next chapter, but for now it is enough to know a thoroughly aroused Congress relieved St. Clair *and* his immediate superior, Major General Philip Schuyler.[71] John Adams, never known as an unusually bloodthirsty revolutionary, was livid and would have done more. "Don't you pitty me to be wasting my Life," he grumbled to Abigail, "in laborious Exertions, to procure Cannon, Ammunition, Stores, Baggage, Cloathing &c. &c. &c. &c., for Armies, who give them all away to the Enemy, without firing a Gun."[72] Less delicately he moaned to Horatio Gates: "We shall never hold a post until we shoot a general." The loss of Ticonderoga "Calls for Inquiry," he demanded. Innocent officers should be acquitted, but those guilty should "meet their Deserts. I see no Medium, I confess, between honourable Acquittal and capital Punishment."[73] As far as we know, Adams was the only member of Congress to suggest shooting someone, but others were just as angry. Thus, even prior to the defeats around Philadelphia, patriots were in a sour mood regarding the performance of their officers, and they were saying as much.

There was more. In October patriot troops, inhibited by poor weather and questionable planning, bungled an attempt to force the British out of Rhode Island. The Continental commander, Major General Joseph Spencer, had cancelled the operation before anyone fired a shot. Once again Congress was aghast. An investigation exculpated Spencer, who resigned under a cloud in 1778, but the entire affair was yet another example of a war effort that appeared stalled and incapable. Rhode Island delegate Henry Marchant could not contain his exasperation: "How long are we to be ruined by false Delicacy!" he wrote Richard Henry Lee. "I wish that Congress would in some self Evident Cases exercise the Sovereign Right of removing [incompetent officers]." "The public Good is sufficient Cause," he insisted. Marchant conceded that Spencer was a decent man—"a sober Man, a religious Man, and a Friend to his Country—but is this enough?"[74] For Marchant and many others the answer was an emphatic, *no*, it was not. It is no stretch to see a causal link between this atmosphere of malaise and the vituperative postures of Mifflin, Lovell, and Sergeant, if not other frustrated Whigs.

Washington's senior officers and closest aides those "gross ignoramouses," according to Kalb—were fully aware of these sentiments. They had not seen the private letters of Lovell, Mifflin, and others, but the critical mood in Congress was no secret. The view from headquarters was realistic; the officer corps knew the general was under political fire. They were painfully aware of the public acclaim being heaped on Horatio Gates, as well as the fact that Gates and Washington already distrusted one another (about which there will be a great deal more to say). Luckily, however, men like Major General Nathanael Greene and chief of artillery Brigadier General Henry Knox, among the officers Washington trusted, were smarter (or with experience would become smarter) than Kalb allowed. So were many other senior officers. While angry, they refused to panic and let the political situation cloud their military judgment. They insisted the chief do nothing precipitate in the field—and specifically that included not mounting a risky assault on Philadelphia—simply to assuage an anxious public and a frustrated Congress. They were rightly concerned another defeat would only make things worse.[75]

Regarding Philadelphia, Greene counseled patience. "I have seen of late, the difficulty your Excellency seemed to labour under, to satisfy the Expectations of an ignorant Populace, with great concern." The Continental Army was in no state to attack Howe, and Washington, it appeared to Greene, "has the choice of but two things." They were difficult choices. He could "fight the Enemy without the least Prospect of Success . . . or remain inactive & be subject to the Censure of an ignorant & impatient populace." If he attacked and failed, public condemnation would follow. If he didn't attack, and instead took the army into winter quarters, he would gain only "the Approbation of your own mind" and, for what it was worth, the appreciation of "all future Generations." In the meantime, it was best to use the break in the fighting to rebuild the battered army. Greene conceded that popular censure was bound to wound Washington's sensibilities (and Greene assured his chief he would share those wounds); but he argued "the cause is too important to be trifled with to shew our Courage, & your Character too deeply interested, to sport upon unmilitary Principles."[76] In seven months' time, in June 1778, Greene would change his tune and argue for action on very nearly the same grounds he urged caution in November 1777—"to shew our Courage, & your Character"—but for the moment his advice was sound.

So was the counsel of Henry Knox, although it was of a somewhat different character. Knox, a Boston bookseller, had learned much of what he knew of martial affairs from his own books, and his advice to Washington was something of a disquisition—with a tedious compendium of historical examples—on the foibles of attacking a stronger foe with a weaker army. It was advice, of course, the commander in chief didn't need; and the history of Roman generals, the deeds of French marshals, and the lessons of storming the "redoubts at Pultowa" [!] made for painful reading. Knox was probably lucky Washington liked him. But there was more than a kernel of truth in what Knox wrote when he stressed the futility of attacking Philadelphia in late 1777; and unlike Greene, he was optimistic the consequences of that decision would not harm Washington. Knox was convinced most Americans still revered the general; he did not think Washington's reputation would suffer if he chose not to fight a winter campaign. Yet the artillerist conceded "I believe perfectly that there are some people who speak disrespectfully of your Excellency, but I . . . believe that these people . . . have never given any unequivocal evidence of their attachment to our rights."[77] In this last Knox was clearly wrong; plenty of firm patriots were speaking "disrespectfully" indeed.

While Congress ultimately accepted Washington's resistance to waging a winter campaign as final, delegates continued to question aspects of the general's leadership—and in pointed terms. Washington had complained bitterly to Congress about the deplorable state of supply operations, correctly explaining that logistical problems had blunted the army's offensive capabilities. But Congress now pushed back. It fully agreed the army desperately needed forage and supplies of all kinds to remain operational, but it brusquely reminded the general it twice—in September and November—had authorized him to impress whatever he needed from regional loyalists. Why hadn't he done so? While the delegates agreed using military power against citizens was normally repugnant—the very reason Washington had shied away from aggressive impressments—a new resolution of December 10 told the general his "delicacy" at this critical period was "prejudicial to the general liberties of America." There was a whiff of umbrage in this resolution, which went on to bluntly direct the commander in chief to confiscate anything "which may be beneficial to the army or serviceable to the enemy" and destroy virtually everything else. He was to leave only a bare minimum a pillaged family needed to survive.[78] Lovell quite enjoyed voting for the resolution, admitting almost gleefully to Samuel Adams the "Resolve was meant to rap a Demi G— over the Knuckles." One can see him shaking his head as he wrote: "What a fatality attends some men in the choice of their favorites!" Lovell was true to form: He simply could not resist an opportunity to stick in a needle.

It remained to be seen what all of this talk, so much of it so angry, really meant. Defeat, as we have seen, especially when unexpected, changes perspectives. Certainly it did for the likes of James Lovell, Benjamin Rush, Elbridge Gerry, Thomas Mifflin, and others. During the "season of hope" they had sung the praises of the commander in chief—but no longer. True, Washington's record in command compared poorly to that of Horatio Gates. It is well to remember, however, that comparisons to Gates were only part of the story. For Washington an equal difficulty lay in comparisons to his own sterling performance in New Jersey during the early months of 1777. Victory had seemed within his grasp. Now, with the earlier expectations of victory dashed, how far would Washington's critics go if a viable alternative to him appeared to offer rebel arms a brighter prospect for success? Would they try to relieve the commander in chief or maneuver to force him from command? And if they tried, how much influence did Lovell, Mifflin, Sergeant, Rush, and those of a similar frame of mind actually have? Before answering such questions, however, it is time to look more carefully at these men who thought they knew more about fighting the war than General Washington. What were their motives; and what were their understandings of their relationships to the generals they hired, including the commander in chief? Perhaps then we will get a better appreciation of the general's growing chorus of critics.

THREE

IDEOLOGUES AND GENERALS

Of Politics and Perspectives

> *Resolved*, That whenever any expedition . . . shall fail in the execution . . . it shall be an established rule in Congress to institute an enquiry into the cause of the failure . . . and into the conduct of the principal officer or officers of the expedition so failing.
>
> —*Journals of the Continental Congress*, November 28, 1777[1]

> I should despair of our cause if our country contained 60,000 men abandoned enough to enlist for 3 years or during the war.
>
> —Benjamin Rush to Samuel Adams, October 1, 1777[2]

No one, it seems—not in the army, not in Congress—was happy when Washington broke camp at Whitemarsh and trekked with his men toward Valley Forge. The new encampment was on the banks of the Schuylkill River some twenty miles above Philadelphia, close enough to cover much of the countryside but far enough from Howe to stay out of trouble. The troops arrived on December 19 and immediately began preparations to spend the winter. That winter, of course, became an epic of endurance and, finally, of revival—now deservedly a staple of America's founding narrative. The thread we will follow is woven throughout the Valley Forge story but distinct in itself: During this winter the general fought not only to save his army but, in his view and in the view of many other rebels, his job as well.

Coming to grips with the battle for Washington's reputation, however, as well as his position as commander in chief, requires an appreciation of the men who made that battle necessary. So this chapter is not about intrigues or plots. That has to wait. It deals instead with individuals and motives and their historical context. In fact, it is time to name names. We need to ask *who* Washington's detractors were and *why* they felt the way (or *ways*) they did about the general. We also need to avoid pre-judging these men. For, in general, Washington's critics—let alone his actual enemies—have not fared well in the public memory of the Revolution. For that matter, they have done little better among historians. Their often shrill tone—how else can we describe Benjamin Rush?—sounded strident to the point of zealotry, and sometimes it was. Their assumption that they held the moral high ground, or that they simply knew better than Washington how to fight a war, still smacks of arrogance. The fact that events ultimately proved them wrong-headed (and in some cases foolish) has not helped their image. Yet these men were patriots; they were *not* the "bad guys" in some period drama.

To evaluate these men "looking backwards," however, is unfair. Most historians now recognize that Washington's leadership was essential (if not "indispensable," as historian James T. Flexner so famously phrased it) to the ultimate American victory.[3] But that was anything but clear in late 1777 or early 1778; nor was American victory under any circumstances or leadership assured. That being the case, we need to look at the actions and motives of Washington's critics from the perspectives of 1777 and 1778, not from the perspective of what we know today. They deserve an evaluation based in their own times and contexts.

DEFEAT IN BATTLE, of course, and the general military "malaise" were the issues most troubling patriots. We know it was the disappointments of late 1777 that led directly to doubts about Washington's leadership. The situation was analogous to the situation in late 1776, when defeat had prompted trepidations about the abilities of the commander in chief. The difference was that in late 1777 there was no Trenton or Princeton to restore confidence in the general. Instead there was Germantown. When Major General Kalb expressed his concerns about American leadership, he did so with the practiced eye of an experienced soldier; he had no political axes to grind. He simply did not see Continental generals of a caliber sufficient to beat Howe's regulars. Loyally, however—and he *was* loyal to Washington—he confined his criticisms to private correspondence. Yet undoubtedly he mirrored the observations of many of the French officers with Continental commissions who also questioned the ability of the American regulars to take on the redcoats, which was much the same thing as questioning Washington's ability to produce a winning army.[4] The skeptical postures of Anthony

Wayne, Daniel Brodhead, Samuel Hay, and other American officers toward Washington derived from the same practical concern: the rebel war effort appeared to be going nowhere, at least in Washington's theater.

The story was the same in Congress—and for all we know, among Americans at large. Congressman William Duer (1743–1799) of New York was a good example. He had nothing personal or ideological against Washington; in fact, Duer was on the conservative spectrum of the Revolution. But he was a successful entrepreneur with mercantile, timber, real estate, and milling interests; and as a businessman the disorganized state of army logistics operations perplexed him no end. So did problematic military leadership.[5] In mid-February 1778 Duer wrote Francis Lightfoot Lee a long letter lamenting what he saw as mismanagement at every turn, and he laid responsibility for the mess at the top: "For my own Part, when I consider the Character of our present Councils, and that of the principal Leaders in our Army, I am induced to prepare My Mind for an Event (which unless a Miracle interposes) will certainly happen, the Dissolution of the Army." Duer's attitude caught his New York colleague Gouverneur Morris, a firm Washington loyalist, by surprise. The "Set of Scoundrels" seeking to undermine the general, Morris concluded, "have made a {*tool* of Duer}" (bracketed text originally in cipher).[6] Abraham Clark of New Jersey was a zealous republican and on the left wing of the Revolution—Rush noted him as "uncommonly quick sighted in seeing the weaknesses and defects in public men and measures." But like Duer, Clark's complaints about the general were purely practical. He worried about the location of the 1777 winter encampment, concerned Washington would leave New Jersey unprotected; and he was vexed at chaotic army administration. "We may talk of the Enemy's Cruelty as we will," Jonathan Dickinson Sergeant reported Clark as saying, "but we have no greater Cruelty to complain of than the Management of our Army."[7] Then there was the lack of any military decision. According to Mercy Otis Warren, other Whigs were simply fed up with the pace of the war even if they admired Washington's undoubted patriotism. The general's seeming "constitutional want of ardency" was damning; they wanted a commander with a more aggressive temper and a quicker end to the conflict.[8]

The Lee brothers, Richard Henry and his younger sibling Francis Lightfoot, were the most ambiguous of Washington's critics. Washington and the Lees were among the era's most notable Virginians, and they had been acquainted for years. Indeed, they were friends.[9] But what of friendships in times of crisis? It is reasonable to assume that Richard Henry and Francis Lightfoot knew that another Lee brother, Arthur, as early as May 1776 had hinted at persuading a ranking French officer to take command of Continental forces. The Lees probably did not know that Washington eventually found out about it and let the matter pass.[10] As the patriot war effort faltered, however, it appears the bonds of friendship frayed; for Richard Henry and Francis Lightfoot had some less-than-complimentary things to say about the general's leadership. It was Francis Lightfoot, we remember, who characterized the end of Washington's 1777 campaign as "disgraceful"; and about the same time Richard Henry found himself in sympathy with one of Washington's most determined antagonists. He wrote Samuel Adams that he (Lee) agreed with Thomas Mifflin in thinking the fortunes of war might improve with "some indispensable changes in our Army"[11]—and we already know of Mifflin's animosity toward Washington. And certainly Richard Henry, as a close political ally and frequent correspondent of the radical New Englander, knew of Adams's qualms about Washington. Lee did not (that we know of) demur when Adams wrote him in disgust of the army's "miserable Set of General Officers" and asked Lee whether failure to get rid of "these worthless Creatures" wouldn't reflect poorly on Washington. Adams's implication, of course, was that it already had.[12]

Indeed, what the Lees *did not* say during the Cabal controversy was as significant was what they did. They were never publicly vocal in Washington's defense nor were they in their letters (at least in their surviving letters)—this even as they corresponded with the general on other topics. In contrast, other Washington partisans, such as Henry Laurens, Lafayette, Alexander Hamilton, and Robert Morris, left no doubt as to where they stood as the Cabal unfolded. Where were the Lees? This did not go unnoticed among the general's allies, who suspected the worst. In early January 1778 James Craik, a senior army physician and Washington's personal physician and friend, sounded a warning. The doctor was "exceedingly" alarmed at what he believed to be accurate reports of a conspiracy against Washington that leagued Richard Henry Lee with Mifflin and Gates. Lee, Craik noted, had earlier denied any opposition to Washington, but now there seemed to be a general understanding that Lee had turned against the general. When he wrote to Washington the doctor was traveling south from Valley Forge, and he claimed he found the threat to the commander in chief was public knowledge along his route through Pennsylvania and Maryland.[13] By this time Washington knew he was under fire, but such a report about an old Virginia friend must have stung.

Questions about Richard Henry Lee's intentions toward the commander in chief were indeed abroad. In two letters in February and March 1778

Lund Washington, the general's cousin who was then managing Mount Vernon, wrote of strong rumors of Lee's ill will toward the general. According to Lund Washington, several Virginia patriots challenged Lee on the matter, with militia general (and future governor) Thomas Nelson aggressively accusing Lee of disloyalty to Washington. These challenges brought "solemn" denials from Lee, who understood his alleged posture toward Washington had put his political future at stake. In fact, local suspicions of Lee were strong. The voters of King William County threatened to withhold support for any candidates who supported Lee for public office; and some militia refused to be drafted for Continental service unless assured Washington would head the army. Lund could not assure his famous cousin of the truth of any of the charges against Lee, but despite Lee's protestations of innocence many Virginians obviously believed them.[14]

Suspicions of Richard Henry persisted. In mid-December 1777 Benjamin Harrison, a Virginia patriot and Signer wrote to Robert Morris (then in Congress at York) that talk abounded in Virginia about Lee. Supposedly Lee had urged a congressional measure to divide command of the army—evidently to make Gates the co-equal of Washington.[15] Harrison was no friend of Lee, and his letter has a whiff of calumny. But it was also of a piece with similar worries. In mid-March 1778 one of Washington's principal aides, Lieutenant Colonel John Fitzgerald, wrote the general of a telling incident in Congress. A delegate reportedly had taken the floor to criticize the general—and it may have been the only time a delegate had done so. (Was this the incident Harrison had mentioned to Morris?) The delegate's remarks went unrecorded, but if he had reckoned his remarks would draw support he was badly mistaken. Reactions were quite the reverse. "The Gentleman was so warmly replied to from different quarters," Fitzgerald reported, "that he has been since Silent upon that Head." Fitzgerald "thought it too delicate a point to ask who this was, but [I] have some reason to believe it was your friend from this State [Fitzgerald was writing from Alexandria, Virginia] whose good intentions you have for some time suspected."[16] Clearly the lieutenant colonel meant Richard Henry Lee, and just as clearly he indicated the commander in chief entertained doubts about Lee.

Washington never broke with the Lees. He maintained a correct, if not cordial, relationship with the brothers, even corresponding at length with Richard Henry about a series of forged letters circulated in London and Philadelphia alleging Washington was critical of Congress and wanted a negotiated peace.[17] Yet Washington's communications with the Lees became relatively scant during the war; and while Richard Henry and Washington exchanged letters in 1781 assuring one another of mutual esteem, the notes have a distant tone. Lee told the general he hoped "the arts of wicked men" bent on sowing "discord and dissension among the friends of America" would not affect their friendship. Lee had not written to the general, he claimed—and this truly has a tinny ring—because, having "little but his good wishes to send to him," Lee didn't want to bother him. By this time, with the turmoil of the Cabal long past, one can imagine Washington asking himself where his old "friend" had been when he had needed him. Certainly the general would have appreciated a little bother of reassuring sentiments from Lee during his political trials rather than long afterward. Actually, the real motive behind Lee's missive was not to restore frayed bonds of friendship but to beg Washington for help while an unprepared Virginia reeled under British invasion. "Our country is truly Sir in a deplorable way," he pleaded, "and if relief comes not from you it will probably come not at all."[18] Lee had to ask Washington for help because there was no one else—as Gates was long out of the picture after his shattering defeat in South Carolina the previous year.

Washington's reply was gracious. "Unconscious of having given you just cause to change the favourable sentiments you have expressed for me," he told Lee, "I could not suppose you had altered them—and as I never suffer reports, unsupported by proofs, to have a weight in My Mind."[19] Actually, as we have seen, doubts about Lee had been a considerable "weight" in his mind. But why pursue an argument with an influential Virginian when he was no longer a danger? Washington had better things to do. On Richard Henry's part, however, and for that matter on Francis Lightfoot's, we can note that their reactions to the situation in late 1777 and early 1778 were hardly unique. The military situation was too bleak to overlook. So was it censurable to be candid at such a time, even when that meant being critical of a friend? That the Lees and others spoke their minds should not be surprising; victory brings few complaints, but defeat breeds discontent in any age. But so do suspicions of disloyalty, and hostility toward the Lees never fully dissipated among the general's friends.[20]

THUS IT WAS NO SURPRISE some patriots concluded the Continental Army could not win with George Washington at its head. That much is clear from all we have considered so far; but there is another facet to consider. All of the controversies surrounding the disappointments of 1777—the capabilities of the commander in chief, the ideological and practical debates over how best to wage war—took place in a well-known historical context. This was the military history of the British Empire, including that of the American colonies, which taught a fairly consistent lesson: Unsuccessful officers frequently lost their commands, and just as frequently they deserved the criticism they received. Congressional delegates and colonials generally, including American officers, were fully aware of British experience in this regard, and we need to consider it.

British officers served in a context of subordination to civilian masters; the day was long past when generals called the political tune in Britain. The British army and the Royal Navy were the tools of civilian government; civilian ministers were responsible for the various military departments, and officers served at civilian pleasure. That said, officers frequently played politics and actively sought the patronage of influential connections in government and the aristocracy—anyone able to help advance an army or navy career. Senior officers "were members of an oligarchy," historian Andrew Jackson O'Shaughnessy has observed, "but they competed within that oligarchy and were fiercely ambitious." They used every advantage they could to get ahead. Sir William Howe, for example, was born into the English nobility. His father was Emanuel Howe, 2nd Viscount Howe, a political notable who served for a time as royal governor of Barbados. William's mother, Charlotte, was popular at the courts of George II and George III. Young William easily purchased a commission in a prestigious regiment, and his career took off from there. Howe's successor in America, Sir Henry Clinton, was a protégé of the Duke of Newcastle.[21] None of this necessarily meant that incompetents were more likely than other men to land the choicest commands. Far from it. In the cases of William Howe, Henry Clinton, and John Burgoyne, Lord North's ministry sent the best officers it could find (or thought it did) to deal with the rebellious colonies.[22] But all of these men had excellent contacts in Parliament; indeed, Clinton and Burgoyne were members. In short, senior commanders generally had solid military backgrounds, but they were equally likely to have considerable political connections—and they knew how to use them.

Political influence, however, went only so far in the face of military failure. Civilian leaders had expectations of the generals and admirals they hired: Officers were supposed to produce acceptable military or political results. Failing that, the consequences of martial failure could be serious, and there was little better demonstration of this than the experience of the senior commanders in America during the Seven Years' War. After Edward Braddock's defeat on the Monongahela in 1755, William Shirley became

British commander in chief in North America (he was already governor of Massachusetts Bay colony). But Shirley was recalled when he ran afoul of colonial political in-fighting and after he failed to achieve decisive results in the field. (A young William Alexander of New Jersey, the future Lord Stirling, had served on Shirley's staff and traveled to Britain with the general to "vindicate, by his testimony, the conduct of his commander.")[23] The British then sent John Campbell, Lord Loudoun, to serve as North American commander in chief and simultaneously as governor of Virginia. When Loudoun failed to get results, the British replaced him with James Abercrombie; and when Abercrombie failed disastrously in battle, he gave way to Jeffrey Amherst.[24] Amherst proved a war-winner and orchestrated the final defeat of French Canada; but had *he* failed, another general would have replaced him. In fact, although Amherst was a hero, the ministry brought him home anyway, supposedly to consult on North American affairs. Instead, he found himself forced to defend many of his military decisions and to explain his failure to pacify the Indians.[25] His replacement in America was Thomas Gage, and when it became clear that Gage could not contain the colonial rebellion, his fate was sealed as well. Lord Germain wisely concluded: "I must lament that General Gage, with all his good qualities, finds himself in a situation of too great importance for his talents."[26] The ministry recalled Gage and sent William Howe. Standard practice was clear: Unsuccessful commanders could expect to be relieved or otherwise called to account.

There were fates worse than relief or political censure. In 1757 the British shot Admiral John Byng on his own quarterdeck for failure "to do his utmost" to prevent the French capture of Minorca.[27] Byng's execution was a sensation in the empire, and it is not too much to speculate that John Adams had Byng in mind when he wrote so scathingly of St. Clair's conduct at Fort Ticonderoga in 1777. In fact Byng's sentence aimed at precisely the result Adams wanted: the "encouragement" of other commanders. The unfortunate admiral had died, as Voltaire so famously put it, "pour encourager les autres." And perhaps it did. Naval historians have seen Byng's fate as one source of an aggressive spirit in the Royal Navy, a predisposition to fight "which set British officers apart from their foreign contemporaries." Moving to battle, enemy sailors knew their British opponents expected to win or sink trying.[28] Better to go down fighting than in front of a firing squad.

The British shot none of their commanders in the American theater during the Revolution, but Americans took some pleasure in learning of royal officers called to account for their performance. Learning of Howe's departure for Britain, Lieutenant Colonel Richard Kidder Meade, another of Washington's aides, gleefully wrote his brother, "I shall not be surprised to learn that Howe is put to death by the populace on his arrival." Of course, no such fate awaited Sir William; but he and his brother, Admiral Lord Richard Howe, endured scathing public criticism for failing to defeat the rebels. So did the vanquished John Burgoyne, also to patriot delight.[29] Then there was the affair of Admiral Augustus Keppel. In July 1778 Keppel led a Royal Navy fleet against the French at the First Battle of Ushant. It was the first fleet action against the French since the advent of the Franco-American alliance. The fighting was indecisive and led to recriminations between Keppel and his subordinate, Admiral Hugh Palliser. The admirals were of rival political factions, and when they accused one another of misconduct at Ushant their respective Parliamentary friends took up the cudgels. Separate courts-martial acquitted both men—but not before the controversy ignited turmoil in Parliament and the press. Americans were fascinated, and before news of Keppel's acquittal crossed the Atlantic some patriots predicted a replay of the Byng affair. John Adams thought Parliament would at least censure Keppell.[30] In fact, misleading reports indicated trouble for several British officers. One announced "that Admiral K—ple was Shot, the Genls Burgoyne and Prescot *Broke* & that Genl H—e was on his tryal before a Court Martial."[31] None of this was true, but patriots hoped it was.

This was the military heritage American rebels largely shared. At least in terms of what they expected from their senior commanders and in their political relationships with those commanders, they differed little from the British. Military subordination to civilian authority was part of that tradition, and in George Washington patriots had a commanding general as wedded to that principle as the most ideological republican radical (not that all radicals appreciated as much). The civilian appointment of generals was a settled matter as well. Between February 19 and 21, 1777, Congress, after spirited debate, decided on criteria for appointing general officers. After rejecting suggestions that the army's general officers choose new major generals, Congress resolved to appoint according to "succession" (seniority), ability, and the quota of troops from each state.[32] Congress would listen to the commander in chief in such matters, but it jealously guarded its prerogative. Washington made no protest. As in Great Britain, in America civilians hired the generals.

Given army subordination to civilian authority, Continental officers naturally looked to Congress for preferment. If the rules for appointment seemed clear enough in theory, in practice there were plenty of ambiguous situations and loopholes. Senior officers quickly adopted the European code of personal honor associated with military rank (they believed they were officers *and* gentlemen) and also acted the part of European officers in courting political contacts as they argued over assignments and, most particularly, seniority and promotion. As historian Jonathan Rossie has explained, such controversies drove Congress and Washington to distraction, and the examples were endless.[33] To cite only a few:

Brigadier George Weedon of Virginia had a commission in 1776, which he resigned. He then got another commission in 1777. So did his seniority stem from his first commission or his second? Weedon had his congressional partisans who argued for his seniority beginning in 1776, but the vote went against the brigadier. He was miffed when Congress decided his seniority began *de novo* from the date of his latter commission, thus ranking Weedon's seniority below men who may not have been generals in 1776 but whose 1777 commissions bore an earlier date. Disgusted, Weedon went home.[34]

Benedict Arnold of Connecticut was infuriated at being passed over for promotion to major general. He finally was promoted with considerable support from Washington and delegates who appreciated his combat leadership, but he then had to fight to regain his seniority within rank. Arnold found the experience humiliating and demeaning, and it did nothing to endear Congress to the major general—with results infamously apparent in 1780.[35]

Over late 1777 and early 1778 Brigadier General Thomas Conway lobbied Congress incessantly for promotion to major general. He claimed, rightly as it turned out, that he had come to America with the understanding that no French officer serving with the Continental Army who was junior to him in the French army would be senior to him in America. When Congress appointed Johann Kalb, Conway's junior in France, a major general, Conway was livid. Conway had excellent contacts in Congress and pressed his case with (as we will learn) ultimate success. Conway had been the Continental Army's junior brigadier, and his promotion caused an explosive reaction among the more senior brigadiers.[36]

Horatio Gates was never shy about cultivating political allies. As a British veteran he knew the value of friends in high places in advancing a military career. By late 1776 Gates was playing the game. Pleading illness, he skipped the action at Trenton and rode to Baltimore to convalesce and make the political rounds with Congress. He went as far as to suggest the army come south to reorganize—perhaps under General Gates?[37] He made it a point to stay close to John and Samuel Adams as well as other New England delegates; and he relied on them in battles with Major General Philip Schuyler over command of the Northern Army.[38] In fact Gates was in touch with congressional friends as much as he ever was with the commander in chief. If ever there was a politically adept general, it was Horatio Gates. (The only general better at the political game was Washington. And he played the game hard—but that's for later.)

If Congress commissioned generals and tried to sort out their squabbles, it also held them accountable for their performance. Like Parliament, Congress had expectations of the men who wore epaulets; and, like Parliament, those expectations centered on producing satisfactory military or political results. Citing British precedent during the Seven Years' War, Eliphalet Dyer of Connecticut noted that Prime Minister William Pitt had not hesitated to relieve underperforming generals.[39] Congress never doubted its responsibility to do the same, and the delegates underlined the point in a resolution of November 28, 1777. The resolution required an investigation of any failed expedition or the surrender of any post, including an inquiry into the conduct of the officers concerned.[40] And with or without investigations, Congress was willing to act if officers failed to perform. Again, a few examples are instructive.

Major General John Sullivan of New Hampshire was a hard-luck commander. By late 1777 he had seen plenty of action. In 1776 he had tried against terrible odds to retrieve the hopeless American situation in Canada. Some in Congress, seeking an explanation for the disaster, grumbled about Sullivan, although a review of the facts found him blameless. Still, the incident was the first in a series of troublesome interactions between the general and Congress. Sullivan was captured at Long Island, and when exchanged he carried a message from Howe asking for peace negotiations with Congress. The general was only the messenger, but there were delegates who eyed him suspiciously. Sullivan then commanded an unsuccessful raid against Staten Island, resulting in another congressional demand for an inquiry. Delegates from Maryland, whose troops were heavily involved in the Staten Island operation, went so far as to insist Maryland troops would never again serve under Sullivan. Once more an investigation cleared Sullivan of wrongdoing. The general was now convinced that a faction of Congress was allied against him (he was right), and his further ill fortune at Brandywine only added to his troubles with the delegates. North Carolina's Thomas Burke was virulent in his denunciations.[41] But Sullivan had done well at Trenton and Princeton, and Washington and most of the officer corps, thinking Sullivan had done as well as anyone could have in difficult assignments, stood by him. Yet if anyone thought Congress was not looking hard at the performance of patriot generals, Sullivan's example should have dismissed any such notions.

The evacuation of Fort Ticonderoga in 1777 was a genuine *cause célèbre*. On the night of July 5 Major General Arthur St. Clair abandoned the post without a fight. The British, under John Burgoyne, had mounted artillery on high ground commanding the fort; and St. Clair wisely concluded the only way to save his small army was to pull out. He did so knowing he would face a firestorm of criticism. He was right. Patriots had thought the northern front secure and that Ticonderoga would stop Burgoyne; they reacted to news of St. Clair's retreat with a mixture of dismay and fury.[42] Congress had Ticonderoga very much in mind when it passed its resolution demanding investigations of military setbacks. In the meantime the political fallout that followed ultimately cost St. Clair and his superior, theater commander Major General Philip Schuyler, their jobs. On July 26 eleven of the thirteen state congressional delegations voted to recall them. The delegates asked Washington to send the name of a replacement, but the general demurred. He noted Congress had treated the Northern Army as a separate command and suggested the delegates name the new commander.[43] Congress immediately (on August 4) appointed Horatio Gates.

In leaving the choice to Congress Washington had skirted a political imbroglio. Gates had wanted the northern command for months and earlier in the year already had come to loggerheads with Schuyler over the issue. He had lobbied hard in Congress—to the scandal of some delegates—and he had enlisted the firm and clamorous support of most New England delegations. The New Englanders claimed their militia would not fight for Schuyler, who they claimed was a haughty New York patrician (which he was) who was inept (which he was *not*) and who simply could not connect with the yeomanry of the militia. They insisted on Gates. Washington had faith in Schuyler and St. Clair, but if he had suggested anyone other than Gates he would have faced a showdown with his political masters. At the time he was preparing to face Howe in Pennsylvania, and a major dispute with Congress was the last thing he needed. For that matter, with Howe marching from Head of Elk and Burgoyne coming south, it was the last thing the rebel cause needed. The general knew when *not* to pick a political fight, especially one he might well have lost.

We already have mentioned the case of Major General Joseph Spencer of Connecticut, but we deal with him here in a somewhat different context. A lawyer and politician, Spencer was a veteran of the colonial wars against the French and Indians; he was an early patriot and in 1775 he had led Connecticut militia to the siege of Boston. Appointed a Continental brigadier, Spencer served at Long Island and White Plains before promotion to major general later in 1776. He then failed his first test commanding a major operation. In late October 1777 Washington tasked him with ejecting the British from Newport, Rhode Island; but Spencer, after organizing some nine thousand men, cancelled the operation before engaging. He complained of bad weather and claimed one of his brigade commanders had failed to come up on time. Congress was furious at another apparent miscue by a Continental general and demanded an inquiry. So did Spencer, trusting it would exonerate him. It did. But the major general's reputation was beyond repair and he resigned his commission the following year.[44] It was a wise decision, as neither Congress nor Washington would have trusted him further with a significant command. The Rhode Island expedition had failed, Richard Henry Lee explained to Patrick Henry, "by the Misconduct, 'tis said, of old Spencer." "I am exceedingly mortified on the Occasion" was the reaction of Rhode Island's William Ellery—which seemed to sum up congressional sentiments.[45]

There were other examples, of course. After his poor performance at Brandywine, Congress informed another French officer, Brigadier General Philippe Hubert, chevalier de Preudhomme de Borré, that there was no further need for his services. Major General Adam Stephen was cashiered for alleged drunkenness at Germantown, to the applause of at least some members of Congress.[46] After problematic performances Major Generals Israel Putnam and William Heath were shunted to less-important commands. In 1779 Continental Navy commodore Dudley Saltonstall was court-martialed and cashiered, blamed (scapegoated, actually) for the disastrous defeat of the Massachusetts expedition against Penobscot, Maine. Saltonstall bore his share of the blame, but the Massachusetts commanders, including artillery lieutenant colonel Paul Revere and expedition commander and militia brigadier general Solomon Lovell (a relative of delegate James Lovell), were every bit as culpable.[47] But Massachusetts would not accuse its own and threw everything on the senior Continental officer. Saltonstall appealed to Congress in December 1779, but James Lovell thought things were too busy to deal with the matter—and there is nothing in the record to indicate Congress ever did.[48] The fact is that Saltonstall, up against the state of Massachusetts, lacked the political clout to get his appeal heard.

In a more dramatic development Congress dismissed Commodore Esek Hopkins, commander in chief of the Continental Navy. Appointed in November 1775, Hopkins compiled a controversial record. In early 1776 he disregarded discretionary orders to sail against the Royal Navy squadron off Virginia, instead raiding the British post on Nassau in the Bahamas. The Nassau raid was a partial success, and Hopkins captured a large store of gunpowder sorely needed by the patriot cause. But southern delegates were angered over the failure to drive the British ships from their area. In August Congress censured Hopkins, doing so over the vociferous objections of John Adams and other delegates, and despite vocal support for the commodore from some of his key subordinates, including John Paul Jones.[49] However, despite the censure and consequent blot on his reputation, Congress left him in command. Hopkins, after drawing additional criticism for refusing to undertake operations he considered unfeasible, then took command of a patriot fleet in Narragansett Bay in Rhode Island. But his ships were woefully undermanned and could not break a Royal Navy blockade of the bay. His seeming inactivity at Narragansett—but what was he supposed to do against an overwhelmingly superior British flotilla?—left him open to further political attacks. Finally the commodore fell out with most of his senior officers, many of whom resented serving with a commander under censure. They sent their various complaints directly to Congress, which brought matters to a head. With a questionable military record and little political support, Hopkins's fate was sealed; Congress suspended the commodore in March 1777 and finally dismissed him in July 1778.[50] Here was a lesson indeed: Congress *could* relieve a vulnerable commander in chief.

All of this is to reiterate a key point: Congress differed little from Parliament when confronted with military disappointments. In questioning the performance of generals and naval officers Congress was doing no more than its job. The delegates had hired the generals, including Washington, and it was the delegates' responsibility to ask *why* if military results failed expectations—and then, if appropriate, to do something about it. And if "doing something about it" entailed relieving, reassigning, or approving the court-martial of a senior officer, then so be it. Congress, like Parliament, had every right to act—and every duty.

In Washington's case in particular, patriots looked to him for more than battlefield leadership. He was no mere general. As commander in chief Washington indeed led the main rebel army in person, but he also was responsible for the organization and training of Continental forces and for determining the broad strategic contours of the rebel war effort. That is, he determined what kind of an army it would be and how it would fight the war. Of course, the story of how he insisted on building a regular Continental Line to oppose European regulars is well known. Washington never wavered from his faith in regular soldiers as the key to victory; only a professionally trained regular Continental Army, he insisted, could stand up to the redcoats and Hessians. Bitter experience had convinced him of the futility of fighting the war primarily with a militia of citizen soldiers.[51] However, his belief never fully overcame the skepticism of patriots who thought otherwise. Indeed, a circle of political radicals took umbrage at Washington's vision of how to fight the war and of *who* should fight it. The questions they raised added another dimension to the controversy over Washington's fitness to command.

Radical arguments went beyond questions of military operations and into the realm of republican ideology. While most Whigs conceded the need for a disciplined army and even accepted the need for some regulars, voices in and outside of Congress questioned Washington's emphasis on professional troops. In fact, they bluntly objected. They did not believe such an army could win, and they did not believe such an army should be the military mainstay of a republic.

Rather, radicals called for primary dependence on militia—theoretically the citizenry in arms—which reflected the essence of their republicanism. They insisted free men fighting for their liberties, homes, and families were infinitely superior to any professional army. Professional soldiers, so this argument went, usually enlisted from the lowest social strata. They had fewer attachments to homes, hearths, and civil virtues; as poor men they served primarily for their pay. In the view of Samuel Adams regulars were the "shoeblacks of Society."[52] And before dismissing these radicals as mere ideologues, it is well to remember they were sincere in their beliefs, however misguided they may have been from a strictly military perspective. They meant what they said. In an age when many Americans believed devoutly in republicanism and when militia service was long a part of colonial tradition, ideology was not simply cant.

Of the radical Whigs in Congress, the most outspoken was delegate James Lovell of Massachusetts. We have met Lovell, and by late 1777 it would have been impossible to find a more adamant critic of the commander in chief. But Lovell was no crank; in fact, he was highly intelligent and every bit as dedicated to the success of the revolutionary cause. Born in 1737, he received a first-class education at the prestigious Boston Latin School, of which his father, John Lovell, was headmaster. James graduated from Harvard in 1756, received a master of arts degree three years later, and taught at the Latin School. Lovell gravitated without hesitation to the radical cause. After the Boston Massacre in 1770 he breathed fire on the issue of standing armies, and Boston Whigs selected him to deliver the first anniversary address marking the occasion. Entitled *An Oration Delivered April 2d, 1771: At the Request of the Inhabitants of the Town of Boston; to Commemorate the Bloody Tragedy of the Fifth of March, 1770*, the speech (and subsequent pamphlet) was a quintessential statement of republican belief in the citizenry in arms. He told an appreciative audience "the true strength and safety of every commonwealth or limited monarchy"—this being six years before independence—"is in the bravery of its freeholders, its militia. By brave militias they rise to grandeur, and they come to ruin by a mercenary army."[53] Given the intensity of his feelings it would have been shocking to discover Lovell changing his views while in Congress. He was the very definition of a true believer.

The Revolution fractured the Lovell family. James took up the patriot cause while his father, John, remained loyal to George III. After Bunker Hill, General Howe had James arrested and sent to Halifax, Nova Scotia; John left Boston with the British army when Howe evacuated the city. The men never reconciled. James was exchanged in November 1776, and in December Massachusetts sent him to Congress. Even in the darkest periods of the war his revolutionary zeal never dimmed. Lovell served diligently until 1782; in fact he was one of the longest-serving congressmen, and colleagues justly admired his work ethic. Lovell was deeply involved in foreign relations—he had more experience in the area than any other delegate—and he was a self-taught cryptologist. As such he was deeply concerned with the security of congressional communications, and later in the war he broke British ciphers for the Continental Army.[54] That such a man came to question the performance of Washington was testimony to how serious doubts about the general had become.

Like other critics of Washington, Lovell was disappointed in the string of Continental defeats.[55] But Lovell's anger had deeper roots. Reflecting his animosity toward regular armies, he was furious with Washington's determination to build a Continental Line on the European model. The general's resolve to put the Continental officer corps on a European footing incensed him. In particular, Lovell denounced Washington's advocacy of half-pay pensions for the officers, a common practice in European militaries. The radical delegate considered the proposal nothing less than extortion and a "mode of introducing into Society a set of haughty, idle, imperious Scandalizers of Industrious Citizens & Farmers." The issue was controversial, and Lovell had plenty of company in his aversion to the measure. Abraham Clark of New Jersey was only typical in arguing, like Lovell, that officers should be content with victory as a reward and forego pecuniary incentives for their service. The sentiment did not endear Clark to the officer corps.[56] Washington himself had opposed the idea in 1776; but conditions had changed by late 1777. Complaints of financial hardship within the officer corps, especially among the junior officers, were reaching alarming levels; and the general rightly feared the impact of mass officer resignations if Congress failed to approve the measure. Congress reluctantly came around, the majority of delegates conceding that ideological preferences had to give way to practical realities. In early 1778 Congress offered a compromise, voting the officers half-pay for seven years after the war; enlisted men serving for the duration of the war would receive a year's pay or eighty dollars. (This settlement did not end the matter. In 1780 Congress agreed to provide officers half-pay for life if they remained in the service throughout the war—a plan replaced in 1783 with an issue of certificates for five years' pay bearing 6 percent per annum until cashed.)[57] But Lovell was having none of this—he was never reconciled to any pension plan. He reminded all who "have not forgotten that this *was* in its beginning a *patriotic war*." After the war the officers could farm like anyone else.[58]

Lovell also objected to Washington's seemingly untouchable status in the army. In this, of course, he was not alone. Great men, republicans took as a matter of faith, always bore watching. French observers were astonished at how some ideologues held even Washington's evident patriotism against him: "*His virtues were spoken of as an additional cause of alarm*," noted the chevalier de la Luzerne, the French minister to Congress, because patriots deemed it unwise "*to expose even the most virtuous man to the subtle temptations of ambition*."[59] Lovell breathed this sort of thing, and he was not reticent in preaching his faith. The general, he fumed in a letter to Samuel Adams, who needed no convincing on the point, had become "a Demi G——," the "one great Man, whom no Citizen *shall* dare even talk about say the Gentlemen of the Blade."[60] And Lovell was consistent. Later in the war, "a few days" after listening to Adams excoriate Washington—"the more popular Washington is on account of his services, the more dangerous does Mr. Adams regard him"—Luzerne dined with a party of delegates. After the meal one of the delegates, a "pupil" of Adams (certainly Lovell) launched into a vitriolic "denunciation of General Washington, declaring that distrust is the guardian of republics" and "that Washington's virtues, real or apparent, form one demerit the more, that he himself had voted against every motion to extend his authority." Who else but Lovell? The other delegates had to calm him down.[61] The man was a splendid ideologue.

Whatever his objections to regular armies, however, much less to popular generals, Lovell never envisioned the militia as a rabble in arms. He found ill-disciplined troops and logistical failings as alarming as anyone else, and he knew success depended on armed forces properly trained, organized, equipped, and "ready for action." He differed with Washington in that he saw no reason why militia could not fill that role. In Congress Lovell had urged patriots to establish a military academy to train officers, and when the delegates transplanted to York he retained his interest in the project. He even discussed the idea with fellow militia devotee Samuel Adams, who thought such a school might take root in Boston (although Adams never pursued the matter). Radicals had no qualms about well-trained citizen-soldiers.[62]

Lovell's faith in militia was shared widely. Samuel Adams warned professional troops were "apt to consider themselves as a Body distinct from the rest of the Citizens. . . .They have their Arms always in their hands. Their Rules and their Discipline is severe. They soon become attached to their officers and disposed to yield implicit obedience to their Commands. Such a power," he concluded, "should be watched with a jealous Eye." John Adams, whose patriotism was beyond reproach, took an equally dim view. A professional army would enlist "the meanest, idlest, most intemperate and worthless, but no more." The yeomen farmers and mechanics, the backbone of republican armies—that is, of the militia—would never serve in a standing army. "Was it creditable that men who could get at home a better living, more comfortable lodgings, more than double the wages, in safety. . .would" join Washington for the duration of the war? "I knew it to be impossible."[63] Major General Charles Lee, certainly Washington's most radical lieutenant, warned "when the soldiers of a community are volunteers [that is, regulars], war becomes a distinct profession. The arms of a Republic get into the hands of its worst members."[64] Such an army was a Whig nightmare.

Benjamin Rush, already known to us as another of the Revolution's most zealous republicans—not to mention as one of the commander in chief's bitterest critics—put the matter of regular armies as well as any ideologue: "I should despair of our cause if our country contained 60,000 men abandoned enough to enlist for 3 years or during the war [that is, for the duration]."[65] It was such statements that labeled Rush as perhaps the most insufferable of all Washington's detractors. Yet, like Lovell, his commitment to the Revolution was total.

For all of his bluster Rush was a formidable member of the founding generation. He was a leading figure of the American Enlightenment, and he shared the intellectual curiosity of Benjamin Franklin while lacking Franklin's sense of humor or self-control. In 1760 he earned a bachelor's degree from the College of New Jersey (now Princeton University), and after working as an apprentice doctor in Philadelphia Rush completed his MD at the University of Edinburgh in Scotland in 1768. He practiced in Philadelphia, was active in civil affairs, and as an army doctor served at Princeton and in the field with the Pennsylvania militia. As a patriot politico he signed the Declaration of Independence for Pennsylvania, did his best to build a credible Continental Army medical department (although creating turmoil in disputes with other doctors), and worked ceaselessly in person and in print to promote popular support for the cause. He was ahead of his time as an advocate for abolition, women's rights, penal reform, medical research, public education, and temperance.[66] The man was no lightweight.

Rush's greatest liabilities were his mouth and his pen: He couldn't keep his mouth shut and he could be utterly reckless on paper—his "anonymous" letter to Patrick Henry was only one instance in this regard. One of his chief biographers has labeled Rush a "gadfly," and historian Thomas Fleming has sketched the doctor, not unjustly, as a runaway mouth.[67] Both of these unflattering characterizations were true enough, but the "gadfly" was also a model of ideological consistency. Like Lovell, he saw no reason to alter his stance on how to wage the war: "The militia began," he wrote John Adams, "and I sincerely hope the militia will end the present war."[68] That is, his military preferences were diametrically opposed to Washington's.

This was fine with other Whigs. They insisted the record showed that enough militia, ideally stiffened by regulars (very few patriots totally rejected the use of regular troops in time of war) but alone if necessary, could deny the enemy safe access to the American interior. They could overwhelm British forces who ventured there. Militia advocates could point to some real militia successes in this regard: Lexington and Concord, the rising in New Jersey in late 1776 and early 1777, Bennington, and, most recently, the militia role in the defeat of Burgoyne at Saratoga. In Congress, Rhode Island's Henry Marchant had thrown up his hands as the 1777 campaign ended. He wrote it off as a disaster. But looking forward to the coming spring he predicted doom for Howe if patriots could rally ten thousand militia.[69] Samuel Adams waxed almost rhapsodic about the prowess of militia when led by competent officers. If only this had been the case in New Jersey early in 1777, he mused, when "so great an Animation prevaild" among the militia, "who knows but that they wd have destroyd" Howe's army.[70] This may have been wishful thinking, but the likes of Marchant and Adams believed every word.

This faith in militia became part of the debate over the waging of a winter campaign in late 1777 and early 1778. At the time republican radicals were the dominant voice in the Pennsylvania government, and they saw militia as the key to prolonging the fighting after the loss of Philadelphia. They even had notions, as diarist Christopher Marshall reported, of calling "out the strength of this State" and retaking their capital city with "a bold push." Marshall hoped Washington would help, but not everyone thought Continental assistance necessary.[71] In December, when the state assembly actually endorsed the plan, it failed to even reference the Continental Army.[72] Recall Elbridge Gerry pondering the loss of the Delaware River forts and wishing the seat of war was in New England: There, he was sure, New England militia would overwhelm the British. Lovell wanted the regular army to adopt the militia practice of electing officers annually; and, casting about for even better ways to organize militia, he joined with Richard Henry Lee in asking the American commissioners in Paris to forward a "plan of the militia of Switzerland" as quickly as possible.[73] If events later proved them wrong, the militia partisans were articulate in pressing their case.

Belief in militia prowess was not the sole province of ideological purists. Others shared it, if not with the zealotry of a Lovell or a Rush. In spring 1778 a supposed French traveler, "Monsieur De Lisle," composed a letter to a (fictitious) French nobleman offering an account of military affairs in America. Actually "De Lisle" was one of many pseudonyms for Governor William Livingston of New Jersey. Livingston, scion of one of the most prominent political families of New York before transplanting to New Jersey, was a devoted patriot but certainly no zealot, at least not of the caliber of Lovell or Rush. In fact, over the course of the war Washington enjoyed the governor's stalwart support.[74] Yet on the matter of regular armies *versus* militia Livingston sounded remarkably like a dedicated militia partisan.

The "De Lisle" letter appeared in the *New Jersey Gazette* of April 23, 1778 (although "De Lisle" dated it December 25, 1777); but thereafter it circulated through other Whig newspapers. Livingston conceded Americans were "divided in their opinions as to the method of carrying on the war by troops enlisted during the war [that is, for the duration], or by militia." In Europe, he wrote, "luxury and a variety of mechanical employments have unfitted a majority" of inhabitants "for the toils and dangers of a military life." But Americans were different. They were still freedom-loving yeomen, used to serving in local militia—but unwilling to "forego the sweets of domestic life for three, four, or seven years service." He cited the dangers "to a free state" in introducing distinctions "between citizens and soldiers"; and, in a line very similar to one Benjamin Rush used privately, Livingston wrote he "should have taken leave of the liberties of this country" had the army succeeded in "raising 80,000 men to serve during the war." The present Continental Army—the one Washington was then training and reorganizing at Valley Forge—had "exhausted America of that class of men who compose the common soldiers of Europe." The only recourse for the Revolution was clear: "A choice therefore is no longer left to the United States of a regular army to serve during the war. They must depend finally upon the militia or yeomanry of the country. The exploits that have already been performed by them, are sufficient to give a full confidence in them." Here Livingston named Lexington, Bunker Hill, Saratoga, New Jersey, and other militia victories as proof "that most of the laurels that have been earned since the commencement of the war, have been gathered by militia." Like Lovell, he wanted militia well trained, and he suggested they serve for a minimum of six months (his experience had taught him that shorter tours of duty often counted for little). With the right leadership "De Lisle" thought they would prove virtually invincible against an enemy of "mercenary banditti."[75] No one ever put the case for—or at least *faith in*—militia any better.

Yet even when such arguments came from friends (although Washington and his allies probably were unaware of the true identity of "De Lisle"), advocates for a regular American army remained unpersuaded of militia capabilities. For them military reality was simply incompatible with ideological purity, and the situation at Valley Forge seemed the unfortunate proof. Patriots were barely able to support Washington's small band at the winter encampment; indeed, the Continentals were struggling to survive amid endemic supply shortages and health crises. This being the case, more realistic Whigs asked how the cash-strapped Congress or states could afford to mobilize, feed, pay, and equip a massive militia army.[76] And if the militia had performed wonders during certain periods, what about its failures? The Pennsylvania militia had failed to rally during Howe's invasion of Pennsylvania, and militia alone could not have stopped Burgoyne. Indeed, Continental regulars had played the key combat roles at Saratoga. Convinced republicans, however, casually ignored such questions. The wishful thinking of Rush, Lovell, and their like-minded friends, while anathema to George Washington, remained potent reminders of the power of ideology.

PRACTICAL DOUBTS and ideological critiques of the commander in chief's generalship were never fully distinct, but by January 1778 they had become fully entwined. Although William Livingston was a friend of Washington's there were practical and republican political aspects of the "De Lisle" letter; and, we should recall, there were similar sentiments in John Adams's various criticisms of Washington. True, Adams was enthusiastic about militia and skeptical of professional soldiers; but whatever his ideological preferences he was also a realist and the defeats of 1777 had utterly dismayed him. However, the most glaring example of this linking of the practical with the ideological emerged in an anonymous tract, "The Thoughts of a Freeman," dated January 17, 1778. But the "Freeman's" argument was of a different order, for it combined practical (Washington was a bad general) with ideological (Washington disparaged the militia) in an articulate and direct call for the relief of the commander in chief.[77] This was something new: No previous critic of the general had gone that far—at least not publicly.

The identity of "Freeman" was, and *is*, a mystery; well over two centuries later he remains anonymous. Was the tract really the work of a single author? Or the statement of a group of like-minded individuals? We simply don't know, and even the discovery of the tract was curious. The "Thoughts" came to light while Congress was in session. Supposedly a delegate (we have no name) entered and handed an envelope to Henry Laurens, by then president of Congress. The nameless delegate had "picked it up on the Stairs" outside the meeting room. This was on January 26, well after the author had dated it; there was no explanation for the delayed delivery. The handwritten document was enclosed in a cover addressed "To the Honble the President of Congress & every member thereof." Laurens glanced at the pages, and if anyone wondered about the delivery Laurens put them off. He told the delegates "it was an anonymous production containing stuff which I must be content with, as perquisites of office." The author clearly intended a wide reading. In this he was disappointed, as Laurens held it close. Instead of burning it, which he considered, he sent it on to Washington the next day (January 27). Laurens hoped that in dispatching the tract he would not be "troubling" the general.[78]

But Washington was troubled. The tract was a scathing analysis—disparagement is a better word—of the general's leadership. The "Freeman" savaged virtually every decision Washington had made over the course of the 1777 campaign; and there was equal contempt for patriots who tolerated such alleged ineptitude. The "Freeman" wondered why the general had allowed

Howe to march so freely from Head of Elk and why the British had outflanked the Continentals at Brandywine. He criticized the loss of the river forts, a calamity that allowed Howe to consolidate his hold on Philadelphia; and he charged that the "evacuation of red bank fort [Fort Mercer] is very mysterious." The war was going nowhere, the "Freeman" alleged, because "the proper methods of attacking beating and conquering the Enemy has never as yet been adapted by the Commander in C—f." The army's medical and supply services, he continued, were a disgrace.[79] So much for practical concerns.

The "Freeman" also pursued a virulent ideological quarrel. He not only mistrusted Washington's partiality for Continental regulars, he was as adamant on the point as Lovell. "The general contempt shown to the Militia by the standing forces is a dangerous Omen," he warned; and he insisted that "the Militia" was responsible for "every" American victory. He demanded Congress recognize that the victory at Saratoga "was owing to a change of Commanders"—the firing of Arthur St. Clair and the relief of Philip Schuyler by Gates—and that a similar change, the relief of Washington, would have seen the main army win around Philadelphia. His conclusion was unambiguous: "That the people of America have been guilty of Idolatry by making a man their god—and that the God of Heaven and Earth will convince them by woeful experience that he is only a man. That no good may be expected from the standing Army until Baal and his worshipers are banished from the Camp—I believe that. Verte."[80]

This was strong stuff. One doubts the "Freeman" (whoever he was, or *they* were) would have written and distributed such a rant without some confidence the message would find a fair number of favorable readers. Having written such a lengthy composition the "Freeman" clearly intended his opus for a significant readership. However, we don't know how widely the "Freeman's" tract circulated. There are copies in at least three archives today, including the Library of Congress (a transcription from the original by Washington's military secretary Robert Hanson Harrison); and Jared Sparks got hold of a copy, source unknown, for his published collection of Washington's papers.[81] There was some public knowledge of it, and some of the earliest historians of the Revolution certainly knew about the "Thoughts." Mercy Otis Warren (1805), Carlo Botta (1809, in Italian), and David Ramsay (1807) all referred to the anonymous communication as well as to Rush's letter to Patrick Henry. According to Botta the "Freeman's" strictures left Washington "cruelly lacerated," while Warren believed the general refused to allow such calumnies to upset him.[82] Either way, the "Freeman" had loosed a heavy barrage.

The bitterness of the criticism hit home, and the general wasted no time in doing some venting of his own. The mail from York probably reached Valley Forge no later than January 30, and Washington replied the following day. He thanked Laurens for sending the anonymous epistle and conceded its contents were something "in which I am so deeply interested." The general told the South Carolinian that he "was not unapprized that a malignant faction had been for sometime forming to my prejudice; which, conscious as I am of having ever done all in my power to answer the important purposes of the trust reposed in me, could not but give me some pain on a personal account." But his chief worry was not personal; his concern lay in "the dangerous consequences, which intestine dissentions may produce to the common cause." The "Freeman's" charges were serious, he admitted, and he felt Laurens should share the document with Congress "as the suppression, or concealment, may possibly involve you in embarrassments hereafter; since it is uncertain how many, or who may be privy to the contents."

Yet Washington was angry not so much at criticism; what really galled him was what he considered unfair play: "My Enemies take an ungenerous advantage of me—they know the delicacy of my situation and that motives of policy deprive me of the defence I might otherwise make against their insiduous attacks. They know I cannot combat their insinuations," he complained, without disclosing information possibly useful to the enemy. The general knew that occasional public "censure" was "the unfailing lot of an elevated station"—criticism came with the job. And he was candid about his performance. "My Heart tells me it has been my unremitted aim to do the best circumstances would permit; yet, I may have been very often mistaken in my judgment of the means, and may, in many instances deserve the imputation of error."[83] Still, Washington was furious with the "Freeman" in particular and his critics generally.

Laurens decided against Washington's advice: He never showed the document to his colleagues. Why? He never explained, but his reasoning likely centered on avoiding an open controversy in Congress. Confronted with an indictment of Washington's leadership, what would Congress have done? Attendance was slim. Only thirteen delegates were present when the "Thoughts" appeared, so a vocal few might have carried undue weight in any debate over the tract's merits. Perhaps Laurens chose not to chance a debate because he was leery of the possible results. But from then on, as he dealt from day to day with his fellow delegates he must have wondered which one of them was the "Freeman." If he ever suspected, he never let on.

HERE WE COME BACK to Major General Horatio Gates. We need to say a bit more about him, as he has had a central place in the traditional history of the Cabal. Indeed contemporaries and many historians often depicted Gates as the alternative to General Washington if a critical mass of patriots became convinced the Virginian could not win the war. A more extreme view sees Gates as an actual rival for Washington's command. But we need to put a finer point on the matter—especially in light of contemporary expectations of senior officers and the ideological preferences of many of the Revolution's more passionate republicans. For viewed in these contexts Gates had considerable appeal.

History has been unkind to Gates. His links to Washington's critics—indeed, he was one—and his disastrous performance in 1780 in South Carolina tarnished his reputation among contemporaries and among many historians. Yet his disappointments lay in the future. In late 1777 Gates was a deservedly popular man. Born in Great Britain in 1727, his mother was the housekeeper of the Duke of Bolton, and in 1745 he secured a commission through the duke's patronage. He saw duty in the French and Indian War—like Washington, he survived Braddock's bloody defeat in 1755—and served competently in various posts in America, Europe, and the Caribbean. He was promoted to major without purchase, a relative rarity in the British army and clearly the mark of an accomplished officer.[84] With experience in combat and army administration he had military credentials far in advance of most colonial officers.

In 1769, however, facing dim prospects for further advancement in a peacetime military, he sold his commission. Then in 1772 he immigrated to America and settled on a modest estate in Virginia's Shenandoah Valley, "Traveller's Rest." The soldier became a planter and, while never rising to the social status of Virginia's old families, Gates took his place in regional social and political affairs. He became reacquainted with Washington, and he met the Lees and other notables, including another transplant from the British army, retired Lieutenant Colonel Charles Lee (no relation to the Virginia Lees). Gates loved his new country and he had no second thoughts about old loyalties as the imperial crisis deepened. He declared early for the colonial cause, and given his military record Congress quickly commissioned him a brigadier general.[85]

During the first years of the war Gates served ably although in circumstances offering little chance for distinction. Gates was the army's adjutant general under Washington, a position to which Gates brought invaluable expertise. He was a first-rate organizer and paper-pusher (hardly a glorious task, but essential) and he worked harmoniously with the commander in chief. Washington was grateful for his service.[86] In 1776 Gates commanded at Fort Ticonderoga, and he did a commendable job of reorganizing battered patriot forces after their painful retreat from Canada. Subordinate officers thought well of him and credited Gates with restoring much of the shattered Northern Army's organization and morale. "Generalship is now dealt out to the Army," the First New Jersey's Colonel Matthias Ogden apprised his friend Aaron Burr, "by our worthy and esteemed General Gates, who is putting the most disordered Army that ever bore the name into a state of regularity and defence."[87] Gates also did his best to support Benedict Arnold as Arnold prepared to meet the oncoming British invasion. After the critical Battle of Valcour Island, in which Arnold's small fleet fought a superior British flotilla to exhaustion, Gates was among the foremost in Arnold's praise.[88] Thus the transplanted Briton was a seasoned professional and no military lightweight, and had Washington been killed or disabled early in the war Gates was by no means an illogical choice as a successor.

Yet the relationship between Gates and Washington soured. While Washington never knew it, by late 1776 Gates's correspondence with Major General Charles Lee revealed a wavering faith in the commander in chief. And Gates's conduct on the eve of the Trenton operation must have given Washington pause. Having marched reinforcements south to link up with Washington only days before the Trenton attack, Gates pleaded illness and promptly left for Baltimore—where he recovered quickly enough to make the rounds with the exiled Congress. In spring 1777 Gates subsequently became embroiled in a controversy with General Philip Schuyler over command of the Northern Department. Washington supported Schuyler and was anything but happy with his former adjutant general. Despite Washington's preferences, in July Gates won the Northern Department command after St. Clair evacuated Fort Ticonderoga and Congress relieved St. Clair and Schuyler. The commander in chief watched all of this with deep reservations, if not private dismay. He still had faith in Schuyler but knew defending him would have ignited a political firestorm. Recall that Washington sidestepped a congressional request to appoint a new commander for the Northern Department, and thus Gates went north as Congress's man, not Washington's.

The aftermath of Saratoga was a turning point in the Gates-Washington relationship. While Gates basked in popular acclaim, he did not immediately see himself as a rival for Washington's job. At least he was *not* intriguing to replace the commanding general. Nevertheless the man was no fool; he fully understood other patriots shared his dim view of Washington's performance. This was especially true among the more zealous republicans. They had faith in Gates, a man who seemed to have everything a good republican could want in a general. Gates had not only triumphed, but he was also genuinely popular with the militia so beloved of radical Whigs. He was a winner in battle *and* politically acceptable.

There is no question that the more ardent republicans wanted him. Samuel Adams had been singing his praises even before Saratoga. Gates "is *honest and true*, & has the Art of *gaining the Love of his Soldiers*," he asserted. After Saratoga Adams could not have been more effusive in his admiration for the major general: The victory of the Northern Army reflected "the highest Honor on yourself & and the gallant officers & Soldiers under *your* Command." That italicized "*your*" left little doubt of Adams's preferences in generals. Lovell was of the same mind. "We want you in different places," the zealous delegate wrote directly to Gates, lamenting the dismal state of military affairs in the Philadelphia theater.[89] And these hosannas were only typical; we have seen the sentiments of other republican purists in the previous chapter. Other patriots of a less radical persuasion—those simply tired of losing battles and a stalled war effort—would have understood a turn to a winning general. Recall the spate of November letters to Gates expressing dismay at Washington's defeats. Nor was Gates bashful about making friends with the commander in chief's detractors; and without openly saying as much, at least that we know of, the radicals understood their hero was amenable to an appointment as Washington's replacement. For the first time a reasonable number of patriots saw a credible alternative to the Virginian. This was not a matter of any malice against Washington—it was about winning the war.

THUS DOUBTS ABOUT the patriot commander in chief had risen to a serious level even as the prestige of Horatio Gates soared. But there is something to bear in mind before looking at the actual Cabal—or what the general and his partisans were convinced was the Cabal. In their criticisms of Washington men such as the Adams cousins and Major General Lee, or even a busybody like Rush, *never* meant harm to the American war effort. Indeed, these men had risked their lives in declaring for independence. Of the men who, at one time or another, expressed misgivings about Washington's leadership, at least seven—John and Samuel Adams, Richard Henry Lee, his brother Francis Lightfoot Lee, Elbridge Gerry, Benjamin Rush, and Abraham Clark—were Signers and had pledged their "Lives," "Fortunes," and "sacred Honor" to the cause. Jonathan Dickinson Sergeant would have signed the Declaration, but he had left Congress to return to New Jersey where he was instrumental in drafting the new state constitution.[90]

A few also had a family stake in the war. While Lovell and Samuel Adams criticized Washington, their sons served in the general's army. Young Samuel Adams was a doctor who served with the Continental artillery; he saw some dangerous duty, including stints near the front lines during combat.[91] The junior James Lovell was an infantry officer with a Massachusetts regiment until transferring to the Continental dragoons.[92] Two of Clark's sons, Aaron and Thomas, were militia officers in artillery; both were captured and suffered cruelly, imprisoned aboard the infamous prison hulk *Jersey* in New York Harbor. Conditions were so bad for one of the brothers that Congress threatened to retaliate against a British officer if young Clark's conditions were not improved (they were).[93] To suggest these men had any desire to impede the patriot military effort is absurd. They wanted to win the war as badly as anyone else, but they had honest doubts about Washington's ability to produce victory.

Part 1 of *Cabal!* is at an end. So far we have traced patriot assessments of the war and Washington's leadership from the optimistic days of the "season of hope" to the gloom of late 1777. We also have identified some—for there will be others—of those who came to question the commander in chief's leadership; and we have explored the motives of their censures, as well as the context of contemporary expectations of senior officers. It is now time to see which of the general's critics chose to act on their doubts.

PART 2

THE USUAL SUSPECTS

-wherein General Washington and his allies come to believe in a Cabal and identify its alleged plotters, and Washington picks his moment to confront General Gates and make their quarrel public, and

-wherein the true threat to Washington's command emerges from the Board of War and forces Washington to confront the board and General Conway; and

-wherein the board attempts an "administrative coup" and compels Washington to defend not only his position as commander in chief but the very meaning of "commander in chief."

FOUR

POISON PENS

The "Classic Cabal"

> Sir,
> a Letter which I received last Night, contained the following paragraph. In a Letter from Genl Conway to Genl Gates he says—"Heaven has been determind to save your Country; or a weak General and bad Councellors would have ruind it." I am Sir Yr Hble Srvt.
>
> —George Washington to Thomas Conway, November 5, 1777[1]

This is the first of three chapters devoted specifically to the Cabal—this one to early events in which Washington finally clashed openly with his chief critics. In essence it is the story of a single letter and the political fallout that ensued once the commander in chief became aware of some of its contents. Penned in mid-October 1777, it was a private missive from Brigadier General Thomas Conway to Major General Horatio Gates; it was critical of Washington, and for the general and his partisans it seemed proof-positive of what they already suspected—a cabal was rising against Washington's command. And not only that. As far as Washington was concerned the Conway letter also confirmed the identities of the actual conspirators. If Washington chose to counterattack—to fight openly to keep his job, or at least his authority as commander in chief—he now had targets.

I have called the episode the "Classic Cabal." It comprises the well-worn narrative of Washington's confrontation with Conway and Gates, and indirectly with Thomas Mifflin. And the story is "well-worn" because the activities of this trio garnered considerable attention from contemporaries, not to mention more ink from historians than any other aspect of the Cabal controversy. As an intrinsically interesting tale, the Classic Cabal has been worth the ink. The events following the disclosure of Conway's letter revealed the depth of tensions rending the American war effort, including a shocking (or entertaining, depending upon one's point of view) level of political skullduggery and personal animosities among virtually everyone involved—Washington not excluded. In fact some authors have seen this affair as the core of the Cabal, with criticisms of Washington largely evaporating as the storm over the letter died.

Interesting as it was, however, the controversy surrounding "the Letter," as Henry Laurens came to call it,[2] was only an opening skirmish in a wider and more serious contest reserved for following chapters. Yet the story of the Conway letter needs retelling. The hullabaloo was extended, spanning a period from October 1777 through February 1778, and it overlapped and was intertwined with more weighty challenges to Washington's command. This chapter, however, will follow the thread of the letter separately, tracing Washington's changing stance on how to deal with those he identified as his antagonists among his fellow patriots. If Washington had suffered the slights of his critics in silence for fear of harming the rebel cause, the affair of "the Letter" changed his mind. The Virginian emerged from the contretemps as a commander in chief willing and able to wage a political campaign as effectively as any he ever waged in the field. Washington had always been a good politician, but now Gates, Conway, Mifflin, and others of their frame of mind would find out just how good.

In his perceptive history of the War for Independence historian Eric Robson credited Washington with a cardinal virtue: patience. The general, often of necessity, was willing to wait for his moment. Impatient for victory, too many of Washington's critics mistakenly took his patience for indecision or irresolution—the "constitutional want of ardency" Mercy Otis Warren mentioned.[3] As we know, it was anything but. In reality Washington was as impatient for victory as anyone else. He knew that the longer the war, the greater the social dislocation and perhaps the greater the chance war-weariness would lead Americans back to the King. Necessity also counseled patience in the political realm, especially as Washington dealt with critics of his leadership. The general was not oblivious to the controversies swirling around his conduct of the war. How could he have been? As we have seen, he even thought some patriots wanted him gone. And considering the tenuous state of the patriot war effort, the concerns of Congress, the emotions of the officer corps, and the bewilderment of much of the public at the reverses of 1777, it was a rare individual level-headed enough to think the turmoil surrounding the commander in chief might be more smoke than fire. By November 1777 Washington certainly believed there was fire, and he was sincere when he later wrote his old friend and fellow Virginian Landon Carter that there was "no doubt" some sort of "scheme" had existed "to see me superceeded in my Command." He even hinted Major General Horatio Gates was the intended beneficiary of the "scheme."[4]

The commander in chief was only human. As Douglas Southall Freeman pointed out long ago, the attacks hurt on a personal basis, but he accepted the slings and arrows that came with senior responsibility in a free society.[5] That didn't mean the general held no grudges on a personal basis. His chief concern, however, lay in the damage high-level controversies posed to the patriot war effort. As commander in chief he was loath to voice his concerns publicly, let alone strike back at his critics. As the "Freeman" incident revealed, the general feared a public airing of squabbles within patriot military and political leadership could only benefit the British.

Yet the general could not ignore political realities indefinitely. Under the circumstances patience could last only so long before it appeared to betray weakness. This was something the commander in chief (or *any* commander in chief) could ill afford. Consider the fate of the politically impotent commander in chief of the Continental Navy, Commodore Esek Hopkins, who indeed Congress did fire. Thus, with the conviction that a plot, or at least some inimical political maneuvering, was afoot, Washington and his friends kept a wary eye on his critics. Some critics, however, bothered the general more than others inasmuch as they appeared especially active as political adversaries or were simply persistently troublesome on other counts. Three names were of most concern: Horatio Gates, the man Washington's doubters saw as the hero of the day; Thomas Conway, a brigadier with genuine talent but also a craving for promotion and influence; and Thomas Mifflin, a friend of Gates and Conway and, of the three, the one who harbored the deepest personal resentments toward the commander in chief. These were the men most closely identified with the Cabal—the "usual suspects"—and at this point they rate a closer look.

The relationship between Gates and Washington had indeed gone off; the friendship and mutual respect they had enjoyed earlier in the war had vanished. In October 1777, in the aftermath of Saratoga, Washington's attitude toward the now-popular major general hardened. Washington was alive to Gates's newfound popularity as well as to the many unflattering comparisons between himself and the Saratoga victor. But it was Gates's now casual attitude toward the commander in chief, probably born of hubris, that widened the breach between the generals. As Gates basked in public acclaim, he failed to officially notify Washington of Burgoyne's surrender; instead Gates sent his dispatch directly to Congress. Washington was miffed on two counts. First, Gates's action seemed a violation of the chain of command, even a deliberate slight of the commanding general. Washington shared the blame in this. In July he had left the appointment of Schuyler's replacement to Congress, and at the same time he had failed to make explicit that he expected any new northern commander (although he knew Congress would name Gates) to be his subordinate. Perhaps Washington simply assumed everyone would conclude as much—but Gates did not, or at least took advantage of the ambiguity of the situation in choosing to deal directly with Congress. Either way, Washington was offended.

Second, Washington considered the failure to promptly report on developments in the Northern Department a dereliction of duty. Prudence, if not courtesy or the military chain of command, dictated that theater commanders keep their comrades informed of significant events. Washington's theater remained active, and who knew what impact the Saratoga operations might have on actions to the south? On October 30, after learning informally of the outcome at Saratoga, Washington wrote Gates a congratulatory letter; but the general pointedly told Gates that he (Washington) could not "but regret" Gates's failure to forward an official report.[6] Gates replied three days later, blithely informing Washington he (Gates) had sent his dispatches to Congress at Congress's request, and that he was sure "Your Excellency has long ago received all the Good News from this Quarter."[7] Washington had, but that wasn't the point.

There was yet another problem. As Burgoyne's invasion loomed, Washington had detached sizeable reinforcements from the main army to the Northern Department. These were the Continentals that bore the brunt of the heaviest and most decisive fighting (although republican purists were loath to admit it). Now, with the Saratoga campaign over and with his army still facing the possibility of active operations around Philadelphia, Washington wanted those regiments returned. The matter of a winter campaign against Howe still hung in contemplation, but without significant reinforcements any offensive was out of the question. For every good reason, as we know, the winter campaign never took place; but there was a moment when Washington hoped that with enough regiments he still might land a punch against Howe.[8] Gates had promptly sent Colonel Daniel Morgan's riflemen south after Burgoyne's surrender; but Morgan's men, fine as they were, were hardly enough. In fact, after discussing the situation with his generals in an October 29 council of war, Washington decided he wanted an additional twenty regiments from Gates, although the commander in chief worried that Gates seemed less than willing to hurry other units after Morgan.

Washington considered it imperative that Gates understand the situation. While he was in no position to speak personally with Gates, he thought the matter too pressing to trust solely to a written dispatch. Thus he directed his young aide-de-camp, Lieutenant Colonel Alexander Hamilton, to ride north and personally explain Washington's reasoning. Hamilton was authorized to speak in Washington's behalf and to convince Gates, then at Albany, to send as many men as practicable to the main army—and immediately. Hamilton was also to see Major General Israel Putnam, then commanding in the Hudson River Highlands at New Windsor, New York. Gates, Putnam's immediate superior, had sent some 2,500 men to Putnam, voicing concerns about British threats to the vital Hudson River defenses. These were troops the main army had been expecting. Washington was unconvinced of Putnam's need for so many men; and, as a young major James Monroe—the future president—noted, while the commander in chief waited impatiently for the tardy units the enemy threat to Putnam's area "prov'd abortive" in any case. Thus Hamilton was to pry reinforcements from Putnam as well.[9]

Hamilton's mission proved difficult. There is little doubt Gates was anxious to continue in an independent command, and neither he nor Putnam graciously acceded to the lieutenant colonel's sometimes pressing entreaties. Hamilton was an urbane young man, but he felt it his duty not to mince words in explaining Washington's position. He found Gates skittish about sending Washington the requested reinforcements, arguing such a large detachment to the main army would leave New England open to British assault. Along with Putnam, Gates accused the insistent Hamilton of impertinence—who did this twenty-year-old think he was?—knowing full well Hamilton was acting under Washington's orders. As forceful as Hamilton was with Gates, he warned Washington he dared not push the major general too hard, and he alluded to Gates's political support. The northern commander, Hamilton wrote, "has influence and interest elsewhere; he might use it, if he pleased, to discredit" Washington's request. "On the whole," he cautioned, "it appeared to me dangerous to insist on sending more troops from hence while General Gates appeared so warmly opposed to it. Should any accident or inconvenience happen in consequence of it, there would be too fair a pretext for censure."[10] In other words, as badly as Washington needed additional troops, it was no time to pick a fight with the Hero of Saratoga.

Ultimately Gates did release substantial reinforcements to Washington's army, then at Whitemarsh, but in numbers too small and too late to support any major venture against Sir William. And Hamilton had been right to warn of possible political complications in dealing with Gates. Even as the lieutenant colonel was meeting with Gates and Putnam, Congress got into the mix. On November 5, the delegates framed a resolution confirming Gates's command in the Hudson Highlands and stressing the need to keep the Hudson clear of the British. To do so Gates was to call on the eastern states for any necessary militia, marine, and material resources, while Putnam was to join Washington's main army with no more than 2,500 men. The rest of Putnam's troops were to remain in the Highlands under Gates. If Washington wanted further troops from the Hudson region he could have them only after conferring with Gates and New York governor (and major general) George Clinton. In an added pro-Gates effort, five New England delegates—John and Samuel Adams and Elbridge Gerry of Massachusetts, Henry Marchant of Rhode Island, and Eliphalet Dyer of Connecticut—tried to amend the resolution. They wanted to require the "concurrence" of Gates and Clinton before dispatching additional regiments to Washington. But that was going too far for the remaining eighteen delegates, who voted against further curtailing Washington's authority.[11] Still, the resolution was a serious restriction on Washington's freedom of action as commander in chief and the Virginian could not have been pleased.

The controversy over reinforcements from the Northern Department was no mere quibble. While Gates may have felt justified in his opinion on what he considered sound military grounds, the fact is that he and Putnam felt free to openly differ with the commander in chief. One doubts they would have done so without some expectation of popular or political support. Gates may have sincerely believed sending more regiments to Washington would imperil New England, no matter how unlikely that scenario was in reality. But sincerity was no excuse for his conduct toward the commander in chief. The situation was analogous to Lee's evasion of Washington's orders to march his troops to the main army in December

1776. Like Lee, Gates felt he had a better grip on military realities than Washington; and also like Lee, he relished operations independent of a commanding general in whom he had lost faith. Congress, intentionally or not, did little to discourage Gates in his recalcitrance, as its resolution of November 5 was hardly a vote of confidence in Washington. In effect the resolution treated Gates as a theater commander virtually co-equal with the commander in chief; and although Gates did not get to keep all the regiments he had wanted, it is reasonable to surmise he was not altogether unhappy with the regard Congress accorded him. As for General George Washington, it is a reasonable surmise that by this time he had had about enough of Major General Horatio Gates.

Then there was Brigadier General Thomas Conway. We should remember that the Irish-born French officer had made a good impression earlier in the year. Conway had led his brigade capably during the "season of hope," and he had fought well at Brandywine and Germantown. Members of Congress respected his opinion on military matters, and at least initially so did many ranking Continental officers. In their early acquaintance in America Lafayette thought well of Conway, and the Frenchman also earned the respect of other American generals. Brigadier General Anthony Wayne and Major General John Sullivan in particular considered Conway enterprising and fair-minded. They had reason: Conway had served on an official inquiry into Sullivan's conduct during an unsuccessful operation against the British on Staten Island; he had also sat on Wayne's court-martial after the disaster at Paoli. Sullivan and Wayne were found blameless, both with Conway's support.[12] Conway, as we know, came to America in part for careerist reasons—a way to advance in the French army—not necessarily through any attachment to the Revolution. In this he was like many of the French and other foreign volunteers. That said, he had served well and was loyal, and that was the point for most patriots.

Yet as time went on another side of Conway emerged, and many Americans found it less attractive. Richard Peters, a member of the Board of War, put his finger on it when he wrote fellow Pennsylvanian Anthony Wayne. Conway, he confided, "I believe . . . is a good Officer tho he has not the Address to please Everybody."[13] Indeed he did not. Conway was an accomplished professional who knew his business, and he missed few opportunities to let everyone know it. And like other European officers, he thought little of criticizing what he considered unprofessional conduct; unfortunately he often did so in terms perhaps not unusual in Europe but which grated on American ears. For example: Rather than stating matter-of-factly that there were better uses for patriot cavalry than mundane messenger duties, he had to add that the practice was "absolutely ridiculous."[14] He was right. But did Americans, still learning the military trade, really need to hear such barbed reminders of their amateur status? Conway's scathing comments on the failures of the rebel army came to encompass its leaders, including the commander in chief. He made free with his opinions in private letters, but there were also slips of the tongue or instances of careless braggadocio; and Conway's attitudes gradually drifted into the communal sphere. They did not endear him to Washington's friends.

Nor did most Americans appreciate Conway's persistent clamor for promotion to major general. Conway was the army's junior brigadier, and as such every other Continental brigadier ranked him. By mid-October 1777, however, rumors that Congress was considering Conway's promotion caused dismay in the officer corps. It was a turning point for Conway, and it cost him much of the respect he had enjoyed earlier in the year.

Conway was not shy about stating his case for major general's rank, and at least in his eyes he had a good case. On November 14, he laid it out in a long letter of self-justification to Maryland delegate Charles Carroll of Carrollton. It was a lament of distress and frustration, written upon learning that Carroll, whom Conway had considered a friend, was unsympathetic to his promotion.[15] The brigadier began with notice of his resignation—only a ploy, for he was either bluffing or hoping to force Congress's hand on his grievances. He was completely serious, however, as he addressed his case in detail. "I will undertake to show that my request of being made a major general had nothing in it so unreasonable as to cause your astonishment." Conway repeated what he had said previously to anyone who would listen: He had come to America with the understanding that no French officer inferior in rank to him in France would rank him in the Continental Army. Silas Deane, the rebel commissioner in Paris, indeed had promised as much; yet in September 1777 Congress broke that promise when it named Johann Kalb a major general. Kalb was a capable officer, but he had ranked behind Conway in the French army; Kalb's promotion came through the influence of his young friend, the Marquis Lafayette. Conway never got over what he considered a gross injustice.[16]

Kalb's promotion, however, was only part of Conway's complaint. He also pointed out that he had recruited other French officers to accompany him to America and that he had done so more economically for Congress than most senior French volunteers. Again he was right. Other officers had received generous reimbursements or stipends for their expenses or initial services, while Conway had asked for and received relatively little. But he then lapsed into the questionable "address" Richard Peters had noted. The angry brigadier told Carroll he had repeatedly offered professional advice to his inexperienced American colleagues, although it seemed he had "not been understood" and that consequently he "saw no alteration [in the Continental Army] for the better." He also pointed to his combat record, insisting immodestly that he was one of the army's best brigade commanders (which he was) and that he could contribute even more as a division commander—that is, as a major general. In fact, based upon what he had seen at Brandywine, Conway considered he was "more qualified to command a division than such major generals who had never seen a line of battle" before Brandywine.[17] Translation: He would be a better major general than his American peers. Conway did not lack self-esteem.

Nor did he lack champions. If his manner—his "address"—irritated many, others felt Conway was just what the army needed. Benjamin Rush, for one, considered him one of the best in the service, the equal of any major general in Europe. After Germantown Rush wrote John Adams of Conway's merits. "For God's sake," he entreated the Massachusetts delegate, "do not suffer him to resign." Overlooking Conway's tendency to abrasiveness, he told Adams Conway was as smart as Major General Charles Lee, another darling of patriot radicals (but then a prisoner of war). Rush admired Conway's reputation as a disciplinarian, and he had no problem with the Frenchman's scathing opinions of American leadership. "Some people blame him for calling some of *our Generals* fools—cowards—and drunkards in public company. But these things are proofs of his integrity, and should raise him in the opinion of every friend to America." "He is moreover the idol of the whole Army," Rush insisted in a gross exaggeration, and he advised Adams to "Make him a Major General if Nothing else will detain him in your Service."[18] Rush's testimonial in Conway's behalf had come as faith in patriot generalship at all levels was falling to new lows, and Rush was not alone in thinking Conway would be an improvement.[19] Certainly Conway was in the good graces of many in Congress, even if not in graces quite good enough to grant him his coveted promotion—at least not yet.

Washington's take on Conway was quite different. By mid-October he had lost any early confidence he had in the French officer. He was probably aware of Conway's low estimate of his (Washington's) leadership, and it was no secret that Conway was friendly with some of the commander in chief's most astringent critics, including Thomas Mifflin. Although he never questioned Conway's competence, he also believed the outspoken brigadier thought too much of himself. But those matters, bothersome as they were, were not Washington's chief concerns. Rather, he considered Conway's constant importuning for promotion a genuine threat to the morale and stability of the officer corps. When the general learned, or at least thought, Congress was taking the Frenchman's request seriously, he felt he had to respond. On October 16, almost two weeks after the disappointment at Germantown, a weary Washington addressed the matter in a letter to an old friend—or a supposed friend—in an attempt to make Congress understand what he saw as the dire consequences of creating a Major General Thomas Conway.

Washington unburdened himself to fellow Virginian Richard Henry Lee. If the general subsequently came to question Lee's personal loyalty, as it seems he did, he had not done so quite yet or else he hardly would have been so blunt and forthcoming in his comments on Conway and the state of the army.[20] As it was, his message to Lee was a plea for congressional restraint on the Conway matter. Apparently ("apparently" because earlier letters from Lee to Washington have not survived) Lee had queried the general on his opinion of Conway because there was growing interest among some delegates in promoting him. Washington was appalled, telling Lee such a promotion would "be as unfortunate a measure, as was ever adopted—I may add (& I think with truth) that it will give a fatal blow to the existance of this army." Conway's merits as a soldier and his value to the army, he told Lee, "exists more in his imagination than in reality"; and he asked why Congress would promote the most junior brigadier in the army "over the heads of the oldest." To do so would be a catastrophic blow to the morale of officers who held their seniority dear and would probably drive many to resign. Indeed, beset with worries about dwindling personal resources, all in the context of a faltering war effort, officers were resigning in troubling numbers. Washington informed Lee he had received twenty resignations in the past six days alone. He warned matters would only get worse if Congress granted a promotion that most of the officer corps felt unjust. "I must therefore conjure you to conjure Congress to consider this matter well, & not by a real act of injustice, compel some good officers to leave your service, & thereby incur a train of evels unforeseen and irremediable."[21]

For Washington this was an uncharacteristically blunt letter. In fact, it was an epistle from a frustrated and drained man who had endured criticisms and sniping to which he felt he could not respond, who worried about his officer corps dissolving in anger and disgust, and who felt he had done his best for the cause even as popular faith in his leadership eroded. Washington was tired of the bickering, tired of the constant controversy, and especially tired of those at the bottom of it all—Conway in particular. He said as much to Lee. "I have been a slave to the service," he avowed, "I have undergone more than most men are aware of, to harmonize so many discordant parts but it will be impossible for me to be of any further service if such insuperable difficulties are thrown in my way." All he wanted was the "public good." The general declared he had "no prejudice against Genl Conway," nor any desire "to serve any other Brigadier, further than I think the cause will be benefitted by it." To finish the war quickly was all he wanted: It "is the most fervent wish of my Soul."[22] His letter was a plea not to let the Conway affair stand in the way of that wish; and the line "it will be impossible for me to be of any further service" in the midst of the discontent surrounding Conway was the closest Washington had ever come to hinting at resignation. Although written in a private capacity to an old acquaintance, the public import of Washington's letter was clear. In fact, it was one of the most serious communications he had penned to that point in the war.

Conway would have to wait for his promotion. Too many delegates, as his letter to Carroll indicated, were hesitant. No doubt Richard Henry Lee had shared Washington's concerns with fellow delegates; and no doubt Washington made his feelings known through other channels. Certainly Congress was aware of the discontent in the officer corps. In the meantime Conway, who by this time had little use for the commander in chief, had remained on duty. He sat on courts-martial, attended councils of war, and carried out the normal responsibilities of a brigade commander, at least until his threat to resign in mid-November. He also kept some questionable (in Washington's view) company; the Frenchman was not at this point personally acquainted with Gates, but he certainly knew Thomas Mifflin.

Mifflin and Conway saw eye-to-eye on Washington. Mifflin's blistering critique of Washington's leadership (recall his letter to Gates of November 17) matched anything Conway had to say, at least that we know of. And as we have seen, Mifflin was a formidable man. His opposition to a radical new Pennsylvania state constitution had caused a breach between himself and many Pennsylvania patriots, but he had many friends in Congress. That eastern Pennsylvania, Mifflin's home bailiwick, was the seat of war over late 1777 and early 1778 probably magnified his importance with the delegates. His opinions mattered, and he shared them freely as he entertained military and political luminaries at his Reading country seat, conveniently close to the exiled Congress at York. Indeed, Mifflin kept influential company. Gates, Conway, and other officers partook of his hospitality over the winter. At various times John and Samuel Adams, James Lovell, Richard Henry Lee,

Benjamin Rush, and kindred spirits were frequent correspondents with Mifflin and occasional dinner guests. While the army struggled against cold and hunger at Valley Forge, there seemed no shortage of warmth and fine fare at Mifflin's table.

Mifflin's dismissive regard for Washington's leadership was no secret, and he sincerely believed the patriot war effort would be better off in Gates's hands. Yet most of his attacks on Washington were oblique. Instead of damning Washington personally, as he had in his missive to Gates, he heaped calumny on subordinate officers. Nathanael Greene was a favorite target, and the calumnies had reach. From Virginia one of Washington's aides, Lieutenant Colonel John Fitzgerald, reported "misrepresentations" by Mifflin and Conway had poisoned "the Opinion of the people" against Greene "in these parts."[23] Such jibes at Washington's lieutenants fooled only the most naïve (if anyone was really *that* naïve)—the real mark was clear enough. It was also clear that Mifflin was an intimate of others who now questioned Washington. Sensing a dangerous opponent in Mifflin was not paranoia on the part of those close to the commander in chief. In fact the Pennsylvanian, having largely neglected his post as quartermaster general, retained his commission as a major general and was in good standing with key members in Congress, especially Lovell and Richard Henry Lee. Of all those involved in the Cabal, Mifflin would prove the most dangerous, although this was not apparent in early October. Indeed, the politically astute quartermaster general would play the least visible role in events as the breach between Washington and his antagonists finally became public—as it was about to do.

THUS WASHINGTON KNEW who his enemies, or supposed enemies, were. At least he thought he did. Here it is well to bear in mind that people in any age react not so much to what is demonstratively true as they do to what they *believe* is true. In the mid-autumn of 1777 Horatio Gates could honestly deny participation in any intrigue against the rebel chief, but that no longer mattered. Washington and his partisans now firmly believed the worst of Gates as well as Conway, and they knew Mifflin was no friend. But if these "calumniators"—as Hamilton later called them[24]—were in some way moving against Washington, what could anyone do about it? As no one had made an overt move in Congress to challenge Washington's command—and such an action would have to come in Congress—the general had little opportunity to confront his critics. This, however, was about to change.

Late on November 4, Washington received a letter from Lord Stirling. Dated November 3, the communication was nothing short of explosive. The message was actually quite lengthy. The river forts below Philadelphia were still holding out, and the major general briefed the commander in chief on the situation. Stirling was optimistic, thinking Howe would be hard-pressed to successfully attack Fort Mercer. He also wrote of forwarding recruits to the main army, supply matters, and his own health (Stirling had taken a spill from his horse). All in all it was a fairly ordinary communication, a routine update—until the very last sentence. It was an astonishing line: "The enclosed was Communicated by Col. Wilkinson to Major MacWilliams, [and] such wicked duplicity of Conduct, I shall alway's think it my duty to detect." "Col. Wilkinson" was Lieutenant Colonel James Wilkinson, an aide to Major General Gates. "Major MacWilliams" was Major William McWilliams, one of Stirling's aides. The enclosure Stirling referred to was a quotation attributed to Brigadier General Thomas Conway, supposedly an extract from a letter Conway had written to Gates, probably in the first two weeks of October 1777.[25] The letter has not survived, but it was one of the many flattering letters Gates had received in the aftermath of Saratoga. Conway had sent it from Reading *via* Lieutenant Colonel Robert Troup, another of Gates's staff officers, then returning to Albany after a visit to York.[26] The original message praised Gates, supposedly extolling his generalship in effusive terms. Then, like others who had communicated with Gates, Conway allegedly took a swipe at Washington, which Stirling quoted as follows: "Heaven has been determined to save your Country; or a weak General and bad Councellors would have ruind it."[27]

Anyone reading the passage could not have mistaken its meaning, and certainly Stirling did not. Neither did Washington when he read it. This was bad luck on Conway's part. Had Washington seen the letters to Gates from Wayne, Brodhead, or Ward, much less St. Clair, he certainly would have been upset. But this was Thomas Conway's letter, and Conway had become a major thorn in Washington's side. It was *enough*: At this point the commander in chief's vaunted patience ended. At last he would counterattack.

The Conway letter has a curious history, and it merits a look before dealing with Washington's reaction. Nothing was more curious than how Stirling learned of the inflammatory excerpt. The key was Wilkinson, and so we need to know him better. A bright young man and the scion of lesser Maryland gentility, he had completed his medical studies in Philadelphia just before the outbreak of hostilities. He had planned to open a practice, but instead he joined the army in 1775. Commissioned a captain and then promoted relatively quickly to major and lieutenant colonel, he impressed his superiors with his charm and efficiency. Wilkinson proved a good soldier, and he compiled a creditable military record as he served variously on the staffs of Nathanael Greene and Benedict Arnold. He also capably commanded an infantry company, fought at Trenton, and even got on well with Washington. In 1776, at nineteen years old, he joined Gates's staff.[28] Wilkinson then ably served the major general during the Saratoga campaign; and as a reward Gates entrusted him with a mission as much ceremonial as practical: He was to carry Gates's official report on the victory over Burgoyne's army to Congress. Such an assignment in those days was an honor, and his orders were to report directly to the delegates in York. There was no mention of Wilkinson's reporting to the commander in chief as well, much less doing so first.

The Marylander turned out to be a poor choice of messenger. Incredibly, entrusted with one of the most important dispatches in the nascent republic's history, Wilkinson attached little urgency to his mission. Albeit he travelled through some nasty weather, even so he took his time stopping to visit acquaintances and dealing with some personal matters, including a two-day visit to his future wife, Ann Biddle, in Easton, Pennsylvania.[29] A week into a journey that should have taken only days, a driving rain forced him to shelter in Reading, Pennsylvania. As fate would have it, Stirling was headquartered in town, and on October 27 Wilkinson joined the major general and his staff for a "pot luck dinner." It was a small party: Wilkinson, Stirling, McWilliams, and another aide, Major James Monroe. Wilkinson recalled the evening as fairly boring; Stirling told war stories, but there was plenty of drinking. Eventually the tipsy general retired, leaving the three young officers alone. The talk then turned to army gossip. When McWilliams asked about rumors supposedly circulating in York that linked Conway and Gates in correspondence critical of Washington, Wilkinson dropped his bombshell. He confided to McWilliams the import of the Conway letter. In doing so Wilkinson was unwise, but he meant no harm. He had not been snooping around his boss's desk. To the contrary, Gates, evidently very pleased with Conway's message, had shared it with his trusted aide.[30] And as events would later prove, Wilkinson's recollection of the damning phrase—"Heaven has been determined to save your Country; or a weak General and bad Councellors would have ruind it"—was faulty. But once imparted to McWilliams, the precise wording hardly mattered.

Mixing alcohol and confidential information is always a bad idea, and under the influence Wilkinson had talked too much about something he had no business talking about at all. He later admitted to being free with his liquor that evening, although he steadfastly denied saying anything damaging to Washington's reputation.[31] Perhaps he honestly did not see what he told McWilliams as anything more than gossip. Who knows? But the proverbial cat was out of the bag. The next morning he rode off, apparently without a thought to what had passed the night before and seemingly unaware of the furor his besotted remarks were about to unleash. One assumes he was no sooner out of sight when McWilliams, as a loyal aide should have, reported the gist of Wilkinson's comments to Stirling. Regarding Wilkinson, one is reminded of the World War II injunction against being free with sensitive information: "Loose lips sink ships." Or perhaps the more pointed German equivalent is better: "Schäm Dich, Schwätzer!"—*very* roughly, "Shame on you, blabbermouth!"[32] Indeed.

And where was the oblivious Lieutenant Colonel Wilkinson while McWilliams was reporting to Stirling? He was on his leisurely way west. The journey took so long some delegates feared Wilkinson had been intercepted. John Adams was near frantic, writing Abigail of his "tormenting Uncertainty concerning our Affairs at the Northward."[33] Wilkinson arrived in York, some fifty-five miles from Reading, only on October 31; the trip from Gates's headquarters had taken twelve long days. The tardy messenger then took until November 3 to assemble Gates's papers and deliver his dispatches to an anxious Congress. While grateful for the (at last!) official report from Gates, Wilkinson's horsemanship had impressed no one. Samuel Adams was seldom noted for his sense of humor, but if his cousin John's memory serves, Samuel got off a memorable line when he quipped, "it would be proper to present the Courier with a horsewhip and a pair of Spurrs."[34] Nevertheless Wilkinson's reward was considerably better: a brevet promotion to brigadier general—but that story is for later.

While Wilkinson made his way to York, for a full week Stirling did nothing with his astounding information about Conway and Gates. One can only wonder why it took him so long to write to Washington; he must have known Conway's letter would gall the commander in chief. There is little doubt Stirling would have enjoyed seeing Conway embarrassed, as he openly detested the brigadier. Like other Washington loyalists, Stirling shared his chief's distaste for Conway's importuning for promotion, although the rebel "lord's" animosity had more personal motives as well. Before Germantown, when Stirling was ill, Conway had temporary command of Stirling's division. Seeking to field as many men as possible, Conway ignored Stirling's request for a detachment to form a personal bodyguard; the brigadier also forbade subordinates to follow any orders from Stirling unless he (Conway) approved them. Stirling was enraged. Washington let the matter pass, but he was well aware of Stirling's dislike of the willful Frenchman.[35] No doubt Stirling felt he was doing his duty in reporting the excerpt from Conway's letter to Washington, but it was duty he must have enjoyed.

Washington, while outraged and exasperated, recognized Conway's letter for what it was: a gift. For the first time he had hard evidence—or what he chose to interpret as evidence—to prove machinations against him were real. The general could even put names on those behind the schemes: Conway and Gates. And by striking at Conway as the letter's author, at the same time he could put its recipient, Gates, on the spot. It was a "two-for-one" opportunity. Washington would not strike with a bludgeon, however; for maximum effect the matter called for finesse. And Conway and Gates were about to find out how well the commander in chief could play the card Conway had so inadvertently dealt him.

Unlike Stirling, Washington did not need a week to deal with the situation. The general had received Stirling's note on the evening of November 4, and the next day he wrote directly to Conway. The letter was two short sentences, a masterful demonstration that less can be more:

> Sir,
> a Letter which I received last Night, contained the following paragraph.
> In a Letter from Genl Conway to Genl Gates he says—"Heaven has been determind to save your Country; or a weak General and bad Councellors would have ruind it."
> I am Sir Yr Hble Srvt.[36]

Washington had accused Conway of nothing, but the truculent brigadier now knew the commander in chief saw him openly as an enemy and linked to Major General Gates. Much now depended on how Conway reacted.

If Washington was looking for a fight, he held the initiative from the start, for the general's brief note had blindsided the brigadier. Conway was at a loss to know what Washington had really seen, much less how he had come to see it. How did Washington, then at Whitemarsh, Pennsylvania, see a private letter sent to Gates at Albany, New York? Certainly Gates would not have shared it with the commander in chief. And what about the excerpt Washington had quoted? While the sentiments were right—Conway *had* deprecated Washington's leadership—the wording was not. The entire business left the surprised brigadier in the dark. Under the circumstances, how was Conway to respond? A cautious man might have waited to learn more before replying to Washington's curt note. Or perhaps an equally short and vague note was in order, one that simply and truthfully denied authorship of the exact words (although avoiding the issue of sentiments). But Thomas Conway was not a cautious man.

In fact, he responded immediately and in detail. He wrote to Washington the same day (November 5), mounting a remarkably cogent defense. He was not belligerent, but he apologized for nothing. He explained he had written Gates a congratulatory letter after the victory at Saratoga and that in this letter he had commented frankly on the sorry state of operations around Philadelphia. "I Spoke my mind freely, I found fault with several Measures pursued in this army; but," the brigadier insisted, "I Will venture to say that in my Whole Letter the paragraph of Which you are pleas'd to send me a copy can not be found." A few lines later Conway returned to the same point: "I Believe i can attest that the expression Weak General has not slipped from my penn."[37] Of course this was arguing a technicality if the Wilkinson account had captured the spirit of Conway's letter.

What, then, was the actual wording? With the full letter missing we will never know (unless, of course, a copy turns up). Still, it seems the spirit of the extract Wilkinson recited was accurate. As early as late October none other than Benjamin Rush had somehow learned of Conway's letter, or at least the section of it in question. Rush was overjoyed with Conway's sentiments. In a letter to John Adams, in which he excoriated the commander in chief and gushingly proclaimed his "pleasure" at Gates's "unparalled success" at Saratoga, Rush offered another version of the controversial quote: "'A great and good God (says Genl. Conway in a letter to a friend) has decreed that America shall be free, or —— [the long dash obviously represented Washington] and weak councellors would have ruined her long ago.'"[38] It wasn't exactly what Wilkinson reported, but it was close.

There is yet another and apparently more accurate excerpt. Conway, or someone close to him, entrusted a copy to Daniel Roberdeau, a radical Pennsylvania politico. Roberdeau later claimed (dubiously) he had shown the letter only to Henry Laurens and an unnamed "French Gentleman"—and he had let Laurens see it only after the president of Congress virtually begged. "I gained a perusal," Laurens plaintively wrote, "by intreaty!" Learning from Laurens that Roberdeau held a copy, one of Washington's aides, Lieutenant Colonel John Fitzgerald, then visiting York, asked the Pennsylvanian a for look. Roberdeau politely refused, citing the private nature of the correspondence. A frustrated Fitzpatrick then found that Laurens had copied an extract, which the South Carolinian readily allowed him to transcribe. Fitzpatrick then sent the copy to Washington. The few lines verified that Wilkinson's recollection to McWilliams was indeed inaccurate as to wording but fully confirmed Wilkinson had accurately reported the essence of Conway's opinion of Washington. "What a pity there is but one Gates!" it read, "but the more I see of this Army the less I think it fit for general Action under its actual Chiefs & actual discipline. I speak sincerely & freely & wish I could serve under you." Moreover, according to Fitzpatrick, Laurens characterized the whole of Conway's letter as rife with "the most bitter Invective" against the commander in chief. Laurens himself, in a letter to a South Carolina friend, noted Conway's actual language was "ten times worse in every view" than Wilkinson reported.[39] If Laurens is to be believed—and his account appears trustworthy—Conway's attempt to skirt the issue of what he actually wrote to Gates was utterly disingenuous.

Yet Conway never denied criticizing the American war effort, and tacitly Washington. He fully admitted to Washington that he believed the commander in chief trusted too much in the opinions of subordinate generals Conway considered second-rate. Although he did not name names, by these he no doubt meant at least Greene, Knox, and *certainly* Stirling. Conway lauded the Virginian's patriotism and personal virtue, but reading between the lines the French officer's skepticism of Washington's leadership was clear enough.

Conway then moved into more dangerous territory. He revealed he had spoken his mind to officers other than Gates. These included Thomas Mifflin and Doctor James Craik. Obviously such an open admission was not the stuff of conspiracy. Conway knew Mifflin was a kindred spirit regarding Washington and that the Pennsylvanian was not in the commanding general's good graces. Yet the fact that Conway would denigrate Washington's closest subordinates in conversations with other officers was no comfort to the commander in chief. That the Frenchman would do so in front of a man known to be the general's friend and personal physician (Craik) must have been infuriating. So was the potential for turmoil within the officer corps—but to this Conway seemed oblivious. In fact, he felt justified in his actions. The brigadier maintained that candor "between General oficers in all army's is encourag'd rather than Discountenanc'd, because from this intercourse of ideas something usefull might arise."[40] True enough, but hardly calculated to ease Washington's wounded feelings when he believed his command was under political fire.

Conway was not done. He assured Washington there was nothing in the letter to Gates he (Conway) would not say to the commander in chief personally. He added he knew some of Washington's aides had accused him of authoring some "Discourses Which i never utter'd"—possibly a reference to a recently published De Lisle (William Livingston) tract lauding Gates's triumph at Saratoga—and he promised to write "an impartial account of the operations Which I saw During this campaign." Again, he would write nothing he would be unwilling to share openly with the general.[41] It all boiled down to: *Yes, I wrote to Gates and told him candidly what I thought—and I've said the same to other senior patriots. But I never meant disrespect to you.* In his mind Conway had made a clean breast of things; but he was hardly so naïve as to think an obviously ruffled commander in chief was going to forget the matter.

In fact Washington did not forget the matter, but for the time being he did not pursue it. He had scored on Conway and knew it, and for the moment that was enough. Besides, he was busy and Conway was a distraction. On November 5, the day he and Conway had exchanged letters, Washington also dealt with at least eight other correspondents on business as diverse as the British prisoners taken at Saratoga, operations around Philadelphia, militia activities in Pennsylvania and New Jersey, and matters of logistics, camp security, ammunition supplies, and the other mundane but necessary minutia of maintaining the army.[42] The general had little time to devote to a feud with a man he now despised.

In fact, within two weeks it seemed Washington's luck regarding Conway had changed. On November 16, the general received what must have seemed a providential letter: The Frenchman informed Washington he had asked Congress for permission to resign. With France likely to enter the war, Conway thought, "along with some other reasons," he wanted to return home. His tone was obsequious; he wished the American cause well and thanked "your Excellency for the civilitys you have shew'd me while I had the honour of being under your orders."[43] But again he was hedging. Along with his letter he enclosed a copy of his eight-page message to Charles Carroll (written only two days earlier on November 14)—the exposition of his case for promotion to major general. This was hardly necessary if all Conway wanted was to leave Continental service. Carroll had sent his copy to Congress, where delegates still impressed with Conway were soon mulling what to do. They did not want to lose an officer they considered a cut above many American generals, and Conway knew he had friends in York. Washington apparently ignored the lengthy enclosure, but he quickly replied that if Congress agreed to the resignation, he had no problem with it. (No surprise there!) But he tactfully refused to allow Conway to leave the army until Congress officially accepted the resignation. When Conway wrote again asking for leave to collect his papers in preparation for a return to France, Washington had one of his aides send approval. At last it seemed the commander in chief would be rid of the bothersome Frenchman. And he was—but only for a few weeks.

YET THE FUROR surrounding "the Letter" (to recall Henry Laurens's term) was only beginning. Having dealt (or so he thought) with Conway, Washington now found the affair expanding. Since his communications with Conway, Washington had continued to correspond with Major General Gates on several important matters, including Burgoyne's captured army and the defense of the Hudson Highlands.[44] The commander in chief never mentioned the Conway letter. Perhaps he was being cagey, waiting to learn what role, if any, Gates may have had in dealings with Conway. If so, Washington waited for over a month before hearing from Gates on the matter. It was not until the second week of December, in a letter dated the eighth, that he received a message from a perplexed and obviously angry Gates. Having learned his private correspondence had leaked to outside parties and was now part of a public controversy, the major general was livid. And no wonder. It was a dispute Gates, no matter how he felt about Washington's leadership, had had no intention of initiating. It certainly took him by surprise. But how had Gates discovered one of his letters, or at least an extract from one of them, had "gone public"?

As far as we know, before the Conway-Washington exchange Gates and Conway were at best casually acquainted, although they certainly knew of one another. Exactly when Gates learned about the extract from Conway's letter, and of Washington's response, is a bit murky. Gates dated the discovery from "About the Beginning of Decemr." This would comport with a letter he received from Mifflin on November 28. Mifflin, then engaged with Congress in reorganizing the Board of War, found the situation acutely disturbing. There is no question of his preference for Gates over Washington and, as the reader will find in the next chapter, he would do his best on the board to elevate Gates at Washington's expense. But astute politico that he was, Mifflin knew "the Letter" controversy was fraught with political risk. He warned Gates of the spreading public knowledge of the Conway-Washington affair: "An extract from General Conway's letter to you has been procured, and sent to headquarters," he reported. Mifflin evidently referred to the "extract" as related from Wilkinson to McWilliams, because he reported Washington had enclosed a copy in his message to Conway, thus ruling out the extracts supplied by Laurens or reported by Rush to Adams. Mifflin continued that he agreed completely with Conway's opinion of Washington, telling Gates "the extract was a collection of just sentiments." But he cautioned Gates never to share such private communications with his aides or, unmentioned but implied, with anyone else. Conway's response to Washington, he noted, was fully appropriate. "It was supported, and the freedom of the sentiment was not apologized for; on the contrary," the approving Mifflin continued, "although some reflections were made on some people, yet the practice was pleaded boldly, and no satisfaction given"—meaning Conway did not back down. But Mifflin concluded with a warning: "My dear General," he counseled his friend, "take care of your sincerity and frank disposition; they cannot injure yourself, but may injure some of your best friends."[45] It was good advice; the situation indeed suggested a measured approach. Washington was, after all, commander in chief, and even amid his difficulties he still had his partisans.

But was Gates really in the dark until early December? It is questionable. Conway was talkative and had friends in the army and in Congress; it is difficult to believe the controversial brigadier had kept the import of his reply to Washington (November 5) to himself. In fact, we know he did not. Judging from his letter to Gates, Mifflin, frequently in Conway's company, clearly knew about it. By late October so did Benjamin Rush and, *via* Rush's letter, so did John Adams. And given Rush's prolix and zealous nature, who else had he confided in? It is hard—more likely *impossible*—to imagine a blabbermouth like Rush keeping such sensational news to himself. Then there was Roberdeau and the unnamed "French Gentleman." The circle of those in the know was not necessarily small. And by this time Conway, by his own admission, was making free with his opinions about the commander in chief. Still, the Frenchman was concerned enough about the controversy to seek reassurance about what he actually had written to Gates. Sometime in (probably) mid-November Conway met privately with Wilkinson in camp at Whitemarsh. He asked the young officer if he had seen the letter, and when Wilkinson said yes, Conway asked him about the paragraph Washington had seen. Did it really say "heaven has Determin'd to save this country or a weak general and Bad Counsellors would have ruined it"? He was relieved to get Wilkinson's assurance "that such a paragraph Was not in my letter."[46]

Wilkinson, of course, was less than honest with Conway, never disclosing that he was the source of the leaked extract *and* of the reported wording. But if Conway was trying to be sure of his ground—he had, after all, insisted to the commander in chief he had not written the offending paragraph—it clearly indicated that talk of Washington's anger was making the rounds. So who else knew about the letter? Army gossip being what it was, word of the controversy easily could have reached Albany by mid-November. If it had, Gates could not be blamed for hoping the matter would blow over without further complications. Mifflin's alert, however, indicating that the matter had become public knowledge would have ended any such hope.

Gates obviously felt he had to react. He chose to contact Washington directly, and in so doing the major general waded into a mire of embarrassment. The Conway affair would inflict the first wound to his public image since Saratoga. His letter to Washington (December 8) made no mention of Conway's obvious slights of the commanding general; instead Gates raised the "disagreeable Situation, [into] which confidential Letters, when exposed to public inspection, may place an unsuspecting Correspondent." That is, Gates presented himself as *the victim* in the affair: He was the "unsuspecting Correspondent." Moreover, he wanted "all the Assistance" Washington could provide in tracking down who had leaked the extract of Conway's letter. "Those Letters have been stealingly copied; but, which of them, when, or by whom, is to me, as yet, an unfathomable Secret." In fact, the "by whom" question, as the reader will see shortly, was disingenuous. But "Letters," plural? Perhaps Gates was unsure of how much of his correspondence was involved in the leak. It seems so. He told Washington he was sure none of his aides were involved, but under the circumstances he reasonably worried about whom he could trust.

Interestingly, however, he believed that Washington was the key to discovering the "Wretch" who not only had betrayed Gates but whose indiscretion could easily damage "Operations under your immediate direction." The implication was clear: Gates suspected Washington knew or could easily find out the culprit's identity. The "Crime" was so important, Gates continued, so fraught with implications for "the Safety of the States," that he had sent a copy of his letter to Congress as well. He drove home the point in his conclusion: "Crimes of that Magnitude ought not to remain unpunished."[47]

In copying his letter to Congress, Gates doubled down on his determination to find the "Wretch"—and to insinuate Washington had some understanding of who it was. Gates's covering note to Henry Laurens again focused on the dangers security breaches posed to the cause. If it was known that the papers of senior officers were pilfered, he asked rhetorically, who then would write candidly or entrust important intelligence to paper? How could secrets be secure? Gates had a point. But why share his letter to Washington with Congress? Gates claimed congressional knowledge of the situation would speed detection of "the Criminal," and that he could not "believe that the traitorous Thief will long escape Detection, after the patriotism of the Delegates shall have been Alarmed." All of this was flattering to Congress, but Gates did not mention how Congress might help in detective work. Was Congress supposed to pressure Washington to name the "Wretch"? (If Gates hoped as much he was disappointed; there is no evidence President Laurens circulated the communication to Congress.)[48] Gates did not say a word about Conway's derogatory remarks about the commander in chief. The import of Conway's slights of the commanding general did not seem to concern him; nor did the fact his letter to Washington, which Gates intended Congress to see, not-so-subtly suggested Washington could finger the source of the leak.

Gates was right about security: Leaking the papers of a senior general was (and is) a grave intelligence risk, not to mention a breach of eighteenth-century conceptions of gentlemanly honor. Nor should unauthorized disclosure of such documents escape punishment. The contents, or even the gist, of Conway's letter would have been a prize for British intelligence; and the British *were* watching specifically for cracks in American unity. Indeed, Howe's officers had picked up signals of the mounting controversy over the American chief. Given the extent and public nature of Washington's escalating tribulations, it would have been astonishing if the enemy had missed them. By November, as news of the Conway-Washington exchange seeped into the public domain, rumblings of discontent among the rebels became known in occupied Philadelphia. Hessian captain and diarist Friedrich von Muenchhausen, an aide-de-camp to General Howe, recorded what must have been common knowledge among the British officer corps: "We hear that Washington is no longer on good terms with Congress." Muenchhausen kept his ear to the ground on the matter, later reporting continuing friction between the delegates and the American commander in chief, as well as the fact that Gates had entered the mix and was "meeting with Congress in York."[49] Major General Charles ("No Flint") Grey had heard more than that. On November 28, the exact date when Mifflin was writing Gates, Grey informed an unidentified correspondent of "a strong report" that a hostile combination in Congress was about to force Washington's resignation and that "the contest of Commander in Chief is between Generals Greene, & Gates."[50] If Grey was wrong, there was no denying British interest in the turmoil within senior American ranks. Although royalists were never able to gauge the full extent of Washington's predicament, much less find a way to exploit it, those were things Washington and his allies hardly wanted to risk. Nor, to his credit, did Gates.

But Washington and Gates were playing games, fencing with one another as it were. Washington was framing the dispute in terms of personal insult and a challenge to his command. And of course he had known since early November the culprit was Wilkinson. Yet in his various dealings with Gates over November he quite deliberately failed to relate the stunning fact that one of Gates's most trusted aides was at least a genuine security risk, if not, as we will see, actually a liar. In either case, this was information a senior general ought to have shared with a key subordinate.

On the other hand, Gates's indignation was hardly righteous. A candid Gates would have told Washington why he suspected the commander in chief could finger the leaker: It was because Gates was convinced his own investigation had identified the guilty man, and that in fact the "Wretch" was a prominent member of Washington's inner circle. It was none other, Gates was convinced, than Lieutenant Colonel Alexander Hamilton, the impertinent young officer who had so offended Gates the month before at Albany. Gates was probably more interested in obtaining a measure of payback against Hamilton than in embarrassing Washington. But Washington would have felt the slap at one of his favorite and most talented aides.

Gates was confident in his suspicion of Hamilton. Having read Mifflin's letter of November 28, the major general reacted appropriately in trying to identify the source of the leak. He did two things. First, he wrote to Conway. He thanked the Frenchman for his flattering letter and agreed with his critique of operations in Washington's theater. He also mentioned Conway's now public intention to resign and expressed his hope Congress would refuse to accept the resignation. Clearly Gates valued Conway. Then, in a "P.S.," Gates told him of the letter extract now in Washington's hands. Actually, Gates referred to "letters," again raising the possibility the letter at the heart of all the excitement may have been only one among others in a more extended Gates-Conway correspondence. "I entreat you, dear General," Gates queried, "to let me know which of the letters was copied off." In whatever communications were involved, Gates assured Conway that in writing he (Conway) had "acted with all the dignity of a virtuous soldier." Now, however, Gates wanted Conway's help in tracking down whoever was responsible for the "act of infidelity: I cannot trace him out," the Northern commander wrote, "unless I have your assistance."[51] There is no indication Conway was able to help, but Gates's letter certainly hinted at a greater familiarity with the brigadier than he would later admit.

Next, Gates questioned his staff officers. How this came about remains a bit cloudy, but again Wilkinson was at the center of things. On December 8, Wilkinson returned to Albany from his mission to York as a newly minted brevet brigadier general.[52] He arrived *before* Gates sent Washington his letter of the same date. Learning of the Conway letter controversy, Wilkinson, according to his notoriously self-serving *Memoirs*, claimed astonishment at hearing Gates confide a scandalous version of how the leaked extract had reached the commander in chief. Gates supposedly accused Hamilton, who allegedly had found himself briefly alone in Gates's headquarters during his October visit. Seizing the opportunity, the tale went, Washington's emissary "purloined" Conway's letter from a "closet," copied it, and secreted the copy to Washington. Wilkinson claims he tried to argue Gates out of this theory, suggesting instead that Lieutenant Colonel Robert Troup, another of Gates's aides and an old friend of Hamilton, might have innocently disclosed the contents of the letter in a casual conversation. But supposedly Gates was not to be dissuaded. Not only that, he planned revenge. Wilkinson quoted Gates as claiming he "had adopted a plan, which would compel Washington to give him [Hamilton] up, and that the receiver [Washington] and the thief would alike be disgraced."[53] Most of this account, of course, was ridiculous. Would Hamilton have known to look in Gates's "closet"? Did he even know about Conway's letter? Would he have risked a theft? But there was enough in Wilkinson's fiction to be intriguing. In his letters to Washington and to Laurens, Gates *did* hint broadly that Washington knew the secret of the Conway extract, which also would have implied the general was protecting Hamilton. It seems Gates did give thought to putting Washington on the spot.

But Wilkinson was lying. Gates did *not* originally suspect Hamilton. In fact, it was Wilkinson who planted the idea of Hamilton's perfidy; there is no evidence Gates had any such notion until Wilkinson's return from York. This is clear from Robert Troup's account of events, which was quite credible. Years later Troup recalled the commotion at the Northern Army's headquarters when Gates learned of the notorious letter. The discovery "excited such unpleasant feelings in the breast of General Gates, as to impel him to strict inquiries among the gentlemen of his family to discover the

Traitor who had betrayed him." All of the aides firmly denied responsibility for the leak "and declared their inability even to suggest any clue" as to who the guilty party might be.[54] Of course one of them was grossly dishonest.

Gates had trusted Wilkinson, or "Wilky," as the major general's inner circle referred to the likeable young officer. And why not? Wilkinson had proved a competent aide and Gates had no reason to think anything but well of him. When "Wilky" returned from his mission to York, Gates queried him about the Conway leak. The new brigadier was in a tight spot. At least three men knew he was the source of the extract: McWilliams, Stirling, and Washington for sure, and probably Monroe—and likely others of Washington's inner circle. (Washington later disclosed Conway had shared a copy of his letter to Gates with Lafayette "under injunctions of secrecy." But Wilkinson could not have known this.)[55] What to do? Essentially Wilkinson had three choices. He could fess up and explain the situation: Make an honest breast of the incident at Stirling's headquarters, blaming alcohol and *very* humbly begging pardon and hoping for the best from the amiable general who had so trustingly fostered his career. *Mea culpa. Volui et non malum* [I meant no harm]. But was a furious major general likely to overlook such a *faux pas*? Maybe not. Or Wilkinson could join the rest of Gates's family in professing ignorance. But if he did claim ignorance he ran the risk of the truth coming out from someone around Washington. Forget that. Finally, he could try to pin the leak on someone else. This, in a precursor to a public career of astounding dissimulation and duplicity that reached well into the nineteenth century, was the course he chose.

Wilkinson spun what on the surface seemed a convincing story. He reminded Gates of Hamilton's October visit—his mission conveying Washington's concerns over recovering Northern Army troops for the Middle Theater. Did the general remember that Hamilton had spent considerable time with Robert Troup? Wilkinson pointed out that Hamilton and Troup were the closest of friends. It was true. The two young men had been roommates at King's College (now Columbia University); they enjoyed a warm relationship, and when Hamilton had come north they had done a lot of catching up. Decades later a still-indignant Troup recalled that Wilkinson, "to screen himself, insinuated to General Gates that the secret of the correspondence had probably been disclosed" by Troup "in an unguarded moment, to his friend Col. Alexander Hamilton." Hamilton then, "by various motives," relayed the story to Washington. It was all a blatant fabrication that also ran the risk of exposure by Washington's camp. But even the offended Troup had to admit circumstances initially gave the lie a ring of truth. After all, Troup had carried Conway's letter to Gates, so perhaps he had seen its contents? The obviously desperate Wilkinson was digging himself in deeper, but for the moment Gates fell for his story.[56] And it was after falling for it that he wrote his December 8 letter to Washington—his call for Washington to "detect" the "Wretch."

Belief in Wilkinson proved costly. On January 4, 1778, Washington finally replied to Gates, and he took the opportunity to deal his rival—and by now Washington saw Gates as such—a stinging rebuke. Eschewing niceties, he came right to the point: He had not appreciated the fact that Gates had sent Henry Laurens (and thus Congress) a copy of his December 8 letter. Why Gates had done so the Virginian claimed he could not fathom. Yet two could play the game. He told Gates that inasmuch as Gates "doubtless" had some important reason for sending a copy of his letter to Congress, Washington would do the same. This was necessary "lest" any delegates "should harbor an unfavorable suspicion of my having practiced some indirect means, to come at the contents of the confidential Letters between you & General Conway." This was surely an allusion to Washington's supposed understanding of Hamilton's alleged duplicity. Washington was probably enjoying himself as he then ambushed Gates with the secret he had kept for two months. "I have to inform you then," he announced, that he *did* know the source of the Conway excerpt: It was Gates's own "Colo. Wilkinson." The general explained the entire sequence of events from Wilkinson's visit to Stirling's headquarters through his (Washington's) exchange of letters with Conway. It was the last thing Gates expected to learn, and it is not difficult to imagine his shock.

The commander in chief was not finished. He again emphasized that his staff had had nothing to do with digging up Conway's letter, and he summarily dismissed the rest of Gates's rejoinder. Washington agreed that dissensions within the army ought not to reach British ears, but he was not persuaded that Wilkinson meant any deliberate harm or "an act of infidelity." Instead of indicting Wilkinson, he directed his wrath at Conway, and thus indirectly at Gates. Washington insisted that until Stirling alerted him, he had no idea Conway had been in touch with the northern commander. "Much less," he added, "did I suspect that I was the subject of your confidential Letters." Again, "*Letters*." Washington had clearly suggested the possibility of a wider Gates-Conway correspondence. Contradicting Gates, the Virginian insisted the leak would not harm the rebel cause in the least. In fact, he wondered why Gates had called upon him "in such solemn terms to point out the author." With distilled sarcasm,

Washington claimed that he thought Wilkinson had acted as Gates's intermediary in speaking with McWilliams! Gates's aide had so freely recited the "extract," Washington mockingly averred that he believed Gates was warning him against Conway's machinations. "I considered the information as coming from yourself"; he solemnly declared, "and given with a friendly view to forewarn, and consequently forearm me, against a secret enemy." That enemy, of course, was Conway, who the general now denounced as "a dangerous incendiary; in which character, sooner or later, this Country will know" him. And the implication was: Everyone else with an ounce of brains knew what Conway was, even if a foolish Gates didn't. "But—in this, as in other matters of late, I have found myself mistaken."[57] The general had dealt Gates the back of his hand. When he wanted to, Washington could skewer an opponent as neatly as any polemicist.

Gates waited until January 24 to get back to the commander in chief, and his letter can only be described as a mixture of cowed dissimulation and, at the end, a bit of gumption. Gates refused to deal with Washington's real concern: That is, he sidestepped Conway's insinuations about Washington's leadership and his supposed involvement with other critics of the patriot chief, including Gates. Instead Gates clung to his insistence that Conway's letter was "perfectly harmless." He even used Conway's explanation. The letter was just a normal exchange of confidential and candid thoughts among senior officers, a practice common "in every Service," although Gates did not want the letter made public for fear of igniting controversies within the officer corps. He was right about that. "Various Reports have been circulated concerning its Contents," he conceded; and to prevent further circulation he intended to return the original letter to Conway (which he did). Like Conway, he glossed over the sentiments of the extract and stressed the actual wording, which he proclaimed "Spurious" and "a wicked forgery." In short, he refused to allow that Washington ought to be upset about whatever Conway had written.

But Gates could not defend Wilkinson. He claimed he had "concealed from him [Wilkinson] the Measures I was persuing, to unmask the Author." The claim rings hollow. There was no cloak-and-dagger investigation at Gates's headquarters; the best evidence (Troup's) indicates the major general had simply and directly asked his staff what they knew about the leak. Gates, as we have seen, considered the young officer one of his most trusted aides, and certainly he was not trying to entrap him. Yet Gates told Washington he (Gates) never had believed Wilkinson's "Insinuation" against Hamilton and Troup. This was nonsense. He had swallowed it whole, and his chagrin with his aide, unmentioned in his letter to Washington, was real and justified. In a paragraph he did not send Washington—Gates struck it from his letter; it exists only in draft—Gates admitted Wilkinson was at fault and asked whether Washington thought the lieutenant colonel "would scruple to make such a Forgery as that which he now stands charged with, and ought to be exemplarily punished." In deleting these lines he probably had in mind Washington's earlier sarcastic treatment of Wilkinson's action. If the major general sensed Washington simply didn't care that much about "Wilky," then there was no point in pursuing that channel.

Yet Gates, even after absorbing Washington's literary ridicule of January 4, would not throw over Conway. He stood by the Frenchman, even writing that he wished Washington had not damned the man in a communication sent through Congress. "I hope," he concluded, "always to find that Gentleman a firm, and constant Friend to America."[58] That took a bit of courage. Horatio Gates had been embarrassed, but he was not a wimp. There was also a real sense that Gates wanted a truce, at least when it came to the Conway affair. It was not to be—not quite yet.

In fact, Washington was in no mood to give Gates the last word on Thomas Conway. Gates's letter of January 23 only stoked the commander in chief's resentment, a resentment reinforced by other developments which, for all the commanding general knew, may have been related. Only a day earlier the general had received disturbing news from Virginia delegate Joseph Jones. Jones was resigning from Congress to return home. His planned departure, however, followed a trip to Valley Forge as part of a congressional delegation charged with conferring with Washington on army affairs. There Jones learned from unnamed officers of rumors of serious political antagonism toward the commander in chief. Returning to York, he became convinced the rumors had a basis in fact. Without naming names, Jones made clear to the general the identities of the alleged culprits. "I had the first intimation given me of the conduct and language of a certain popular pensylvanian lately appointed to the New Board of War." This was Mifflin, who was "of the disposition and Temper of another Gentleman of that Board whose Name the fortunate events of last fall, hath greatly exalted." And this, of course, was Gates. The retiring delegate left no doubt he believed opposition to Washington was real, but he was equally sure the activities of Mifflin and Gates would "redound to their own disgrace." Public opinion would "shield and protect" the commander in chief "from the shafts of Envy and malevolence." Nevertheless Jones wondered if there were not "instances" when the "public welfare may be injured if passed over in silence."[59] Jones's letter reached Washington about the same time, or perhaps a day earlier, than Gates's message of the twenty-third—and the missive from Gates was an "instance" Washington was not about to "pass over in silence."

Then came added concern. Only days later Henry Laurens notified the general of the "Freeman" tract. At headquarters the recent sequence of events now seemed ominous indeed: first the suspicious correspondence between Conway and Gates, with Gates refusing to distance himself from Conway or even to acknowledge Conway's slights of the commander in chief; next the grim news from Jones; and then the mysterious appearance of the "Thoughts of a Freeman," which called outright for Washington's relief. Washington could be forgiven for connecting the dots.

Thus when he replied to Gates on February 9, Washington's tone was of an order beyond anything he had penned to this point in the war. In a literary sense he was taking no prisoners (some clichés *are* appropriate). He turned on the vitriol, spurning the issue of the "genuineness of the paragraph in question" behind which Gates had sought refuge. He pointedly insisted Gates seemed only concerned with finding out who had leaked the Conway letter, no matter what the "genuineness" of its wording. Washington's anger was palpable: The "extracts" indeed had conveyed the letter's spirit, the general bluntly told Gates, "and your only solicitude was to find out the person, that brought them to light." If Conway's letter was so harmless, Washington demanded, why was Gates really so averse to sharing it? If Gates was so worried about "anxiety and discontent" in the officer corps, wasn't "suppressing" the letter—already the stuff of speculation—likely to increase tensions? Weren't Continental officers reasonable enough not "to take offence at a performance [Conway's letter]" supposedly "so perfectly inoffensive"? And what about Gates's protest that the letter was a confidential communication? Ridiculous. Hadn't Conway admitted he had shared its contents with others? And what about the major general himself? Gates, the commanding general scathingly observed, had complained at first that he didn't know if Washington had learned of the extract from a member of Congress or from an "officer." This, Washington accused, "plainly indicates that you originally communicated it to at least one of that honorable body." And Washington could not conceive why Gates would impart to Congress Conway's "strictures . . . on the operations of the Army, under my command."[60]

Finally, there was Gates's defense of Conway. Washington was having none of it, and he stood by his condemnation of the Frenchman. Was Conway critical of recent Continental generalship? Did he think he knew better? Then, he challenged Gates, why did Conway not speak up in any of the councils of war? In modern parlance, he accused Conway of being a Monday-morning quarterback—better at pointing out errors and "advantages that have been lost" than at foreseeing and avoiding difficulties. In the general's scorching opinion Conway was just not that smart, no matter what Gates thought. And contrary to Gates's favorable opinion of Conway, Washington predicted the Frenchman would prove "capable of all the malignity of detraction, and all the meanesses of intriegue, to gratify the absurd resentment of disappointed vanity, or to answer the purposes of personal aggrandizement, and promote the interests of faction."[61]

Over the course of his public career Washington wrote some stinging letters, but this epistle to Gates revealed him at his most belligerent. As for the recipient, it is likely Gates had never received a communication of this tone and severity, and perhaps never would again. Washington, of course, concluded with the normal "I am with respect—Sir Yr most Obedt Servt." It was laughable. But Washington's blistering offensive had hit home. While the rebel chief didn't know it, Gates, dismayed by the continuing bad blood over the Conway letter and other conflicts with the commander in chief, was now ready to end hostilities, at least when it came to "the Letter."

THE AFFAIR OF "the Letter" would drag on through February 1778, and its associated legacy of ill will would frame much of the context of the wider struggle between Washington and his political antagonists. The acrimony would be inextricably entwined with a series of more serious matters—"the Real Cabal" I have referenced earlier and which will occupy us in subsequent chapters—but for the present we should trace the course of the Conway letter to its conclusion.

As the matter became public knowledge even some congressional radicals were disturbed. To snipe anonymously at Washington was one thing; but to have him return fire at two senior officers, and to have the controversy go public, was entirely another. Two months later Abraham Clark, a heatedly zealous delegate from New Jersey and no friend of Washington's leadership, was alarmed. Fervent Whig that he was, Clark understood "a dissention among the principle Officers of the Army must be very injurious to the Publick interest." And "a dissention," to put it mildly, was exactly what Conway's indiscretion had brought about. Clark knew what had to be done: "The Authority & Credit of the Commander in Chief must be Supported."[62]

Thus it was a chastened Horatio Gates who responded to Washington. Ten days later (February 19) the major general offered an olive branch, expressing a sincere wish that "no more of that Time so precious to the public, may be lost upon the Subject of General Conways Letter." Abandoning his previous benign view of Conway, Gates now blandly stated he had no personal connections to the Frenchman. His correspondence with Conway, the major general shamelessly pleaded, was intended only to verify that he (Gates) understood the contents of the now-notorious letter. Conway had to be responsible for any wounded feelings. Gates said he wanted no further controversy (that was certainly true) and apologized if Washington felt anything he had written had offended. He "Solemnly" declared "that I am of no Faction" and hoped the commander in chief would see nothing to "induce you to Spend another moment upon this Subject."[63] Much of this was utter dissimulation, and Washington saw through it. Gates gave up on Conway, as a later chapter explains, only in the face of Washington's counterattack and only after a series of subsequent events made Conway a political liability. But Gates was clearly on the defensive, and Washington, busy at Valley Forge, accepted the truce. He was as "averse to controversy, as any Man," he answered, and had entered the fray only reluctantly. He assured Gates his "temper" led him "to peace and harmony with all Men," and that he hoped any antagonisms would be buried "hereafter in silence."[64] Gates could be forgiven for wondering how a man who preferred "peace and harmony" could wield a pen like a rapier.

Gates had other problems with "the Letter": There was still the matter of James Wilkinson. Before the discovery of his deception, Congress, at Gates's urging, had brevetted Wilkinson to brigadier general in gratitude for bearing the official news of Burgoyne's surrender. A brevet commission was temporary, valid for a given campaign or, in Wilkinson's case, apparently for the war. Afterward a brevet officer reverted to his previous rank. But the promotion made Wilkinson the army's youngest general officer, much to the disgust of Continental colonels with more seniority. Indeed, Congress never would have promoted Wilkinson without Gates's blessing—such was the Hero of Saratoga's prestige. Yet the uproar over the promotion continued to such an extent that, feeling the heat, Congress sought a way out of the mess. Rather than have the new brigadier serve in the field, which would only engender continued friction within the officer corps, the delegates offered Wilkinson the position of secretary to the reorganized Board of War. He accepted the post on February 3, 1778. He would be working under Gates, who had taken up duties as president of the board in late January.

The new assignment seemed to solve all of Wilkinson's difficulties, and at first Gates was pleased for his protégé. That soon changed.

Indeed, "Wilky" became nothing but trouble. Until Washington blew the whistle on him, Wilkinson remained in Gates's good graces. Gates sent the young brigadier—he was still only twenty years old—on an inspection tour of western New York defenses. But problems rose quickly upon his return to Albany. As "the Letter" affair continued, Stirling, concerned that he had reported accurately to Washington, now wanted confirmation of the actual wording. He wrote Wilkinson asking that he verify what he had told McWilliams, and the message reached Wilkinson only two days after he had accepted his new position with the Board of War. Wilkinson replied that given the nature of the evening in question—there had been plenty of alcohol—he couldn't recall exactly what he had said, but he noted Conway had since confirmed the spirit of the sentiments he (Wilkinson) had mentioned to McWilliams. However, he professed shock that Stirling would ask him to comment on a private letter; he insisted that while he had been "indiscreet" with McWilliams, he was not "dishonorable." Wilkinson then (February 22) sent copies of his correspondence with Stirling to Congress in an obvious attempt to shift the focus of the controversy to the rebel "lord."[65] All of this from the man who had blindsided Conway and Gates about the source of the extract and had tried to implicate Robert Troup and Alexander Hamilton in the affair.

By then Washington and Gates had just completed their correspondence on the Conway affair, and Gates had learned the worst about Wilkinson. When Gates confronted him, Wilkinson took the offensive. He accused Gates of wounding his honor, blamed Stirling for the entire business, and then, in a colossal display of arrogance, told Gates that Stirling "shall bleed for his conduct, but it is proper I first see you." For a twenty-year-old to challenge a major general to a duel was shocking by itself, but to threaten two of them in the same sentence was truly remarkable. Gates fired back: "I am astonished if you really gave McWilliams such information how you could intimate to me, that it was possible Colonel Troup had conversed with Colonel Hamilton upon the subject of General Conway's letter."[66] The next day Wilkinson *did* challenge Gates; and the two officers met on the morning of February 24 with pistols and, per the *code duello*, accompanied by seconds. But there was no shooting. Wilkinson claimed a tearful Gates made things up at the last minute. However dubious Wilkinson's account of Gates's behavior, the men did manage some sort of reconciliation, and Gates did agree to have "Wilky" remain as board secretary.[67]

If Gates thought his problems with his aide and secretary, and with the Conway letter, were over, he was dead wrong. Wilkinson was simply too turbulent an individual to let things go. He had enough sense, however, to appreciate how deeply his promotion had offended the officer corps. Rather than face continuing hostility from brother officers, and, as secretary to the Board of War without the prospect of a field command, he wisely decided to resign his brevet. This he did on March 3, 1778.[68] Yet he felt he had a score to settle with Lord Stirling. While friends dissuaded him from challenging the earl—something Wilkinson had considered—in mid-March he wrote Stirling demanding that he (Stirling), in effect, mitigate Wilkinson's role in leaking the controversial paragraph from Conway's letter. Specifically, he wanted Stirling to acknowledge Wilkinson had revealed the extract only innocently during a casual conversation. Stirling complied, but then for reasons unknown he went further, spinning an unlikely account of his decision to contact Washington in the matter. He told Wilkinson he had reported the extract to the commander in chief only after hearing someone (unnamed) claiming he had overheard Wilkinson asserting he had never spoken of the Conway letter. Stirling even claimed he wrote to Wilkinson inquiring about his remarks to McWilliams but received no answer, although no such letter has ever come to light.[69] This convoluted story was rubbish, and of all people Wilkinson probably recognized a self-serving lie when he saw one. He told Washington that "the Authenticity of the Information recd thro Lord Stirling I cannot confirm";[70] but as it seemed to shift some of the onus for the controversy from Wilkinson's shoulders, Stirling's blatant fabrication apparently satisfied the bellicose brigadier.

Here we can pause and total the "score" of who had done what to whom in the affair of "the Letter." Conway, in admitting authorship, dubiously denied any demeaning comments about the commanding general. Gates disingenuously professed to see nothing serious in Conway's observations while knowing full well of the Frenchman's hostility to Washington. Mifflin endorsed Conway's sentiments on Washington and warned Gates to be careful with his correspondence. Washington was coy with Gates about his knowledge of Wilkinson's involvement and then ambushed Gates with the information. Wilkinson played everyone false with the nonchalance of a professional confidence man; and then Stirling, whose letter to Washington had ignited the controversy in the first place, related an absurd version of events to Wilkinson. Virtually everyone's pen was poison while they jockeyed for advantage or sought to evade embarrassment or blame. No single letter of the revolutionary generation matched Conway's for resulting drama—or perverse comedy. Spiced with a bit of humor the affair could have been a Marx Brothers movie.

At the time, however, no one was laughing. Bruised sensibilities, anger, and dissimulation reigned as the Classic Cabal revealed strengths and weaknesses among the main actors. Certainly Washington, his patience with his critics exhausted, emerged with a stronger hold on the army than he had enjoyed since the "season of hope." His principal lieutenants had rallied to him, and he found support among key members of Congress. Horatio Gates had stumbled badly. The Conway letter had tarnished the halo he had worn since Saratoga; with all of his political contacts, in what in fact became a political fight with the commander in chief, Gates had looked like an amateur. Still, Washington was hardly home free. Despite the claims of some historians, the end of "the Letter" controversy was *not* the end of the Cabal. Far from it. Gates may have been humbled, but he retained the support of most congressional delegates and other influential patriots. Among these were the two Thomases: Conway and Mifflin. Conway did not resign. Indeed, in later December 1777, as the furor over his letter raged, he would prove an even more serious impediment to Washington's command. And Mifflin, who had played only a supporting role in "the Letter" affair, would take stage center in the ensuing "Real Cabal."

FIVE

"BE WARE OF YOUR BOARD OF WAR"

The Real Cabal Begins

I hinted some time ago my discovery of party in our Councils. The events which I dreaded & in many instances predicted are now coming to maturity.—Henry Laurens to John Laurens, January 8, 1778[1]

The General is fully inform'd of all these Cabals, they prey on his Constitution, sink his Spirits, and will in the end I fear prove fatal to him. . . . with a few words more I shall finish this painful Subject, *Be Ware of your Board of War.*

—Benjamin Harrison to Robert Morris, February 19, 1778[2]

IN 1809 Italian-born physician and historian Carlo Botta published one of the earliest detailed accounts of the War for Independence. Botta shared the European revolutionary fervor of the 1790s, and with the fall of the French monarchy he adopted French citizenship, served with the French military in Italy, and later sat as a French legislator. Given his political leanings it was no surprise that Botta admired the young United States and its successful revolution. An astute observer of his times and an avid writer, his *Storia della guerra dell'Independenza degli Stati Uniti d'America* (*History of the War of the Independence of the United States of America*) won critical acclaim from many Americans. The book was "well written," one of Jefferson's friends assured him, "and contains information not found in any other narrative on the same Subject." And the historian was a sympathetic character:

"his principles are just and liberal, and he is a most amiable man." Upon reading the volume Jefferson agreed, and so did John Adams.[3]

One wonders, however, what Adams in particular—that devout republican often so despairing of Washington's generalship—thought of Botta's treatment of the Cabal episode. For the historian was blunt in assessing the controversies roiling American political and military affairs over the Valley Forge winter. He took it as a given that Washington's command was in serious jeopardy; indeed, he was convinced some Americans wanted the Virginian out. The general's critics, Botta explained, "enlarged upon the victories of Gates, whom they placed far above Washington, and were continually extolling the heroic valor of the Americans, which rendered them capable of the most splendid achievements, when they were led to battle by an able commander." According to Botta, while Washington's antagonists wielded considerable influence in patriot councils, they stopped short of an organized political plot to remove the commander in chief. Yet their "machinations" were real enough. Instead of orchestrating any overt congressional move against Washington, Botta claimed they aimed at throwing "so many disgusts" in his way that he would "retire from the head of the army and thus make room for the immediate promotion of Gates to that exalted station."[4] Botta's explanation of the Cabal remains controversial, but there is no question that, calculated or not, a series of "disgusts" dogged the commander in chief. And there is no doubt about the source of the worst of them: It was the Board of War, the congressional department established to support the patriot war effort.

In fact the Board of War is the chief concern of this chapter, and we will find the board at the crux of the Cabal controversy. Matters of what Congress intended and allowed the board to do, how the board functioned, who staffed it, what initiatives it pursued, and, of course, its relationship with the commander in chief are vital to our story. While the Conway letter had ignited fireworks among patriots—as well as grabbing the attention of generations of historians—the attendant Washington-Gates drama was only a reflection of the angst engendered over late 1777 and early 1778 as the Board of War began to define its role *vis a vis* the American armed forces, meaning primarily the Continental Army. The question before us is to what extent the board's collective actions posed a genuine challenge to Washington's authority and whether this challenge was innocent or hostile. Was it no more than the board members taking legal steps (and they *were* legal) they deemed necessary to reinvigorate the patriot war effort? Or along with those steps, did the board, for whatever reasons (as Carlo Botta thought) *deliberately* seek to compromise Washington's role as commander in chief? If it did, we can fairly conclude the board's actions, including those "many disgusts," constituted the "Real Cabal"—a matter far more serious for Washington and the Revolution than any letter by Thomas Conway or any other disgruntled patriot officer.

This chapter is the first of two to address the efforts of Washington's critics to take control of the Board of War—and in so doing to bring key training, discipline, and logistics functions, and even operational decisions, under the board's purview. These measures would have expanded the board's original and intended responsibility as a support body (a matter explained shortly) to include a direct and authoritative role in the army's day-to-day activities. The board's success in any of these areas—traditionally the bailiwicks of the commander in chief—would have constituted an "administrative coup" at the expense of Washington's authority. "Commander in chief" would have been little more than a hollow title.

Our immediate concern is with the Board of War's first such initiative. This was a bold attempt via congressional resolution in December 1777 to appoint Thomas Conway to the new position of inspector general of the army. Washington, of course, wished only anathema on Conway, and the affair of "the Letter" loomed large over the new imbroglio (the general was not in a forgiving mood). But the new controversy was vastly more important than Congress foisting an unwanted officer on the commander in chief. Rather, in framing the nature and authority of Conway's new office, Congress and the board set in motion a series of bitter reactions from Washington's headquarters; and the resulting fracas over the inspector generalship signaled the gravity of what was to come as patriots grappled not only with how to restore the effectiveness of American arms but with whether or not Washington would remain commander in chief in anything but name.

CONGRESS ESTABLISHED the Board of War and Ordnance in June 1776. The step was long overdue. Until then the delegates had tried to manage the war with a series of *ad hoc* congressional committees, an effort that was problematic from the start and ultimately dangerous as the conflict expanded. Maintaining supply; recruiting, legal, personnel, and other administrative arrangements for the Continental Army; and coordinating military affairs with the thirteen states were daunting tasks in the best of circumstances—and by mid-1776 circumstances were not the best. The rebel invasion of Canada had failed disastrously, and surviving rebel forces in the Northern

Theater, concentrated mostly at Fort Ticonderoga, were struggling to regroup and rebuild. Worse, patriot armies faced a looming British invasion from Canada and, Washington was sure, the enemy was gathering for a strike against New York City. In Philadelphia the delegates were multitasking. No single committee held the reins of the war effort. Instead the delegates divided their time between urgent financial and diplomatic matters, relations with various Indian tribes, dealings with the states, and trying to define Congress's position as a nascent national government, all while fighting a war and with virtually all of the delegates learning how to raise and maintain armed forces as they went along. Creation of the Board of War was an effort to bring administrative order out of chaos and to place military support tasks in the hands of a single body.

In a resolution of June 12 Congress spelled out the new Board of War's responsibilities in considerable detail. Its function was to support the army, not to actually manage its operations. The board—often called the "War Office"—was to compile and maintain an "accurate register" of all Continental Army officers; to keep records of "all the artillery, arms, ammunition, and warlike stores"; and to maintain custody of all arms, munitions, and stores not in service with the armies. In addition the board would forward all congressional military correspondence and funds to the armed forces and the states, keep all appropriate records, take charge of prisoners of war, and "superintend the raising, fitting out, and dispatching of all such land forces as may be ordered for the service." Nowhere in this charge, however, was there provision for the War Office to assume a direct role in logistics, strategic planning, training, field operations, or other daily activities. These were matters left to Washington and his staff officers and to the established departments of the army—or so Washington assumed. Washington reported directly to Congress.

The resolution called for a Board of War of five members, all of them congressional delegates. The initial members represented the various sections of the rebellion as well as the states with the largest number of men under arms. The chairman was John Adams of Massachusetts, with the other seats filled by Roger Sherman of Connecticut, Edward Rutledge of South Carolina, Benjamin Harrison of Virginia, and James Wilson of Pennsylvania. Congress named Richard Peters, a prominent Philadelphia lawyer and political figure, board secretary.[5] With its organization established the new board set to work.

The board's record was mixed. It could claim some successes. In September 1776 Congress, pressed by an adamant Washington, agreed to a controversial board recommendation to raise a long-term Continental Army along with recruiting incentives that included bounties for enlisted men and officers. These were the men Washington would mold into his new regiments at Morristown. The War Office also drafted new articles of war designed to assure better discipline in the new battalions. But the board struggled mightily to keep up with its various duties. The myriad military records and correspondence; financial accounts and inventories of all types, troop movements, prisoners of war, captured enemy spies; and the other minutia of keeping the army functional were a daily trial. The War Office also dealt with the complaints of officers as they argued over rank and precedence. Reports from the board on every conceivable subject related to the army flowed to Congress almost every day. Without interfering with the commander in chief, board members monitored Washington's progress at Morristown as he rebuilt the Continental Line. It also made some tough calls. In an especially contentious case, in May 1777 the board advised Congress to leave Major General Philip Schuyler in command of the Northern Department. Congress confirmed the decision but, as the reader knows, later reversed it in favor of Gates after the subsequent loss of Fort Ticonderoga. From time to time board members expressed interest in specific troop deployments, although they never meddled with actual operations.

But the original problem with the Board of War remained: As all board members were also delegates, the burdens of divided attentions again became intolerable. Members frequently missed meetings as they dealt with other congressional responsibilities, and membership was far from stable as board seats changed among the delegates.[6] Adams, as chairman, was overwhelmed and exhausted as he tried to keep up with War Office duties. Looking back on his experience, he thought he never had worked so hard.[7] As a steward of the war effort, the Board of War, try as it might, was not working out as planned.

Congress, to its credit, recognized as much. "The business of a Board of War is so extensive, so important, and demanding such constant attention," Richard Henry Lee told Washington, "that Congress see clearly the necessity of constituting a new Board, out of Congress, whose time shall be entirely devoted to that essential department."[8] To their discredit, however, the delegates moved slowly—almost glacially—on a reform measure. Distracted by the uncertain military situation in the Middle Theater, and then preoccupied by their move to York in the face of Howe's invasion of Philadelphia, they toyed with a number of ideas over the summer and early fall of 1777.[9] They finally agreed on a new board configuration only on October 17. The reformed Board of War would consist of three members; but, as Lee predicted, this time none of them would be members of Congress. The secretary's position would remain and, recognizing the volume of business the original board encountered, with congressional approval the new War Office could hire as many clerks as necessary to keep up with business.[10] The reform was a step, however tentative, to put the administration of the war effort on a professional basis.

Washington greeted news of the reform warmly, hoping any administrative change in managing military affairs would be for the better. The general also had no objections to the proposed appointees.[11] On October 20, Richard Henry Lee informed him of the three leading candidates: Pennsylvania politico and former adjutant general and aide to the commander in chief Joseph Reed; the army's adjutant general Timothy Pickering of Massachusetts; and Lieutenant Colonel Robert H. Harrison of Virginia, a successful attorney before the war and a long-serving aide to Washington. In May 1776 Harrison had replaced Reed as the general's military secretary.[12] While Washington had only a tepid relationship with Reed, he saw the suggested board members as men with whom he could work. "The three Gent[leme]n you have in contemplation for constituting a Board of War . . . are, in my judgment, equal to any you could make choice of," he told Lee. They knew as much as any Americans, the general continued, about "the business" of war; and "the advantages of having able Members solely confined to this department are too obvious & important; & the benefits to my self, & the army at large, too diffusive & extensive, to suffer local conveniencies to interpose; for which reason if Messrs Harrison & Pickering should Incline to accept the appointment, it will meet with my ready concurrance."[13] So far, so good.

The fly in the ointment, however, was Thomas Conway. Lee reported talk in Congress of appointing the troublesome Frenchman as adjutant general in place of Pickering when Pickering took his seat on the new board. Lee was interested in learning Washington's opinion on all of the new board members, but he especially wanted his fellow Virginian's thoughts on Conway's possible advancement—although Washington already had informed Lee of his disdain for the self-promoting brigadier.[14] He replied to Lee that while Conway might have the makings of an adjutant general, any promotion in rank would still upset the more senior brigadiers. Besides, Washington observed, Conway was a "bad scribe," hardly a recommendation for an officer tasked with drafting orders and dispatches and keeping records. In fact, in the event Pickering joined the Board of War, the commander in chief could think of better men than Conway to replace him as adjutant, and he pointedly told Lee as much. Lee, however, evidently thought Washington's concerns were academic because, he advised the general, rumors in York held that Conway was simply angling for a title and promotion in order to enhance his career prospects upon a speedy return to France.[15] Still, after all that had passed, Washington could properly wonder at Conway's seemingly inexplicable staying power with so many members of Congress.

Any thoughts Washington may have entertained on the new Board of War or, for that matter, Conway, quickly became moot. Delaying even further as the military outlook deteriorated, the delegates appointed the new members only in early November, and they were not the members Lee had named in October. Of the original three, Pickering was the only one remaining. The fate of Reed's possible appointment is obscure. He was becoming heavily involved in Pennsylvania politics—in 1778 he was elected president, the titular governor—so perhaps a seat on the Board of War didn't appeal. In any event, when Congress inclined toward former commissary general Joseph Trumbull of Connecticut, Reed, privately annoyed, made no public protest. In selecting Trumbull over Reed, Congress also was aware Reed and Trumbull were not on friendly terms and could not have served together amicably.[16] Besides, Trumbull was a capable man with experience in vital supply operations and his appointment made sense. Harrison ultimately declined to serve, preferring to remain on Washington's staff. His place went to another Pennsylvanian—a familiar name that more than caught the attention of the commander in chief.

Enter once more Richard Henry Lee. Fully aware of Washington's low opinion of Thomas Mifflin, but nevertheless convinced of Mifflin's worth, Lee proposed Mifflin in place of Harrison. On November 2, 1777, Lee contacted Mifflin with what can only be described as an exceedingly generous offer. Obviously speaking for Congress, or at least a majority of delegates, Lee not only invited Mifflin to serve on the board but promised the Pennsylvanian he could keep his commission as a major general as long as he collected only his War Office salary.[17] Mifflin—the poor health of which he had complained now seemingly improved—leapt at the chance. Five days later he tendered his resignation as quartermaster general, a position to which he had devoted but little recent attention, and accepted his appointment to the War Office.[18] One can only imagine Washington's reaction.

Indeed, one who *could* imagine it felt he owed the general an explanation. Thus on November 22 Lee again wrote to his fellow Virginian. His tone and message reflected his understanding that the commander in chief would blanch at news of Mifflin's appointment. Lee knew of Washington's low opinion of Mifflin's performance as quartermaster general, and he addressed it directly. He told Washington that Mifflin did not want to serve in the quartermaster department, but with his health on the mend Mifflin was "willing to continue his aid to the public cause." In a clear reflection of Mifflin's influence with Congress, no matter what Washington thought of the man, Lee insisted the Pennsylvanian would be an asset to the new board and that Congress appreciated Mifflin's "uniform, vigorous, and well founded patriotism." "The skill and industry of this new Board," Lee soothingly continued, in future promised the commanding general "great relief." And Lee did have a nugget of good news: There seemed to be no further talk of Conway as adjutant general.[19] All in all, with the new Board of War in place, Lee thought military affairs were looking up; one doubts Washington saw things that way.

What was Congress thinking in its embrace of Mifflin, a known critic of the commander in chief? Kenneth R. Rossman, Mifflin's principal modern (1952) biographer, sees nothing untoward, and certainly nothing reflecting any conspiracy aimed at undermining Washington. Rather, Rossman sees Congress acting with an appreciation of Mifflin's military background and experience in quartermaster operations. Moreover, the Pennsylvanian's commitment to the Revolution was genuine and his ambition, the historian insists, was only "normal and natural" in a man trying to do his utmost for the cause.[20] Indeed, there is no gainsaying Mifflin's patriotism—patriotism, the reader will recall, Washington's other critics shared. Even so, Mifflin's doubts about the commander in chief were no secret, and it is difficult to believe Congress did not know exactly what it was doing when it put Mifflin in a position that would share (with Congress) support for the war effort. Congress wanted the disarray in American military affairs put right, and most delegates clearly thought Mifflin could help do so.

Couple with this the Anglo-American military heritage of which Congress was also well aware: Generals worked for civilian authority, and civilians held military leaders accountable for satisfactory performance. Civil authorities also had the power and responsibility to make leadership changes when necessary. Mifflin's appointment did not necessarily mean Congress was looking to make such a change, but it *did* mean patriots were willing to listen to voices other than Washington's. As Lee's letter to Washington (November 22) unmistakably indicated, many in Congress were listening to Mifflin; and Lee probably was not alone when, the next day, he wrote Samuel Adams expressing his faith in Mifflin, and specifically in Mifflin's insistence that Washington's army needed a shaking-up—"some indispensable changes."[21]

Indeed, with the ear of Congress, the Pennsylvanian was pushing an agenda even before formally taking his seat on the Board of War. His initial focus was a complicated reform of quartermaster operations. According to Lee, Mifflin proposed dividing the quartermaster department into civilian and military branches, with the military branch subdivided "into Commissaries of Teams, of Forage, of Tents &c. &c. to be governed in their purchases by estimates from the Quarter Master general who is to touch no money but a moderate tho sufficient salary." The civilian post, however, "to be filled by a person well qualified to discharge its duties," would hold the key fiscal and administrative authority.[22] In other words, ultimate control of army logistics would reside in the War Office, to whom the civilian quartermaster would report, and *not* with the commander in chief. Whatever the theoretical merits of Mifflin's reforms, no one—and certainly not Mifflin—discussed them with Washington before they became fodder for congressional debate. Given the strained relations between Washington and Mifflin, and the general's low opinion of Mifflin's performance as quartermaster general, the commander in chief would have placed little confidence in any Mifflin proposal anyway. But the fact that Mifflin would go directly to Congress with a plan—no matter how well intentioned—concerning a vital logistical function, and that Congress would consider it without serious discussion with Washington, boded ill for army relations with the new Board of War and for the general's authority as commander in chief. Washington saw Mifflin's initiative in just this light, and he would fight it—but not yet.[23]

Mifflin's next move was more dramatic and, from Washington's perspective, positively alarming. Given the expected volume of business confronting the new board, Mifflin suggested expanding the body to five members. Congress readily agreed. A new seat went to Richard Peters, secretary to the old board and an experienced hand at dealing with the complexities of military administration (his promotion left the secretary's position open for James Wilkinson). Then the bombshell: At Mifflin's urging on November 27, Congress enthusiastically appointed the Hero of Saratoga, Horatio Gates, to the board. And there was considerably more. In a message to Congress the old Board of War, which Congress had asked to stay on until the new board could get properly organized, further revealed Mifflin's influence. The War Office members begged "leave to represent that General Mifflin has expressed a warm Sollicitude that Major General Gates should be appointed President of this Board, from a Conviction that his Military Skill would suggest Reformations in the Different Departments of the Army essential to good Discipline, Order, and Œconomy, and that his Character and Popularity would facilitate the execution of such Reformations when adopted by Congress." Congress quickly complied.

While the board presidency was technically a civilian position, the appointment allowed Gates to keep his rank and, if he chose, to serve "in the field, as occasion may require." Gates had, the delegates concluded, a "peculiar fitness" for his new post, "upon the right exertion of which the success of the American cause does eminently depend."[24] It had been some time since Congress had said anything so complimentary to Washington. Moreover, while Washington had not yet confronted Gates about the Conway letter business, by late November "the Letter" controversy was becoming a public matter. At this point, however, the letter hullabaloo made little difference to Congress, even among the more conservative members. Delegate James Duane of New York was one of them. In mid-December, while on a congressional mission dealing with northern Indian affairs, he wrote Gates a reassuring note: Duane hoped to meet with Gates before the major general left for York in order, he said, to "ease your mind on a Subject which, without any Reason, has given you Pain." It was an obvious reference to "the Letter." "You may be assurd," Duane confidently told the general, "that you hold a high Place in the Esteem and Confidence of Congress."[25] Gates was their man—and given the context of the day, Gates was their man seemingly for every good reason.

Mifflin got what he wanted with Gates's appointment. Readers will recall that it was only ten days earlier that Mifflin had sent Gates a scorching criticism of Washington and a plea for the major general to come south and rescue the faltering patriot cause. The letter was quoted extensively in Chapter 3, but part of it bears repeating: "This army will be totally lost unless you come down & collect the virtuous Band, who wish to fight under your Banner, & and with their Aid save the southern Hemisphere. Prepare yourself for a Jaunt to this Place [York]. Congress must send for you." Lovell was of the same mind. "Come to the Board of War," he wrote Gates, "if only for a short Season."[26] There was even some enthusiasm in camp at Whitemarsh. In the Tenth Pennsylvania Regiment, Lieutenant Colonel Samuel Hay (whose letter we cited earlier) wrote joyously to his friend Colonel William Irvine of the Seventh Pennsylvania: "God Speed the Brave old fellow [Gates] and send him safe back to us, for I fear we cannot do much good without him." Hay still had some faith in Conway as well, and the Pennsylvanian feared mistakenly that the Frenchman had returned to Europe.

Mifflin and Lovell had longed to see Gates in charge of the war effort, and as president of the Board of War it appeared he would be. In fact, as board president Gates would be Washington's chief. To those who lamented the state of patriot arms, it finally appeared there would be a chance to redirect the American war effort and remedy the misfortunes of late 1777. And these were misfortunes and mistakes that Mifflin and kindred spirits—James Lovell, William Duer, Samuel Adams, Jonathan Dickinson Sergeant, Benjamin Rush, apparently the Lee brothers, and certainly other patriots in and outside of Congress—laid at Washington's feet. That may explain why, as Congress named members to the reconstituted War Office, *it left the commander in chief entirely out of the loop*. That is, the delegates never consulted the commander in chief on the final composition of a body charged with supporting critical aspects of the patriot war effort. This was too large an omission to attribute to some innocent oversight, and we can reasonably conclude Congress thought it was time for some fresh thinking on how to fight the war.

Thomas Mifflin had played a brilliant hand. Yet, contrary to the popular lore of the Conway Cabal, there was no subterfuge, secret plot, or underhanded political maneuvering involved. *There was no need*, for Mifflin had not acted alone. His efforts to expand the Board of War and install Gates as president would have gone nowhere without congressional support. And there would have been no such support had Congress and other ranking patriots not harbored serious doubts about Washington's leadership. In addition to Richard Henry Lee, the board appointments received the hearty endorsements of Connecticut delegate William Williams, who saw the board as of "vast importance for the Regulation & supply &c [etc.] of the army, & highly honorable," and of Lovell, who called the new board "the first Board upon the Continent."[27] Indeed, only a day earlier Lovell had written Gates imploring him to come south and rescue patriot arms. "Good God! what a Situation are we in! how different from what might have been justly expected! You will be astonished when you come to know accurately what numbers have at one time and another been collected near Philada. to wear out stockings, shoes and breeches. Depend upon it for every ten Soldiers placed under the Command of our Fabius 5 Recruits will be wanted annually during the war."[28] If Lovell was prolix other delegates certainly shared his alarm, and there is no public record of anyone in Congress objecting to the new board members. The delegates were not fools; justly concerned about the fate of the cause, they were not "tricked" or misled into anything in acting as they did.[29] Mifflin was fully aware that his appointment and initiatives would not sit well with the commander in chief, but so were many in Congress.

HORATIO GATES arrived in York on January 19, 1778. He had delayed travelling south until wrapping up his personal affairs and settling command arrangements in the Northern Department and Hudson Highlands. He entered the town to the hosannas of patriots who looked to him as the hero of the day, the man who would retrieve the fortunes of the faltering war effort.[30] Gates honestly hoped to live up to expectations.

Service on the Board of War, however, quickly proved a trial. By the time he reached York his differences with Washington were common knowledge, and the Conway letter affair was in full stride. Moreover, Thomas Conway was now a problem of an entirely different order. On November 14, Conway had submitted his resignation to Congress (to Washington's relief), and the delegates had sent it on to the Board of War. The board, however, sat on it—and one suspects the board did so on the advice of Mifflin, who held the Frenchman in high esteem. How high became stunningly apparent. Rather than accept Conway's resignation, on December 13, well before Gates arrived in York, Congress named Conway inspector general of the army. The delegates also promoted the Frenchman to major general, the promotion the importuning Conway had coveted for so long.[31] Congress had acted at the recommendation of the Board of War. This was over a month after Washington had confronted Conway over "the Letter."

The elevation of the much-hated Conway shocked army headquarters, then still at Whitemarsh and contemplating the move to Valley Forge. If Botta saw the Cabal as a sequence of "disgusts," nothing could have disgusted Washington and most of the senior officer corps more. Gates could honestly say he had no part of the business; but at least initially he saw no reason to distance himself from Conway. In fact, we know from Gates's correspondence with Washington that at this point Gates stood by the Frenchman. Nevertheless, Washington saw the promotion of Conway as an affront, and Conway's appointment as inspector general only seemed to underscore the tedious new major general's ties to Gates. All this was playing out, of course, while the commander in chief still seethed over "the Letter" and only days after Gates had learned his private correspondence had leaked. Relations between the two senior generals hardly could have been worse. Thus Gates would have to decide how to handle Conway and the new inspector generalship in an especially difficult context.

No one, we should note, had objected to establishing the position of inspector general. It was not even the War Office's idea. In October 1777 Washington had assembled a council of war in which he pointedly asked if an inspector general, tasked with "establishing one uniform set of maneuvers and manual, be advisable."[32] That is, Washington wanted a single officer responsible for training the army to uniform standards. Until then the adjutant general, Timothy Pickering, had carried out these duties along with his other various responsibilities. The council unanimously agreed that training functions were too important to leave to the partial attention of the adjutant (and in any case Pickering would soon leave the adjutant's post to join the new Board of War). Conway, one of the generals present, made haste to let Congress know he was interested in the job and, Washington was convinced, even intimated the position was his (Conway's) idea.[33]

Congress was well aware the Frenchman had linked his star to Mifflin and Gates—no demerit in late 1777 and early 1778. On November 9, Conway had informed Gates of his intention to resign, but he again hedged, noting a willingness to work with Mifflin. This was clearly a reference to Mifflin's interest in bringing discipline and order to Continental ranks; that is, Conway was alluding to the inspector generalship.[34] He told Mifflin as much, too. On November 11 he wrote the Pennsylvanian a flattering letter offering congratulations on Gates's appointment as board president. With Gates in place, the Frenchman continued, necessary "amendments in the frame of our army" could begin. He went on at length about the discussions in the October council of war, and he pointed out his extensive experience in training European soldiers. Conway assured Mifflin he would offer Gates advice on reorganizing the Continental Army, including "practice in the austrian, prussian and french service."[35] It was an obvious expression of interest in the new post, and all but openly saying he wanted the job. The letter revealed an equally obvious understanding on Conway's part that Mifflin was the go-to man on the matter.

Washington initially had no inkling of Conway's approach to Mifflin, but the general later had no doubt that Mifflin touted Conway's supposed talents and availability to the delegates. For members of Congress concerned about Conway's various threats to resign, the inspector generalship seemed a perfect way to satisfy him. This made some sense, especially since Conway *did* have a good reputation as a disciplinarian in the French army and, in all fairness, he had done an admirable job of training his Continental brigade. And unpopular as Conway was among senior officers, the training needs of the army were such that some Continentals would have tolerated him. "We want some kind of general tutoring in this way so much," Lieutenant Colonel John Laurens wrote his father Henry Laurens, "that as obnoxious as Conway is to most of the army," training under his direction would be better than none at all.[36] Inasmuch as the colonel was a loyal member of Washington's inner circle and despised Mifflin, Gates, and especially Conway, this was quite a concession on the young man's part.

Even so, Conway's appointment was explosive on several counts. First, with Conway's letter to Gates an open sore with Washington, it was improbable the new inspector general could have established a *modus vivendi* with the commander in chief. Common sense or a moment's thought would have shown that Conway's appointment held the potential for a confrontation between the commander in chief and the board—if not with Congress. In that case forcing Conway on Washington would test the Virginian's patience with civilian authority.

A more immediate problem was the reaction of the officer corps. Concerns over a possible Conway promotion already had the army's brigadiers on edge, a fact of which Congress was fully aware. All of the brigadiers were senior to Conway, and Washington had predicted the Frenchman's promotion to major general would provoke consternation. He was right. The brigadiers, with the sympathy of most of the major generals, responded angrily. After heated discussion of how to frame their protests, they sent letters of grievance to Washington and to Congress. In a long missive of December 31 the brigadiers assertively told the commander in chief that "Promotions without any apparent reason have taken place, which reflect disgrace & dishonor upon us." These promotions, they complained, favored "persons who have never distinguished themselves as soldiers, and who have nothing more to boast of in the present contest, than that they have modestly trumpeted their own praise to Congress, have ventured to cross the Atlantic to seek that bread, in America, which they failed to obtain in their own country, or have been the lucky messengers of good news [meaning James Wilkinson]." While the letter did not mention Conway and Wilkinson by name, it was clear enough who the brigadiers meant. The situation "must give disgust & dissatisfaction" to officers who had served long and well but who were now contemplating leaving the service. The generals wanted Congress to investigate and correct what they considered an egregious injustice; and without saying so directly, they clearly hoped Washington would send their letter to Congress.[37] A week later nine brigadiers sent a petition of similar language directly to Congress, but this time they specifically protested Conway's promotion. "As soldiers and Men of Honor we doubly feel the Indignity," they wrote, and concluded with the hope "we shall receive the Approbation and Relief of Congress." They received neither. On January 19 Congress tabled the memorial with, as Henry Laurens glumly reported, "Contempt."[38]

The commander in chief stood aloof from these actions. He frowned on anything that might reflect a military challenge to civilian authority; thus he did not send a copy of the officers' letter of December 31 to Congress. Nor did he endorse their later petition. But his feelings on the Conway business were no secret. Most of Washington's senior officers had stood by him as he endured the mounting criticisms of his leadership, and he returned their loyalty. That his civilian masters would promote Conway over them was galling in the extreme. As David Clary and Joseph Whitehorne, historians of the army's inspectors general, have so aptly put it, by December 1777 "the Continental Army was no longer big enough to hold both Thomas Conway and George Washington."[39] And we can add that both Congress and the Board of War should have known it.

Beyond the anger of the officer corps, however, was the matter of the inspector generalship itself. Washington clearly valued the improvements such an officer could bring to the army, but he just as clearly intended any inspector general to be his man, a staff officer to assist the commander in chief in training and disciplining the Continentals. As Congress had framed the new office, however, the inspector general was *not* to be a staff officer under the commander in chief. Rather, he would be an agent of Congress and the Board of War within the army and reporting directly to Congress and the board. It was an arrangement that struck directly at Washington's authority: He would command the army in the field—and hopefully an army much improved through the efforts of the inspector general—but he would have no direct control over what those improvements would be or how they were to be implemented. In effect the inspector general would be, if not a rival, at least a parallel commander of the army.

The legislation establishing all of this was actually quite complex, and the legal remit of the inspector general was very broad, even hazy, in its parameters. Congress actually provided for two inspectors general, although Conway was the only one appointed. The inspectors were empowered to implement standards of training and maneuver approved by the War Office, and they were responsible for seeing that officers "strictly observed" them. The inspector general also would directly task regimental commanders with holding periodic regimental reviews and with compiling detailed records on virtually all areas of regimental status. Required record-keeping included returns of clothing and of "arms and accoutrements"; accounts of recruiting, pay, and rations expenditures; rosters of sick, wounded, and other casualties.

The inspector also wanted a "return of all the officers of each regiment, with observations upon the behavior, capacity, and assiduity of every individual." Regimental commanders were to report all of this information on forms designed by the Board of War. All data was to be "carefully scrutinized by the inspector general," who would then make appropriate comments before sending everything on to Congress—which would, per its normal practice, refer reports to the board. All of this would take place at the beginning and end of each campaign, or at any other time the inspector thought necessary; Washington could order similar reviews. Pay records would also fall under the inspector's purview. Finally, Congress asked the board to suggest any other regulations that might "extend its [the Board's] utility."[40] It was a potentially dangerous suggestion as, in effect, it allowed a new and untried body the latitude to define its own mission and authority.

It was actually extraordinary; the arrangement was the antithesis of what the October 29 council of war had decided. The inspector general, as the council had envisioned the position, would be a staff officer tasked with implementing a training regimen drafted and approved within the army. The officers were quite specific: "The manual [of] manœuvres, or any regulations to be established, previously to be settled or agreed to by the Commander in chief, or a board of officers, appointed by him for that purpose."[41] But the congressional resolution placed the inspector general virtually at the heart of the army's day-to-day operations without reference to the prerogatives of the commander in chief. Congress all but obliterated the chain of command as it made regimental commanders subject in so many matters to the authority of the inspector. There was no provision even for copying all of the required reports to the commander in chief. Then there was the business of the "observations upon the behavior, capacity, and assiduity of every individual" officer. Was Washington not to be responsible for the evaluation and conduct of his own subordinates? This was a slippery slope toward making the inspector general the Board of War's political commissar. "Taken to its logical conclusions," Clary and Whitehorne have correctly observed, "the resolution of December 13 would have effectively eliminated the command authority of the Commander in Chief."[42] It was a significant "disgust" indeed.

Equally important was the fact that Congress knew exactly what it was doing on December 13. It was no legislative fluke or oversight. With the new Board of War still assembling, members of the old board—without consultation with Washington—made their recommendation to Congress after considering written communications from Conway (which apparently have not survived).[43] The old board members concerned were Francis Lightfoot Lee (Virginia), William Duer (New York), John Harvie (Virginia), and Jonathan Bayard Smith (Pennsylvania). They would sit intermittently on the board through the spring of 1778. Of these, Lee and Duer were known critics of the commander in chief, with Duer (the businessman so upset with the chaos in army administration) probably quite pleased with the meticulous record-keeping mandated in the congressional resolution.[44] Two days later Lee informed his brother Richard Henry, who had returned to Virginia, that "Conway is made a Majr. Genl. & Inspector of the Army." Richard Henry probably received the news without surprise. Delegates not on the board seemed just as pleased; Connecticut's Eliphalet Dyer certainly was. "Congress," he wrote his friend Joseph Trumbull, "have great hopes & expectations from this New Constituted Board of War." (Trumbull was soon to be appointed a member of the new board, but he never served due to illness.) Every military department needed a "total reform," Dyer insisted, and the appointment of "Inspectors Genll" would see to it. Dyer made it clear the inspectors (he did not mention that only one, Conway, had been appointed) would be the "Executors & Assistants" of the War Office, *not* the army. William Ellery of Rhode Island noted approvingly the appointments to the new Board of War, including Gates as president, and Conway's new promotion and assignment as inspector general. He expected the new arrangements to "rectify the errors & disorders" in the various army departments.[45] If any delegates had second thoughts about the new War Office or the new inspector generalship, much less Conway as the new inspector general, evidently they never said a word.

Whatever the attitudes of Congress, Washington saw the new inspector generalship for what it was—a direct threat to his command authority. This was not paranoia. The appointment and promotion of Conway, an officer Washington now considered nothing less than a bitter personal antagonist *and* a menace to the stability and morale of the army, made the situation even more unpalatable. Washington, already in a contentious mood over the Conway-Gates correspondence, felt he had no choice but to fight back, and his staff officers were aboard in opposition. Alexander Hamilton captured staff sentiments when he later explained the army's objections to William Duer who, as we have seen, was one of the Board of War authors of the inspector generalship. "The novelty of the office excited questions about its boundaries," Hamilton wrote. "The extent of its operation alarmed the officers of every rank for their own rights." True, the army needed reforms, but "the plan established by Congress, on a report of the Board of

War when Conway was appointed appears to me exceptionable in many respects. It makes the Inspector independent of the Commander in Chief," the young aide pointed out, and it "confers powers, which would produce universal opposition, in the army, and by making the previous concurrence of the Board of War requisite to the introduction of every regulation which should be found necessary opens such a continual source of delay as would defeat the usefulness of the institution." It would be much better, Hamilton insisted, to let Washington introduce reforms that Congress could review. "Perhaps you will not differ much from me, when I suppose, that so far as relates to the Board of War, the former scheme was a brat of faction, and therefore ought to be renounced."[46] The "brat of faction" comment may have been telling. Hamilton, who had made it his business to learn who Washington's critics were, probably had fired a none-too-subtle shot across Duer's bow.

But how to renounce the new inspectorship without an imbroglio with Congress? Washington wisely fell back on patience. He waited for the new inspector general to make the first move, and Conway obliged. On December 29 the Frenchman sent Washington a letter proposing to get right to work. In fact Conway was quite the optimist; he suggested he could whip the Continentals into shape easily and quickly. "The Method I thought the Most efficacious," he explained, "is to assemble one or two officers and non-commission'd officers from each Regiment . . . [and] instruct them in all Manœuvres necessary for a Battalion, a Brigade, a Division, this I think I can with some assiduity effect in a Month's time. when the officers and non commission'd officers are thoroughly instructed, they are to repair to their respective Regiments in order to spread the instruction." The plan was not necessarily bad, and in fact the French and other European armies had employed it successfully.

Conway then added fuel to the fire. Raising one of the sorest points of all with the officer corps, he asserted that his promotion was only logical given his post as inspector general. He rather lamely claimed he had "accepted of the office . . . with the view of being instrumental to the Welfare of the cause, and to the glory of the commander in chief in Making his troops fitt to execute his orders." The major general then insisted he had not solicited his new job, a statement which, if technically true, was as disingenuous as his claim not to have denigrated Washington in his famous letter to Gates. And Washington must have winced at Conway's concern for the "glory of the commander in chief." This was arrant rubbish. Was it sarcasm? Conway finished on what he no doubt considered a high note: If Washington found his appointment in any way "Disagreeable," he pledged he would happily go back to France.[47] The tone of the letter was self-assured, even condescending. But if Conway thought that Congress had settled the matter of his position and rank, and that Washington would fall in line after a bit of sweet talk (or a bit of a sulk), he had the commanding general all wrong.

Washington replied the next day, in effect telling Conway "not so fast." He pointed out that the Board of War had issued no new regulations for Conway to implement and that, until the board did so, he (Washington) would issue no orders in cooperation with any steps Conway might attempt to initiate. The commanding general was hiding behind a technicality; had he wished he could have allowed Conway to take at least preliminary steps toward a training program. Washington effectively had stiff-armed the inspector general. As to Conway's appointment, Washington feigned indifference. "Your appointment of Inspector General to the Army, I believe has not given the least uneasiness to any Officer in it." If this wasn't distilled sarcasm, nothing ever was. But on Conway's promotion to major general, Washington was more pointed: "by Consulting your own feelings upon the appointment of the baron de Kalb you may judge what must be the Sensations of those Brigadiers, who by your Promotion are Superceded. I am told they are determin'd to Remonstrate against it." The general informed Conway he would respect any officer Congress appointed, but the tone of the letter was chilly enough to freeze water.[48]

Washington's tone was colder still when Conway actually showed up at Valley Forge. The Virginian was no more than formally civil when the inspector general made two visits to headquarters. Conway immediately saw that without the full weight of the War Office in back of him he would get nowhere with Washington, and on December 31 he departed Valley Forge for York to rally political support. The same day he also sent another note to the commander in chief, this one with more than a whiff of wounded belligerence. Conway plaintively told Washington that, per his instructions from the Board of War, he had every intention of drawing up appropriate regulations for the disciplining and training of the army. These he would submit for the board's approval. In the meantime he wanted to get to work and save time. Once again he defended his new rank as appropriate to his status as inspector general. "What you are pleas'd to call an extraordinary promotion is a very plain one. there is nothing extraordinary in it, only that such a place was not thought of Sooner." Conway then became positively snarky. He noted that few newly promoted officers of any rank shared the "universal merit" that Washington clearly wanted to see in senior commanders, although it was amply in evidence in "the *great frederick* in europe, and the *Great Washington* in this continent. I certainly never was so rash as to pretend to such a prodigious height; neither Do I pretend to any superiority in personal qualitys over my Brother Brigadeers for Whom I have much regard. but *you* sir and the *great frederick* Know perfectly well that this trade [the training of armies] is not Learn'd in a few Months."[49] Washington read the sarcastic comparison to Frederick the Great as the calculated affront it was. It was as bad as Conway's unflattering remarks in "the Letter." If Conway was less subtle in his barbs than the commander in chief, the Frenchman could play the insult game equally well.

Having in effect turned Conway out of camp, Washington took up the political cudgels. If Conway saw Congress as his territory, the commander in chief chose to confront the inspector general on Conway's own ground. With the turn of the new year the general dispatched a letter to Henry Laurens. Dated January 2, 1778, the brief message met Conway's pretensions head-on. Washington informed Laurens, and through him Congress, that the Frenchman was not the inspiration for the inspectorship. The general pointed out that in fact the October 29 council of war had collectively agreed on the utility of such an officer, and that he had another officer in mind for the post. He mentioned the Prussian volunteer Henry Leonard Philipe, the Baron d'Arendt, as a qualified officer, and he noted d'Arendt was among the first to mention the potential benefits of appointing an inspector general. As to Conway's reception at Valley Forge, Washington candidly told Laurens "that I did not receive him in the language of a warm and cordial Friend, I readily confess the charge. I did not, nor shall I ever, till I am capable of the arts of dissimulation. These I despise, and my feelings will not permit me to make professions of friendship to the man I deem my Enemy." For Washington this was unusually blunt language, and he was not finished. "At the same time," he continued, "Truth authorises me to say, that he was received & treated with proper respect to his Official character, and that he has had no cause to justifye the assertion, that he could not expect any support for fulfilling the duties of his Appointment."[50] Laurens, as Washington knew, was a friend, but the general was a bit less than forthcoming with the South Carolinian in this last statement—he had made it abundantly clear to the Frenchman that he (Washington) would cooperate with him only grudgingly and only if Conway first produced a copy of the required board-approved regulations. If he had ever returned to camp as inspector general Conway would have faced what today we would call a "rulebook slowdown."

Yet it never came to that. Conway would never rejoin the army as inspector general, although he would hold the empty title for another several months. In the face of Washington's forceful opposition, Conway's politicking with Congress and the board met with indecision in both bodies. No resolution of the dispute was immediately forthcoming. That was fine with Washington. In the Frenchman's absence the army was not idle. Training, albeit piecemeal, went on in some brigades,[51] and Washington's staff set to work defining the position of inspector general both in functional and administrative terms. That is, they spelled out what an inspector general would actually do and how the position would fit into the army's command structure. Plans mirrored the recommendation of the council of war of the previous October. As the army envisioned the new post, the inspector general indeed would be responsible for implementing a uniform regimen of training, discipline, and maneuver; but he would be a staff officer reporting to the commander in chief and operating directly under the commander's authority.[52] The Board of War would have no role in the day-to-day operations of the inspectorate.

Congress ultimately agreed with Washington. The Virginian's opposition to Conway and the board's formulation of the inspector generalship finally prompted some second thoughts among the delegates. Abraham Clark of New Jersey, a veteran congressman, originally had voted to promote Conway and appoint him inspector general. But the ensuing furor shocked the New Jersey radical. Other delegates had told him that the Frenchman was a good officer. If he had known about Conway's bad blood with Washington (the congressman claimed not to have heard about "the Letter"), Clark wrote apologetically to Lord Stirling, he never would have voted for Conway's promotion. Readers will recall that Clark was no fan of many of Washington's military decisions; nevertheless Clark dreaded the potential consequences of turmoil among the army's senior officers, and he would support the general's authority as commander in chief from that point forward.[53] Clark's reasoning hit home. The need for army reforms was so evident and pressing that, in the face of Washington's determined stance, Congress backed away from Conway. The delegates withdrew neither his promotion nor title as inspector general; but they acquiesced when, in late February, a solution to the army's training problems presented itself in the person of a pretended Prussian noble, Friedrich Steuben.

Steuben's arrival was unexpected. Like so many European officers looking for work after the Seven Years' War, he came to America seeking to better his fortunes. He had served as a captain on the staff of Frederick the Great and he was not a nobleman, but his resume said differently. In Paris, Steuben had impressed Benjamin Franklin; and Franklin doctored the Prussian's credentials. Steuben then presented himself to Congress as a former lieutenant general under Frederick with the title of baron. After this grandiose introduction, however, the Prussian showed considerable humility. Unlike Conway, he asked for neither rank nor title; he offered to serve as a volunteer with the understanding that appropriate rewards would follow if he proved himself. Congress and Washington were impressed, and in March Steuben unofficially assumed the role of inspector general. The Prussian instituted a regimen not dissimilar from that Conway had planned; but Steuben simplified European drill and maneuvers, and he launched his program by training a model company. Subordinate officers then spread the new drill throughout the regiments. Steuben proved his worth, and with Washington's enthusiastic endorsement Congress confirmed him in the post in May. Congress also named him a major general, but by then his popularity in the army was such that the promotion raised few objections (although earlier some officers had groused about Steuben exercising what they considered too much control over their units during training operations).[54] Washington gave Steuben his unstinting support, and the Prussian deserved it—although it is easy to suspect Washington would have happily worked with any capable inspector general as long as his name wasn't Conway.

Washington eventually won a complete victory in the matter of the inspector generalship. On May 5, in addition to confirming Steuben, Congress eliminated the resolutions of December 13 that the army had found so obnoxious. Instead it endorsed a plan the commander in chief had submitted on April 30 and had already set in motion. It was simple: Following instructions drawn by Steuben, sub-inspectors would supervise two or more brigade inspectors who would train individual infantry brigades. The army would appoint all of these officers and all would be within the chain of command. The War Office was out of the picture, and the authority of the commander in chief was intact. It took time to bring Congress around—five months of procrastination and indecision—but for Washington it was a political triumph of the first magnitude.[55]

IN ADDRESSING THE entire matter of the inspector generalship, and the issue of Major General Conway specifically, Washington notably avoided dealing with the Board of War. He was in touch with the board even as he first wrote to Congress complaining about the Frenchman, although he confined that message and all subsequent messages to matters of army supplies, enlistments, and civil-military relations. But he *never* brought up the matter of the inspector general.[56] The Virginian had no reason to trust the War Office. He was more than aware of Mifflin's central role in the new War Office and of the close relationship Mifflin and Conway shared; and if Gates had not yet arrived to take up the board presidency, Washington considered the Saratoga victor fully in league with the former quartermaster general and the new inspector general. His correspondence with Gates over "the Letter" affair left no doubts on that score. As far as the commander in chief was concerned the board was the tool of his enemies even if not all of its members were necessarily inimical to him. Whatever the case, he was not about to surrender his authority to the board without a fight.

It is no small point to note the commanding general's preference for communicating directly with Congress. While he had critics among the delegates, he also had friends, not the least of whom was the new president of Congress Henry Laurens. In going over the board's head to Congress Washington could at least get a hearing, and a sympathetic one in some quarters. From this point forward, skirting the board and dealing directly with Congress would be Washington's standard tack in confronting the board's initiatives. Congress became the arbiter of disputes between the army and the board—a battleground, as it were, on which competing military and civilian stakeholders would make their cases for control of the patriot war effort, or at least for control of the Continental Army. Washington never deviated from his commitment to military subordination to civilian authority, but the controversy over the inspector generalship showed he could play hardball with civilians when he felt he had to. And in fighting off the Board of War, he successfully played off the War Office and Congress—two civilian bodies—against one another. Quite a demonstration of political finesse.

However, there remains the question of why Congress initially had gone along with the board's formulation of the inspector generalship. That is, was the threat to Washington's authority an unintended result of an otherwise innocent attempt to bring needed reforms to the army?[57] The answer must be no, and that to the contrary the Board of War and Congress, as these pages have noted, knew exactly what they were doing. An argument for an innocent oversight fails on several counts. The first is personified in Thomas Mifflin. Mifflin's antipathy toward Washington is a now familiar theme. True, it had a personal dimension as Greene replaced Mifflin in Washington's confidence; but Mifflin's antagonism also was borne of an honest concern for the patriot cause and a fear that Washington was not the man to set things right. The Pennsylvanian eagerly accepted the solicitation of Congress (or at least of Richard Henry Lee, which was likely the same thing) to join the reconstituted Board of War, and Congress specifically framed its resolution on the inspector generalship on the advice of Conway—Mifflin's favorite for the new post. Can we really conclude Mifflin didn't know precisely what he was doing?

And what of Conway's appointment? Congress made the appointment, of course, but no doubt after consulting Mifflin and in full knowledge of Mifflin's relationship with the Frenchman and of Conway's low opinion of Washington. Indeed, it was Conway's skeptical posture toward the commander in chief that appealed to Mifflin. Given Mifflin's concerns about the state of the army, it is unlikely he would have recommended an inspector general with close ties to Washington. Mifflin wanted an inspector able and willing to exercise independent judgment, and he saw Conway as such a man. Freeing the inspector general from Washington's authority, as the December 13 resolution did, was yet another means to assure the inspector general actually could implement board-approved reforms should the commander in chief raise objections. Under the circumstances Conway was a logical choice.

Then there was the matter of Congress. The fact is that, early on, the delegates saw the inspector general's position in the same light as Mifflin. Until Washington launched his political counterattack at the end of December there was no reason to believe otherwise. The *Journals* of Congress and the available papers of the delegates reflect no hint of dissent as Congress approved the December 13 resolution. In fact all evidence points in the opposite direction. The reader will recall the approving comments of a number of delegates. To argue that Congress overlooked the full implications of the resolution is to argue for congressional naiveté of a considerable scale; and men like James Lovell, William Williams, and Francis Lightfoot Lee certainly had been in Congress long enough to know what they were doing. They were *not* naive. They *were*, like Mifflin, worried about the state of the war effort. So it makes more sense to see the December 13 resolution for what it was: an aboveboard effort to restore stability and efficiency to the army, even if the mode of doing so seriously ruffled Washington's feathers.

WE SHOULD NOTE at this point that no one was talking about relieving Washington. As the debate over the inspector general unfolded, the Board of War's plan aimed at curtailing the commanding general's authority in a critical area, not at getting rid of him. To threaten the commander in chief in *any* way, however, was also to invoke the wrath of the general's partisans. Chief among these were the young staff officers of his military "family," and they not only reacted defensively, they had no trouble identifying the source of the threat. They pointed to Mifflin. On January 3, Lieutenant Colonel John Laurens, then at Valley Forge, angrily wrote his father, Henry Laurens. He brought the senior Laurens up to date on the army's views of the controversies swirling around Washington's command and the consequent indignation gripping much of the officer corps. At the center of it all, he wrote, was "a certain party, formed against the present Commander in chief, at the head of which is Genl. Mifflin"; and Conway, the junior Laurens insisted, had advanced under cover of the "weight" he enjoyed with Mifflin's friends.[58] Alexander Hamilton, perhaps John Laurens's closest friend in the army, shared the same dark views of the Pennsylvania patriot and the Irish-French major general. These he shared with New York governor George Clinton in a letter of February 13. In earlier correspondence Hamilton already had mentioned his suspicions of "the existence of a certain faction," but over January suspicions had given way to certainty. "I have discovered such convincing traits of the monster," he assured the governor, "that I cannot doubt its reality in the most extensive sense . . . . I believe it unmasked its batteries too soon and begins to hide its head; but as I imagine it will only change the storm to a sap; all the true and sensible friends to their country, and of course to a certain great man [Washington], ought to be upon the watch, to counterplot the secret machinations of his enemies." He then let loose on Conway. "He is one of the vermin bred in the entrails of this chimera dire, and there does not exist a more villainous calumniator and incendiary."[59] A brilliant young man, Hamilton was also a good hater.

Other officers felt the same (although without Hamilton's literary flamboyance), and thus we come back to the issue of perceptions: Were they reporting reality or, as Nelson and other historians have suggested, overblown fears of nonexistent conspiracies? In fact, even allowing for Hamilton's overheated rhetoric, seeing the threat to Washington's authority in the proposed inspector generalship was not the stuff of overactive imaginations. Mifflin and Conway were not friends of the commanding general and the resolution of December 13 spoke for itself, so why should we not accept the reactions of Laurens, Hamilton, and others—and for that matter, of Washington himself—as reactions to the realities of the day?

Henry Laurens offered a very sober assessment of exactly this question. The senior Laurens, president of the Continental Congress since November 1, 1777, was firmly in Washington's camp; and he was well informed on military affairs in large part through frequent and intimate correspondence with his son. Henry shared John's resentments of Washington's critics, and no one outside of the army was more irritated with Conway. During "the Letter" incident Laurens had considered Conway's slights of the commander in chief deeply troubling, and he also considered Conway's snarky comparison of Washington with Frederick the Great "unbecoming" and "unpardonable." Yet as president of Congress he tread carefully, concerned with keeping the peace between fractious colleagues lest the business of Congress become even more difficult than it so routinely was. Nor did he want a public fracas that could damage already fragile patriot unity. Yet Laurens did take the floor in Washington's defense at least twice, and he found himself "called to account" for his trouble. He predicted he would face more of the same after any repeat performance.[60] Thus no one was better placed to judge the temper of Congress on questions of the day, and few if any questions were more important than the status of the Continental Army and its commander in chief. So we must ask: Given his "insider" perspective, did the president of Congress think the controversy over the inspector generalship reflected a threat to Washington's command, or at least a threat to Washington's prerogatives as commander in chief?

Later chapters will find Henry Laurens of different minds on how seriously to take any threats Washington's critics might pose; his thinking would change according to circumstances and to whom he was writing. But over the course of the inspector general imbroglio he was of one mind: He feared the worst. He confessed as much in a long letter he wrote to John between the eighth and tenth of January. "I have no body here to whom I can with pleasure and safety unbosom myself," he told his only son. And given the chance to "unbosom" himself he held nothing back. He damned (without naming) his predecessor, John Hancock of Massachusetts, as the source of many political difficulties. Laurens blamed him for failing to deal with the disorganization prevalent in various departments that threatened disaster to civil and military functions. Consequently the South Carolinian faced a gloomy prospect on assuming the presidency, and he was in no mood for false optimism. "Our whole frame is shattered," he warned. "We are tottering, & without the immediate exertions of wisdom & fortitude we must fall flat down."

Looming large in Laurens's concerns was the status of the commander in chief. The accumulating indignities Washington had suffered at the hands of critics alarmed him, and Laurens insisted that without Washington at the helm the American cause was virtually doomed. He conceded that the entire

Conway affair had to be "a little troublesome" to Washington, but he hoped it would blow over when people finally realized the Frenchman's intriguing nature. As president of Congress he had heard out Conway civilly as the then brigadier general defended his inflammatory letter to Gates. But Laurens was uneasy, detecting "something in the manner of his [Conway's] representation which raised doubts in my mind, the correspondence [with Gates] even under favour of his own narrative appeared to me to have been indiscrete & dangerous." In any event, Laurens wished fervently that his son was near enough to discuss the Conway affair privately: "I never wished for you more in my Life than I did upon that occasion."[61] And Conway was only part of the problem. The senior Laurens warned John that there were those in and outside of Congress working to the Virginian's detriment, and there had been for some time. "If my memory does not deceive me," he continued, "I hinted some time ago my discovery of party in our Councils." Then, ominously: "The events which I dreaded & in many instances predicted, are now coming to maturity." The focus of Laurens's immediate concern—"the pivot upon which the late mischiefs have turned"—was probably Thomas Mifflin, just as John had warned only days earlier. There was only one conclusion to draw from this: The opposition to Washington was no illusion and was fraught with potentially serious consequences for the integrity of his command. And if the president of Congress thought so, who are we to differ?

How had things proceeded to such a pass? Laurens had an explanation. "Candour obliges me to say that some" of the "party" did not dislike Washington. In fact they respected him, and Laurens was "persuaded [they] would not wittingly be concerned in a plot against him." But as he explained to John, "they 'want the honour to defend.'" That is, they would not rise to confront Washington's critics. "In all such junctoes, there are prompters & Actors, accomodators, Candle Snuffers, Shifters of scenes & Mutes";[62] and for the time being it was clear that the "prompters & Actors" held the upper hand. He might have added that it was easy for them—the "prompters & Actors"—to do so. Over late 1777 and early 1778 Congress could barely muster twenty or so delegates for most sessions; and Laurens, despite urging the states to send their allotted number of members, was genuinely alarmed for the credibility of Congress. Could so small a group really speak with the authority of the revolutionary cause?[63] Thus a determined handful of delegates, especially if they represented a core of the longest-serving and most experienced members—which certainly describes the likes of Lovell, Duer, Williams, and Francis Lightfoot Lee—easily could wield considerable influence on particular issues. In all likelihood this is precisely what had happened on December 13, 1777, as Congress followed the lead of the Board of War in establishing the inspector generalship and in the promotion and appointment of Conway.

The War Office itself was in a similar situation. In flux between the old and new boards, the advice and leadership of such seemingly sensible men as Mifflin and Conway obviously was telling with board members. As in Congress, for the time being the "prompters & Actors" held the stage.

WHATEVER THE SITUATION in Congress, in seeing off Conway Washington had stymied the Board of War's first attempt on his authority as commander in chief. Viewed in this light, the fight over the inspector generalship was actually the start of the Cabal. And the board's attempt to craft an inspectorate outside of the army chain of command also revealed the nature of the Cabal: It had (and *has*) been hiding in plain sight. It was never a secret plot, never a hidden conspiracy; the Cabal developed as an open and legal effort to seize control of a key army function at the expense of the authority of the commander in chief. Once more we need to bear in mind the perspective of late 1777 and early 1778: No one knew which side would win the war, and it appeared to many patriots that American chances were anything but bright. In this context the attempt to place the new inspector general under the Board of War's orders was, if not wise from a strictly military perspective, at least understandable. It was an action undertaken by responsible civilian authorities acting under a sense of obligation to their cause, and in doing so they also followed long-standing precedent holding that political authorities had to act in the face of military reversals.

Of course Washington and most of his senior officers saw things differently; and certainly they saw "faction" or "cabal" behind the Board of War's actions. But historians skeptical of the Cabal's existence have scanted the significance of the storm over the inspectorate and Conway's appointment. Instead, in considering the incident—and the Cabal generally—they have parsed the vocabulary of eighteenth-century politics at some length. They have pointed out, rightly, that Americans had adopted the British colloquialisms of "party," "faction," "conspiracy," and, yes, "cabal" in describing the activities of political or other organized opponents. Such terms could encompass a sizeable opposition or just a few individuals allied for a specific nefarious purpose.[64] No doubt traditional republican fears of conspiracies reinforced the use of such terminology. Regarding the Cabal, Paul David

Nelson has nicely summarized the thinking among many recent historians: "It would appear that the commander in chief and his allies seized upon some bits of evidence that proved little or nothing by themselves, combined them into an incomplete story, filled the gaps with conjecture, and came up with an explanation of events that narrowed to a single word: *conspiracy.*"[65]

Yet historians busy denying the existence of conspiracies have missed the point: Under the circumstances conspiracy was unnecessary. Patriots who questioned Washington's leadership no doubt had some private discussions, but in framing the inspector generalship—and in appointing Conway—they made their policy and practical initiatives legally and in the full light of day. *This openness and legality, however, was no less a threat to Washington's command.* The general's friends recognized as much, and their saying so was hardly paranoia or conspiracy-mongering. They were reacting to actual developments, not rumors, suspicions, or innuendo. And to some of these men the chief source of the menace was obvious. Benjamin Harrison, a former Virginia delegate, was such a friend. An early patriot, he had signed the Declaration for the Old Dominion, and in the face of the reverses of 1777 he had remained a committed partisan of the commander in chief. While in Congress Harrison also had served on the old Board of War, and he did not like what he saw as the new board took up its duties. In mid-February he wrote bluntly of his fears to a kindred spirit, Pennsylvania delegate Robert Morris. Harrison warned that Washington was beset by "Cabals," and for the general's allies he had some pithy advice: "Be ware of your Board of War."[66]

It was good advice. The dispute over the inspector generalship was serious enough in and of itself, especially in the context of the heated rhetoric of the day. But it was not an isolated matter. Rather, as subsequent events soon demonstrated, it was part of a broader pattern of behavior in the Board of War as it pursued an agenda that would have left Washington's title of commander in chief virtually meaningless. Indeed, the Cabal would deepen as the number of Carlo Botta's "disgusts" mounted—and it is to those further "disgusts" we now turn.

John Adams (1735-1826), one of the first to recommend Washington as commander in chief in 1775, had despaired of the general's leadership by late 1777. Not as publicly vocal as some of Washington's detractors, his skepticism became known anyway and, among some patriots, even haunted him after the war. Engraving after a portrait by John Singleton Copley, 1783. (*Library of Congress*)

Benjamin Rush (1746-1813) was a committed revolutionary, a Signer for Pennsylvania, a diligent but argumentative army doctor, and, postwar, an ardent reformer in many fields. Like Samuel Adams, Rush had a republican faith in militia and mistrusted Washington's preference for a regular army. He was impressed with Conway, Gates, and Charles Lee, and his writings contained some of the most virulent criticisms of the commander in chief. Portrait by Charles Willson Peale, c. 1783, from the original in the Winterthur Museum, Wilmington, Delaware

"The Battle of Brandywine River, September 11, 1777," by Johann Will, c. 1777, from his "Ten maps and views of the battlefields of American Independence in the state of Pennsylvania and New York." Brandywine was the first in a series of defeats that shook patriot faith in Washington's leadership. It came as a shock after Washington's fine performance in New Jersey earlier in the year. (*Library of Congress*)

"Surrender of General Burgoyne," by John Trumbull, completed 1821. Saratoga was one of the truly decisive engagements of the War for Independence. Burgoyne's surrender to Gates on October 17, 1777 deservedly made the American commander a patriot hero and opened the way for formal French recognition of the United States. (*Architect of the Capitol*)

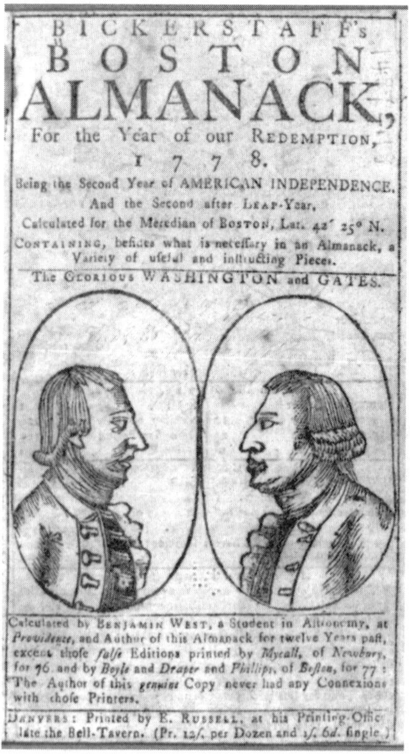

BICKERSTAFF's
BOSTON
ALMANACK,
For the Year of our REDEMPTION,
1778.
Being the Second Year of AMERICAN INDEPENDENCE.
And the Second after LEAP-Year.
Calculated for the Meredian of BOSTON, Lat. 42° 25' N.
CONTAINING, besides what is necessary in an Almanack, a Variety of useful and instructing Pieces.
The GLORIOUS WASHINGTON and GATES.

Calculated by BENJAMIN WEST, a Student in Astronomy, at *Providence*, and Author of this Almanack for twelve Years past, except those *false* Editions printed by *Mycall*, of *Newbury*, for 76 and by *Boyle* and *Draper* and *Phillips*, of *Boston*, for 77: The Author of this *genuine* Copy never had any Connexions with those Printers.

DANVERS: Printed by E. RUSSELL, at his Printing-Office late the Bell-Tavern. (Pr. 12/. per Dozen and 1/. 6*d*. single.)

Above, George Washington by John Trumbull, 1780. (*New York Public Library*) Left, *Bickerstaff's Boston Almanack, For the Year of our Redemption, 1778.* The cover featured woodcuts of "The Glorious Washington and Gates," with the generals, no doubt inadvertently on the almanac's part, glaring at one another. (*Library of Congress*)

William Alexander, Lord Stirling (1726-1783). It was Stirling's letter to Washington dated November 3, 1777 (Washington received the following day) that first revealed the existence of the controversial Conway-Gates correspondence and set in motion months of acrimony between Washington and Gates. (*New York Public Library*)

Lieutenant Colonel Alexander Hamilton (1755 or 1757-1804) thought the worst of Gates, considering the Hero of Saratoga a political threat to Washington. As one of Washington's closest aides, Hamilton played a prominent role in rallying political support for the commander in chief and in denigrating the general's critics. He was positive the Cabal was real. (*New York Public Library*)

Major General Nathaniel Greene (1742-1786) of Rhode Island emerged as one of Washington's most talented and loyal subordinates. Unpopular with Washington's critics, Greene's rising influence with the commander in chief was partly responsible for Mifflin's falling away from Washington. Appointed quartermaster general, replacing Mifflin, Greene was instrumental in alleviating the army's supply problems by the late spring of 1778. (*Independence National Historical Park*)

Marie-Joseph Paul Yves Roch Gilbert du Motier, Marquis de Lafayette (1757-1834), a French aristocrat volunteer in the Continental army, was a major general and an intensely loyal member of Washington's military family. Lafayette firmly believed in the Cabal. When the Board of War named him to command the "Irruption into Canada," he refused to have Conway as his second in command and he insisted that he lead the operation as a subordinate of Washington, not as an independent commander reporting directly to the board. (*New York Public Library*)

The Golden Plough Tavern, left, and adjoining Joseph Chambers House, center, in York, Pennsylvania. Congressional delegates frequented the tavern and Horatio Gates was a guest at the Chambers house while ensconced at York. (*Library of Congress*)

Henry Laurens (1724-1792), as president of the Continental Congress, quietly defended Washington against his congressional critics. Through his son, Lieutenant Colonel John Laurens, one of Washington's closest aides, he kept informed of sentiments in the army as the Cabal played out. In turn he kept John (and thus Washington) informed of the temper in Congress. (*Library of Congress*)

Horatio Gates (1727-1806) was an accomplished professional soldier with considerable experience as a British officer in North America before Independence. After immigrating to America he was an early patriot, and he brought valuable administrative experience to the rebel army even as he became critical of Washington's leadership. His victory at Saratoga in October 1777 stood in stark contrast to Washington's defeats in Pennsylvania and, in the eyes of many patriots, made him a viable alternative to Washington as commander in chief. (*Independence National Historical Park*)

Early in the war Thomas Mifflin (1744-1800) had been one of Washington's intimates. Disillusioned with the commander in chief by late 1777, Mifflin was one of the first to see Gates as an alternative to Washington. Washington was critical of Mifflin's performance as quartermaster general, which did not help their relationship. Mifflin played a key role in reorganizing the Board of War and in recruiting Gates as board president—and in crafting the board initiatives that so disturbed Washington and his allies. (*Library of Congress*)

Thomas Conway (1735-1800), one of the many French volunteers in Continental ranks, was actually a competent brigadier general; but he had an intriguing nature that brought him into the orbit of Horatio Gates and Thomas Mifflin. Washington had resented Conway's importuning for promotion even before identifying him as a central figure in the Cabal. The commander in chief hated the man. (*New York Public Library*)

Washington's Headquarters, Valley Forge. When the Board of War appointed Conway inspector general, he arrived at Washington's headquarters expecting to take up his new duties. Washington met him here with little more that icy civility. (*ZeWrestler/Wikimedia Commons*)

Friedrich Steuben training troops at Valley Forge. After Washington refused to deal with Thomas Conway as inspector general, Steuben loyally filled that role as a member of Washington's staff, not as an adjunct of the Board of War. The pretended Prussian noble was instrumental in retraining the Continental Army at Valley Forge as it evolved into an effective regular army. (*New York Public Library*)

James Wilkinson's (1757-1825) tipsy gossip at Major General Stirling's headquarters set in motion the controversy over Thomas Conway's letter to Horatio Gates. He meant no harm in his comments, but his subsequent efforts to avoid responsibility for the ensuing furor led to a pattern of duplicity that deepened the antagonism between Washington and Gates. (*Library of Congress*)

Gouverneur Morris (1752-1816), congressional delegate for New York, had no sooner taken his seat in Congress than he traveled to Valley Forge as a member of the Committee at Camp. Active on the committee, he supported Washington as the committee helped the general fend off the various initiatives of the Board of War that threatened his command authority. (*Library of Congress*)

Lieutenant Colonel John Laurens (1754-1782) of South Carolina, a close friend of Alexander Hamilton and a member of Washington's inner circle, was convinced the Cabal constituted a genuine threat to Washington's command. Laurens kept his influential father, Henry Laurens, informed of Washington's thinking on the individuals and events connected to the Cabal. Like Hamilton, Laurens saw Mifflin, Conway, and Gates as the Cabal's prime movers. (*New York Public Library*)

Richard Henry Lee (1732-1794) and his brother, Francis Lightfoot Lee, were prewar friends of Washington's. Yet Richard Henry spoke well of Conway and Washington's allies were skeptical of Lee's loyalty to the general. Neither of the Lee brothers rose to Washington's defense during the Cabal months, and Richard Henry professed his attachment to the general only when Virginia patriots challenged him on the matter. (*Library of Congress*)

Robert Morris (1735-1806), a Pennsylvania congressional delegate and the financial genius of the Revolution, was a staunch Washington ally and warned repeatedly about political machinations against the general. Even so, he managed to maintain cordial relations with some of the general's critics, including Major General Charles Lee. (*Library of Congress*)

William Duer (1743-1799), a conservative businessman and New York delegate, held no ideological brief against Washington. Rather, he was appalled at what he considered the poor management of the patriot military effort, for which he held Washington and other senior officers responsible. (*New York Public Library*)

Washington rallying troops at the Battle of Monmouth. The battle, fought on June 28, 1778 in and around Monmouth Courthouse (Freehold), New Jersey, silenced most of Washington's severest critics. The battle was a tactical draw, but it seemingly reversed Washington's losing record of 1777 and showed that his regular Continental Army could fight effectively. (*Library of Congress*)

SIX

"DISGUST" UPON "DISGUST"

The Struggle for Command

> . . . finding that the inactivity of the Army, whether for want of provisions, Cloaths, or other essentials is charged to my account, not only by the common vulgar, but those in power, it is time to speak plain in exculpation of myself. . . . Since the month of July we have had no assistance from the Quarter Master General, and to want of assistance from this department, the Commissary General charges great part of his deficiency.
>
> —George Washington to Henry Laurens, December 23, 1777[1]

> How strange it is that Men, engaged in the same Important Service, should be eternally bickering, instead of giving mutual aid. Officers cannot act upon proper principles who suffer trifles to interpose to create distrust, & jealousy—All our actions should be regulated by one uniform Plan—& that Plan should have one object only in view, to wit, the good of the service.
>
> —George Washington to James Mitchell Varnum, November 4, 1777[2]

We have met Henry Laurens, president of the Continental Congress, and Benjamin Harrison, a Virginia Signer, former delegate, and member of the original Board of War; they were reasonable and well-informed men not prone to overreactions or inordinate fears. And as we now know, in late 1777 and during the early months of 1778 they were imagining nothing when they saw political trouble brewing for the commanding general. Harrison was certainly right when he located the chief threat squarely in the Board of War. Without question the board's plans for the new inspector generalship, including Conway's appointment, aimed at bringing a key facet of army operations under board control. That the board had done so openly and for reasons it thought good and proper made little difference to General Washington. He recognized the obvious: An inspector general responsible to the board would have significantly diminished his authority as commander in chief. This was precisely what Alexander Hamilton had explained to New York delegate William Duer.[3] In their correspondence neither Laurens nor Harrison specifically mentioned the acrimony over the inspectorship in terms of Washington's status, but they knew of his resentments; and they just as clearly sensed a tide running against the general in York.[4] Moreover, the further actions of the board seemingly confirmed as much. Its designs on the inspector general's post were no "one-off"; in fact the Board of War's offensive in behalf of its authority in military affairs was far from over.

The offensive was sweeping; over the first two months of 1778 the board's initiatives constituted the heart of the Cabal. Beginning in January 1778 the War Office made a determined effort to assert control over several critical army departments and functions, the success of which would have secured the board's role as the dominant player in military affairs. Targets included the commissary and quartermaster departments, troop deployments, and strategic initiatives. That is, the board under Mifflin and Gates sought control of logistics and field operations; and as in its attempt on the inspector generalship, it tried to do so at the expense of the commander in chief. In pursuing this aggressive course the board would raise the stakes in what we must now see as nothing less than a struggle to wrest control of the army from the commanding general.

Here the narrative of the Cabal intersects with that of the Valley Forge winter. The story of Valley Forge, of course, is an American epic—an epic of endurance, suffering, and survival in the face of periodic food and supply shortages, foul weather, and too frequently political ineptitude. It has a literature all its own.[5] We need note here only that as the commissary and quartermaster departments struggled to feed and supply the Continentals, and as Congress for various reasons failed to resolve these problems, the Revolution's military fortunes fell to one of their lowest ebbs. The gross mismanagement of critical patriot logistical operations threatened to do what Sir William Howe had failed to accomplish—destroy the Continental Army. By late December 1777 a desperate commanding general stated the case bluntly in a now-famous letter to Congress: "I am now convinced beyond a doubt," he informed Henry Laurens, "that unless some great and capital change suddenly takes place in that line [the commissary department] this Army must inevitably be reduced to one or other of these three things. Starve—dissolve—or disperse, in order to obtain subsistence in the best manner they can."[6] Laurens had not always shared Washington's correspondence with all of his fellow delegates, but this time he certainly did. The general's fraught letter put Congress on notice: Fix the logistics nightmare or risk losing the army. There was no higher priority, for losing the army meant losing the war and the death of independence.

In military usage the word "logistics" encompasses "the procurement, maintenance, and transportation of military matériel, facilities, and personnel."[7] For our purposes the acquisition, storage, and delivery of food, forage, and supplies of all kinds also fall under the logistics. Logistical functions are detailed and, to the nonprofessional, often arcane; they are hardly the most scintillating aspect of military history. But the board's gambit into logistics operations demands our attention, albeit at some (and often complicated) length. It was, and is, a maxim that whoever *supplies* an army, in effect, *controls* the army. We have this on the best of authorities: It was Napoleon who observed in so many words that armies travelled on their stomachs and Erwin Rommel who sagely pronounced that the quartermasters had won or lost the battle before anyone had fired a shot.[8] In their day Mifflin and Gates, both with considerable experience in army supply administration, certainly knew as much. So did Washington. Often overlooked when things go well, the importance of logistics becomes glaringly apparent when supply operations break down, as they did so grievously at Valley Forge.

In most eighteenth-century armies, including the Continental Army, the separate but related commissary and quartermaster departments handled logistics functions. Although mostly staffed with civilian administrators and personnel, the commissary department was formally attached to the army and tasked with feeding and clothing the troops. Initially headed by a single commissary general, the job proved too much for one officer. After the New York campaign of 1776 Congress divided it between a commissary general of purchases, who procured foodstuffs and clothing, and a commissary general of issues, who managed storage and distribution. The competent Joseph Trumbull, son of Connecticut governor Jonathan Trumbull, was the original commissary general; he stayed on as commissary general of purchases until his resignation in 1777. Congress then appointed William Buchanan, a former Maryland militia officer, whose performance would prove lackluster if not disastrous. Charles Stewart, a prominent New Jersey politico and former congressional delegate, became commissary general of issues. Hardworking and generally effective, Stewart remained on the job until after the Yorktown campaign. In December 1776, following the division of the department, Congress also appointed a clothier general, and subsequent appointments placed separate commissary officers in charge of hides, bread, forage, accounting, and management tasks. The delegates also authorized the purchase of hundreds of army wagons and teams and appointed a wagon master to manage transportation arrangements.[9] Thus commissary operations comprised a massive and demanding undertaking.

The quartermaster department was responsible for the procurement and distribution of army supplies other than clothing and foodstuffs. The department also was in charge of troop movements and "route reconnaissance; the repair and maintenance of roads and bridges; the layout, organization, and construction of camps; and the supply and maintenance of wagons and teams and of boats for water movement." It was a herculean task, and the quartermaster general held senior military rank and reported directly to the commander in chief. Major General Thomas Mifflin was the first to hold the post, and with the exception of a brief period under Stephan Moylan in the summer of 1776, the department remained formally under Mifflin until his resignation in October 1777.[10] As these pages have explained, his performance was controversial and his attention to departmental operations only nominal after mid-1777; but his undoubted knowledge of quartermaster operations accounted for much of his popularity with Congress.

Efficient logistics operations depended on the coordination of commissary and quartermaster resources. Quartermaster teams, for example, often had to transport commissary shipments to encampments or to storage magazines. In the first year of the war the novice supply services did remarkably well. Washington's army around Boston never had everything it needed, but it had enough. (The case was far different for patriot forces operating in Canada, where conditions would have challenged even mature logistical services.) When operations shifted to the Middle Colonies, however, patriot logistics gradually proved unequal to the task. Combat in and around New York and New Jersey was extremely fluid, and commissary and quartermaster services were barely functional by the time Washington's bedraggled forces escaped to the Pennsylvania side of the Delaware. The supply departments healed as Washington rebuilt the army at Morristown, and they kept the troops reasonably well supplied in early 1777. But subsequent active campaigning wore out equipment, shoes, and clothing and consumed tons of munitions, food, and animal forage. Operations during the Philadelphia Campaign would have taxed even veteran supply officers. Indeed, British officers, who enjoyed supply services beyond anything available to patriots, bemoaned logistics difficulties even as they repeatedly battered rebel forces.[11]

However, some of the worst wounds to patriot supply efforts were self-inflicted. Lack of central oversight hurt military procurement in particular. Congress was late in issuing clear instructions on departmental responsibilities to Trumbull and Mifflin, and these officers were never able to sort out their precise relationships. Neither was Buchanan after he replaced Trumbull. With lines of authority hazy, commissary and quartermaster agents frequently competed for the same supplies; and because Congress had no authority over the states, there was competition with state purchasing agents as well. In fact, while Pennsylvania agreed to provide commissary and quartermaster support to rebel forces in the state, state and congressional officials botched initial efforts to coordinate operations, especially purchasing. They sorted things out too late to avoid the logistics failures at Valley Forge—and I will say considerably more about this mess. Muddled departmental responsibilities also hindered magazine (warehouse) management; inventory records were abysmal, and there was virtually no way to quickly ascertain how much of anything was on hand or the status of requisitions or shipments in transit. In June 1777 Richard Peters, secretary of the original Board of War (and future member of the reconstituted board), informed Washington that he had tried repeatedly "to procure exact Accounts of the Receipt & Distribution of Military Stores, arms, &c received . . . but have not yet been able to do it with any Degree of Precision." The situation resulted in considerable waste. Food, forage, arms, tools, blankets, and other stocks too frequently rotted, molded, rusted, or fell prey to vermin as they sat in storage through oversight or the inability to transport them.[12] The grim circumstances of the Continental Line at Valley Forge offered a classic example of the relationship between inadequate supply operations and poor combat effectiveness; wars could be lost as much through mismanagement as defeat in the field.

By December 1777 the situation had become dire. Buchanan labored under enormous difficulties, but at best he was a poor administrator who failed to demand accountability from his subordinates. Many of his duties, especially at camp, fell to his chief deputy Ephraim Blaine. Blaine was competent, but he was often close to despair from inadequate funding for transport and matériel, broken-down wagons and equipment, starving and dying horses, and uncooperative or incompetent assistants (and getting blamed for it all).[13] Washington and his officers were bitterly critical of commissary operations, and Buchanan's officers were the butt of considerable hostility at headquarters. Feelings were even more acute among the hungry soldiery, who vented at commissary personnel and even threatened violence. In mid-February Thomas Jones, one of Charles Stewart's deputy commissaries, wrote Stewart in a near panic after irate troops cornered and threatened him with physical violence at Valley Forge. "Its by the greatest Chance that I have Escaped Being made an Example of owing to the Neglect of the Comy [Commissary] & the Purchasing Departmt." The army would not last another week, he warned, without "an immediate Supply of Provisions." Jones told Stewart he had had enough. "You may Depend on't I will not stay here longer than the last of this month if I can live so long."[14]

Quartermaster operations were little better. With Mifflin's official departure in October, the struggling department fell largely to his deputy, Colonel Henry Emanuel Lutterloh, who already had been trying to do much of Mifflin's job. No administrative wizard, Lutterloh could only do his best within a collapsing system.[15] At Valley Forge supplies of all kinds, including clothing, blankets, medical stores, and especially meat, arrived only irregularly. Morale plummeted, sickness and hunger began to take their toll; discipline suffered and desertion was rife. It was in this atmosphere that Washington penned his "Starve—dissolve—or disperse" letter to Henry Laurens.

WASHINGTON'S DRAMATIC LETTER hit Congress like a lightning strike. The general had intended it for shock effect—*anything* to finally get delegates safe and warm in York to recognize how imperiled the army really was—and it had precisely the desired impact. It finally sparked a congressional awakening. Previously Congress had dispatched delegates to meet personally with Washington on various issues, but visiting delegates spent relatively little time at camp. The situation now called for a more extensive congressional inquiry. Thus Congress determined to send a delegation to Valley Forge to scrutinize firsthand and at length the condition of the army. On January 10, Congress named a Committee at Camp (also called the Committee of Conference, or Conference Committee) charged with investigating Washington's dire reports on the army's organizational, supply, and other problems. The committee was then to recommend remedies.[16]

Committee membership was interesting. Congress originally intended to appoint six members—three delegates and three members of the Board of War—but then quickly added a fourth delegate member. The delegates were Joseph Reed of Pennsylvania, Francis Dana of Massachusetts, Nathaniel Folsom of New Hampshire, and John Harvie of Virginia. Mifflin, Gates, and Timothy Pickering would represent the board. Seeing those last three names probably was cold comfort for Washington.

In fact there was little predicting how the committee would get on with the general. James Lovell, that most ardent of Massachusetts republicans, was doubtless pleased with the initial committee membership, for which he had voted. It seemed safely in the hands of individuals unlikely to hold Washington in awe. He could count on Mifflin and Gates, at least, to take a hard line with Washington as they set "upon the great Business of introducing Discipline and Œconomy into the army."[17] This was at a time when Lovell remained in full cry against Washington. Only days later, convinced the Virginian was dragging his feet on the issue of impressing supplies, Lovell joined other delegates in registering displeasure. They passed a resolution, Lovell gleefully wrote Samuel Adams, "meant to rap a Demi G— over the Knuckles." "What a fatality attends some men in the choice of their favorites!" he mused in frustration.[18]

Lovell, as a long-serving delegate, was among the best informed on the political drift of the day, especially when it came to attitudes toward the commander in chief. So he may well have known that Pickering also had grave doubts about Washington's leadership. Having served as Washington's adjutant general through the disappointing 1777 campaign, Pickering considered the general anything but infallible. Indeed, he simply did not see the general as the leader essential to rally a faltering cause. "The present situation of public affairs," he confided to another officer, "reminds me of the distracted state of Britain [in] the first years of the last war [the Seven Year's War]. Would to God we had some great, some patriot Pitt, to rescue us from impending danger, and conduct us to victory and glory, by a wise management and vigorous execution of public measures! But where shall the man be found?"[19] Pickering's biographer, Gerard Clarfield, was surely right when he concluded Pickering "was not . . . among Washington's greatest admirers."[20]

In addition to Mifflin, Pickering, and Gates, Lovell probably also saw a kindred spirit in Dana. This was a misjudgment. While Dana did have some misgivings about the Virginian's performance, the Massachusetts delegate brought an open mind to his committee service.[21] Folsom was something of a blank slate; like other New Englanders he was no fan of Schuyler, but the historical record reveals no pronounced feelings he may have held about the commander in chief.[22] Reed and Harvie were generally favorably disposed toward Washington. Reed's relationship with the general had suffered when Washington had accidentally seen a letter from Major General Charles Lee to Reed in December 1776, when Reed was the army's adjutant general. The letter was critical of Washington and indicated Reed shared Lee's doubts about the commander in chief. But Washington seemingly had put the matter behind him. John Harvie, a successful Virginia lawyer and close friend of Jefferson, had arrived at York in October 1777; for most of his term he was the only delegate attending for Virginia. During his time at Valley Forge (January 24 to February 27, 1778) no one represented the Old Dominion in York. He was not especially close to the Virginia Lees, and Washington apparently saw no reason to mistrust him.[23] Still, if the committee was not stacked completely against the general, he would have to be careful as he met with its members, especially those from the board.

Ten days later, however, events took a startling turn. Congress had second thoughts about sending Mifflin, Gates, and Pickering to Valley Forge. In fact, it decided *not* to send them. The politics of the Cabal was at work. Officially the board members would not go to Valley Forge because the press of business in York supposedly demanded their presence. The real reason, of course, was quite different, and everyone knew it: Mifflin and Gates were at loggerheads with the commander in chief and including them on the committee would have been asking for trouble. Gates fully understood he should not accompany the committee.[24] Richard Peters, secretary to the board and soon to be a member, minced no words in explaining the state of affairs. "Congress," he told Robert Morris, "have thought it most prudent considering the State of Parties at Camp to keep General Mifflin and Gates here." He could have said the same of Pickering. At Valley Forge the snarky comment of Connecticut brigadier Jedidiah Huntington easily confirmed Peters's observation: "I fancy they [Mifflin and Gates] don't like us well enough to come."[25] Henry Laurens, who fervently wished for a cordial collaboration between the committee and Washington, was just as pleased the board members would be absent. Congress, he wrote Lafayette, had "stripped" the committee delegation "of all their intended Military Coajutors & will consist [only] of members of Congress."[26]

There is no evidence Congress took this course in order to tilt the committee in Washington's favor. Indeed, over the following weeks the delegates would endorse a series of board initiatives Washington considered nothing less than hostile. But juggling the committee membership was a sign of how seriously Congress was now taking the crises at Valley Forge. As Laurens noted, Congress indeed had named a committee entirely of delegates. It replaced the three board members with two more congressmen, Charles Carroll of Maryland and Gouverneur Morris of New York.[27] Carroll and Morris were members of a different caliber, and their appointments may have taken some of Washington's critics by surprise. They were openly pro-Washington. As replacements for the Board of War members, they could hardly have pleased Lovell or anyone else who thought well of Mifflin and Gates. Carroll, a veteran member of Congress, was on notice as a Washington man; his aversion to Conway was a matter of record. And while he may not have said as much to his fellow delegates, to his father he revealed his doubts about the leadership of Horatio Gates at a time (November 8, 1777) when most patriots were singing the praises of the Saratoga victor.[28]

Morris was new to Congress. The delegates had "summarily" (Morris's word) put him on the Committee at Camp the very day he took his seat in York (January 21).[29] Not quite twenty-five years old, Morris was brilliant but with a reputation as unpredictable. William Duer, the New York businessman and a fellow delegate, wondered about Morris's appointment. Duer, who periodically sat on the Board of War as a delegate member, and who (the reader will recall) had little faith in Washington's ability to straighten out the army's problems, thought Morris should have remained longer in York. "Parties run pretty high in the Army," Duer wrote a New York friend, and he feared Morris had not been with Congress long enough to grasp the intricacies of the controversies dividing Washington and his critics. Morris, he warned, was "like an Elephant in War [and was] often times more destructive to his Friends than his Antagonists."[30] Morris was also something of a rake, unashamedly chasing any woman who caught his eye (and apparently with some success). With this in view the New Yorker was just as glad to leave York for Valley Forge. He wrote his friend John Jay that the temporary rebel capital was a dreary place; it was no fun and most of the delegates were "Disagreeables." Worse, he complained, "there are no fine Women here at York Town. Judge then of my situation."[31] Did he count on improving his love life with the Continental Line?

WITHOUT WASHINGTON'S chief antagonists along—that is, without Mifflin, Gates, and perhaps even Pickering—the committee reported to Valley Forge in late January and set up headquarters at a substantial private home, Moore Hall, some three miles from Washington's headquarters. Carroll missed the initial meetings. Learning his wife was ill, he had left for Maryland and would not reach Valley Forge for some weeks.[32] At full or partial strength, however, the committee, with Dana as chair, would work closely with Washington until March. Members examined virtually every facet of army operations and evaluated Washington's extensive recommendations for organizational and administrative reforms. It was a relationship entirely suited to Washington's purposes. He was dealing with an official arm of Congress that included some political friends; and given the relatively few delegates attending Congress, the committee members represented a sizeable and potentially influential block of allies if Washington could consolidate their support. In addition he would have the committee's undivided attention; and unlike the delegates in York, the committee could see the problems at Valley Forge firsthand—and Washington and his officers made sure that they did. Even better, as he hosted the committee the commander in chief did *not* have to deal with the Board of War.

In meeting with the committee Washington followed the old (probably even then) political rule. In so many words: "He who sets the agenda—wins."[33] The general was taking no chances on this score. Prior to the committee's arrival Washington had Alexander Hamilton draft a lengthy and closely argued compendium of the army's problems, a missive which included Washington's suggested reforms. The committee first assembled at Moore Hall on January 28, and Washington attended with his aide John Laurens. Not waiting for the delegates to get deeply into questions or concerns of their own, the next day the general presented them with his manifesto. As Washington hoped, the document guided the committee's work for the next two months and, in effect, served as the blueprint for the army's revival at Valley Forge.[34]

Washington's reform agenda dealt with a number of contentious issues. One of the touchiest, of course, was the nagging matter of half-pay pensions for officers (and for their widows and orphans), which the general considered essential for keeping the best officers in the army. He also wanted matters of rank and promotion standardized, and he pressed for restructuring army organization, including the size and number of regiments. With voluntary enlistments too few, the general urged the committee to endorse plans to draft men from the state militias into Continental service. Eventually the committee generally agreed with Washington's positions on all of these concerns, and it said as much in various reports to Congress. Congress, however, would debate many of them well into the spring before reaching any final decisions. It took until April, for example, for Congress to reach a compromise solution to the pensions issue. Other matters could not wait.

The supply crisis was the immediate worry, and it occupied most of the committee's initial meetings with the commander in chief. Washington blamed the sorry state of logistics operations squarely on the dysfunctional quartermaster and commissary departments. In frank terms, in late December Washington already had registered his anger over the performance of these departments—telling Henry Laurens, and through him Congress, that he (Washington) was tired of taking the blame for the failures of the commissary and quartermaster generals.[35] Now he told the Committee at Camp much the same thing. Without naming the man, although it was clear who he meant, Washington's document execrated the conduct of commissary general William Buchanan. Washington wanted Buchanan gone. "Unless a very considerable alteration shortly takes place, I see no prospect of adequate supplies for the succeeding campaign. To attempt supplying the army from hand to mouth (if I may be allowed the phrase) scarcely ever having more than two or three days provisions beforehand, and sometimes being as much in arrears, is a dangerous and visionary experiment." Military operations would be impossible, the general warned, without adequate stocks of food, liquor, and other supplies, all in magazines properly positioned to support army movements.[36] These arrangements depended on strong and active supervision of commissary agents working with the army and procuring supplies in the states, and the hapless Buchanan was not the man to supply the necessary leadership.

The general was no less displeased with the quartermaster department. The department was critical, he noted, as it "comprehended, Forage Masters, waggon masters, artificers &c. with all their appendages." As such "it is a department of great trust and magnitude, on the due administration of which all the operations of an army essentially depend." Washington had high expectations of a quartermaster general, insisting he must be "a military character—a man of abilities, of business and activity, well versed in the resources of the country and of sufficient prudence and rectitude, to exercise his office, in drawing the necessary supplies, in a manner least distressing to the inhabitants."[37] The general detailed what he expected of the quartermaster department, but as with the commissary department, he located the key to success in leadership. A quartermaster general had to weed out surplus and unproductive deputies, demand performance from his subordinates, and make the most of departmental resources. Implicit in all of this was the fact that, with the quartermaster department essentially rudderless since Mifflin's departure, the administrative mess in the department had become intolerable. Indeed, quartermaster failures were at the crux of the supply crisis at Valley Forge.

Thus Washington wanted major changes in the logistics departments, and he wanted them fast. But he wanted to be sure of something else as well. As with the inspector general, he expected that any reformed commissary and quartermaster departments would operate under *his* authority. New commissary and quartermaster generals would be *his* people; they would be in and of the Continental Army. As a civilian, the commissary general would probably keep his office close to Congress inasmuch as he would routinely be handling government contracts. But he would still be an army employee taking direction from the commander in chief, and his subordinates would travel with the army. As a military officer, the quartermaster general would be a key staff officer working directly with the commanding general. There was no mistaking Washington's intentions: In whatever reforms eventuated he would insist on unity of command—*his* command.

Unity of command was no small concern. Eighteenth-century military writers offered no uniform definitions of the principles of war, but they did devote considerable thought to identifying the essential elements of warfare and how to apply them. Washington and other senior officers were familiar with many of these works, although exactly what they found useful is open to question.[38] As a practical matter, however, the fight over the inspector generalship revealed Washington's fears of the consequences of divided command. Shortly before that dispute irrupted the general had related his thinking on the subject to one of his brigadiers, Rhode Island's James Mitchell Varnum. "How strange it is that Men, engaged in the same Important Service," he mused, "should be eternally bickering, instead of giving mutual aid. Officers cannot act upon proper principles who suffer trifles to interpose to create distrust, & jealousy—All our actions should be regulated by one uniform Plan—& that Plan should have one object only in view, to wit, the good of the service."[39] The modern American military has defined unity of command in similar terms: "Unity of command means that all forces operate under a single commander with the requisite authority to direct all forces employed in pursuit of a common purpose."[40] Washington would have fully understood.

In fact, Washington saw unity of command as central to his authority as commanding general. Without clear authority to coordinate the army's key logistic operations and to hold accountable the civilian and military officers tasked with the execution of logistics functions, the title of commander in chief would mean little. He would never lose sight of this point as he dealt with the Committee at Camp and reacted to measures proposed by the Board of War.

AS MUCH AS Washington and the Committee at Camp agreed on the need to reform the supply departments, the hope of improved logistics in the future could not feed hungry men and animals in the short run. The situation was such that the general simply could not wait for the committee to propose logistics reforms and for Congress to discuss and enact them. Thus in the interim Washington personally took over supply operations. That is, he functioned as his own commissary and quartermaster generals, and for a time the tasks seemed all consuming. He urged the states to forward any available provisions, and he sent senior staff officers to speak directly with governors. They pleaded not only for emergency supplies but also for amending price controls and other legislation impeding procurement operations. Washington harried commissary and quartermaster personnel insisting they get wagons moving to camp; he held them accountable for timely deliveries of food, blankets, forage, and other supplies. He and his staff officers pushed purchasing agents, commissary officials, and civilian patriots to search out stocks of provisions of all kinds in private hands.[41] Activity bordered on the frantic: "For Gods sake," one of Washington's chief aides wrote a commissary deputy, "exert yourself."[42]

These emergency measures included impressments. The general had resisted congressional calls to seize supplies from regional farmers, fearing a popular backlash inimical to the cause. But the collapsing logistics functions compelled a change of heart. Responding to congressional pressure, over January and February he sent foraging expeditions into the Pennsylvania, Maryland, and New Jersey countrysides; troops swept up anything edible, even searching in woods and swamps to find livestock secreted away by farmers reluctant to accept promissory notes. Tories felt the heaviest hand of these operations, but Washington made sure the impressment process was orderly. Officers issued receipts for impressed goods, and impressments ceased when the supply crisis eased. In the pinch these *ad hoc* measures prevented the army from starving and freezing,[43] but they were no substitute for properly organized and efficient quartermaster and commissary departments. And a commander in chief forced to run his own supply operations had little time for much else. It was no way to run an army.

It *was* no way to run an army. On this at least Washington and the Board of War agreed. Board members saw the same administrative chaos in the supply services, the same hungry and sick soldiery, the same dying animals, and the same danger of the army actually dissolving. *They differed fundamentally, however, on what to do about it.*

Having surveyed the questionable, and sometimes egregious, performance of the army's commissary and quartermaster departments, the board concluded that repairing the situation was beyond the capabilities of current army leadership. That being the case—and with Mifflin, Gates, and Pickering having extensive experience in military administration—the board felt it had to intervene directly to put supply operations back on track. As it had in the matter of the inspector generalship, it decided that it should do so without reference to the commander in chief or the official army commissary and quartermaster departments. Once again the board's actions were clearly efforts to exert its authority over the patriot war effort at the expense of Washington's command authority. Moreover, while the board knew full well that the Committee at Camp was supposed to address the supply crisis, it consciously decided to act before the committee could make any recommendations. *And it is noteworthy that no evidence indicates any board member or congressional delegate disagreed with any of the board's subsequent actions.*

What followed was one of the most inexplicable episodes in the Cabal narrative, and one of the most confusing in the story of the American war effort. As Washington fumed over his dysfunctional logistics departments, and as the members of the Committee at Camp looked ahead to their travels to Valley Forge, the Board of War took some dramatic steps. Instead of stepping in to force quick changes in the commissary department—perhaps starting with pressing Congress to fire Buchanan—it convinced the delegates to authorize a completely new commissary service. On January 15, after consultation with the board, and more than two weeks *before* the Committee at Camp even could begin to consider the matter, Congress effectively put Mifflin and, upon his arrival in York, Gates in charge of commissary functions. In a sweeping resolution the delegates ordered the War Office to employ "one or more proper persons" to purchase thirty thousand barrels of flour or "wheat equivalent," have the wheat "ground into flour," and then establish storage magazines in four Pennsylvania locations. Board personnel would deposit twelve thousand barrels at or close to Lancaster, six thousand barrels at Bethlehem, two thousand at Downingtown, and two thousand at Pottsgrove. Board agents, called superintendents, were empowered to use all available mills, employ necessary coopers, and "hire or impress" wagons to carry flour to the magazines. Congress also gave the board authority to set prices for flour, wheat, and other commodities provided those prices contravened no Pennsylvania or other state price control laws.[44]

This new service would exist separately and in parallel to the existing commissary department. The board never thought of coordinating its plans with the Committee at Camp or the army; in fact it had created a competing commissary organization and put in charge a man, Gates, widely recognized as one of Washington's chief rivals. Moreover, the new superintendents also would be competing with Pennsylvania's state procurement officers. Thus instead of simplifying commissary operations, patriots now had *three* of them in the field, all looking to procure supplies in the same region at the same time. It was a potential administrative nightmare—and certainly one of the grossest violations of unity of command in American military history.

Washington was consulted on none of this beforehand. Of the initial four magazines, the closest one to Valley Forge was at Downingtown, some twenty miles away; the farthest, Lancaster, was over fifty miles away. Moreover, the commanding general was to keep his hands off. The congressional resolution *specifically forbade* the army's established commissary department from meddling with the board's new arrangements: "That these magazines, being established without the interference of the commissary general, or his officers, shall, when necessary, be ordered under the direction of the issuing commissary general by the Board of War." The board was running the show, and the commissary general of issues, Charles Stewart, would get involved only if the board told him to. Thus the lackluster Buchanan, commissary general for purchases, was out of the loop as far as the board's efforts were concerned. This was perhaps not a bad thing, as Washington had no more regard for the man than did Mifflin or Gates. But why did Congress not just fire Buchanan and hire an effective commissary general? The answer was simple: *Because a new commissary general in the established commissary department would have had a direct relationship with Washington, and the board had lost faith in that arrangement.* Obviously Mifflin and Gates had convinced most of Congress likewise.[45]

Historian Jacqueline Thibaut, whose exhaustive study has established her as the closest student of logistics operations during the Valley Forge winter, has called the congressional resolution of January 15 "extraordinary."[46] She was certainly right. The Board of War had inserted itself into a critical facet of the war effort, no doubt sincerely hoping to do a better job of supplying the army than William Buchanan's struggling department. It is noteworthy, however, that Congress granted the board this "extraordinary" authority knowing full well of the strained relations—actually the animosity—existing between Gates and Mifflin and the commander in chief.[47] Again Congress had deferred to the Board of War at the expense of Washington's authority at a time when unity of command was essential to the recovery of supply operations. It was an obvious "disgust"; it was the Cabal in the form of an administrative coup.

Gates, however, wasted no time in launching the new effort. He appointed nine superintendents, placing each one in charge of a purchasing district in Pennsylvania, Delaware, Maryland, or northern New Jersey. He issued detailed instructions on what to purchase, where to establish additional magazines, and how to interact with Pennsylvania procurement agents. The superintendents were "empowered to instruct and direct" the Pennsylvanians, and to make sure they obeyed. Gates reminded his men to pay no more for supplies than prices set by Pennsylvania and New Jersey authorities, but if people wouldn't sell the superintendents were "authorized to seize."[48] Clearly Gates took his commissary undertaking seriously; and just as clearly he intended it to be the critical factor in relieving the Continental Army's distress—and all of this was to happen under his purview.

If further evidence of the board's determination to gain control of patriot logistics was necessary, it came during the next two weeks. With its foot firmly in the door of commissary functions, the board then persuaded Congress to reorganize the quartermaster department. On January 28—the very day the Committee at Camp first convened at Moore Hall—Mifflin, Gates, and Peters met (the board required a quorum of three members to act) and drafted a report for a departmental reorganization. Congress took up consideration on the thirtieth.[49] The report stressed the fiscal tribulations of the department—"large sums of money are immediately wanted"—and presented Congress with two choices for quartermaster reforms. One was simple, the other complicated.

Option one would have Congress appoint an experienced ranking officer to the post of quartermaster general. The new man would have the "power to arrange the Department, with the approbation and concurrence of the Board of War."[50] Note the absence of any reference to the commander in chief, whose "approbation and concurrence" the board apparently considered unnecessary. The appointee, even if technically a staff officer of Washington's, in reality would have been a creature of the board. The arrangement smacked of the proposed (and defeated) plan for the inspector generalship.

The second option was considerably more complex. In fact it was complicated enough to prompt the question: "What were they thinking?" The plan envisioned dividing the quartermaster department into four independent branches. First, there would be a quartermaster general whose realm would be "The *Military Line*." He would plan routes of march, manage army transport, establish campsites, maintain an order of battle, and deal with anything else ascribed to quartermasters "in all the books of the profession." But the quartermaster general would handle no public funds other than "small occasional sums" necessary "to defray petty expenses." This virtually penniless officer was hardly the strong quartermaster envisioned in option one. A second section called for a "quartermaster of *Forage*," who would deal only in "that article in his purchases." Third was a "quartermaster for Horses and Waggons"; and finally there would be an "Agent" in charge of tents, entrenching tools, barracks construction, and "all the smaller supplies of the Department, such as paper &c." All of these individuals would plan their purchases based on directions from the quartermaster general or the Board of War—not the commander in chief.[51] Given the myriad difficulties patriots already had experienced trying to coordinate logistics efforts, whatever made the Board of War and Congress think this bizarre administrative structure had any conceivable promise is anyone's guess.

Yet the board's report was a serious matter. Historian Wayne Bodle, who has produced a remarkably detailed and insightful study of the army's experience at Valley Forge, has called the report "a bold-faced attempt by the board to expand its authority from a supportive role into the day-to-day operation of the army itself."[52] It surely was, especially in conjunction with the attempt to capture the inspector generalship and the more successful move to control commissary operations. At least some delegates must have realized the implications of the situation, as the report sparked debate and Congress postponed discussion for a day. It did no better the following day (January 31): Presented with a motion to adopt the board's first option—to appoint "an officer of rank" as quartermaster general—Congress again put off a decision.[53]

Why the delay? The *Journals* of Congress are silent on the reasons, as are surviving letters of delegates. The probable answer, however, lay in the first substantive communication to Congress from the Committee at Camp, which arrived on the thirty-first. In the view of most delegates it was not good news. Reacting to Washington's request for an effective quartermaster general, the committee recommended Major General Philip Schuyler for the post. It was not a unanimous choice. Nathaniel Folsom dissented, the only recorded dissent during the committee's work at Valley Forge.[54] And by any measure Schuyler was a controversial nomination. He and Gates had no use for one another, and Schuyler was still under a cloud after the debacle at Ticonderoga the previous year. A later court martial would acquit the

New Yorker with "honor," but that wouldn't come until September. Yet Washington had never lost faith in Schuyler, and even after Gates had relieved Schuyler, he (Schuyler) had continued to efficiently channel vital supplies to Gates's army. It was a contribution essential to the victory at Saratoga. Washington wanted a capable staff officer as his subordinate, and Schuyler fit the bill. The committee members (except Folsom) agreed; and while noting the controversy surrounding Schuyler, they clearly followed Washington's lead in considering him the best man for the job. Given the deplorable state of the quartermaster department, the delegation informed Laurens, and stressing "how much depends on filling it up in a proper Manner, we cannot help mentioning General Schuyler, & for the Benefit of the Service we could wish he would undertake it."[55]

Congress was unconvinced. Gates was too popular and Schuyler too unpopular, no matter what Washington wanted. Murmuring among the delegates held Schuyler liable to "an intrigueing mind; a temper unfriendly to the dispositions of officers in the army & its peace"—a clear reference to Gates and probably Mifflin. There were also concerns that Schuyler, while a man of "influence & knowledge" in New York State, was otherwise limited in his understanding of the country at large and thus would not be up to the job.[56] Unstated was the fact that Schuyler was Washington's preferred candidate.

Congress had appointed the Committee at Camp—composed entirely of their own members—only three weeks before, but now the delegates held it at arm's length. They failed even to respond to the committee's recommendation. Indeed, they buried Schuyler's nomination by sending it to the War Office, where predictably it was never heard from again. Then, likely in reaction to the recommendation of Schuyler, on February 5 Congress dropped the notion of a strong quartermaster general presiding over a unified department. Instead the delegates voted to reorganize quartermaster operations using the Board of War's second alternative model: a departmental division into four sections with a quartermaster general closely beholden to the board.[57]

This action had Mifflin's fingerprints all over it, and the commander in chief realized as much as soon as he learned of it. Washington had seen the plan long before. In fact he had read its key points over two months before in a letter from Richard Henry Lee. Knowing of Washington's growing aversion to the Pennsylvanian, readers will recall that Lee had tried to explain his enthusiasm for Mifflin's appointment to the new Board of War. He was taken with Mifflin's experience and especially with his proposed reorganization of the quartermaster department. "General Mifflin has proposed a plan for the Quartermaster department that appears judicious, and well fitted to answer the purpose of good service and Œconomy at the same time," Lee told the commander in chief. "He would divide this department into its military and civil branches, the former to be filled by a person well qualified to discharge its duties, and the latter, again to be divided into Commissaries of Teams, of Forage, of Tents &c &c to be governed in their purchases by estimates from the Quarter Master general who is to touch no money but a moderate tho sufficient salary."[58] This was precisely the remarkably complicated plan Congress approved on February 5, and (no surprise) without any consultation with Washington.

THE MODERN AMERICAN ARMY has warned its officers against the dangers inherent in "mission creep." This occurs when commanders tasked with a certain mission receive "guidance or change in mission for which the unit is not properly configured or resourced; or if it is beyond the legal remit of the Army." The problem also "occurs when a unit attempts to do more than is allowed in the current mandate."[59] In other words, mission creep occurs when an organization, for one reason or another, sets out to do things it originally never intended to do or was never even created to do. Mission creep can happen innocently as an organization identifies tasks it feels it can or should handle, even if those tasks were not part of its original responsibility. Or it can occur less benevolently if an organization seizes an opportunity to increase its own political, military, business, or other influence at the expense of another organization. In other words, a "power grab." In either case mission creep (modern management jargon calls it "scope creep") can lead to unanticipated complications and organizational conflicts detrimental to the original mission and to everyone concerned.[60]

In the case of the Board of War "mission creep" was not incidental or benign. It was a power grab. When Congress established the Board of War in 1776 it had defined the board's mission in terms of a support organization. It would maintain records, see to the storage of equipment not in field service, superintend prisoners of war, produce reports, handle Congress's military correspondence, and deal with mundane tasks that would otherwise burden the delegates. But Congress had never envisioned the board as an active participant in the army's daily operations. Certainly Washington, who had welcomed the establishment of the board, never imagined the organization in anything other than a supporting role—much less did he foresee it emerging as a threat to his authority. But the reconstituted Board of War obviously saw things differently.

With its mandate ill defined, the new board, as organizations in such circumstances sometimes do, set out to test the limits of its authority. It did so aggressively. The first step in this direction, of course, was the attempt to create an inspector generalship under its control. Had this been a solitary incident, perhaps we could excuse it as a political misstep but not necessarily part of any wider political or military ambitions. While frustrated in the matter of the inspector generalship, however, the move into commissary and quartermaster operations leaves little doubt about the board's intentions. As of early February the board had obtained legal authority to control essential supply and logistics functions, and in so doing it had expanded its remit well beyond a supporting role. It had established itself as a direct participant in the army's daily activities—and seemingly with veto power over any decisions the commander in chief might make in these critical areas. Without clear command authority on logistical matters, Washington could undertake no major strategic initiatives without board approval.

The political skill of Thomas Mifflin, the popularity of Horatio Gates, and the acquiescence of a Congress desperate to reverse the fortunes of war had deepened the challenge to Washington's command. In a very real sense the Board of War was asserting its authority as the commander in chief's superior. And Washington understood as much.

In allowing the Board of War free rein with logistics arrangements, however, Congress had opened a Pandora's box. While Congress initially wanted Pennsylvania to concede a leading role to the board's superintendents and their deputies, the state, after deliberating for three weeks, announced it would not abide by the board's directives and would not cease its procurement efforts. The state would not accept a secondary role. Thus for vital weeks the three bodies in the procurement business—the board superintendents, commissary department personnel, and Pennsylvania purchasing agents—were in direct competition for a diminishing supply of regional provisions and forage. The effect was to drive up prices, thus spurring inflation and creating ill will between the competing agencies. The three parties never fully worked out collaborative arrangements, and too often the left hand had little idea of what the right hand (much less a *third* hand) was doing. It would be difficult to conceive a more complicated situation. There was simply no central management—no unity of command—in critical procurement and distribution efforts when the army's very survival depended on effective administration of logistics operations.[61]

Then in mid-February Congress made things even worse. The delegates ordered three superintendents in eastern Pennsylvania (including Jonathan Mifflin, Thomas's cousin) to halt all purchasing. Congress gave two reasons for its abrupt action. In a change of stance it decided not to pick a fight with Pennsylvania. It noted that state purchasing commissioners were now active and could handle procurement operations, at least in eastern Pennsylvania. Congress also professed alarm that the three board superintendents had ignored state price controls and were paying too much for provisions.[62] There was a resulting chain reaction. Gates, unsure of how to proceed, and perhaps misunderstanding congressional intent, directed the superintendents to suspend *all* activities, including deliveries of supplies to Valley Forge.[63] With activities halted, state personnel, who had impressed wagons at the request of the board superintendents, had to return the wagons pending new instructions from the state executive council. Gates then further muddied the waters. He told Laurens that some other superintendents, those west of the Susquehanna River, had stopped work in protest over what they charged was unfair competition from state procurement agents. They reportedly refused to go back to work until someone addressed their complaints. The sources of all of this confusion remain obscure, although Pennsylvania authorities suspected the worst. Had the Board of War engineered the mess deliberately in order to reinforce the authority of its superintendents? Gates had done no such thing; but as Thibaut has correctly observed, whatever the source of the confusion it is certain "that the army suffered as a result."[64]

As all of this transpired the established commissary department was almost completely in the dark. Its personnel didn't know what to make of the board's venture into army supply or of Gates's seemingly inexplicable actions. Blaine, a man who was not only diligent but thoughtful—much later he would draw up a comprehensive plan to reform commissary operations—could not understand developments. What was the Board of War up to? He did know that his boss, the ineffectual Buchanan, had no clue. Blaine wrote Stewart that Buchanan was "quite blind to the intensions of the Board respecting himself and those in his employ."[65] It is clear that Blaine, and no doubt others in the formal commissary department, were unclear of what their relationships to the board's superintendents were supposed to be. But in mid-February, at a time when the army desperately needed functioning commissary and quartermaster support, this is how matters stood.

Washington was aghast at all of this. The general had wanted reformed and effective army commissary and quartermaster departments under his command as keys to solving the supply crisis. Instead, at the Board of War's behest, Congress had delivered anything but. If these logistics "reforms" stood, Washington would have been reduced to little more than a field commander operating at the sufferance of the Board of War—just another general.

Thomas Conway seemed to think so. After his embarrassment at Washington's hands in late December he seemed to care little about what anyone thought of his relationship with the commander in chief. On January 5 Lafayette reported that Conway was busy in York. The disgruntled inspector general (for he still technically held the post) was chatting up other French officers as well as political contacts; reportedly he was singing his own praises to appreciative audiences. According to Lafayette Conway was, in effect, looking for a job. He mooted himself variously to Congress as the leader of an expedition against St. Augustine, commander of patriot forces in Georgia, or even as American ambassador to France.[66]

But not everyone listening to Conway approved. Some two weeks later deputy commissary Ephraim Blaine, on business near Valley Forge, learned of other Conway remarks. By chance an innkeeper he knew at nearby Windsor Forge overheard a boasting general officer—certainly Conway—openly disparaging Washington in conversation with other officers. Washington, Conway's alleged comments held, "was not the man people Imagined, and by no means a great general"; in fact the Virginian acted more like an "old woman." Blaine, after double-checking details of the episode, sent two reports to Lieutenant Colonel Robert Hanson Harrison, a member of Washington's "family" (and the officer who chose to remain on the general's staff rather than serve on the new Board of War).[67] While the commissary officer suggested not mentioning the incident to Washington, reasoning that criticisms of the general would only rebound on the critics, one doubts Blaine was serious. Why bother to inform one of the commanding general's closest aides? In any event Harrison jotted down a memorandum of Blaine's letters and (as Blaine had not) the lieutenant colonel *did* specifically name Conway.[68] More disturbing than Conway's carping—Washington, after all, had checkmated the Frenchman's ambitions—was the fact Conway would feel so free to publicly demean the commander in chief. Conway was angry and reckless but not necessarily stupid; one can suppose he carried on as he did feeling he enjoyed allies in high places.

Then Conway went a step further. Earlier in the month Washington had issued a "passport"—a safe-conduct pass—to a British and Hessian party coming from Philadelphia with supplies, primarily clothing, for redcoat and German prisoners. The party was headed for prison locations near Reading and then on to internment camps in Virginia. (Both sides were supposed to provision their prisoners of war or pay for their upkeep.) On January 21, the traveling British lodged at the establishment of a "Mr. Herbert, Inn Keeper" outside of Lancaster; Herbert charged them less than the amount specified under Pennsylvania price controls for bed and board because they paid in specie rather than Continental currency. Almost immediately Pennsylvania authorities found out about the transaction and compelled Herbert to present the British with a new bill; state law made no provision for adjusting prices based on specie payments.[69] The situation became politically messy when a British officer complained of the matter to delegates Gouverneur Morris and John Harvie, who were in the area travelling to join the Committee at Camp at Valley Forge. On the twenty-fourth Morris and Harvie, thinking the incident made rebel authorities look picayune, wrote the Pennsylvania council at Lancaster and suggested that Congress ought to decide the issue. They reasoned that Continental currency and prisoners of war fell under congressional authority.[70] Pennsylvania authorities, however, refused to budge and Congress, not looking for a fight with the state, did nothing. Harvie and Morris proceeded to Valley Forge with the issue unresolved and probably unaware that their attempted intervention had stirred up a minor hornets nest.

In fact the affair was far from over. Three days later an American patrol intercepted and arrested the British party shortly after it had left Lancaster. The officer in charge, New York lieutenant colonel William Stephens Smith, who had just assumed command of one of the army's "Additional Regiments,"[71] was under orders from the Board of War. The board had acted after receiving erroneous intelligence that General Howe had prevented patriots from shipping supplies to American prisoners in British hands. Washington quickly informed Gates the report of Howe's action was wrong and insisted his passport be honored. The commanding general directly ordered Smith, who had contacted Washington requesting orders, to release the British party.[72] But officers at Lancaster objected, goaded by Major General Conway. There were questions over the composition and size of the British party, suspicions over the party's true mission when some members were found with counterfeit Continental currency, doubts as to Washington's full knowledge of the British party's intentions, and anger among the rebels over

British mistreatment of American prisoners.[73] And in any case Conway and others argued that orders from the Board of War trumped Washington's passport. Conway had words with Lafayette when the latter, on his way to York, inadvertently walked into the situation and insisted the passport be honored. Congress, instead of ordering some quick resolution of the matter, decided to conduct a formal inquiry. It never happened. Frustrated, the supply party returned to Philadelphia in disgust.[74]

Washington could not ignore the incident. For whatever reasons, Conway and other Continental officers—that is, some of his own subordinates—had consciously declined to honor a passport he had issued, citing the authority of the Board of War. Given the temper of the times Washington could hardly see the business as an innocent misunderstanding. The Conway letter affair remained current, the fight over the inspector generalship was a fresh memory, and the entire matter of army logistics was shaping up as another point of contention with the board. Whether or not he saw the passport incident as a deliberate insult—another case of the Board of War flexing its muscles at his expense—Washington let Gates know he was unhappy. On January 27, he informed the board president that he (Washington) saw nothing amiss with the size or conduct of the British and Hessian supply party. Furthermore "I should have been happy," he continued, "if the Officers and Cloathing had not been seized, as it destroys that confidence which should ever be had in passports and involves consequences of a delicate & interesting nature." He reminded Gates "that there is a particular agreement between General Howe & myself, under the sanction of which they [the British and Hessians] came out."[75] The note to Gates was curt, but Washington had held his temper, although probably with difficulty. He could reasonably wonder if his ability to deal with his British counterpart was now under question.

The passport incident was more than an annoyance for the general. It was an instance of the Board of War issuing orders directly to Continental troops, ignoring Washington and thus (again) doing violence to the normal chain of command, or at least to what Washington would have considered the normal chain of command. Nor was the incident isolated, for Gates had taken to more sweeping and—from Washington's view—more intrusive initiatives.

In fact Gates had begun directly deploying and even raising Continental units on his own initiative. In late January the board president had ordered the recruiting, organization, and equipping of three new artillery companies for the Northern Department. Gates never told Washington about the plan, and the board's orders specified that the new units were to be independent of Knox's command. This order came while Henry Knox, the army's chief of artillery, was doing his best to reorganize the Continental artillery.[76] It was also a time, Washington felt constrained to tell Gates, that we "stand in need of a much larger [artillery] train than we now have in the field, and ought besides to have a reserve to answer the demands of contingencies." With this concern in view the commanding general questioned another of Gates's unilateral moves. For reasons unknown to Washington, Gates had ordered twenty-seven artillery pieces stored at Albany, New York, and readily available to the main army, shipped almost one hundred miles to Farmington, Connecticut.[77] Gates also had detailed a Continental regiment to guard the artillery. Why, Washington queried him, had he done so? The commanding general had every reason to wonder what was going on.

The Board of War may have considered Connecticut farther from harm's way should the British consider a raid on the stockpiled guns, but that wasn't the point. The point was that the board again had intervened directly in army deployments without consulting the commander in chief. The action not only ignored the army chain of command, but the transfer of the artillery and an infantry regiment was disruptive at a time when Washington's army needed every available soldier and when Washington and Knox were deeply involved in reforming the artillery arm. Knox, then in Boston arranging the delivery of a shipment of French arms and munitions to the army, was perplexed. "Genl Gates might have had some particular operation in view by ordering the Cannon to" Farmington, the artilleryman wrote Washington, but in early February Knox had no idea what it might be.[78]

By mid-February, however, Knox had learned something else of what Gates had in mind. The Hero of Saratoga was looking for new laurels; he intended to raise a new army of six regiments and a small corps of rangers—at least some 2,500 men—to invade Canada.[79]

THE "IRRUPTION INTO CANADA" was Gates's idea. In theory it had merit. After the defeat of Burgoyne in 1777, what could deliver a greater shock to the British than a rebel army pushing north? As early as December 1777 Gates and some interested delegates had mulled sending Brigadier General John Stark of New Hampshire, the victor at Bennington, on a raid up Lake Champlain toward Montreal.[80] As interest in the idea grew, however, the projected operation assumed larger proportions. Intelligence indicated British defenses were weak, and Gates's plan envisioned seizing the Lake

Champlain to Montreal corridor, taking Montreal itself, capturing supposedly abundant supplies there, and issuing a call for Canadians to join the Revolution. And even if the Canadians didn't rise, at the very least patriot forces could destroy much of the British military capacity in the North and divert enemy attention from other fronts. There seemed to be little downside. It was on this basis that Gates convinced the Board of War and Congress to back the scheme. Congress formally endorsed the venture on January 22 and, save for a skeptical Henry Laurens, support for the "irruption" apparently was unanimous.[81]

Congress did more than approve the venture. Acting on a report from the War Office, it specifically placed the entire enterprise in the hands of the board. It did not ask Washington what he thought of the plan; it did not ask the general who ought to command the invasion; it did not ask what impact the diversion of resources to support the "irruption" might have on the operations of the main army. It never officially notified the commander in chief of what was going on; Congress left that to Gates, which Gates did two days later. Congress did, however—again on the advice of the board—name the Marquis de Lafayette to command the new army, seconded by Major General Thomas Conway and Brigadier General John Stark, the victor at Bennington the previous year. The choices were actually good ones. Congress trusted that Lafayette and Conway, being French, would appeal to the largely French-speaking Canadians; and Stark, from New Hampshire, knew the territory and had been involved in the earliest discussions of a new Canadian venture.[82]

The commander in chief may have picked up signals on what was afoot from his friends in York, but he received the first official notification of the "irruption" from Gates in a letter of January 24. Acting very much as Washington's superior, he simply told the commanding general what Congress had resolved and referred him to a separate enclosure with full particulars of the planned operation. Gates assured the Virginian that the main army would suffer no manpower shortages as a result; the major general said he would replace any regiments detailed from Washington's troops with units from elsewhere. Washington must have winced. The Continental Line needed to dramatically increase its numbers, not hold at its current levels. Indeed, Gates's letter arrived only days before the commander in chief would tell the Committee at Camp the army could fill its regiments only if the states drafted militia into Continental service. Gates then had the temerity to soothingly invite Washington to comment: "Should your Excellency think any Steps are wanting or any Directions omitted, which may be necessary upon this important Enterprize, the Board will be happy on this, as well as every other Occasion, to recieve your Opinion & Advice."[83] Washington must have shaken his head. Where was such an offer *before* the Board of War and Congress had settled everything?

Gates then requested Washington's "Permission" (could the general really say no?) for Lafayette, by now a favorite member of Washington's "family," to leave Valley Forge for his new assignment.[84] The request was a sham: The same day Gates had written Lafayette *directly* stating it was "the Wish of the Board that you would immediately repair to Albany [the expedition's headquarters], taking with you . . . such other gallant French officers as you think will be serviceable in an Enterprise in that Quarter." So much for the chain of command. Gates also wrote independently to Stark and Colonel Moses Hazen explaining their roles in the "irruption" and ordering them to Albany as well. The men in Hazen's regiment ("Congress's Own"), then under Washington, were mostly Canadians who had joined the Americans during the ill-fated patriot invasion of Quebec in 1775–76. Credit where due: Gates wisely thought Canadians would be appropriate in a new invasion and told Washington to send the regiment to Albany.[85] The impending effort would be the Board of War's largest operational undertaking.

Washington's reaction to all of this—he considered the "irruption" a fool's errand, and no doubt he saw Gates as the fool—will concern us in the next chapter. For now there is the matter of what the Board of War intended in bypassing the commander in chief while planning such a significant mission, one that would entail the commitment of considerable manpower and precious resources. There is a fine but important line between deliberately not informing someone of something and simply considering it unnecessary to inform them. The former suggests a calculated snub or premeditated insult, while the latter is just as bad—or perhaps worse. It implies the neglected party simply has no business knowing or has nothing to contribute. So why did the board keep Washington in the dark?

Some historians have dismissed the notion that the board deliberately snubbed the commander in chief. They have pointed out that Northern Army commanders had operated more or less independently since 1775 and that the planned "irruption" envisioned a similar command arrangement. But this argument hardly justifies the failure to contact Washington. While never directly in command of the Northern Theater, Washington always tried to remain briefed on events there. Responding to Burgoyne's invasion in 1777, for example, his decision to send major reinforcements to Gates, including some of the army's best units, accounted for the victory at

Saratoga. And certainly Washington considered that, as commander in chief, he should have received timely official notice of Burgoyne's surrender. As he explained to Gates, events in one theater could vitally affect those in another.[86] Paul David Nelson has suggested that Gates's plan for the "irruption" was not unreasonable, and if mounted quickly as a winter campaign it stood a chance of success. He noted Laurens's explanation of the delay in notifying Washington: With January already well advanced, time was of the essence in mounting the invasion; and this supposedly precluded bringing Washington into the planning process. It would have taken too long.[87] But this is a highly speculative observation. Had the Conway letter and other rifts between Washington and Gates not clouded their relationship, there was nothing to prevent notifying Washington the minute the "irruption" became a matter of serious discussion. And if, as Nelson believes, Congress saw its support for the Canadian venture as "a healthy assertion of civil control over the military,"[88] that possibility *would* point to a deliberate snub of the commander in chief.

Other authors have speculated that in naming Lafayette commander of the "irruption" the board was trying to wean the young Frenchman from his attachment to Washington. Lafayette, as we will see, came to believe this, or at least to think the board had callously disrespected Washington in failing to consult him about the operation and Lafayette's appointment beforehand. But this scenario is unlikely given the invasion's obvious need for senior French-speaking officers, and Congress was fully aware of the value of the name recognition Lafayette would bring with him into Canada.[89]

Barring the discovery of some smoking guns, there is no way to answer these questions with certainty. What we can say is that Washington saw the "Irruption into Canada" as one more incident in a train of incidents challenging his authority as commander in chief. He was right. The proposed Canadian venture, like the board's smaller moves into troop deployments, was another step (albeit a bigger one) from a supporting role to that of a key player in active operations. It was "mission creep" *redux*, and yet another fracture of command unity. Further, it was clearly an indication of the board's energetic attempt to take charge of the war.

One outside observer, if he could not provide a "smoking gun," at least offered the view of a man charged with reporting the contemporary scene accurately. This was Conrad Alexandre Gérard de Reyneval, the first accredited diplomat to represent France in America. In 1778 in Paris Gérard had led the negotiations with Silas Deane, Benjamin Franklin, and Arthur Lee that hammered out the Franco-American military alliance and the Treaty of Amity and Commerce, in which France recognized American independence. He arrived in America in March 1778 to take up his diplomatic mission. Vergennes, the French foreign minister, tasked Gérard with reporting regularly on American affairs, and the military situation—including the status of General Washington—was second to none in importance. Gérard was grim on this account. Washington, "whose conduct seems to have merited the esteem of Europe, and who couples virtue with talents, has been vigorously attacked with all the arms that envy can supply." The diplomat had no doubt that the threat to the general's command was real, and he told Vergennes that the proposed Canadian invasion was part of "the Cabal against Washington."[90] Gérard had no reason to report anything but the truth as he saw it, and as Vergennes's eyes and ears in York he made it his business to see and hear as much as he could.

LIKE GÉRARD, Joseph Reed viewed the "Irruption into Canada" ominously. For the Pennsylvanian learning of the Canadian operation was something of a catalyst, forcing him to review and tie together the various developments he had witnessed over the past couple of months. Reed was less than two weeks into his service on the Committee at Camp when he pulled his thoughts together in a long letter to his friend and fellow Pennsylvania delegate Jonathan Bayard Smith. The epistle remains one of the most revealing documents of the Cabal narrative.

The letter marked Reed as a convinced pessimist. He lamented the tension between the army and Congress and thought regular contact between civil and military authorities might have prevented the recent ill will. Much of the blame lay on Congress. It was hard to get delegates to camp long enough to really sort out problems; the Spartan existence at camp was "not very agreeable to Gentlemen accustomed to the Conveniences of domestick Life." As a result Washington's relationship with the Board of War and much of Congress had deteriorated to such a point Reed didn't want to commit "particulars" to paper. Who knew who would eventually see such a missive? Still, he wrote quite a bit for a man claiming reticence. "It is too plain that a general Idea prevails thro the Army & Country of a Want of Harmony between the principal Characters in our political Drama," he told Smith. "I should be extremely happy to be perswaded that it was groundless but some Events have happened & they seem to multiply so fast that as a Lover of my Country & feeling an Attachment to its Interests superior to all other Considerations I cannot but perceive & lament it. And the more so as Experience shews how difficult it is to heal such Breaches." Reed had referred to events as far back as the defeats of 1777 and probably the inspector general imbroglio, and he was sorely distressed by their impact on the reputation of "a very high Character." Washington was under fire, but Reed considered the general's critics wrongheaded in drawing out the controversy. The cause suffered amid the acrimony, so it was better to make a decisive choice: Get rid of Washington or back him. "To permit Power to remain in any Hand upon which much depends," he wrote almost in despair, "& at the same Time to adopt Measures to thwart & enfeeble its Exertions I can never agree to—either change the Hands, or support them with your greatest Weight."[91] In Reed's view the choice was obvious: Back Washington. It was also obvious to Reed that some patriots indeed were out to "thwart & enfeeble" the general. In other words, and by whatever term, there was a Cabal.

Congress needed to behave; to undermine the commanding general was to undermine the Revolution. "I apprehend our Path is plain, to take Care the publick Interest does not suffer in the Justle. In the Course of Events, the Enemy have become possessed of this Intelligence. It is publickly talk'd both in New York & Philada. that our leading military Characters are hostile to each other, & they draw no small Degree of Consolation from the Circumstance." Then Reed excoriated the "irruption." "The Characters of Men are too delicate to discuss on Paper," he insisted (while still going on at considerable length), but the entire business of the Canadian expedition "must wound, & very sensibly too, the Man with whom while possessed of supreme military Powers it is our Duty as Members of Congress to be on the most harmonious Terms." Then a darker fear: "If it should prove a Part of a systematical Plan to lessen a great Character, by drawing off the necessary Supplies of Arms & Provisons, & render his Exertions feeble & ineffectual," even a success in Canada would mean little if the main army suffered. But Reed considered a northern success unlikely, and that "by attempting to support an Army here, & carry on an Expedition there, we starve & fail in both[.]" In that case "we shall never forgive ourselves or be forgiven by others." He urged Smith to do everything he could to abort the invasion, and he wanted "Those who are bold enough to think of a Change" of generals "to reflect upon these Circumstances." Until they could find a "superior Character"—a better general—Reed thought everyone "bound by every Principle of Honour, Interest, & Gratitude to discourage every Attempt to lessen his [Washington's] Character, & weaken or counteract his Measures. If there should be any such System formed as I have hinted, &

any farther Marks of it appear, let me intreat you, my dear Sir, to oppose it with your best Interests, you can never serve your Country more effectually."

Reed closed with a final and distinctly unflattering observation on the board: "As I have never known the Powers, & Duties of the Board of War, I confess myself very incompetent, to judge of the Nature & Extent of the Evils, which will flow from Division between it and the Commanders of our Armies, but it seems pretty clear that its Influence & Utility must be very limited, if the publick Cause will not be much injured by such a Conflict."[92]

Reed's stridency took Smith aback. While Smith conceded that recent congressional actions appeared "injurious" to Washington, he responded that the "zealous" patriotism of the delegates "almost forbid any suspicions of undue motives." Yet Smith conceded it was necessary to "prevent the body of the people," especially Pennsylvanians, from "losing their confidence in the Commander in Chief"—a fairly clear indication that confidence was waning. And Smith added that the roots of much of the trouble lay with the Board of War's procurement agents—the superintendents—whose often high-handed conduct had caused such offense among Pennsylvania authorities. Reed was in accord with his friend on this point, but he never lost his mistrust of the board's motives.[93]

Reed's letter was in fact a concise summary of the state of the Cabal in late January and early February. The "Irruption into Canada," as he saw it, was a capstone of a consistent series of events that threatened Washington's authority as commander in chief. It is hard to disagree. In aggregate the fight over the inspector generalship, the board's assertion of its authority in commissary and quartermaster functions, and finally its decision to move into actual military operations constituted a march to command—and all at the expense of the ostensible commander in chief. We can debate whether or not all of this comprised a conspiracy of some sort, whether it was a nefarious collaboration to bring down or force the resignation of the Virginian—Carlo Botta's train of deliberate "disgusts." That point matters only to those who insist on seeing the Cabal strictly in terms of some underhanded plot by devious individuals. What really mattered was the grave reality of the threat—with or without a conspiracy—to Washington's command authority. Was the title of commander in chief to be meaningless?

Washington saw matters in precisely these terms. The question now is: What was he going to do about it?

PART 3

END GAME

~wherein the Cabal crumbles before a sustained and skillful counterattack from an aroused General Washington and those loyal to him; and

~wherein scores are settled and a measure of vengeance is wreaked upon Washington's critics, and the general's place in the army and the Revolution is assured; and

~wherein the events and importance of the Cabal are assessed and observations made on Washington as a political general—a commander in chief—and how the Cabal shaped his subsequent role in history.

SEVEN

COUNTERATTACK

The Politics of Patience and the Collapse of the Cabal

I can assure you that no person ever heard me drop an expression that had a tendency to resignation. The same principles that led me to embark in the opposition to the arbitrary claims of Great Britn operate with additional force at this day; nor is it my desire to withdraw my Services while they are considered of importance in the present contest.—George Washington to William Gordon, February 15, 1778[1]

Proceed, heaven-guided Chief, nor be dismay'd
At foreign myriads, or domestic foes,
(The best have foes, and foes evince their worth.)
—William Livingston as "Hortentious," April 1, 1778[2]

DURING THE FIRST TWO MONTHS of 1778 the Board of War, with the acquiescence of Congress, was having its way. While the driving forces of the Cabal were Mifflin and Gates, Pickering was in no frame of mind to differ with their plans. Neither were such delegates as William Duer and Francis Lightfoot Lee, who occasionally sat on the board in the absence of the ill Joseph Trumbull (whose absence turned out to be permanent). The Board of War—the War Office—had maneuvered skillfully as it inserted itself into key facets of the army's daily operations. The commanding general could think what he liked, but for the time being he was on the defensive.

Yet Washington remained committed to the patriot cause and to his job, and frankly he saw the two as inseparable. Whatever his critics supposed, the general sincerely believed he *was* the man to see the war through; he also considered any threat to his authority as commander in chief more than a personal slight—it was a threat to the final success of American arms and thus to the Revolution itself. He did not lack for allies in the army and in Congress, but with few exceptions at this point his congressional friends were not vocal. That would change, but as Henry Laurens put it so delicately, for the present those friends lacked "the honour to defend" and were mostly "Candle Snuffers . . . & Mutes."[3]

Washington was on a rough political road, made no easier by the demands of active military operations and the struggle to provision his army. Over January and February the "disgusts" had been frequent, but he never thought of quitting. In January a letter from a relatively new friend, the Boston reverend and future historian of the Revolution William Gordon, warned the general of rumored moves in Congress to replace him. Washington professed disinterest, which we know wasn't true. He was very concerned although he would not publicly admit as much; but he was candid with Gordon on another score. "I can assure you that no person ever heard me drop an expression that had a tendency to resignation," he told the reverend. "The same principles that led me to embark in the opposition to the arbitrary claims of Great Britn operate with additional force at this day; nor is it my desire to withdraw my Services while they are considered of importance in the present contest." He knew there were those in Congress who wanted to replace him and that they were "endeavouring to effect a change." He also knew their favorite was Gates. But Washington would resign only if the "voice" of the public called for it but "not that of faction."[4] The general never considered a surrender in the field, nor would he in the political arena. He would fight back.

WHILE WASHINGTON pondered his situation he consciously chose not to confront the Board of War head-on. He had done so with Gates and Conway in "the Letter" contretemps, and he certainly had thrown those gentlemen on the defensive. He had done so, however, only after patiently enduring long weeks of criticism and only when he thought he had a clear advantage over Gates and Conway. Fighting with subordinate generals was one thing, but fighting with his political masters was entirely another. The commanding general was averse to doing anything that might lead to an open breach with Congress. This was a matter of principle as well as practicality. Washington would do nothing that smacked of disrespect for civilian authority, and he relied on Congress for financial support and the legal basis for his own authority. He knew he had skeptics among the delegates, as well as some out-right antagonists, but any sort of showdown with them would be ill advised at a time when the army needed all the support it could find. Besides, he had the Committee at Camp to deal with, and over February and into the spring he would plead his case with its members. In the meantime he elected to be patient—*somewhat.*

Patience does not imply inactivity or any lack of concern. If Washington sought to avoid any personal clash with Congress and considered an "above-the-fray" posture the best public course, he was not willing to leave the field to his critics. Quite the opposite: The general was more than willing to let his partisans carry the battle in his behalf. And given the intensity of what transpired it is inconceivable to think the general was unaware of the political war his military subordinates and other friends declared on Mifflin and Gates.

Over January 1778 the political atmosphere in York and at Valley Forge had turned increasingly passionate. The Conway-Gates correspondence remained a point of contention—that ever-present background of animosity—and following the inspector general and Conway episodes Washington's partisans turned up the heat. It is difficult to date the advent of the truly angry fire directed at the Board of War with any precision. While it gradually became a public matter, the Conway letter affair largely involved personal communications among a limited (albeit growing) circle of men. The inspectorship mess widened the circle as more individuals reacted to events. But the board's move into logistics and actual military operations was a tipping point; it confirmed the expanding influence of the board—"mission creep," if you will—at the general's expense. Washington's army and civilian allies, already leery of Mifflin, were now absolutely convinced the Board of War, if not moving to force Washington's resignation or relief, was at least out to usurp his command authority. Thus the period between January and March 1778 saw an astonishing level of communications among the general's associates warning of plots and urging them to rally in Washington's defense. And we need to remind ourselves that if Washington's associates thought they saw a conspiracy afoot, in fact they were reacting to real events. The threat of an administrative coup was a figment of no one's imagination.

There was a consistency to these concerns, and they were not the fulminations of frenzied political partisans. In early January, probably on or about the second, Major John Clark, Jr. became convinced that Washington's command genuinely was at risk.[5] Clark was not an ordinary officer. A Pennsylvania Continental, he was wounded early in the war and unable to return to active field duty, although for a time he served as an aide to Nathanael Greene. Thereafter Clark became involved in patriot intelligence activities, but how he drifted into the murky doings of espionage remains obscure. Exactly how he met Washington is equally unclear; but the general, who functioned as his own spymaster, somehow decided Clark was the man to organize intelligence operations in and around British-occupied Philadelphia. This Clark did with success, running a spy ring and reporting regularly to Washington on enemy activities.[6] Clark also had his ear to the ground among patriots, and there is no reason to doubt the sincerity and veracity of his belief that support for the commander in chief was eroding in Congress and among some rebel leaders.

Others were equally sure, or at least were concerned enough to make enquiries. On January 4 Brigadier General Henry Knox, chief of artillery and a member of Washington's inner circle, was one of them. He was aware of the rumblings of discontent over Washington's performance, but in early January he may have learned something more concrete. We have no idea whether Clark had reported his fears to headquarters, but timing suggests he may have and that news from Clark prompted Knox to action. Knox did what Washington would not or felt he should not do himself. The brigadier wrote directly to a member of Congress and asked point-blank if there was a movement against the commander in chief. Knox sent his letter to Massachusetts delegate Elbridge Gerry, an old acquaintance, probably not knowing Gerry had made some less-than-flattering observations on the commanding general in late 1777.[7] The artillery chief came right to the point: He told Gerry that no one else in the service enjoyed a level of confidence approaching that accorded Washington. Yet Knox feared "intrigue, misinformation, caprice, and unsuccessful efforts combined"—implying there had been efforts—might have led "good men" to doubt the general. Congress needed to know, he advised Gerry, that "every military character on this continent, taken collectively, vanishes before him; and he is not only a soldier, but a patriot in the fullest sense of the word."[8] Only a brigadier very worried for the fate of his superior would have written such a letter, and Knox was no needless worrier.

Knox waited just over a month, until February 7, for Gerry's response. It was not completely reassuring. The congressman told the brigadier the delegates supported the commander in chief and insisted there was no evidence of a plan to "injure the Reputation of, or remove from office, the Gentleman hinted at [Washington] in your Favour of Jany the 4th." This was true enough, at least from Gerry's perspective. But this leads back to the question of definitions: What constituted a "plan" or conspiracy? Gerry skirted—in fact he entirely failed to mention—Congress's support for the Board of War's various initiatives. He never touched on the attempt to create an inspector general independent of Washington's command or on the board's efforts to assert control of commissary and quartermaster operations. He never discussed Gates's move into troop deployments or the "Irruption into Canada."[9] These were certainly among the events that triggered Knox's concern; but with Gerry they either failed to register as anything inimical to Washington or, because the board's actions carried the imprimatur of Congress, the Massachusetts delegate refused to see them as any sort of underhanded political maneuver. "Dissensions"? "Party Spirit"? Gerry saw plenty of them—but in the army and not in Congress. He went so far as to warn Knox to vigilance against any "artful General" who might threaten the cause. The Massachusetts delegate defended congressional handling of the thorny issues of rank and promotions, and he specifically condemned disputes within the officer corps over these matters, lamenting the army's "mistaken Notions of Honor." In effect Gerry had delivered a classic republican lecture (it bordered on a polemic) on military threats to liberty.[10] If Knox responded to Gerry his letter has not survived, but we can imagine the brigadier's reaction. Something like: "Gee, thanks a lot."

We can only assume Knox shared Gerry's response with Washington, but it probably brought little comfort. In fact the January angst evident in Knox's letter not only continued, but news from other quarters directly contradicted Gerry's message. On January 22, Washington received a message from a fellow Virginian, delegate Joseph Jones. This is a letter we already have seen in chapter 4; now we need to recall its ominous alert to the activities of Mifflin and Gates. It was during a committee mission to camp (then at Whitemarsh) that Jones learned of the army's suspicions about the War Office.[11] Upon his return to York he found those suspicions confirmed. The reconstituted Board of War was on the march, and the Virginia delegate feared its direction. In fact he even considered postponing his departure from Congress so that he "might possibly be of some use in obstructing or endeavouring at least to prevent the mischevous consequences of those base Acts and machinations that are but too prevalent among some people." And "some people" prominently included Mifflin and Gates. Unlike Gerry, who had seen nothing in York inimical to Washington, Jones now saw more than enough. He had found the Cabal. Jones was sure that whatever Mifflin and Gates were up to eventually would "redound to their own disgrace."[12] Nevertheless Jones felt the situation merited a prompt warning to the commander in chief, and like others he had identified the Board of War as the source of the Cabal.

Another warning, almost two weeks earlier than Jones's, indicated news of the Cabal had spread well beyond York and Valley Forge. On January 6, Doctor James Craik, Washington's personal physician and friend, sent his truly alarming message to headquarters. This was the letter, already cited in these pages, Craik sent after travelling from Valley Forge to his home in Port Tobacco, Maryland. Like Jones's letter, it is worth a longer look. Craik warned the general, based on what he claimed was good authority, "that a Strong Faction was forming Against you in the New board of War and in the Congress." Craik had heard the same story at various stops along the way from Valley Forge, and he believed it was "pretty general over the Country." No one could offer details, but there was a consensus that "Eastern & Southern Members" were involved, including Richard Henry Lee. Then Craik zeroed in on Mifflin, and here he did provide specifics (and please pardon his spelling):

> G——l M——n in the New Board of War was a very Active person. This Last I am affraid is too true, I think I have reason to beleive him not your Freind from many Circumstances—The Method they are taking is by holding up General G——s to the people and making them beleive that you have had three or four times the number of the Enemy, and have done nothing. that Philadelphia was given up by your Mismanagement and that you have missed many opportunities of defeating the Enemy, and many other things as ungenerous & unjust—These are the low Artifices they are making use of—It is said that they dare not appear openly as your Enemy, but that the New Board of War is Composed of Such leading men as will throw Such obstecles and difficulties in your way as to force you to Resign.[13]

While Carlo Botta never cited Craik's letter, it is difficult to believe he hadn't seen a copy, for it stated plainly the historian's belief in board-manufactured "disgusts" as the key to forcing Washington from command.

In fingering Mifflin and the Board of War Craik was both right and wrong. Certainly the doctor was right placing Mifflin, with the acquiescence of the board and Congress, at the center of the Cabal—or "party," or "faction," or "junto" or whatever accusatory term contemporaries chose to use. But it was less sure that Mifflin's goal was to get rid of the general; the Pennsylvanian was smart enough to realize such a goal was probably political overreach. To make Washington truly subordinate to the board, however, did seem attainable; and the board's actions left little doubt Mifflin was maneuvering to bring it about. Again we can use the term "administrative coup"—the effort to establish the Board of War as the policy-making body of the patriot war effort. Mifflin therefore became the lightning rod for counterattacks. Even as Washington's allies vilified him, however, the former quartermaster still had plenty of friends. Desperate army commissary officials still contacted him seeking help in arranging supply shipments.[14] As the days of January rolled by Mifflin remained a man to reckon with.

The Pennsylvanian's critics, however, were gathering steam; and they were persistent and well placed. Lieutenant Colonel John Laurens, son of Henry Laurens and a popular member of Washington's military "family," had named Mifflin as the "head" of "a certain party, formed against the present Commander in chief." On January 8, the young Laurens even conveyed a belief held at headquarters that Gates was only a stooge of Mifflin: "only the instrument of more dangerous and inveterate persons."[15] John knew he could count on his father to defend the general in York (indeed, as we have seen, Henry Laurens already was doing so), and it is unlikely Washington was unaware of his young aide's efforts. Like Knox, Lieutenant Colonel Laurens was doing what Washington felt he could not or should not—meddling directly in the political theater.

It is *very* unlikely the general missed what another of his aides was doing. Tench Tilghman was the scion of a well-to-do Maryland family, and the Tilghman name was a fixture in Maryland society. Tench was educated in Philadelphia where he subsequently went into the mercantile business with his uncle. He was an ardent patriot and early in the war he served the cause in various political and military capacities.[16] Older than most of Washington's aides, Tilghman was thirty-two years old in mid-1776 when he joined Washington's staff as a volunteer aide-de-camp. He brought a level of maturity to the general's headquarters, and Washington frequently entrusted him with delicate missions. It was Tilghman the general sent to confer personally with state governors and other senior patriots on matters of emergency army supply, and Tilghman the general trusted to deal with clandestine intelligence operatives.[17] The Marylander was one of the commanding general's longest-serving aides and was thoroughly loyal.

Tilghman harbored an implacable animosity toward Washington's critics, and Mifflin and Gates attracted his special contempt. Over January and February he targeted them in a vigorous letter-writing campaign that featured scorching denunciations of the two generals. He warned Pennsylvania delegate Robert Morris "of a party forming against" the commander in chief, and Mifflin's "unaccountable behavior" left no doubt that the former quartermaster general was "at the bottom of it." The British "have already heard of and exult at this appearance of division and faction among ourselves," he warned, and he added that Washington was feeling the pressure but felt he could not publicly respond without "publishing to the world" the divisions in the American cause. Thus it was up to the general's friends, Tilghman told Morris, "to support him against the malicious attacks of those who can have no reason to wish his removal but a desire to fill his place." He asked Morris to keep an eye on things in York and confront any of the general's critics. Challenge them, Tilghman urged the congressman, to move openly against Washington if they so desired, rather than pursue "this rascally method of calumniating behind the Curtain."[18]

This was strong stuff, and Tilghman's message was much the same to another influential friend, Pennsylvania militia brigadier John Cadwalader. Cadwalader, with his brother Lambert, was a successful Philadelphia merchant before the war and another early patriot. While Lambert served in the Continental Line (he was captured at Fort Washington in 1776), John twice refused a Continental brigadier's commission. He was an effective militia commander, however, and fought in several significant actions in the Middle Theater. Cadwalader was one of Washington's favorite militia generals and a fierce partisan of the commander in chief[19] (and in that guise he will figure prominently later in these pages). Tilghman sent Cadwalader a stinging condemnation of Mifflin. At Valley Forge not much was happening "in the military line," he informed Cadwalader, although "in the underhand political [scene] there is a deal of juggling. But I trust the storm will break upon the Heads of those who raise it. Great pains are taking to swell the Character" of Gates and "to depreciate that of our worthy General. Who is at the bottom of this," Tilghman confided, "you I dare say will easily guess"—an unmistakable reference to Mifflin. He condemned Mifflin for leaving the quartermaster department "at a critical time," and he even mistakenly thought Mifflin was the author of the "De Lisle" letters praising Gates (the reader will recall that "De Lisle" was actually New Jersey governor William Livingston). Like John Laurens, the Maryland officer went so far as to claim Gates was just a dupe—"a puppet"—in Mifflin's hands and that Mifflin's ambition lay at the bottom of the "damned faction." He urged Cadwalader to broadcast the word and insisted that the glare of public notoriety was the best "way to stop the poison."[20]

Cadwalader did his best. He sent off a very similar letter—in fact it was a virtual duplicate of Tilghman's letter—to New York governor George Clinton. Clinton, as the reader will recall, already had received Alexander Hamilton's message of similar import after Conway's appointment as inspector general. Cadwalader also dispatched a short letter warning of "Dissentions among ourselves"—certainly a reference to the Cabal—in a note to Benjamin Franklin in Paris.[21] Like Washington, Mifflin had made important enemies.

Other Washington allies continued to focus on the Board of War. In Virginia Benjamin Harrison—the former delegate and member of the original board who had warned Robert Morris to "*Be Ware of your Board of War*"—continued in the same vein. Harrison had served in Congress with North Carolina Signer Joseph Hewes, and he sent Hewes a similar alert. He had it on good authority, he cautioned, that partisans "both in and out of Congress" were maneuvering against Washington in favor of "the Saratoga Hero." "I give greater credit to this, when I consider who they are that compose our Board of War, men who are most of them avowedly his [Washington's] enemies." "In the name of wonders," the exasperated Virginian asked, "how came it thus constituted?" He feared that "the good and virtuous of you" had been "taken in," and he predicted "very great confusion" for America if wise men failed to keep their "eyes and ears" open.[22]

In Congress late January found Robert Morris writing letters as well. "For Heavens Sake & for the sake of your Country & of Justice," he urged Richard Peters, newly seated on the Board of War, to do whatever he could to "thwart unworthy attacks on Worthy Characters." Morris assured Peters that Washington's personal character was immune to all assaults, but he warned against attacks on the general's "Military Character." There Washington's record left him vulnerable, and Morris wanted a united front in the commanding general's defense. The "first Man in this *World*" deserved all of their support in raising an army sufficient "to shine with that Splendour he Merits." The general's enemies, he declaimed, "must then hide their Heads & silently witness the Triumph of that Virtue which first excited their Envy." For a hard-boiled financier and businessman Morris could wield a rather florid pen, and he left the subject with a promise to do all he could to foster Washington's success.[23] Thus Washington could count on Robert Morris, and by late January the general also knew the sentiments of Henry Laurens and Joseph Jones. It seems the "Mutes" in Congress were beginning to pay attention.

Surveying the political scene from Valley Forge, where he served with the Committee at Camp, Gouverneur Morris took up the cudgels for the commander in chief. By early March, after more than a month of committee service, he had seen enough to suspect the worst of Gates and Mifflin, and he also was spreading the word. "A Set of Scoundrels," he wrote New York chancellor Robert R. Livingston, were "very busy in an Attempt to ruin" Washington. Morris claimed Gates and Mifflin were leading the effort, and he lamented that fellow New York delegate William Duer had fallen in with them.[24]

Unbeknownst to Morris, however, on the same day Duer also had sent a letter to the chancellor. We have met New Yorker William Duer: He was the no-nonsense patriot businessman who saw the young Morris as something akin to an "Elephant in War," unpredictable and liable to trample anyone. Duer was no novice in military affairs. He had served on the original Board of War, and he sat on the new board as it underwent reorganization. Given this experience Duer thought he had a realistic understanding of the army's problems, and he minced no words in identifying them. He warned Livingston that the Continental Line was infected with "Party" spirit and that it was inactive and undisciplined. Its administrative affairs were a mess. He doubted things could be put right any time soon.[25] What Livingston thought of all of this is anyone's guess; but Duer's letter, if nothing else, seemingly confirmed Morris's report of Duer's alignment with Mifflin and Gates—the usual suspects (long before Claude Rains ever uttered the term).

The timing of this letter-writing campaign was no coincidence. Spanning early January to roughly mid-March, it jibed perfectly with the immediate aftermath of the inspector general affair and the Board of War's subsequent initiatives. The Morrises (Robert and Gouverneur), Harrison, Tilghman, the Laurenses (Henry and John), Hamilton, Knox, Major Clark, Cadwalader, and others had reacted to real events—not mere rumors. And it is noteworthy that they had done so in *exactly* the period the board had mounted its most serious challenges to Washington's authority. The significance of the timing is unavoidable.

Their collective counterfire began to hit home. Conway was convinced he was the victim of a "cabal" seated in Washington's headquarters, where he certainly had no friends. Indeed, Mifflin and Gates were not oblivious to the gathering wave of criticism, and they liked it no better than Washington did the barbs and "disgusts" directed his way. The two officers could be excused for thinking there was an organized cabal out to get *them*—and in effect there was. Lieutenant Colonel Robert Troup, one of Gates's aides during the Saratoga campaign, warned Gates against just such a plot.[26] (This was before, we should note, Troup had learned of Gates's belief in Wilkinson's concocted story of Troup's role in leaking "the Letter.") Feeling the heat, at one point in late January Mifflin left York in a huff. According to his cousin Jonathan Mifflin, he was incensed over increasing talk linking him to efforts to oust the commander in chief. After cooling off at his Reading home Mifflin eventually returned to duty on the board, heatedly disclaiming all hostile intentions toward the commander in chief. In the meantime Pickering complained that Mifflin's absence impeded quartermaster operations.[27]

Meanwhile, at Valley Forge the Board of War generally was in bad odor with Washington's friends. Richard Peters, who as we have seen was ambivalent about the existence of serious opposition to the commanding general, found out just how bad. Peters had no sooner taken his seat on the board when rumors circulated linking him to Washington's detractors. Colonel Daniel Morgan then challenged him to a duel, and the colonel—the celebrated rifleman and a genuine hero at Saratoga—backed off only when a disgusted Peters accepted the challenge.[28] Unless one counts the laughable Gates-Wilkinson encounter, this was one of two affairs of honor born of the Cabal (as we will see, Cadwalader would later challenge Major General Lee). But Major John Clark was all for more. He wrote Nathanael Greene that threats of a "few Oz's [ounces] of Gunpowder . . . will answer a good purpose" in dealing with Washington's critics.[29] As satisfying as taking a shot at, say, a Lovell, Rush, or Mifflin, may have been for Clark, the major of course was wrong. The Cabal, or whatever one wishes to call it, had tempers on edge as never before, and patriots shooting at one another would have done nothing for the cause.

WHILE LETTERS FLEW and tempers flared, Washington and the Committee at Camp dug into their work at Valley Forge—seemingly unconcerned with the literary furor elsewhere, much less with reports of partisans resorting to the *code duello*. After an organizational meeting and its initial sit-down with Washington in the final days of January, the committee hit its working stride in February. Early in the month, based on its observations and conferences with the commander in chief, it began compiling and forwarding reports to the rest of Congress. If Washington ever had entertained doubts about the attitudes or political inclinations of the committee members, any such worries quickly evaporated. The general worked easily with the politicos, and as their relationship warmed Washington found the key to countering the Cabal. He was always scrupulous about military deference to civilian authority. But now he had a *choice* of civilian authorities: the Board of War, the executive body tasked with supporting military affairs for Congress and Washington's titular superior; Congress as a whole, the source of his commission and the legal foundation of his command and of the board's authority; or the Committee at Camp, the select group of delegates he now dealt with personally. Again, as he did while fending off Conway as inspector general, Washington elected to bypass the board whenever possible. Nor would he work directly with congressmen sitting in York. Instead he would carry the fight through Congress's own Committee at Camp—his immediate guests and increasingly (as events would prove) his reliable allies.

Indeed, Washington virtually ignored the board. During the committee's months at Valley Forge he exchanged only some thirty-five letters (most have not survived) with Gates. Of the extant messages only two or three dealt with logistical matters, and it is easy to suspect that one of these in particular was meant to drive home to the board the army's desperation in even the smallest matters of supply. In this instance Washington requested a supply of writing paper and reminded Gates, a former adjutant general, of how vital paper was to army administration. (Gates obligingly forwarded a shipment.) Most letters, however, touched on other matters. There was Conway's troublesome letter to Gates, the passport affair, prisoner-of-war exchanges, the status of Burgoyne's captured army, the Canadian "irruption," and mundane administrative minutia.[30] Over the same period a survey of Washington's headquarters staff papers reveals a complete absence of direct communication with the War Office.[31] It is abundantly clear that Washington was refusing to acknowledge himself as subordinate to the board in the patriot chain of command. And if the board had failed to consult with Washington as it reached important decisions, the general returned the favor as he worked with the Committee at Camp.

Washington's counterattack (for that is what it was) bore fruit relatively quickly. His first success came in contesting the Mifflin plan for the reorganization of the quartermaster department. After adopting the plan to divide the department, on February 7 Congress sent word to Valley Forge asking the Committee at Camp to suggest names for the new quartermaster generalship. Curiously—in fact *very* curiously—that letter somehow got lost. Laurens had sent the note via a "Messenger Barry"; but Barry, whoever he was, brought back no reply from the committee, and there never was any explanation of who received the message from Barry or what might have happened to it. Laurens waited until the twentieth to follow up. He noted fears among some delegates that the message had miscarried (as it mysteriously had), so he enclosed another copy of the February 5 resolution—the Mifflin plan—and asked that the committee send the requested list of nominees "by the return of the present Messenger."[32] The committee replied the same day, acknowledging receipt of Laurens's letter and its enclosures but including no list of candidates. Instead it promised to convey its own "Sentiments" on the proposed quartermaster reorganization in a separate communication. Cagily, however, it did not say when.[33] There was no hint in this that the "Sentiments" of the committee might not jibe with the Mifflin plan adopted in Congress—but in fact that was exactly what was brewing. And one suspects the committee was stalling.

For Washington the lapse of almost two weeks was fortuitous. While Congress awaited an answer to its original message, the Committee at Camp and Washington had been waiting for Congress to signal its response to the committee's recommendation of Schuyler as quartermaster general. With communications at a temporary standstill, the general continued discussions with committee members without having to deal with the February 5 resolution—which raises the question of what *really* happened to "Messenger Barry's" dispatch. Was it conveniently lost? One doubts that any committee member would have deliberately ignored (or worse) a dispatch from fellow congressional delegates. But one of Washington's subordinate officers? Whatever the case, enjoying this gift of time Washington steadily led the committee away from any accommodation with the Mifflin plan.

Indeed, relations between the committee and the board were not the best. Joseph Reed already was on record: He was furious at the board's effort to preempt Pennsylvania's procurement efforts. He blasted board members as "a Sett of Gentlemen in avowed Opposition to the Authority of the State" who were exerting "an arbitrary Power over the Property of the People."[34] Reed was reacting to what he perceived as disrespect for the laws of his home state, but other committee members were no happier. In fact by February 22, at about the same time it received Laurens's communication of the twentieth, the committee already had had enough of the quartermaster conundrum. Without any further communication on the matter with Congress or the Board of War, it "Closed the business of the Quarter Master Genl. Department." And in so doing the committee slammed the door on the Mifflin plan.[35]

The committee damned Mifflin's reforms at length. "In Concert with the General," the delegation concluded that dividing the quartermaster department "into four capital Branches" was, in so many words, nonsense. "Without a controuling Chief" the proposed departmental divisions "must necessarily involve Interference with each other," and Washington would have to sort out the resulting "Confusion" and "Controversies." The arrangement would force the commander in chief again to be his own quartermaster; and it would lead to wasteful cost and peculation as "each of these [four] Officers must necessarily be empowered to draw publick Money, & of Consequence, that the Chance of Frauds, & Amount of Expenditures will be greatly increased by so many separate Departments."[36] Consequently the committee had something completely different in mind. Noting "that it is upon the Characters of Men principally, & not upon Paper Systems that our Success must depend. We propose Sir to have a Quarter Master General, & two Assistant Qr. Masters General appointed by Congress." These officers would be allowed one percent commissions on all purchases. These commissions would annoy republican purists, but the committee knew they could hardly expect to attract capable appointees on any other terms. And the man they wanted in charge as quartermaster general was Major General Nathanael Greene, who would be responsible for the entire quartermaster operation *and* would be on the senior staff of the commander in chief. Unity of command—it was pure General Washington. The committee notified Congress of these "Sentiments" in a long letter to Laurens of February 25.[37]

In just days Mifflin's plan unraveled completely. In York, not yet having received the committee's letter of the twenty-fifth, the delegates became justifiably alarmed at the growing picture of quartermaster and commissary departments completely adrift. At the Board of War Timothy Pickering admitted as much. He reported continued bickering between the board's superintendents and Pennsylvania purchasing commissioners, and he longed for the arrival of fellow board appointee, former commissary general Joseph Trumbull. Trumbull's knowledge of the "Commissary's business," Pickering hoped, would put things right. But Trumbull was sick at home in Connecticut (and in the end he never took his seat).

Quartermaster affairs were no better. Mifflin knew more about quartermaster operations than anyone else, Pickering lamented, but with Mifflin's temporary absence the department was in disarray. "By such means," he warned, "public business, which demands instant attention . . . is postponed" and the rebel cause threatened with ruin.[38] Congress knew as much. It had supported all of the Board of War's recommendations for commissary and quartermaster reforms—and had done so in full knowledge of the poor relations between Gates and Mifflin and the commander in chief—and now the delegates had to backtrack.

Not quite giving up on the Mifflin reforms, the delegates did decide to cut some red tape. On the twenty-first they again sent "Messenger Barry" to Valley Forge with a new resolution, this one authorizing the committee to skip sending a list of nominees for the quartermaster generalship. The committee, this time "in conjunction with General Washington" (*finally* Congress decided the general ought to be involved), was to go ahead and actually appoint a quartermaster general and the heads of the other quartermaster branches. It was a real concession from politicos who jealously guarded their prerogatives in appointment matters. While on this occasion Barry's dispatch found a safe arrival—perhaps because it was more to Washington's or the committee's liking?—it made no difference. No names from the committee or appointments from Congress were forthcoming.

Instead, the arrival of the committee's "Sentiments" in York led to an even more significant and startling change. On March 2, having thoroughly digested the committee's ideas, Congress repealed its resolution of February 5. In its place the delegates adopted the committee's—and Washington's—substitute plan for the quartermaster department, including the one percent commissions. The new plan specifically provided for a strong quartermaster general as a member of Washington's senior staff. Greene was named quartermaster general, retaining his major generalship in the line. Greene's assistant quartermasters general were both sound men: Colonel John Cox, a Philadelphia merchant and owner of a major iron works in New Jersey, and Charles Pettit, a prominent New Jersey lawyer, politician, and secretary to New Jersey governor William Livingston. Greene was to appoint all additional department personnel.[39] All told the fight over the quartermaster department had taken just under a month, and for Washington it was a complete victory—his second against the Board of War after beating back Conway's appointment as inspector general. Gates was finding Washington a wilier adversary than Burgoyne.

All of this was galling for Thomas Mifflin. His plans for quartermaster operations were frankly ill conceived for all of the reasons the Committee at Camp noted. But his plan was not ill intentioned; Mifflin meant it for the best. For better or for worse the Pennsylvania patriot had given the matter considerable thought. Given his antagonistic relationship with the commander in chief, however, nothing Mifflin proposed was going to find favor at camp. To add insult to injury (although the insult was unintended), when Congress repealed his plan it compounded Mifflin's disappointment by ordering him to draw up a report on the status of quartermaster preparations for the 1778 campaign. The report was to note what stores were available, in what quantities, and where they were—and he was to deliver the document to his archenemy, the new quartermaster general, Nathanael Greene.[40]

As REPORTS FROM the Committee at Camp filtered back to York, it became increasingly clear that the committee members—who, as we recall, comprised about a quarter of the Congress—were lining up with Washington on virtually every issue. This became evident as the committee continued its focus on logistics and specifically now on commissary operations. In early March the committee sent Congress a lengthy report detailing the quantities and locations of provisions necessary to maintain the troops over the next several months. The delegates considered the report over several days, and on March 13 they reacted dramatically. In a complete about-face, they passed a resolution striking directly at the board's recently granted authority in commissary affairs. In fact the resolution demolished that authority completely.[41]

Congress directed the board to implement the committee's report and to do so *not* through its own system of superintendents and separate magazines. Rather, purchasing and distribution functions were to revert to the army's established commissary departments and officers. In addition the new resolution restored the chain of command: The commissary general was to "be subject to the orders of the Commander in Chief," and he (the commissary general) would no longer be tied to the seat of Congress. He was to maintain an office and clerk in the neighborhood of Congress, but he was personally to "visit the armies and posts" and remain abreast of actual conditions in the field, something Buchanan had not done. The army would have considerable say in commissary purchases. Supplies considered substandard upon delivery could be reported to any Continental brigadier or major general; these officers were authorized to have deputy commissaries seize any such deliveries and auction them for the public account. The same resolution strengthened the authority of the commissary general of purchases, allowed the deputy commissaries commissions on all of their purchases, and gave them direct responsibility for their assistants. The War Office could still hire people to help the commissary department and would receive periodic reports on inventories and distributions, but its function now was to support—not *supplant*—commissary officials.[42] A week later Congress went further and specifically told the board to do nothing to interfere with Pennsylvania's procurement operations.[43] All of this was another and sweeping admission by the delegates that they had got it wrong in allowing the Board of War to take the lead in logistics matters.

The new resolution presaged the end of the hapless William Buchanan's tenure as commissary general of purchases. Everyone knew he had to go, and there was quick consensus that Washington's preferred candidate, Jeremiah Wadsworth of Connecticut, should replace him. It took a month to work out details with Wadsworth, but he came aboard in April and injected a new rigor into commissary operations. At the same time the delegates also directed Pennsylvania to leave future purchases of flour and wheat to the established commissary department and to submit records of previous purchases to Wadsworth.[44] With new funding, and working in tandem with Greene, Wadsworth soon had his department on the mend and army supply operations along with it. Logistics was again fully in the hands of the army's formal departments; and while supply problems persisted, by early spring the crisis was past and the army was reasonably well provisioned. Credit the Committee at Camp—and the commander in chief.

THE BOARD'S BIGGEST SETBACK, however, came in the area of strategic policy: Gates's brainchild, the planned "irruption into Canada," came to naught. It failed on a number of counts, not the least of which was a balky marquis Lafayette. When offered the command the young Frenchman initially was delighted; he fairly oozed enthusiasm (it was Lafayette's style) when he wrote back to France that he was to command an army. Gates, however, who certainly saw Lafayette as a figurehead calculated to attract French-Canadian support, was no fool. He was not about to entrust such an important mission to a relatively untried young officer; no doubt he saw the experienced Conway as the actual guiding hand of the operation. Upon reflection, however, Lafayette interpreted the appointment of Conway as his second-in-command as a deliberate affront to Washington. It was anything but. In fact, some in Congress saw sending Conway north as a way to get the nettlesome major general out of Washington's hair.[45]

Still, Lafayette was adamant. Traveling to York, he took his complaint directly to Congress. Instead of Conway he wanted Major General Alexander McDougall, then in the Hudson Highlands; or, if McDougall's health was not up to the job, Lafayette wanted Kalb. Moreover, he refused to serve under the authority of the Board of War. He insisted that all orders come through Washington as commander in chief. In late January he wrote Henry Laurens that he wanted his expedition considered a detachment from the commander in chief's army and himself as "an officer under his [Washington's] immediate command."[46] The petulant twenty-year-old threatened to go home, taking other French officers with him, if he didn't get his way. It was hardly a reflection of the military deference to civilian authority Washington usually preferred (although as we soon will see, in this case a cagey Washington was actually complicit in Lafayette's conduct).

Lafayette was no less truculent when on January 30 he arrived in York to meet with Congress. Henry Laurens, one of the only delegates—if not *the* only delegate—to oppose the Canadian venture from the start, reported finding a very angry young Frenchman. The marquis had "discovered a noble resentment for the affront offered to his Commander General Washington, to whom his appointment had not been intimated by Congress." Lafayette insisted that his appointment, and those of other senior officers, "should be through his General."[47] On the thirty-first the marquis had dinner with the Board of War at Gates's headquarters. Mifflin did not attend (he had just left in a sulk for his home in Reading), but in addition to Gates Lafayette dined with Richard Peters, then still secretary to the board and soon to take his seat as a member, and with Francis Lightfoot Lee and William Duer, two holdovers from the old board. According to the Frenchman's (often unreliable) *Memoirs*, at some point during the meal he offered a toast to Washington, which supposedly caused some of the board members to fidget—but they all drank it.[48]

There is a ring of the apocryphal in this story. No other contemporary mentioned it, and Lafayette wrote of it only decades after the war; but over the course of the evening Lafayette did convince the board of his loyalty to Washington. He also reiterated his concerns over command arrangements for the "irruption"; once again he threatened to go home unless he could have McDougall or Kalb as his second-in-command. Except for Duer, Lafayette found the group sympathetic, and the board subsequently reported favorably to Congress on Lafayette's requests.[49] But, perhaps leery of conceding too much to such a staunch Washington loyalist, the board also altered its earlier instructions to the marquis. Instead of an expedition to attach Canada to the Revolution, Gates now mentioned the "irruption" only as a "mere incursion or ravage"—that is, a raid.[50] Thus under the reconfigured mission Lafayette, even if successful, would not be attaching a new colony to the American cause.

If the dinner was a reasonably cordial affair—except, of course, for Lafayette's remembered toast to the commander in chief (if it actually occurred)—there was still plenty of tension in York. Many delegates must have turned purple at the Frenchman's conduct. If any other officer had made such "my way or no way" threats Congress very properly would have called his bluff. But Lafayette was a special case. He was a (if not *the*) key to the French alliance, the link to critical French diplomatic, material, and direct military aide. The delegates tried all sorts of arguments to bring the marquis around. "A good deal of struggle was made to elude the Marquis' demands," a seemingly amused Laurens recalled.[51] Yet Lafayette wouldn't budge.

Most delegates probably had no idea that in arguing with the marquis they were up against more than an obstinate young major general. In fact, Lafayette had plenty of backup at Valley Forge. Before sending his January 26 letter to Henry Laurens, Lafayette vetted it with Gouverneur Morris, then with the Committee at Camp. Morris, who believed the "irruption" was a ridiculous plan, approved and encouraged his French friend to send the letter. Morris then wrote directly to Laurens supporting Lafayette's objections to the command arrangements, and two days later John Laurens wrote to his father along the same line.[52] Before departing for York, Lafayette also met with three members of the committee (probably including Morris) who also endorsed his reservations about the Board of War's command arrangements for the "irruption." In fact, knowing the parlous state of the main army, the committee became gravely concerned about the wisdom of the Canadian expedition as soon as it learned of it.

Then Washington got involved, although behind the scenes. The general, smarting from the board's seeming affront and firmly convinced the Canadian scheme was inane, encouraged Lafayette's misgivings. Recall from the previous chapter that the young general had orders directly from Gates to proceed immediately to Albany. He disobeyed—and there is no other word for it. Instead he received the commander in chief's permission to leave camp to plead his case in York. This was hardly a politically "hands-off" act on Washington's part. Given his technically subordinate position to Gates, Washington's authority to contravene an explicit order from the Board of War was highly questionable. But he did so. Had Gates dared to press the point, Washington's action could have been construed as insubordination on both Lafayette's *and* Washington's parts. In fact, historian Louis Gottschalk has seen all of this activity at Valley Forge as the birth of "a counter-Conway cabal in the army and in Congress."[53] If Gottschalk exaggerated the point, it was true enough for Washington and those loyal to him. Had Congress been reading the signals from Valley Forge, it would have gathered that few officers close to the general, let alone its own Committee at Camp, had any faith in Gates's plan. In fact the Canadian venture was shaping up to be something of a contest between Washington and the committee versus the rest of Congress (save for the doubting Henry Laurens) and the Board of War.

As much as many in York had to grit their teeth, they had to give way to Lafayette's demands (although his status as a "detachment" of Washington's army remained ambiguous). McDougall's health was too frail, so Lafayette took Kalb with him to Albany, where the "irruption" was to assemble. Once at Albany, Lafayette and Kalb found Conway had preceded them on his own initiative; he had departed York before Lafayette and Congress had come to terms. Clever man that he was, Conway knew when to get out of town. His presence, however, as well as the entire *imbroglio* over his participation in the proposed campaign, quickly proved moot. For the "irruption" never got off the ground.

Gates had overpromised. Instead of 2,500 well-equipped troops, there were only a few hundred awaiting Lafayette. Even these lacked the provisions, equipment, and transport to go anywhere, much less attempt a "ravage" of British posts in Canada. In fact, it readily became apparent that the necessary manpower and supplies would not be forthcoming, and even if they were the season was too advanced to allow a rapid march on Montreal. Conway already knew as much. He had corresponded with Benedict Arnold, then still convalescing from wounds suffered at Saratoga but a man with extensive experience in Canada. Arnold's message to Conway was simple: Forget the "irruption." The plan was poor, resources insufficient, and the chances and consequences of failure too great.[54] Livid, Lafayette quickly came to the same conclusion. He wrote to Gates and Laurens expressing his alarm, and he fretted that with any chances of martial glory evaporating he would look the fool having embarked on a mission so poorly planned. The president of Congress responded reassuringly that no one could possibly blame the marquis for the situation, but Laurens probably was anything but surprised to learn of the sorry conditions northward.[55] Besides, while Lafayette fumed in Albany there were growing second thoughts in York about the wisdom of the expedition. Laurens's "mutes" and "candle snuffers" were stirring.

In fact, a report of February 11 from the Committee at Camp gave even Gates's best friends among the delegates at York little choice but to sit up and take notice. Drafted by Morris and signed by Dana as chairman, the lengthy missive went far beyond Lafayette's worries about command arrangements and botched planning. The communication began gently: It acknowledged Congress's desire to foster "a Spirit of Enterprise" in the army and agreed that this was a fine thing. But that was all the good the committee had to say as the report's tone abruptly shifted. The committee expressed deep misgivings about the proposed expedition, and the members insisted the gravity of the matter "forbids us to be silent." They warned that "caution"—surely an elusion to Washington's posture at Valley Forge—was not the same as "Timidity" and that "Enterprize without the constant Eye of Prudence is at all Times hazardous." After this ominous introduction the committee report then ripped into Gates's plan. It was a withering indictment on two broad counts: first, the committee damned chances of the plan's success and, second, it challenged Congress to consider the "irruption's" adverse "Connections with other Transactions"—that is, the Canadian venture's potential impact on the wider war effort.

On the first count, the report argued that the Canadian venture was impractical. While the committee conceded that a small success in Canada would lift American morale, it asked if that would outweigh the consequences of a defeat that would buoy the spirits of America's enemies. And what if the expedition took Montreal? The patriot treasury lacked the money to support a subsequent occupation. And if an initially successful American army consequently withdrew, and *again* gave up an attempt on Canada—the British had ousted them in 1776—what reason would Canadians ever have to trust the patriot cause? The resources simply were not available to succeed in the north, and the consequences of likely failure were too great.[56]

Turning from such practical concerns to "other Transactions," the committee struck even deeper. A failure in Canada would be disastrous to American morale—a blow leading to desertions from the army, a "Disgrace to our Arms," encouragement to the tories, and likely to "an Indian War in all its horrors." "These are the certain Consequences of a Defeat." Besides, patriot resources were barely sufficient to prepare Washington's regiments for a new campaign. "Every Musket carried into Canada," the report claimed, "will be in Effect the loss of a Man to the main Army." Moreover, patriots were finding it hard enough to subsist the troops at Valley Forge without diverting precious supplies to support an operation of dubious practicality. With so few patriot soldiers to spare, those available should remain with Washington or reinforce the vital Hudson Highlands; if Washington could destroy Howe in Philadelphia, even successful peripheral operations would mean little anyway. The committee saw absolutely nothing to justify the "irruption." It concluded that "our Opinion may be ill founded; but you will pardon us when we add that it is possible it may not."[57]

Washington could not have put the case against the Canadian venture any better—and it is a safe assumption that he did not have to inasmuch as the committee report reflected his thinking. It is an equally safe assumption that the committee discussed the matter fully with the general before Morris drafted the document and Dana put his name to it. Once again, the general found the Committee at Camp an effective intermediary with Congress and a foil to the War Office.

Congress received the report on or about February 16, when the delegates read it and referred it to the board. They also showed some previously absent curiosity about the mission and directed the board to send copies of the orders issued to Lafayette.[58] Given the tone and detail of the committee's report, Washington's evident displeasure, and Lafayette's dismayed communications, at least some delegates were no longer content to rely only on information from Gates or others on the board. In fact the board seemed to have nothing to say regarding the growing squeamishness about the situation northward. As far as we know Gates had no official response to the committee's report or to other questions about the parlous state of the "irruption." Rather, after waiting a week the Board of War simply sent the entire matter back to Congress unresolved; and Congress in turn formed yet another committee—its usual response to any problem—to ponder what to do.

This time it was the right response, because the new committee made a quick decision.[59] The next day, February 24, it recommended that the board caution Lafayette against any precipitate action. The supply and manpower situation being what it was at Albany, the Frenchman should not undertake his mission unless he had enough men properly clothed and supplied. The marquis should "regulate his conduct according to the probability of success," and he was not to put his troops unnecessarily at risk. In other words the "go" or "no go" decision was Lafayette's, but the implication was that "no go" was a real likelihood. A week later, however, after further considering the report from the Committee at Camp, Congress put a punctuation mark on the sorry business. "Authentic accounts," the delegates concluded, indicated the Canadian expedition faced insuperable difficulties; the mission now appeared too "hazardous" and "imprudent." Thus Congress ordered the frustrated major general to "suspend for the present the intended irruption."[60] The resolution held Lafayette blameless and commended his dedication and service, but the deflated marquis would have to seek martial glory elsewhere. Congress officially killed the "irruption" on March 13 and ordered Lafayette and Kalb (but *not* Conway) back to the main army.[61] At Valley Forge the commander in chief, no doubt privately, must have breathed a sigh of relief (and probably satisfaction) at the expedition's demise. Indeed, Gérard, the French diplomat, was convinced Washington's influence had killed the "irruption."[62] There is no record of Gates's reaction.

IT HAD BEEN a busy several months. From December 1777 through March 1778 Washington had fenced with the Board of War and its leading members, usually meaning Thomas Mifflin and Horatio Gates. The disputes had been serious: the matters of the inspector generalship and Conway's promotion and appointment; the struggles to control commissary and quartermaster functions; and the board's various efforts to become a player in military operations culminating in the "Irruption into Canada." All posed threats to Washington's authority as commander in chief as the board sought to expand its support mission to assume a leading role in military policymaking. The effort fell afoul of the politically astute commanding general.

The board's defeats marked an end to any major sympathy with Washington's critics. In effect the Cabal had dissolved along with the influence of the Board of War; Congress no longer was willing to champion it in any contest against Washington's authority. Sentiments did not shift abruptly, but Henry Laurens—that bellwether of the mood in Congress—noted the change as Washington made his case through the Committee at Camp. Laurens, only a month earlier so concerned about a "party" forming against Washington, now thought things were looking up for the general. In mid-January he assured Lafayette, who was utterly convinced a conspiracy was afoot, that criticisms of the commander in chief now amounted to little. In fact he now thought Washington had no congressional enemies, or at least that he enjoyed the support of nine out of ten delegates. "Parties" in Congress, he advised, had made the "Road rough but not impassable." (Only days later, however, we should note that Laurens was still concerned about the "dangerous altercations" arising from the Conway-Gates letter.)[63] Laurens even took some snarky pleasure in commenting on the end of the "irruption." If he once thought he was the mission's lone congressional skeptic, he now found an altered mood in Congress. He told South Carolina governor John Rutledge that among delegates recently so enthusiastic about Gates's plan, feelings at the moment were quite different: "Now—well 'I never liked that Canadian Expedition' is unanimous."[64] Canada? What Canada?

Much the same can be said about the Cabal itself. Historian Robert K. Wright, Jr. has seen "the termination of the Canadian 'irruption'" and congressional "dismissal" of Conway's criticisms of Washington as the end of "the challenge to Washington's leadership of the Army."[65] Coupled with the board's failure to secure control of the inspector generalship and to take over Continental logistics, Wright is certainly correct. The general's critics largely held their peace, and his chief antagonists increasingly found themselves without an audience. Thomas Mifflin maintained a sullen silence; he would not officially resign from the Board of War until August, but his stock in Congress had fallen dramatically. Gates also saw his influence waning. Bruised in the Conway letter affair, stymied in efforts to implement any of his major initiatives, and without Washington's regard (to put it mildly), speculation was rife that the Hero of Saratoga would leave the board in the spring and return to the field.[66] As late as mid-March, however, he evidently still had some hopes for the "irruption." On the thirteenth the board asked Congress to promote a Major Thomas Mullens, a French aide to Major General Conway, to lieutenant colonel—the new rank to be valid "in Canada only." It was a routine request—major generals could expect to have lieutenant colonels as staff officers, and in February Congress had so promoted some of Lafayette's aides. But Congress failed to act on Mullens. It was hardly a vote of confidence in Gates or his hopes for the northern expedition (much less in Conway).[67] Bereft of the leadership of Mifflin and Gates the board would have no pretensions to military leadership—the days of "mission creep" were over, and so was the attempted administrative coup.

By late February one senses that Washington felt the political tide running in his favor. On the twenty-eighth, writing to his aide, Lieutenant Colonel John Fitzgerald, Washington seemed more at ease than he had in some time. Conway and Gates, be believed, had shot their bolt. "Matters have, and will, turn out very different to what" those officers had expected. Gates's letters to him (Washington) had caught the major general "in the most absurd contradictions." Mifflin had Cadwalader so angry that Washington thought a duel was possible (it didn't happen), and Conway was stuck in Albany after being sent "upon an expedition which all the World knew—& the event has proved, was not practicable." The commander in chief noted that his opponents indeed had had in mind "getting me out of the way," but with some satisfaction he concluded that "the Machinations of this Junto will recoil upon their own heads."[68] As far as the Virginian was concerned, if he had not won outright over the Cabal, at least he was well on his way to doing so.

Washington now had plenty of help. His relationship with the Committee at Camp was close and productive. Indeed, the committee's reports to Congress on all subjects generally reflected Washington's views; and Dana, Morris, and Carroll at least were his articulate partisans. And friends elsewhere had rallied. In New Jersey, Governor William Livingston—in another of his many pseudonyms, this time the (very bad) poet "Hortentius"—praised the general as "heaven-guided" and beseeched him not "to be dismay'd At foreign myriads, or domestic foes." In a personal letter Livingston pledged his friendship, "all the Devils in hell and all the *envious intrigues* upon Earth, notwithstanding."[69] Indeed, the most prominent *envious intrigues* were quiet. Over March Benjamin Rush and Samuel Adams spoke nary a public word against the general (that we know of—and if Rush was spouting off *someone* would have known). Visiting York in mid-March, Lieutenant Colonel Fitzgerald found Congress coming around. "Those who were endeavoring to Injure you in the Public Esteem," he informed the general, "are become sensible of their own insignificance & [I] earnestly hope they may feel the contempt & Scorn of all good men in proportion to the Iniquitous Scheme which they expected to accomplish." Whatever the "Junto" had in mind, the lieutenant colonel thought most of Congress was now "warmly attach'd" to the commander in chief. In Virginia, Richard Henry Lee, whose loyalties to the general Fitzgerald (and Washington) considered suspect, was fighting for his political life. He had to assure local voters of his allegiance to the general in order to secure reappointment to Congress.[70]

In Congress the impact was evident. By early March even William Duer and James Lovell were quiet, at least as far as any adverse comments about the commander in chief were concerned. Maryland delegate John Henry wrote Governor Thomas Johnson approvingly of the demise of the Canadian operation—a perfect case of Laurens's "'I never liked that Canadian Expedition'"—and he now hoped Continental forces could concentrate under Washington "in the Middle States," which Henry saw as the decisive theater.[71] Eliphalet Dyer of Connecticut, erstwhile no great proponent of Washington's leadership, now saw the sands shifting. With the Committee at Camp solidly in Washington's corner and Gates balked in every direction, Dyer now proclaimed: "there is not the most distant thought of removing Genll Washington, nor ever an expression in Congress looking that way, [it] is a Tory lye from the beginning."[72] Really? Was "The Thoughts of a Freeman" a "Tory lye"? Or perhaps congressional support for an inspector general reporting to the Board of War and outside of the army chain of command? Or maybe Dyer could have explained why Washington and the army were so upset with the Board of War. Perchance Dyer should have compared notes with Henry Laurens back in early January when, as president of Congress, the South Carolinian genuinely feared a "juncto" with its "prompters & Actors." And why should we believe Dyer rather than Laurens? The Connecticut delegate was a firm patriot, but it seems his late discovery of congressional faith in Washington was simply bending with a newly prevailing wind.[73]

Cabal? What Cabal? But the affair wasn't over . . . not as far as George Washington was concerned.

EIGHT

PAYBACK

The Politics of Getting Even

> The General I allways revered & loved ever since I knew him, But in this Instance he has rose superior to himself. Every Lip dwells on his Praise for even his pretended Friends (for none dare to acknowledge themselves his Enemies) are obliged to croak it forth.
>
> —Elias Boudinot to Alexander Hamilton, July 8, 1778[1]

The Cabal had collapsed, at least in any form connected with the Board of War. In late May 1778, having weathered the Valley Forge winter and with his regiments rebuilding, Washington took a spare moment to write to his old friend and fellow Virginia planter Landon Carter. We have seen this letter earlier in these pages. Along with other news of the day, Washington brought Carter up to date on rumors of a "disposition in the Northern Officers to" replace him as commander in chief in favor of Horatio Gates. That threat had passed, he assured Carter, but he was just as sure a conspiracy had existed to remove or discredit him. "That there was a scheme of this sort on foot last fall admits of no doubt," he wrote; and without naming names he obviously had referred to Gates, Mifflin, and Conway. There was no disguising his contempt for all three. But he told Carter all was well for the time being. Publicly exposed, the plotters "slunk back—disavowed the measure, & professed themselves my warmest admirers. thus stands the matter at present."[2] Washington thought he still enjoyed the confidence of Congress, he told his friend, but the letter implied that the matter was not entirely settled.

It wasn't. The general and his allies had foiled all attempts to subvert his authority as commander in chief, but that was no guarantee that critics would not rebound in the event of another disappointing campaign season. In fact, if quiet for the moment, some of the general's most vociferous opponents had adopted a "wait and see" posture. As late as June, before the British evacuation of Philadelphia, James Lovell—that ever-caustic thorn in Washington's side—reassured Gates that many delegates still had faith in the Saratoga hero. He counseled Gates to await the outcome of the impending 1778 campaign, clearly implying that if Washington failed again . . .

Washington needed to avoid just such a scenario, and doing so would involve work on two fronts. The first was the battlefield. The general had to demonstrate that he and his new army could stand the test of combat. That is, Washington had to reverse the sorry results of his 1777 campaign, thus eliminating practical doubts about his generalship. At the same time he needed to prove the worth of his regular ("respectable") army, thus cutting the legs from under his ideological critics and their dreams of militia virtue. Then there was politics. Success on this second front would depend on success on the first. If he succeeded in battle he could use any recovered prestige to settle political scores once and for all. In other words there would be payback for the Cabal.

Spring saw the chief characters of the Cabal going separate ways. In early May Horatio Gates left York—and the Board of War—to resume command of the Northern Department. Without a Canadian front the department was essentially the state of New York, and Gates would make his headquarters initially in the Hudson Highlands. If his dignity was ruffled after the Cabal, at least he knew he still had friends in Congress; he also could take some solace in knowing his contretemps with Washington did not land him in a backwater assignment, at least not at first. There were not quite enough friends, however, to give him fully what he wanted. A number of delegates, no doubt with Gates's blessing, tried to set up the Northern Department as a command reporting directly to Congress—that is, independent of Washington. But Congress, no doubt with Washington's blessing, had had enough (at least for the moment) of a divided command structure and the effort failed.[3] There would be only one commander in chief.

Still, the northern command was an important posting and some of Washington's allies were happy enough to see Gates land there. Even Gouverneur Morris hoped Gates could get along with New York State officials.[4] Washington retained a professionally correct relationship with the major general. He asked Gates to stop in at Valley Forge to discuss the upcoming campaign while on the way to his new assignment, and the commanding general assured New York governor George Clinton that Gates would do his utmost to safeguard patriot control of the vital Hudson River. There was no question, however, of who was in charge: Gates was taking orders from the commander in chief.[5] To his credit Gates initially was cooperative, and he checked with Washington before undertaking anything beyond the operations of his own department. But the Virginian put his foot down whenever Gates's independent streak reappeared. When Congress tried to appoint a French officer, the grandiosely named René-Hippolyte Penot Lombart de Noirmont de la Neuville, as inspector general for the Northern Department, reporting to Gates and independent of Steuben, Washington issued an emphatic veto: "There can be but one head."[6] Unity of command: It was a message fully indicative of Washington's approach to army command generally.

The Highlands saw no major military operations during Gates's command, but fallout from the Cabal continued to haunt the major general—*thanks in large part to George Washington*. In late March, when Washington learned Wilkinson was at Valley Forge, he invited him to dinner at headquarters. During the evening the general shared his correspondence with Gates regarding the Conway letter, including Gates's distress upon learning Wilkinson's role in the business. Why would Washington share what he must have known would be inflammatory information with the volatile Wilkinson? It is easy to speculate that Washington knew he was stirring up trouble for Gates. The affair of "the Letter" already had resulted in a challenge from Wilkinson to Gates. Did the general really think "Wilky" would take these revelations calmly? And Wilkinson certainly didn't. "He seemed a good deal surprised at G——s's Letters," Washington told Stirling, "& was not at all sparing in his abuse of him & C——y." Washington must have relished this; but even better was a subsequent letter from Wilkinson. Wilkinson wrote thanking the general for his "condescension in exposing to me M[ajo]r Genl Gates's Letters which Unmask his Artifice & efforts to ruin me." Now the lieutenant colonel turned on his former benefactor and on Conway: While he "solemnly" assured Washington he could not recall the exact words of the Conway letter, he was positive Conway's "general

Tenor" was as critical of Washington as he (Wilkinson) claimed—this despite Gates's insistence that the offending extract was a "wicked & Malicious Forgery." If ever "the Genuine Letter" surfaced, Wilkinson averred, its words would bear out his damning claim.[7] From cozying up to Gates and Conway in the fall of 1777, in the spring of 1778 he was sucking up to Washington and virtually pleading victim status. True, Wilkinson had meant no harm in talking with McWilliams, but thereafter he had played false virtually every step of the way.

No matter how difficult it is to sympathize with him, Wilkinson may honestly have believed he had been wronged. Ruminating on what he considered Gates's affront to his honor (assuming he had any), Wilkinson decided on a clean break. A month later he wrote Henry Laurens thanking Congress for his appointment as secretary to the Board of War. But life on the board would not do: He explained that the "sedentary life" the appointment would entail would be "ruinous to my Health." If this was preposterous, so was what followed. "Permit me to add," Wilkinson continued, "that I could not consistently do business under Major General Gates after the uncandid, artful, unjust & ungenerous practices he has employed to dishonor me."[8] This was shameful: Wilkinson had been as slippery with the truth in dealing with Gates as Gates had been in dealing with Washington, and now he was being deceptive with Congress. On its part, Congress was only too happy to be rid of the impossible young officer. Laurens responded coldly, noting the delegates had accepted the resignation but considered the tenor of Wilkinson's letter "improper for the cognizance of Congress & inadmissible" for congressional records.[9] Laurens returned the letter as a calculated rebuke. Perhaps he was lucky Wilkinson did not challenge him.

The snub from Laurens did nothing to calm the truculent "Wilky." His animosity toward Gates smoldered, and apparently he was looking for a fight. He got his chance in early September when Gates appeared at Washington's headquarters at White Plains, New York. Gates had reported there to testify at the court-martial of Major General Arthur St. Clair, the result of St. Clair's evacuation of Fort Ticonderoga the previous year. There Gates encountered Wilkinson and angry words passed. The upshot was another duel in which Gates refused to fire and Wilkinson fired and missed three times. (Gates biographer Paul David Nelson has noted that Wilkinson wasn't much of a shot.) The men parted in enmity, and the next day even their seconds drew blades on one another.[10] But for the fact that bullets and swords do kill people, there was a large element of farce in the entire business. Virginia politico Edmund Pendleton, no partisan of Gates, puckishly wrote his friend Brigadier William Woodford that "Gates and Wilkinson have been Cannonading each other."[11] The incident added nothing to Gates's reputation.

In the autumn Congress changed Gates's assignment. Concerned about a possible threat to the Boston area, Congress directed Washington to send Gates there. It proved to be a largely inactive command. While the major general was happy to be farther from Washington, Boston was a comedown for Gates. The British threat never materialized, and Gates had few troops to command. Moreover, Boston itself did not warm to him. He had replaced the very popular Major General William Heath, and he did not get along with powerful Massachusetts politico John Hancock. Public knowledge of Gates's antagonistic relationship with Washington probably did nothing to enhance the major general's popularity. While never Congress's intent, in effect the Boston posting had sidelined Gates. "Hither to," Greene wrote Alexander McDougall, Gates had enjoyed the company of "flatterers." Now "he has been like Samson after his Head was shaved. His strength has been no more than another mans. This is a situation his pride and ambition cannot brook."[12] Greene was right, and for the present Gates labored out of the military mainstream—and the commander in chief was probably quite happy to have it so.

Washington saw no reason to be anything but icily civil to Thomas Mifflin. For the time being Mifflin remained a member of the Board of War, and he retained the respect of some delegates. William Duer, ever the Washington skeptic, still thought Mifflin ought to be quartermaster general. But Mifflin's stock had fallen, and with Gates's departure and the frustration of board initiatives at Washington's hands, the Pennsylvanian posed no further threat. The former quartermaster general did continue his jabs at Greene, protesting the Rhode Islander's supposed undue influence with Washington—and once doing so, according to one witness, while "tipsy" after "a plentiful infusion of the juice of the grape."[13] As Washington put it, the former quartermaster general, like Gates and Conway, had "slunk back" and "disavowed" any intrigue. Still holding his major general's commission, Mifflin tried briefly to resume his army career. The attempt met the sarcastic dismay of some in Congress; but as a major general he was entitled to attend councils of war, although the commander in chief notified him of an April meeting only in the curtest of terms. Senior officers greeted him with the same chilly disdain Washington had shown Conway the previous December, and Mifflin soon left for Congress to defend his financial accounts from his time as quartermaster.[14] With Washington now riding high, with some justification Mifflin feared he was facing a virtual inquisition. In the end he defended himself successfully from any questions of peculation; but in the meantime, to the relief of most delegates, in August he resigned from the army and from the Board of War. Mifflin was nothing if not resilient, however, and after some months in the political wilderness he found his way back into the good graces of Pennsylvania—and eventually back into Congress.[15] But he never again crossed swords with George Washington.

The demise of the "Irruption into Canada" left Major General Conway marooned in the north. Conway's time in Albany had not been the happiest. He had continued to grouse about being junior to Kalb and, since neither Lafayette nor Kalb had wanted him along anyway, he had little to do. (Parenthetically, we should note that even as Conway objected to serving with Kalb, who had been his junior in France, he made no protest to serving under Lafayette, who had climbed no higher than captain in the French army.) When Lafayette and Kalb decamped to rejoin Washington at Valley Forge, Lafayette ordered Conway to remain behind. He was to command the few regiments and stores at Albany, far from Congress or the main army—and far from any hope of an active command as the spring dawned and patriots turned their thoughts to a new campaign.[16]

What happened next left no doubt of Conway's fall from grace in Congress, which actually was a reflection of the wider Cabal's failure. In March Congress ordered Conway to report to Major General McDougall, then at Peekskill in the Hudson Highlands (Gates had not yet arrived to relieve McDougall). According to Laurens, most delegates no longer trusted the Frenchman to hold an independent command.[17] Conway was not there long. In April McDougall sent him back to Albany where, as he complained to Gates and Laurens, "there are no troops, [and] where I will never be able to give the least protection to the Western or Northern frontiers." In May the forlorn major general presided at a celebration honoring the Franco-American alliance, but he could do nothing of military significance.[18] There is little question that he was actually distraught; men Conway had counted on as friends now could not put enough distance between themselves and the divisive officer. Even Gates, to whom Conway had linked his fortunes, had backed away, weary of "the Letter" controversy and Washington's animosity.[19] The Frenchman certainly was feeling sorry for himself: "I have been Box'd about in a Most indecent Manner," he complained, and he simply did not understand why he could not lead a division in any new campaign. "I did not Deserve this Burlesk Disgrace, and my honour Will not permit me to Bear it." "Undeservedly my Character must suffer, therefor, sir, I expect you'll Make my resignation acceptable to Congress." Congress read this letter on April 28 and the same day voted, eight states to one, to accept Conway's resignation. Only Virginia, with Francis Lightfoot Lee at the head of the delegation, voted to keep Conway in the army.[20] (Credit Lee with loyalty to a friend in trouble.) For a man who had played politics with the wrong crowd, bet on the rise of Gates, and made no secret of his lack of regard for Washington, Conway in the end turned out to be something of a political naïf.

And he *was* naïve. Conway had bluffed at resignation before only to have admirers beg him to stay. Perhaps he counted on the same reaction to his letter from Albany. Indeed, he was stunned when he learned Congress had accepted his resignation, and he tried to backtrack. The now former major general had his chief aide, the chevalier de Neuville (the same man Gates would try to have named as his inspector general), write Congress that it had misunderstood Conway's letter. Neuville explained that Conway had meant to express his dismay at his situation, but he hadn't *really* meant to resign. But it was too late. Laurens told Neuville that the delegates certainly would hear Conway's explanation; but if they did there is no evidence Congress ever seriously considered changing its mind.[21] Dejected and angry, Conway drifted back south, ultimately to Philadelphia after the Americans reclaimed the city in late June. There he would try to get a certificate from Congress attesting to his service to the patriot cause, a document he could take back to France and use in his quest for promotion in the Bourbon army. But our story is not yet done with Thomas Conway; he would play a final and dramatic role in the Cabal chronicle. For the moment, however, we must leave him—bereft of command, given up by most friends, and adrift amid a revolution that had considered him a military asset but no longer valued him.

As THE CHIEF ACTORS in the Cabal fell from political favor over the late winter and early spring, another figure emerged to give the story a fateful new dimension. This was Major General Charles Lee. We have mentioned Lee before as an early critic of Washington's leadership—as indeed he was in late 1776—and some historians have seen him as the choice of more radical patriots for Washington's job.[22] Unwittingly he would play a major part in the Cabal's final chapter. Thus we need to know more about Charles Lee.

Lee was born in 1732 near the city of Chester in west-central England.[23] His family was middling gentry, of good social standing but of moderate economic status. Charles's father was Colonel John Lee of the 55th Foot, and the young Lee began his military career as an ensign in the 55th. After a posting to Ireland, he saw considerable action during the Seven Year's War. He was wounded during the disastrous British defeat at Fort Ticonderoga in 1758; then in Portugal he led a daring night attack that routed the Spanish at the Battle of Vila Vehla in 1762. He ended the war as a battle-hardened major with an enviable service record. Lee also emerged as a complex and volatile soldier. He could be genial, brusque, and arrogant in turns. He thought nothing of castigating the foibles of senior officers, caring little if his views became known. He quarreled with brother officers, and an army surgeon actually tried to kill him.[24] Lee certainly ranked as one of the army's most eccentric and contentious officers.

Lee's regiment disbanded after the Seven Years War, leaving him no place on the British roster. For the next eight years he was a military vagabond. He served as aide-de-camp to King Stanislaus Poniatowski of Poland, who made the Englishman a major general in the Polish army. Lee's itinerary also included Constantinople, the Russo-Turkish War (as an observer with the Russian army), Hungary, Vienna, France, and Italy, where he killed a man in a duel. His return to Great Britain was unhappy. Lee found no opening in a British regiment; and although in 1772 he was promoted to lieutenant colonel on the inactive list, his failure to advance left him bitter. Indeed, his resentments overrode his judgment. He publicly approved of colonial resistance to the Stamp Act, and he harbored private doubts about the wisdom of monarchy. When the King failed to promote him, Lee published a biting satire of George III—and in Britain Lee's career was finished.

Like many Englishmen with dashed hopes at home, Lee looked to America for relief. In 1773 he transplanted to Virginia and the following year he purchased a modest estate near the modern town of Leeville (named in his honor) in what is now West Virginia. He had found the property through the advice of an old army friend, Horatio Gates, who also had settled in Virginia. Lee quickly established influential connections with the likes of Richard Henry Lee, Thomas Jefferson, and George Washington.[25] Lee promptly identified with rising colonial resistance to Great Britain. In fact Lee's was one of the earliest voices to call for outright independence. The bitterness he felt toward a Britain that, in his eyes, had unjustly thwarted his military career may have fueled his political leanings; but Lee's radical sympathies were sincere.[26] Recognizing his patriotic and military credentials,

Congress commissioned him a major general, ranking him only behind Washington and Artemus Ward of Massachusetts. When Ward resigned Lee became second in command. He did well during the first eighteen months of the conflict, serving capably under Washington's orders outside Boston, in South Carolina, and in and around New York City.

In December 1776, however, Lee's volatility surfaced. Critical of Washington's leadership—and the commander in chief had made his share of mistakes—Lee unburdened himself in now famous letters to Joseph Reed and Horatio Gates. Both messages unsparingly questioned Washington's generalship. Inadvertently Washington saw the letter to Reed, but he made no issue of the matter as he tried to hold his dissolving army together.[27] But Lee then crossed the line between criticism and insubordination. With Washington's main army crossing the Delaware into Pennsylvania and Lee commanding a following column in New Jersey, Washington ordered Lee to join him as quickly as possible. But Lee disobeyed. He wanted to remain in New Jersey to rally the militia and then fall on the British rear as they chased Washington.[28] Washington was bewildered by the conduct of his second-in-command, but at this point the last thing the patriot army needed was a showdown between its two senior officers.

Fate spared patriots that trauma. Early on December 13 a British patrol captured Lee at White's Tavern, near Basking Ridge. Lee was a prisoner for almost sixteen months, until April 1778 when he was freed on parole.[29] Yet even in captivity he managed his share of drama. After an initial period of close confinement, his captors allowed him comfortable accommodations. They even allowed him pen and paper, a particular joy for Lee. He wrote frequently to Congress, Washington, and friends on all manner of subjects, even offering himself as a go-between for peace negotiations (nothing came of that idea). However, Lee's most unusual letter was never meant for patriot eyes. Addressed to the "Royal Commissioners"—that is, to Lord Richard and Sir William Howe—the document outlined a "scheme" whereby the British could crush the rebellion. The plan called for the Royal Navy to seal off ports between Annapolis, Maryland and Newport, Rhode Island. This, Lee claimed, would encourage loyalists to rise and end the rebellion in two months. Lee's document came to light only in the mid-nineteenth century,[30] and little suggests that the Howe brothers ever saw it. While most modern scholars have dismissed notions of treasonous intent on Lee's part, had patriots learned of Lee's plan they certainly would have considered him a traitor. Why did he write such a document? Historian John Alden has suggested it was a ruse designed to lure Howe into his fruitless Pennsylvania Campaign, although John Shy's guess seems better: that Lee wrote it "simply to become a participant again instead of a bystander."[31] In fact we will never really know.

In the early spring of 1778 the British agreed to swap Lee for redcoat brigadier Richard Prescott. Paroled in April, Lee was formally exchanged and rejoined the army in mid-May. Although he never saw it coming, his release led steadily down a path to professional oblivion. He became a source of friction almost immediately, wasting no time in disparaging Major General Steuben's training regimen.[32] Lee insisted that adopting European tactics was foolish; instead Americans needed tactical and organizational simplicity. Lee called for what was essentially an army of well-trained militia—men "drawn from their Ploughs"—that would fight defensively and wear down the enemy. "Harassing and impeding can alone Succeed," he warned; to stand in the open against British professionals was "talking Nonsense."[33]

Theoretically Lee's ideas were not necessarily bad, but they were completely out of step with Washington's vision for the army. The major general's talk of soldiers "drawn from their Ploughs" and disdain for European tactics harkened back to the republican ardor of 1775 and early 1776. That ardor, as Washington well understood, was long gone. Lee's emphasis on the defensive also fell on deaf ears. Most patriots now wanted a Continental Army that could *fight.* Lee's ideas were simply out of date. Again John Shy: During his months of captivity "the war seemed to have moved beyond Charles Lee."[34]

Lee proved especially obtuse on the political front; his inability to sense new political realities was glaring. He supposedly told Elias Boudinot, the patriot commissary general of prisoners instrumental in negotiating Lee's exchange, that he (Lee) "found the Army in a worse situation than he expected and that General Washington was not fit to command a sergeant's guard."[35] This may be apocryphal, as Boudinot was a Washington loyalist and detested Lee. But on a visit to York the note of discord continued. Lee met with members of Congress, probably including his partisans Richard Henry Lee, North Carolina's Thomas Burke, and others.[36] Indeed, on April 9, the day Lee reached York, Burke wrote favorably of the general to North Carolina governor Richard Caswell: "We are many of us [in Congress] persuaded that some Officers in the Army wish not for the release of General Lee because his enterprising disposition and martial genius will be a strong contrast to their want of both."[37] Lee also met with Henry Laurens, who recalled that Lee seemed uneasy with Washington's leadership. It was hardly an impression to leave with one of the commander in chief's political allies.

Lee followed the meeting with a letter. He expressed his gratitude to everyone who had pressed for his exchange, and went on to note his relationship with Washington was "well." Then, with astonishing insensitivity, he told Laurens "I am persuaded (considering how he is surrounded) that he [Washington] cannot do without me."[38] That was quite a message to a man whose son—Lieutenant Colonel John Laurens—was one of those "surrounding" the commander in chief.[39] If Lee had thought to befriend the congressional president, he had failed miserably.

Lee maintained his old habits, seemingly unconcerned with what others might think of the company he kept or of what he might say. His correspondence with his radical friend Benjamin Rush—one of Washington's most virulent detractors—continued in the same vein. It was "hard to say," he wrote, which side had blundered the most thus far in the war. "Upon my Soul," he added, "it was time for fortune to interpose or We were inevitably lost."[40] Lee's attitude did not go unnoticed, and Nathanael Greene sounded a cautionary note. He allowed that Lee was a fine officer, but he feared the "junto"—the Cabal, and Mifflin in particular—would try to "debauch and poison his mind" against Washington. Greene confessed he thought "no great good" would come of Lee's return.[41]

Less tangible matters also distanced Lee from many peers. His manners and personal conduct were notoriously unpolished. Careless about his appearance, he once came unshaven and bedraggled to table with General and Martha Washington. His alleged conduct the previous evening was worse. Lee supposedly had slipped "a miserable dirty hussy" into his room; and as Lee's room was next to Martha's, the situation was potentially awkward in the extreme. Lee thought it splendid when Gates boasted that in one encounter his son, Robert, had drunk himself silly and contracted a venereal disease. Lee said it bespoke a manly youth.[42] Such sentiments were foreign to Washington; nor did he expect those in his military family to feel differently. These men prized their dignity as officers and gentlemen, whereas Lee frequently did not. Thus there were potential flash points between the army's two senior generals and a rupture was certainly possible—and although neither man realized it, the flash point was not far ahead.

IF WASHINGTON HAD qualms about Lee's return or about the remnants of the Cabal, to the extent he could he laid them aside to focus on preparing his army for a new campaign. As June approached the military situation was evolving rapidly. In Philadelphia Lieutenant General Sir Henry Clinton had replaced Sir William Howe as British commander in chief. With the French now in the war, and the Spanish threatening, London had decided to de-emphasize operations in the northern colonies and redeploy British forces to other fronts. Clinton received orders to give up Philadelphia and get his troops back to New York City, from which many of them would head to other parts of the empire, including the American south. The Royal Navy lacked the shipping to carry the army, its equipment and animals, and any number of frightened tories back to New York, so Clinton would have to march the bulk of his army across New Jersey. He completed his evacuation of Philadelphia on June 18 and set out northeast.

At Valley Forge Washington had the reorganized Continentals ready to react. Part of that reorganization, however, dealt with a military legacy of the Cabal. With Mifflin and Conway gone, the commander in chief gave Thomas Mifflin's former division, which included Conway's former brigade, to Brigadier General Anthony Wayne. No one we know of regretted the absence of the two unpopular officers.[43] Moving quickly, the patriot regiments crossed into New Jersey to pursue Clinton, and on June 24 Washington and his senior lieutenants met to consider their options. Washington knew the Continental Army was much improved. Steuben had instilled new discipline and tactical agility; Greene and Wadsworth had solved most logistical problems; new recruits had fleshed out the regiments; and French arms and equipment had arrived in quantity. But how good was the new army? It lacked the test of major combat, and Washington was wary of committing it to a decisive action unless absolutely necessary. Thus the consensus among the officers was conservative: The rebels should try to land a limited blow without risking a general engagement, and Charles Lee was the most insistent on avoiding a major showdown with Clinton.

Still, there was politics to consider. The Cabal had its roots in perceptions that Washington could not win the war, and another losing campaign easily could revive his critics—in fact it easily could put them in full cry. Thus the general could not afford a major defeat, or even a mediocre performance. But what of allowing Clinton to march unmolested through an entire American state? On June 24, after a council of war in Hopewell, New Jersey, Nathanael Greene (now quartermaster general) put the political case for combat as well as anyone. "If we suffer the enemy to pass through the Jerseys without attempting any thing upon them I think we shall ever regret it," he advised. "I cannot help thinking we magnify our difficulties beyound reallities. We are now in the most awkward situation in the World," he continued. How would it look if the army closed with the enemy but then appeared to lose courage and fail to land a blow? "People expects [*sic*] something from us & our strength demands it. I am by no means for rash measures but we must preserve our reputation." Greene counseled against a general action while insisting some sort of encounter was essential if the army—and by implication *Washington*—was to retain popular and political support. Greene was adamant on the point, even stating that if it came to a general engagement he was willing to fight it out.[44]

While more skittish than his quartermaster general about major combat, the commander in chief agreed that the situation called for fighting, and he progressively sent stronger Continental detachments from the main army toward Clinton. He wanted enough combat to demonstrate the prowess of his Continentals—and thus the worth of his vision of a regular American army—and his own capability in the field. And he wanted it all without losing the regiments that had endured and revived at Valley Forge. In effect the rebel chief elected a middle ground between a major battle and letting Clinton escape scot-free.

The Battle of Monmouth was fought on Sunday, June 28, in central New Jersey near the town of Monmouth Court House, also called Freehold. Clinton had marched slowly to Freehold, slowed by poor roads, blazing hot weather, and torrential downpours. But mostly he slowed the pace hoping Washington would catch up and offer battle. He rested his men for two nights at Freehold, and as he pulled out of town early on the twenty-eighth he found that the Continentals had closed and evidently *were* looking for a fight. And they were led by Major General Charles Lee, the rebel army's second-ranking officer.

Lee commanded an American vanguard of something under four thousand men. He had opposed a large action, but Washington sent him forward with discretionary orders to bring on a limited engagement if an opportunity presented itself. Lee was not to risk a major confrontation, but Washington did want to hit Clinton hard enough to satisfy political objectives. With every intention to fight, Lee attacked what he thought was the British rear guard, but he was promptly surprised to find Clinton counterattacking in overwhelming numbers. Lee wisely began an orderly retreat toward what he hoped would be the approach of Washington's main force. Washington indeed was coming up, and riding forward the commander in chief met Lee sometime around 1:00 p.m. In a famous exchange, he angrily asked Lee the reason for the retreat, and a flustered Lee was barely able to point out the strength of Clinton's oncoming redcoats. Washington checked his temper as he realized Lee was right. He left Lee and Anthony Wayne to fight holding actions while he rode back to form the main army on defensible ground.

Within minutes Lee and Wayne were fighting for their lives. Wayne was overrun, escaping toward Washington with the remnants of his command, while shortly thereafter Lee was able to pull back in good order. The desperate delaying actions bought the time Washington needed to organize his main line. Clinton made one attempt at Washington's position, but Continental artillery shattered an attack by the famed British grenadiers. Washington spent the rest of the day in a long artillery duel with British gunners followed by limited advances against Clinton. Sundown ended the action and, convinced Washington would not give him a showdown fight, Clinton saw no point in reengaging. He pulled out after dark, ultimately reaching safety at Sandy Hook and then locations in and around New York City.

The battle was a hard-fought draw. Clinton's mission was to get his men back to New York for redeployment, and he had done so without so much as the loss of a single wagon from his lengthy baggage train. The rebels, pointing to Clinton's withdrawal and their possession of the battlefield, trumpeted a major victory. In fact the Continentals had fought gamely and Washington had displayed admirable leadership. Washington's officers quickly broadcast a narrative of victory, patriot valor, and Washington's gallantry; the message was that disappointments of 1777 had been erased and the commander in chief's reputation restored. And if anyone dared ask, if the victory was so total, how it was that Clinton had got so cleanly away, there was an answer: Lee's morning retreat had been a blunder that robbed the army of a complete triumph. In short, Lee was the scapegoat for failure to destroy Clinton.

Furious and wounded by rumors of his misconduct, Lee, after an intemperate (on his part) exchange of letters with Washington, quite foolishly demanded a court-martial to clear his name. Washington accommodated, probably quite happily, although he would later claim he only did what Lee demanded. The court found Lee guilty of three charges: failure to attack as ordered, conducting a disorderly retreat, and in his letters showing disrespect for the commander in chief. The first two charges were absurd, and virtually all concerned knew it, but Lee's letters indeed had been disrespectful. Any "not guilty" findings, however, might have reflected poorly on Washington—and that was not going to happen. The court suspended Lee from command for a year and sent the verdict to Congress for confirmation.

What had Lee's court-martial really meant? It had little to do with Lee's performance on June 28; he had fought well under daunting circumstances and against very long odds. Even some of Washington's staunchest partisans admitted as much; and there was public murmuring that if the major general really had been guilty, then his yearlong suspension had been too light a sentence. Lee himself claimed that Washington's headquarters (and thus Washington) had plotted to disgrace him. He was right, and he said as much to his friends—and those friends were his biggest problem. While Congress deliberated the court-martial verdict, Lee pleaded his case to the wrong people. He poured out his side of the story to the likes of Richard Henry Lee and garnered the public support of Benjamin Rush. To say the least, these were not names calculated to sooth the feelings of the commander in chief—nor of those favorable to Washington. From Virginia, Continental colonel Walter Stewart wrote Greene that his (Stewart's) officers were "much Exasperated" with Richard Henry Lee because of his sympathy for Charles Lee. At least, Stewart hoped, the court-martial aftermath would dent Richard Henry's influence and spell the end of "the Junto."[45] To all who cared to look, it was clear that Lee's court-martial was a political event—designed to use Lee as a means of striking back at Washington's opponents and striking *down* the Cabal once and for all.

It took courage to speak up on Lee's behalf. Some did, although in the afterglow of Monmouth they only did so at some risk. Captain Evan Edwards (one of Lee's aides during the battle) learned this the hard way. "I have been almost mob'd in defending you," he told Lee; "ten thousand infamous lies have been spread that I never heard before to bypass the minds of People against you." Edwards saw nothing but injustice in Lee's fate: "In the name of God, what are we come to?"[46] Most of Lee's friends lacked Edwards's gumption and fell into glum silence. In Congress, delegates wrote home or to colleagues proclaiming the triumphal news, some even predicting Monmouth had set the patriot cause on course for a quick victory. It was the "season of hope" all over again. Even Lovell and Sam Adams welcomed the result of the battle, although in muted terms and without crediting Washington. Elias Boudinot seemed to capture the moment in a snarky jibe at Washington's erstwhile critics: "The General I allways revered & loved ever since I knew him, but in this Instance he has rose superior to himself. Every Lip dwells on his Praise for even his pretended Friends (for none dare to acknowledge themselves his Enemies) are obliged to croak it forth."[47] In so many words Gérard said much the same thing. He had warned Vergennes that "the split" between Washington and Gates was "getting to be dangerous." But "the evacuation of Philadelphia and the battle of Monmouth decided the question, and the partisans of General Gates are reduced to silence."[48] Open critics of the commander in chief, once so common, were a rare breed after June 28.

And what of Thomas Mifflin and Horatio Gates? In the weeks after Monmouth Mifflin lay low, a perfect example of Boudinot's observation that "none dare to acknowledge themselves his Enemies." Whatever the Pennsylvanian thought about the commander in chief, he limited public comments to denying that he had harbored any ill will toward the general. He was fully aware that in patriot sentiments the Hero of Monmouth had displaced the Hero of Saratoga. Besides, in the aftermath of Monmouth he was immersed in the details of defending his own conduct as quartermaster general and too busy to comment at length on military affairs. On his part, Gates played the good soldier, sending congratulations to Washington after Monmouth.[49] Any good will on Gates's part, however, was not necessarily reciprocated, as plenty of bitterness lingered among Washington's staff officers. Hamilton, never one to overlook a slight against his chief (or against himself; no doubt he remembered the leaked-letter incident), gleefully commented that Washington had won his own laurels at Monmouth. Unlike Gates at Saratoga, Washington had no Benedict Arnold at hand to do the hard work for him. This, of course, rather pettily neglected Lee's gallant delaying action that allowed Washington the time to form the main army.[50] Lee, enraged at his own disgrace, warned Gates that Washington's partisans were out to get him (Gates) as well. "For God's sake take care of yourself," Lee warned, "there is a mine laid under your feet, and the train [of gunpowder] ready laid, the materials heap'd up from self conceit arrogance ignorance and mean jealousy."[51] Lee, of course, in the midst of his frustration, was exaggerating; but there was no question that Washington's people (and to be candid, Washington) used the aftermath of Monmouth to settle scores.

Lee's ultimate fate demonstrated as much. Had the major general held his tempter after his court-martial and argued the facts of his conduct at Monmouth to Congress, perhaps the delegates would have sought a compromise between the generals. Lee's friends urged him to moderation, and certainly they advised him not to force Congress to choose between himself and the commander in chief. But such advice was foreign to Lee's combative nature and he fought back in letters and in print, denigrating Washington's role at Monmouth and protesting his own innocence. But given Washington's resurgent popularity Lee's was a lost cause. After months of nail-biting delay, during which all concerned did their best to sway popular and private opinion, in December Congress had no real choice but to confirm the court-martial verdict. Lee still had his admirers, and the vote against him was not unanimous. Seven of the twenty-three voting delegates stood by Lee and wanted to overturn the court-martial verdict. But majority support for the verdict was no real surprise. "When a dispute had been carried to so great a height," an observant Briton (probably the great parliamentarian Edmund Burke) commented, "between an officer on whom the Americans reposed there [*sic*] chief consequence, and one subordinate less popular, it is not difficult to divine where the blame will be laid."[52] When the anguished major general finally sent Congress an insolent letter, the delegates announced they no longer had need of his services.[53] Lee never again served as a Continental.

Even before Lee's court-martial, however, feelings ran high among Washington's friends; and for some of them the aftermath of Monmouth seemed opportune to settle scores from the Cabal. Thus we meet again Brigadier John Cadwalader of the Pennsylvania militia, the officer who, at Tench Tilghman's urging, took up his sharp quill in the commander in chief's behalf. Cadwalader had commanded a militia contingent during the battle; but only days later, as Washington marched his army northeast toward the Hudson, Cadwalader and his cousin, New Jersey militia major general Philemon Dickinson, rode to Philadelphia. Their intention was to goad former inspector general Thomas Conway into a duel. Cadwalader supposedly disparaged Conway's courage at the Battle of Germantown (a charge utterly false), and after whatever words passed between Conway and Cadwalader—and we do not know exactly what they were—the former challenged the latter. Dickinson served as Cadwalader's second, and the Pennsylvanian's fire hit Conway through the lip. Initial accounts of the duel reported a mortal wound, but Conway quickly recovered.[54] His American career, however, was finished; and before returning to France he wrote Washington apologizing for any offense he may have given. Washington never replied.

Dueling was never officially sanctioned, but among patriot officers it had become increasingly common. Gérard, the French minister, thought the practice had "reached an incredible and scandalous point." [55] At whatever point, however, Cadwalader's action provoked no public censure. Quite the contrary. Indeed, some two months later Congress offered him a Continental brigadier's commission and command of all American cavalry (which Cadwalader graciously declined, mistakenly believing the war was about over).[56] Upon learning of the duel Nathanael Greene was positively gleeful, and he was sure others felt the same. He cheerfully told the Pennsylvanian

"Your duel made a great noise in the American World. Most People rejoiced at Mr. Conway's fate."[57] It is hard to imagine Cadwalader receiving such applause for shooting a former congressional favorite anywhere but in the afterglow of Monmouth.

Not everyone applauded Cadwalader. Thomas McKean, chief justice of the Supreme Court of Pennsylvania, sternly disapproved; but he was perhaps the sole patriot to record his dissatisfaction, although he dared not do so publicly. Writing to fellow justice William Atlee, McKean dismissed Cadwalader's action as "weaknes and vanity." But the judge could read the sentiments of the day. Any legal action against the brigadier, McKean thought, "might be attributed by uncharitable persons to resentment rather than justice."[58] He was right in doubting the duel served justice, but it clearly illustrated Washington's loyalists were never bolder in defending his reputation. And inasmuch as no one was willing to speak up for Conway, the duel demonstrated the extent to which the commanding general's critics had "slunk back."

It also demonstrated the point to which Washington's partisans would go. Later young John Laurens would exchange shots with Charles Lee, and Lee came close to a duel with Steuben. An unidentified French officer, writing home with what he claimed was "the most impartial veracity," found Virginia torn between partisans of Washington and friends of Gates and Lee. He was sure the two major generals were linked to a "cabal" against the commander in chief but that the effort had "fallen through." The counterattack *versus* the Cabal, however, had proceeded "in too noisey a way—it looks like persecution." The thoughtful Frenchman mused that if carried too far, the treatment of Washington's critics could backfire: "The sort of pity it excites may provide them the means of recovery."[59] That never happened; Washington's victory was too complete.

IF HIS CRITICS were cowed, however, some instances of animosity remained. In particular, Nathanael Greene proved right about Horatio Gates. Whether it was "pride," "ambition," or something else that motivated him, Gates proved unable to sit on the sidelines indefinitely. Gérard had predicted as much as well. At some point after Monmouth, the French diplomat thought, Gates's "proud spirit" would "manifest itself."[60] The major general may have seen a change in congressional leadership as an opening, because after a quiescent several months he again tested his influence *vis a vis* the commander in chief. Henry Laurens had stepped down as president of Congress in December to be replaced by John Jay of New York. In January 1779

Gates wrote Jay an effusive congratulatory letter, florid and fulsome even by eighteenth-century standards. "The choice Congress have made of your Excellency as their president at this most interesting Juncture proves the high sense they have of your Merit;" Gates then added his "most fervent wish" that the coming year "may offer your Excellency the most favourable opportunities for manifesting your Abilities and Patriotism." This was flattery verging on art form. The letter ended with a reference to a subject that had vexed patriots the year before; in fact it had done much to dim the luster of Gates's reputation—and to end the Cabal.[61] There was talk of another expedition to the north—Canada again.

Early in Jay's tenure Canada again became a patriot focus. In the aftermath of the Battle of Monmouth, and with active French participation in the war, there was speculation among patriots about a British evacuation of the rebellious colonies. In that case, the question went, would an American offensive into Canada be feasible? There was even talk of a joint maneuver with a French fleet operating on the St. Lawrence River. The idea was intriguing enough to prompt the formation of yet another congressional committee, this time to confer directly with Washington and Lafayette. In response Washington wrote a lengthy and negative assessment of any Canadian expedition directly to Laurens on November 11, 1778. The general, still gun-shy after the go-round on the subject earlier in the year, thought a northern venture might be possible—but *only* if the British pulled out of the rest of America first and *only* if patriot resources were adequate to support any joint operations with the French. He also objected to certain details in the proposed venture. While there was some interest in an advance on Quebec through Coös in northern New Hampshire, the commander in chief insisted that any operation (on the off chance one actually occurred) should use the traditional corridor up Lake Champlain. In any case the committee concluded, per Washington's detailed advice, that patriot resources simply were not up to the task while the British maintained active operations in America. And the British did not appear to be giving up the contest. The general was emphatic on this point, and consequently on January 1, 1779, the delegates voted to suspend any preparations for a Canadian invasion.[62]

Gates, however, would not give up on the idea—because it was largely *his* idea. Even with the collapse of the "irruption" the major general had never lost interest in Canada; he was honestly convinced attaching the "Fourteenth Colony" to the Revolution was both desirable and possible with the right planning and resources. He had quietly set about that planning as early as May 1778 when he reported to his northern command headquarters in the Highlands. Intelligence he mistakenly believed reliable reported British defenses in Canada were weak (but not as weak as Gates thought) and that Canadians were ready to throw in with the patriot cause (a highly optimistic assumption). Such was his fascination with Canada that Gates neglected to mount serious operations against the Indians on the New York frontiers—operations Washington and Congress had fully expected. Citing advice from officers he considered informed on Canadian affairs, Gates stubbornly thought an invasion through Coös promised success if a French fleet could sail up the St. Lawrence River in support.[63]

Gates continued to argue for the operation even after the January 1 congressional vote and after Washington's feelings on the matter were well known. Now in Boston, the major general chose to dispute the matter in writing, telling the commander in chief of his "Astonishment at the sudden change of your Sentiments, and relinquishment" of the Canadian plan—ignoring the fact that Washington had shown only tepid interest in the first place and that even that interest was predicated on the British abandoning the rest of America. As he had during the Conway letter affair, Gates also wrote directly to Congress, and he elected to send copies of his correspondence with Washington.[64] It was a strategy that had backfired in 1778, and it worked no better in 1779. Gates was no longer the congressional darling he had been, and it was unsurprising that Congress paid him little attention on the matter.[65]

What *was* surprising was Washington's reaction to what he saw as yet another instance of Gates's meddling at his expense: The commander in chief threw a literary tantrum. On April 14, having learned of Gates's communications with Jay, including the fact that Jay had received copies of Gates's correspondence with Washington, the commanding general responded with a blistering missive of some 3,500 words. Jay was a long-time partisan of the general and well aware of the breach between Washington and Gates, but the New Yorker must have taken a deep breath at the length and tone of Washington's message. The Virginian laced into Gates as an intriguer and thorn in his side since early in the war. Some of Gates's "unfriendly views . . . have been too notorious not to have come to your knowledge: others, from the manner in which they have been conveyed to me will probably never be known, except to a very few." But the general thought Jay had "perhaps heard enough, and observed enough, yourself, to make any further explanation from me, unnecessary." He would not bother Jay with these matters but for the fact that again "Genel Gates has endeavour'd to impress Congress with an unfavourable idea of me."[66]

Washington gave full vent to his spleen. He castigated as misleading or false Gates's account of their communications. Gates claimed Washington largely avoided him; Washington produced dozens of recent letters. The commander in chief pointed out that he had never fully endorsed a new Canadian operation—that he always had made such an effort contingent on a British pull-out—and he bluntly rejected Gates's arguments in behalf of the venture. Then Washington trotted out the Cabal—he had neither forgotten nor forgiven. He bitterly recalled the "coldness & constraint in General Gates's behaviour to me—These increased as he rose into greater consequence; but we did not come to a direct breach till the beginning of last year," he told Jay. "This was occasioned by a corrispondance, which I thought rather made free with me between him and Genl Conway, which accidentally came to my knowledge. . . . Besides the evidence contained in them of the genuine-ness of the offensive corrispondance, I have other proofs still more convincing, which having been given me in a confidential way, I am not at liberty to impart." With the end of "the Letter" affair, Washington insisted, he had tried to be civil and professional with Gates, only to "find that this Gentleman does not scruple to take the most unfair advantages of me." The general ended with a long postscript disparaging Gates's criticisms of current army deployments.[67] There was real vitriol in all of this; Washington had written nothing like it since tearing into Gates during the Conway affair. Even Douglas Southall Freeman, perhaps Washington's most sympathetic biographer, thought the general had laid it on a bit thick.[68]

Perhaps Washington's letter to Jay was a chance to unburden, something of a catharsis. He certainly didn't hold back, and the letter clearly reflected the intensity of anger Washington had harbored from his travails during late 1777 and early 1778. The commander in chief was settling scores with Gates. Gates, a patriot and former friend who, with Mifflin and Conway, had become the Cabal personified in Washington's eyes. And if Washington needed assurance his literary blast had hit the mark, Jay promptly supplied it. Whatever "Impression" Gates had tried to make, Jay wrote, "has not taken." The major general's correspondence "passed without a single Remark. Your Friends thought it merited nothing but Silence and Neglect. The Same Reason induced me to take no Notice of it in my Answer." "Gratitude ought to have attached a certain Gentleman"—and here Jay meant Gates—"to the Friend who raised him. a spurious Ambition however, has it seems made him your Enemy." Then the president of Congress waxed philosophical. Gates's conduct, he noted was "not uncommon. To the Dishonor of human nature, the History of Mankind has many Pages filled with similar Instances; and we have little Reason to expect that the Annals of the present, or future Times, will present us with fewer Characters of this Class. On the contrary there is Reason to expect they will multiply in the Course of this Revolution." It was a moment in time "of general Heat Tumult and Fermentation" that favored "the Production & Growth of some great Virtues, and of many great and little Vices. Which will predominate, is a Question which Events not yet produced, nor now to be discerned can alone determine."[69] It was stoic but good advice from a man President Washington much later would appoint chief justice of the new republic's Supreme Court.

Jay's response also signaled Washington's new post-Cabal relationship with Congress. While members of Congress remained free to correspond with military personnel, on important matters Washington enjoyed something akin to a normal chain of command, or at least a new respect for his prerogatives as commander in chief. The discussions over a new effort against Canada had taken place directly with the general, not with the Board of War, a development the general no doubt appreciated. Other signs pointed in the same direction. In May Congress voted a resolution of thanks to Colonel Goose van Schaick and his troops for their successful raid against the Onondaga Indians in New York State. But instead of sending it directly to Van Schaick, Jay, with the approval of his fellow delegates, thought it "most proper that this be communicated to him by your Excellency."[70] A small thing, perhaps, but it was a courtesy Washington had seldom enjoyed the year before and also an affirmation of his status as commanding general. A greater affirmation followed. With the expected arrival of a French fleet in May, with the possibility of joint operations, Congress did something it never would have considered with Mifflin and Gates still in harness: It voted full confidence in Washington to conduct operations as he saw fit. A resolution of May 10 expressed "the Sense of Congress that your Excellency consider yourself at Liberty to direct the military operations of these States in such manner as you may think expedient. . . .Congress confide fully in your Excellency's Prudence and Abilities; and . . . signify to you their wish, that neither an undue Degree of Delicacy or Diffidence may lead you to place too little Reliance on your own Judgment, or persuade you to make any further Communications of your Designs than necessity or high Expedience may dictate."[71] In the spring of 1779 the vote of confidence was all Washington could have wished from a Congress he hardly trusted twelve months earlier.

Thus the Cabal was gone. But defanged and harmless, shades of the prolonged incident, with all of its wounded feelings and charged emotions, haunted patriot circles for some time. Charles Lee continued to defend his conduct at Monmouth, to demean Washington's leadership, and even to champion Thomas Conway well into 1779. His efforts met only with popular hostility. Faced with a threat of violence, a Baltimore newspaper that dared to publish a Lee tract quickly printed an apology. Writing to Nathanael Greene, Virginia brigadier George Weedon still saw Congress as a nest of "designing men" and "creatures"; Weedon hoped the army's virtue would hold the Revolution together while Washington continued to view "the Calumny of such Mortals beneath his notice."[72] In December 1778 South Carolina governor Edward Rutledge called on John Jay, just seated as president of Congress, to remain on guard. Recent experience had shown how important it was "to oppose a Cabal in its Infancy." "Were it in my Power," he advised, "I would stifle it in its Birth." Rutledge thought there was still danger. "Conway, the Lees [Richard Henry and Francis Lightfoot] & M[ifflin] are said to be at the Bottom of this, besides an abundance of Snakes that are concealed in the Grass." Of course this was old news up north, and we can surmise from Rutledge's letter that notice of Conway's wounding, Mifflin's fall from grace, and the fact that the Lees no longer held a whip hand in Congress traveled slowly to Charles Town (Charleston). Be that as it may, the South Carolinian was worried that the "Spirit of Cabal, & unworthy Ambition" would hurt the cause worse than Sir Henry Clinton's army.[73] Greene remained convinced that Mifflin was just laying low, quietly working to revive "the old Scheme," and that he would stir up as much trouble as he could if Washington again should falter on campaign.[74]

In some quarters Washington's newfound popularity was cause for complaint. Major General John Sullivan warned against Gates, Mifflin, and even Joseph Reed, taking up the chant of "the dangers arising from a Commander who enjoys the full and unlimited confidence of his army."[75] If one can doubt the basis of Sullivan's fears, there seems little question that Samuel Adams remained true to form. According to the chevalier de la Luzerne (Anne-César de La Luzerne), who had replaced Gérard as French minister, as late as January 1781 Adams was still beating the drum against the supposed dangers of Washington's popularity: "He devoted himself to exciting alarm against General Washington, and the more popular Washington is on account of his services, the more dangerous does Mr. Adams regard him."[76] Far from being a danger to the general, however, Adams's consternation certainly stemmed in part from his understanding of how little weight his views now carried.

There was no focus to these residual grumblings. With Mifflin and Gates gone the Board of War had reverted to its original and intended supporting role. Washington had won the support of most congressional delegates, and even James Lovell had ceased any overt carping. Lovell remained a champion of Gates and warned him of critics trying to undermine him—but the radical delegate gave up directly attacking the commander in chief. Richard Henry and Francis Lightfoot Lee, like most of Charles Lee's erstwhile friends, essentially gave up on the embittered major general. As far as we know Benjamin Rush—the ideologue's ideologue—had nothing further to say to Washington's detriment. Conway, once such a lightning rod for Washington's critics, had glumly returned to France; Congress, to its discredit (and frankly, also to Washington's), failed even to provide him with a certificate attesting his good service in America. While Washington could not claim every patriot as a friend, he could rest assured that (barring, of course, further disasters on the battlefield) any further challenges to his authority as commander in chief were unlikely.

Indeed, as angry as he had been in early 1778, by late 1779 Alexander Hamilton considered the remnants of the Cabal something of a joke. Ever looking for a fight with Washington's antagonists, whoever they might have been and wherever he could find them, the sharp-witted lieutenant colonel, tongue firmly in cheek, claimed *he* was now their target: "Speaking of Casar & a C[r]omwell," he wrote his close friend and fellow aide John Laurens, "Don't you think '*the Cabal*' have reported that I declared in a public house in Philadelphia that 'it was high time for the people to rise, join General Washington & turn Congress out of Doors.'"[77] No one had done more to fight the Cabal at its height, and his levity was the surest sign of its demise.

EPILOGUE

> For affliction does not come from the dust, Nor does trouble sprout from the ground, Yet man is born to trouble, as the sparks fly upward.
>
> —Job 5:6–7

As Job reminds us, "affliction does not come from the dust." In late 1777 the patriot cause had a very real affliction, and it had not come from the dust. The origin was glaringly apparent: Washington appeared to be losing the war. Efforts to reverse the fortunes of war, however, sent sparks flying upward as the commander in chief clashed with fellow Americans who, for reasons they thought necessary and proper, pursued a series of measures that threatened his command. These pages have explained those measures, in aggregate, as an administrative coup that would have left Washington's title of commander in chief essentially empty. To the likes of James Lovell, Elbridge Gerry, Thomas Mifflin, Horatio Gates, and others these steps were the appropriate actions of responsible individuals trying to save a faltering revolution. No matter what Washington thought about efforts to circumscribe his authority, his critics believed they were doing the right thing. They were not evil men, nor for the most part were they fools. They were doing no more in questioning Washington than William Pitt had done in calling to account faltering British commanders during the Seven Years' War. That history (and Washington) eventually proved them wrong was hardly evident at the time.

Patriot attempts to address these afflictions of military defeat crystallized in the Cabal. If only for a few months, some of the Revolution's most dedicated patriots lost faith in the commander in chief; and they supported actions that, if not aimed at forcing his actual resignation, certainly would have placed him firmly under the thumb of the Board of War. Yet these efforts—collectively the Cabal—ultimately failed. And now, near the end of our story, we are left with the questions of "why" it failed and what impact that failure had on the principal individuals involved—especially General George Washington.

THE CABAL'S FAILURE had several interrelated roots. One of the most obvious, ironically, was the inability of Washington's critics to establish their own version of "unity of command." While the Cabal was centered in the Board of War, it had friends in and outside of Congress. But they never "sang the same song" (to use the cliché). Those who faulted Washington on military grounds did not necessarily disagree with him on ideological grounds, and all of his critics did not necessarily want him removed. Some never even saw their support for the various initiatives of the Board of War—measures that so offended the commander in chief—as inimical to the general. Recall that even in the face of a vehement Washington's objections, Elbridge Gerry refused to see these actions in the same dangerous light as did the army's senior officers. Quite the contrary, Gerry was offended at the army's dismay.[1] Then there were men like Lovell and Mifflin—and we can safely include Benjamin Rush—who had urged the Hero of Saratoga to come to the main army and save the Revolution. Gates, flattered at such regard, knew exactly what he was doing as president of the board, all the while claiming no animosity toward Washington. Others wanted to save the Revolution just as badly but were not so sure that getting rid of Washington was the answer. In this regard we have met New Jersey's Abraham Clark. A republican stalwart, he was not keen on many of Washington's decisions, but he ultimately concluded that the "Authority & Credit of the Commander in chief must be Supported."[2] Thus motives among the general's critics were seldom the same, and the voices of the Cabal were less a choir than a cacophony.[3]

Then there was the question of numbers. In Congress the general's enemies were never sure they had the strength to bring any measure against him to a vote. Henry Laurens may have hinted that trouble of this nature was brewing in early January 1778. We have seen his letter of warning to his son John that matters in Congress appeared to be coming to a head. But they didn't. James Lovell, Samuel Adams, Virginia's Lee brothers, William Duer, and other like-minded men certainly could count, and it is a safe assumption that sometime between December 1777 and March 1778, if they had counted enough delegates with them, a vote might well have occurred. It never did.

Washington's critics had another problem—George Washington himself. They had misjudged the man, failing to realize they were up against a political master. There should be no quibbling about Washington's performance in facing down the Cabal. It was a remarkable display of political acumen. Fortunately the Virginian came to the Revolution well prepared in this regard, for Washington was no stranger to affairs of state. Historian John Ferling's incisive exploration of the young Washington's involvement in the affairs of colonial Virginia has revealed an often underappreciated side of the future general. He took his role as a member of the gentry seriously, serving in local offices and in the House of Burgesses; and he learned early in his career to maneuver between clashing political interests, to cultivate the friendship and patronage of the influential and powerful, and, frankly, to get what he wanted through very practical (and sometimes hardball) political dealing. If Washington preferred the image of a leader above any partisan fray, he was no naïf; he had a healthy ambition and was not reticent about pursuing it.[4] Without this background it is difficult to imagine his success as commander in chief. The position demanded someone with precisely this experience as well as the talents of military command.

The general never hesitated to use his political talents to assure his position as commander in chief. This was to be expected. Washington sincerely believed his vision for the Continental Army—an army of well-trained and properly equipped professionals—offered the best prospect for the success of the Revolution. He was fully aware he needed to carry this point against a strong ideological preference for militia among many patriots, a preference with deep roots in colonial military tradition. The general believed not only in his military vision, but despite the disappointments of later 1777 he also believed in his own ability to lead the cause to victory. These pages have dwelt on these points at length. But it is worth making some final observations on how Washington deployed his political arsenal against the Cabal.

First, we go back to historian Eric Robson's observation about a key Washington trait: patience. In the field, whether or not we accept the "Washington-as-Fabius" view of the general, he was in no hurry to engage. Measuring his strength against that of his opponents, he picked his moments, striking when he thought circumstances favored an attack. He had an aggressive temperament, but he chose to fight on his own terms. As in the field, so in politics. There is no doubt Washington took personally the criticisms he endured during the tense months of late 1777 and early 1778, and he expressed his share of anger and frustration. But for the most part he remained patient even though it hurt. Then, when circumstances were right, he chose his targets. His delayed riposte to Gates during "the Letter" incident was devastating, catching the Hero of Saratoga flat-footed. Gates never effectively countered Washington's ambush and never fully recovered his political equilibrium.

Washington was equally effective in dealing with the Board of War. Dominated by Mifflin and Gates, with some other members being problematic, the board posed a genuine threat. The board's series of measures calculated to bring key military functions under its effective control—the administrative coup—constituted the heart of the Cabal. Washington saw as much. He also saw that neutralizing the board would be more effective than any direct confrontation with Congress. This he did largely by ignoring or bypassing the board. In December 1777 he brushed off Inspector General Conway and disregarded the War Office; and when Congress dithered, Washington did nothing until he was able to find an acceptable inspector—Steuben. And Steuben, unlike Conway, would serve within the traditional chain of command. Washington did not argue with Congress; he simply balked until the delegates gave up on Conway, at least as inspector general. The board and its congressional supporters lost that skirmish decisively.

Washington saw no reason to change tactics. In controversies over the commissary and quartermaster departments, and then over military operations, Washington dealt with the Committee at Camp. Working almost exclusively with committee members—and thus playing off one civilian body against another—he was able to counter virtually every measure the board proposed (and Congress supported) that threatened his authority as commander in chief. It took *time* and as much patience as he could muster, but the general came out with his hold on the army stronger than ever, especially after Monmouth confirmed his stature with the public.

Another of Washington's invaluable traits was his sense of people. He valued talent and loyalty, and he was usually right about those he could trust. He chose his military family and political allies with care. The likes of Alexander Hamilton, John Laurens, Tench Tilghman, Robert Hanson Harrison, and John Fitzgerald formed the nucleus of a talented and completely dedicated staff. Washington also implicitly trusted the loyalty of Lafayette,

Knox, Greene, and Stirling. (He trusted Benedict Arnold as well, and of course he got it notoriously wrong. No one is perfect.) As we have seen, these were the men who carried the political fight with the Cabal while the commander in chief, fully in the know about their activities, seemingly was not directly involved. Recall how he worked through Henry Laurens in Congress and used his aides to carry his message to influential patriots, steadily undercutting Mifflin and Gates. John Laurens made sure his father knew what the army was thinking throughout the Cabal episode, and through John, Henry kept Washington informed of the temper in Congress. Hamilton was not only a capable aide-of-all-work, but he did as much as anyone—and more than most—to combat the Cabal. His letters to delegates and to other prominent patriots warned explicitly of the challenges to Washington's command and urged support for the general. He and John Laurens were the key figures in destroying Charles Lee's reputation after Monmouth, and Lee's disgrace became an object lesson in the fate of anyone who crossed the commander in chief. Tench Tilghman openly called on influential patriots, John Cadwalader included, to rally in Washington's behalf. Washington didn't need to fight his own battles, at least not openly. When it came to brass-knuckle political infighting, the general had the right troops at hand and they were more than willing to take on all comers.

They gave a virtuoso performance while Washington seemingly remained above the partisan battle. He avoided the public prints and, other than in communications with Henry Laurens and later to John Jay, his correspondence with political figures seldom alluded to the Cabal. This reticence extended even to correspondence with men he knew or suspected were not his friends, including the Lee brothers and James Lovell. In the case of Charles Lee, he never uttered a public word against Lee after the disgraced major general's court-martial. In fact, after Congress sustained the verdict Washington insisted that he never demeaned his former second-in-command and that he spoke of Lee only in the line of duty and strictly in neutral terms.[5] As far as most of the public was concerned, General George Washington simply did not dirty his hands with common politics. The entire Cabal episode revealed Washington as a political maestro. It would be difficult to name another revolutionary leader his equal in this regard.

None of this is to suggest that Washington was hiding behind others in dealing with the Cabal (reluctant as he was to get his political hands dirty). Far from it. When he thought necessary Washington could step into the arena and fight as hard and as directly as anyone. With Gates and Conway he was blunt, even confrontational. As we have seen, in the leaked-letter affair the commanding general actually ambushed Gates and subsequently berated him over Gates's regard for Conway and his seeming indifference to the sentiments expressed in Conway's letter. Washington, of course, was furious that Gates, Mifflin, and Conway seemed worried only about how their private communications had become public. There was nothing subtle in Washington's treatment of Conway when he tried to take up duties as inspector general. Washington certainly did not hold back when he castigated Gates in his December 1779 letter to John Jay. By then the Cabal was over but not the hard feelings it had engendered.

The general could also be sly and maneuver behind the scenes as well as anyone. Consider his dinner invitation to James Wilkinson while at Valley Forge—and the dinner conversation in which Washington just happened to bring up the contents of a letter he had received from Gates. It was the letter in which Gates excoriated his former aide's conduct in disclosing the contents of Gates's private correspondence from Conway. An innocent slip of the tongue? Seriously? More likely it was a deliberate attempt to make life as difficult as possible for Gates—a bit of payback. Then there was Lafayette's visit to York in January and February 1778. We will remember that the young Frenchman had received direct orders from the Board of War to report immediately to Albany to take command of the "Irruption into Canada." It was an expedition Washington considered nothing less than idiotic and on which the Board of War had failed to consult him. But Washington gave the young marquis permission to go to York to question the command arrangements; that is, the commanding general directly contravened an order from the board, or at least allowed Lafayette to do so. And while Lafayette lingered with board members at York, at Valley Forge the commander in chief worked with the Committee at Camp to marshal arguments ultimately lethal to the projected "irruption." Imagining Gates's distress at the canceled venture was probably a bonus for Washington. There *was* a touch of Machiavelli in the man.

We must never forget that Washington was a fiercely determined individual. His patriotism was genuine, and so was his belief that his leadership was essential to eventual American victory. Washington would meet people halfway on certain matters, but he refused to give way when it came to core issues: unity of command, the necessity for a professional Continental Line, and his prerogatives as commander in chief. In dealing with the Cabal he backed down on none of these points. Knowing what battles to fight to a finish is a gift, and Washington had it. And recognizing Washington's political skill in dealing with the Cabal underlines a key aspect of the man: George Washington was more than a general—he was commander in chief. This role entailed qualities beyond courage and skill in battle: tact, patience, determination, an ability to balance or reconcile conflicting personalities, and, especially in Washington's case, the subtlety and skill to deal with civilian authorities—even skeptical authorities—in behalf of the army and, frankly, to defend himself and his policies without throwing the army into turmoil.[6] There was no better example than his using the Committee at Camp to influence Congress and to checkmate what he saw as a hostile War Office. Thus, to do his job Washington had to be a politician, and he had to be a *very* good one. Political finesse was (and is) essential in any commander in chief. He was at his best in this role.

But was the Cabal a "conspiracy"? In fact the question is pointless, and historians who have doubted the existence of the Cabal have wasted too much time on the issue. As the reader will recall from some of our earliest pages, a "cabal" was an eighteenth-century derogatory term for virtually any hint of an organized opposition to someone's preferred political position or program. Of course, if you favored those same positions or programs you were a statesman—or at worst a politician. To define a situation or group as a "cabal" depended upon who was doing the defining. And what constitutes a conspiracy? A large or even a small group in collusion for some nefarious purpose? Private political discussions among like-minded individuals before acting through legal, legislative, or other means? The Board of War acted legally and certainly was in conversations with Congress. And we know that Washington's critics spilled plenty of ink *writing* about the general, so are we supposed to think they weren't *talking* about him. Of course they were.

But in any case actions spoke louder than words. Whether or not we want to define their actions as a plot or conspiracy, a majority of delegates *did* support the Board of War at least until the spring of 1778. They did so fully aware that Washington was at odds with the board. And they did so equally aware that the board's actions, if allowed to stand, would have undercut the general's authority. Congress supported or accommodated policies clearly attributable to Mifflin and Gates, men who had lost faith in the commander in chief and who had incurred his enmity. Unfortunately the *Journals* of Congress recorded very few votes, but the resolutions on the inspector generalship, logistics operations, and the "Irruption into Canada" *did* pass, evidently with comfortable majorities. There was at least one incident in which a delegate—almost certainly Richard Henry Lee—took the floor to question Washington's leadership; and Henry Laurens recorded the sour reception he received when, even as president of Congress, he rose to defend the general. That the delegates and board members did these things for what they saw as the best of motives does not mitigate the fact that they did so. The Cabal did not have to be a plot or conspiracy, and those who search for conspiracies have missed the fact that the Cabal was a series of intentional and very visible acts. Whether the political process that gave rise to these acts was a "conspiracy" or merely "politics" was simply a matter of opinion. And in any case such a distinction made little practical difference to Washington and the army.

Of course, those in Washington's camp *did* suspect the worst, and well they should have. What else were they to make of repeated Board of War initiatives impinging on Washington's authority? How else could they interpret congressional support for the War Office and the influence of Mifflin and Gates, much less the delegates' persistent regard for Conway? Is it at all surprising to find talk of conspiracies or plots—or of "cabals," or "parties" or whatever term a given observer chose? In Congress Henry Laurens chose "junctoes," of which, the reader will remember, Laurens warned his son John. For the time being, he confided, the "prompters & Actors" were having their way. He never named names, but it is not hard to assume he meant the likes of Samuel Adams, the Lees, Lovell, Gerry, and other radicals. The "accommodators, Candle Snuffers, Shifters . . . & mutes," even if friendly to Washington, simply had lost the initiative to their more assertive colleagues. As president of Congress, Laurens quietly lent his support and sympathy to the commander in chief, but he never felt free to publicly denounce the "juntoe." But others in Washington's camp certainly did, and the list was long. Among senior officers Greene, Knox, Lafayette, John Cadwalader, and others were certain Washington faced a determined cadre of opponents. So were a number of former or current members of Congress. Benjamin Harrison (remember "*Be Ware of your Board of War*"?), Henry Jones, Robert Morris, and Gouverneur Morris all were convinced the general was under serious political fire. Washington's aides—Alexander Hamilton, John Laurens, Tench Tilghman, John Fitzgerald, and others—also were among those who sounded the alarm *at the time*. John Laurens made no bones about his feelings toward Mifflin, who he saw at the center of the Cabal. Hamilton excoriated the commanding general's critics whenever an opportunity arose. Could they *all* really have been so mistaken, so paranoid, in the face of nothing more than political carping? Why question Washington's certainty on the matter? His sources of information were excellent, and why would he tell an old friend (remember Landon Carter?) that some patriots had been willing to replace him in favor of Gates?

Then there were the reports of the French diplomats, Gérard and Luzerne. Their job included keeping the French court informed of American political and military developments; they were seasoned diplomats and they made it their business to be in the know. The status of the American war effort was perforce one of their chief concerns, and they interpreted the threat to Washington as anything but imaginary. Were *both* of them wrong? Was that remotely possible?

Frankly, denying the Cabal's reality strains credulity. And in the face of all of this, quibbling over the exact meaning of the word "cabal" or conspiracy is simply . . . well . . . quibbling.

WHAT ABOUT CONTEMPORARIES who denied the existence of the Cabal? Their protests had (and have) a hollow ring. Mifflin, as we know, bemoaned talk of his antipathy to Washington, but he led the War Office in directions Washington never wanted to go. Massachusetts delegate Eliphalet Dyer did flatly deny the existence of any congressional movement to oust the commander in chief. But if Dyer meant there was no actual *conspiracy* against the general, which seemingly was the import of his comment, we must again bear in mind that conspiracies existed—or not—in the eyes of the beholder. But Dyer *did* go along with the board's initiatives knowing full well of Washington's opposition to them. Elbridge Gerry did likewise, and both of these Massachusetts men were aware of the breach between Conway, Gates, and Mifflin on one hand and the commanding general on the other.[7] Again, actions spoke louder than words.

Of course there were examples beyond Dyer and Gerry. We have discussed the political difficulties Richard Henry Lee encountered when his name became associated with the Cabal; and although he insisted he was Washington's friend, we can ask where he and his brother (Francis Lightfoot) were when the general came under political fire. They never publicly—or privately so far as we know—rose to his defense until their political survival came into question. In later years Samuel Adams vehemently denied any ill will toward Washington, but his conduct in 1777 and 1778 belied his postwar evasions. The Massachusetts radical remained fixated on the dangers of popular generals. Besides, denials from most of these men came only *after*—

and sometimes *long* after—Washington's counterattacks had sent the Cabal running. So who was going to own up to being part of it or knowing about it and doing nothing to blow the whistle? And why credit the problematic protests of the Gerrys, Dyers, Lees, and Adamses as opposed to the overwhelming testimony of those contemporaries who saw a "Cabal" in congressional support for the orchestrations of the Board of War?

We can end this discussion with the case of John Adams. There was no greater patriot; other than Washington perhaps no one did more to assure the success of the cause of independence. But we know what he was saying about the commander in chief in late 1777 and we know why he was saying it. As patriot military fortunes declined, so did his faith in the man he had proposed as commander in chief in 1775. The loss of Philadelphia, the importance of which Adams had discounted in early 1777, left him mortified when it actually occurred. Contemporaries knew what Adams thought, and his doubts about the general left an impression. A young James Madison joined the Virginia congressional delegation only in 1780, but he obviously learned enough about Adams's feelings toward Washington to make him wonder about the New Englander's political viability after the war. In 1788, as Americans discussed the new republic's first presidential election, Madison wrote Thomas Jefferson a trenchant letter on who might emerge as Washington's vice president. Adams, he thought, was an unlikely contender. Madison considered the Massachusetts patriot especially unpopular in the south; and in the rest of the country, he predicted, too many people would find Adams "*obnoxious*" based on his political positions, his abrasive personality, and (as Madison saw it) a penchant for intrigue. And there was more: Americans also would reject Adams because of "*his cabal during the war against General Washington*" [italics in original].[8] Of course Madison was wrong. Adams was indeed acceptable for much the same reason Washington was acceptable as commander in chief in 1775—the new nation needed a north-south balance. But the ghost of the Cabal obviously lingered in the public consciousness, and that ghost would not have survived to haunt public affairs a decade later had it not been the ephemeral residue of something once quite real.

OTHER THAN GHOSTS (so to speak) the Cabal left in its wake a cast of very human individuals, and the Cabal story would be incomplete without accounting for the fates of at least some of the episode's central actors. Most went on to more-or-less successful post-Cabal political or military careers, although some followed paths more interesting than others.

As nineteenth-century historians eventually labeled the entire episode the "Conway Cabal"—and the first author to use the term was probably Jared Sparks of Harvard[9]—there is no better place to start than with former major general Thomas Conway. The Franco-Irishman healed quickly after his wound from Cadwalader's pistol ball. He returned to France to the immense relief of his anguished wife. She had learned of the duel but not of her husband's fate. Madame Conway entreated the American diplomatic mission to provide any news it had, and not to spare her feelings if the news was grim. But as of September 1778 there was no additional information, and we don't know when she finally learned Thomas was alive.[10] He was not only alive, but he prospered. While Conway never received the coveted certificate attesting to his Continental service (which he told a sympathetic Richard Henry Lee was "extraordinary," the result of a "cabal" against him), he resumed his career in the French army. He won promotion and served with distinction in French India, where he was governor general from late 1787 to 1789.[11] Despite some controversy, Lafayette recommended to Washington that Conway be allowed into the Society of the Cincinnati along with other French officers in Continental service. He returned to France in 1792, but the following year Conway picked the wrong side during the French Revolution. Apparently he never learned from his American experience that he was a poor judge of political winds. In 1793, after commanding royalist troops in southern France, he fled from revolutionary forces with his wife (supposedly, and ironically, with some British help) and died in Ireland in obscurity about 1800.[12] If anyone in America noted his passing there is no surviving public record.

Horatio Gates and Thomas Mifflin fared better than Conway, although Gates came into his share of trouble. After the Cabal, Gates's relationship with Washington was never more than strictly professional. The Hero of Saratoga still had friends in Congress, and while there was no more serious talk of Gates as a rival to Washington there was still some faith in Gates's ability to rally militia. On that basis, and with hopes that he could produce another Saratoga in South Carolina, in 1780 Congress sent him to command the Southern Department after the fall of Charleston. It was a poor decision. On August 16, Cornwallis resoundingly defeated Gates at the Battle of Camden, routing the patriot army and virtually destroying Gates's military reputation. Peevishly, many of Washington's partisans gloated at Gates's humiliation. Gates never faced a court-martial or official investigation after the Camden disaster, but he suffered in limbo, without command or formal exoneration, until allowed to rejoin the army in 1782. At this point Gates was the army's second-ranking officer.[13]

The approaching end of the war found Gates at the center of one of the conflict's most serious affairs. In March 1783 the army, awaiting word of the final treaty of peace, was encamped at Newburgh, New York. After fruitless attempts to negotiate settlements over back pay and pension obligations with Congress, resentments in the officer corps threatened to boil over. Anonymous circulars (actually authored by one of Gates's aides, Major John Armstrong, Jr.) called on the officers not to disband the army and hinted at worse—perhaps some sort of coup?—if Congress failed to do them justice. On March 15, the officers met to discuss their protests with Gates in the chair, when Washington appeared uninvited. In an emotional address the commander in chief reminded them of their duty, called on them not to sully the sacrifices they already had made, and denounced any thoughts of using the army to threaten Congress. With this the so-called Newburgh Conspiracy evaporated. The exact nature of Gates's role, much less the course of any direct action a disgruntled officer corps may have taken, has been a matter of debate.[14] But Gates did himself no honor. Armstrong never forgave Washington's intervention. Soon after demobilization he lamented to Gates that in backing down at Newburgh the officers had lost their best chance to do themselves justice, and years later he wrote the aging major general ridiculing Washington's presidency.[15]

After the war Gates led a relatively quiet life. With the death of his beloved first wife Elizabeth, he moved to New York City and eventually remarried. He did his best for aging Continental veterans, often loaning money he knew he would never see again. As he drifted into the Jeffersonian political camp he lost the friendship of many of the New Englanders, including John Adams and James Lovell, now Federalists, who had been his ardent champions during the war—and during the Cabal. Gates and Washington never reconciled.

Thomas Mifflin, who never again commanded Continentals after 1778, landed deftly on his political feet. By 1782 he had largely mended fences with the more radical Pennsylvania patriots and once again won election to Congress. He served as president from November 1783 to June 1784. Thus it was on December 23, 1783, when Washington appeared before the delegates to resign his commission, that the retiring general presented the commission to Mifflin—a man who likely would have welcomed such a resignation some six years earlier. One wonders if either man saw any irony on the occasion. Mifflin's political trajectory continued to climb. In 1787 he was a delegate to the Constitutional Convention and signed the new Constitution for Pennsylvania. By the following year Mifflin was president of Pennsylvania, then governor upon the promulgation of the new state constitution. He served until 1799, after which he took a seat in the legislature; the tireless politico was in office when he died in 1800.[16] The Cabal had slowed Thomas Mifflin for a time, but it never stopped him. In the end Washington didn't like the Pennsylvanian, but he never underestimated him.

James Wilkinson virtually made a career of cabals. After a stint as clothier general, a post he filled with no distinction but with a strong whiff of peculation, he accepted a brigadier's commission in the Pennsylvania militia and took a seat in the legislature—all the while maintaining a cordial relationship with Washington. One suspects the general remembered how useful "Wilky" had been in humbling Gates. Wilkinson went west after the war and was active in Kentucky politics. There he did his best to sabotage political rivals, especially George Rogers Clark, whose lucrative position as Indian commissioner Wilkinson wanted and eventually got. By 1787 he was secretly in Spanish pay, supplying intelligence and intriguing to attach the American West in some manner to Spain. In 1791 he was back in the army, and he served creditably under Anthony Wayne against the northwest Indians even while surreptitiously trying to undermine Wayne. With Wayne's resignation Wilkinson actually became the army's ranking general.[17]

As if to prove that backstabbing was an exact branch of political science—of which he had made a thorough study—his deceit and dissimulation sought new boundaries. After the Louisiana Purchase President Jefferson made him governor of a major part of the new territory—thus putting Wilkinson in a position to work for and against Spain and the United States at the same time! He was involved in Aaron Burr's conspiracy, but when Burr's plans (whatever they may have been) began to unravel Wilkinson betrayed Burr and turned him in. While suspected of duplicity by any number of authorities, Wilkinson always was able to cover his tracks. He was nothing if not clever—and lucky. He was a major general during the War of 1812, during which he botched two efforts to invade Canada. Again, he survived an army inquiry. Named American envoy to Mexico, he became involved in Texas land schemes before his death in 1825. Wilkinson was buried in Mexico City.[18] He was that rare individual in the Founding generation—a genuine and unadulterated knave. And he got his start in the Cabal.

Major General Charles Lee fell from grace less for what he did than for his choice in friends. True, he had ideological and personal differences with the commander in chief. But in the immediate aftermath of the Cabal to associate with the likes of the Lee brothers, Benjamin Rush, and Horatio

Gates was as politically naïve a step as Lee could have taken. Indeed, his fall was a classic case of guilt by association. Lee continued publicly and privately to protest his treatment, but to no avail. He never disappeared from the public scene, and despite his bitterness at many former brother officers he was magnanimous enough to write Anthony Wayne a congratulatory letter after Wayne's dramatic victory at Stony Point in 1779. He kept in touch with Rush and managed to remain friends with Robert Morris and a number of Continental veterans; he even retained the respect of James Monroe. Beset by debts, in 1782 Lee sold-up in Virginia and moved to Philadelphia to finalize the sale of his Virginia home. He never left the City of Brotherly Love; he died there of some sort of fever later in the year. Although not mourned by most Washington loyalists, Lee's funeral was well attended. The president of Congress, John Hanson of Maryland, and even Gouverneur Morris were there as Lee was laid to rest with military honors in Christ Church graveyard.[19] At final rest, the turbulent soldier was as quiet as he ever had been.

The Virginia Lee brothers went on to successful post-war careers, although their relationships to the general were quite different. Despite post-war denials, their differences with Washington during the war were no secret. Aside from defending themselves against accusations of animosity toward Washington, they never rose to defend him during the height of the Cabal. After the war and into Washington's presidency, Richard Henry Lee and Washington continued a normal acquaintance with a fairly regular correspondence and an occasional visit. Washington's communications with Francis Lightfoot, however, were scant. During all of this there is no indication Washington ever brought up the Cabal as the Lees continued their political careers in state, Confederation, and national offices. There was no point in opening old wounds as the former general and the Virginia brothers labored to get the new ship of state safely launched.

Other post-Cabal stories were similar; as Washington looked forward he saw little sense in fighting old battles. He never had a close relationship with Samuel Adams anyway, and given Adams's unrelenting republican hard line during the war and post-war alignment with Thomas Jefferson, Washington and the Massachusetts radical essentially ignored one another. That was fine with Washington. Even after he became the nation's first vice president, John Adams and the president shared only a formal relationship. Benjamin Rush, later ashamed of his former attacks on the commander in chief, fully repented. He did his best to convince early historians, notably John Marshall and Bushrod Washington, not to mention his attacks on the general; he made no mention of them in his autobiography. His children suspected he got rid of any personal papers linking him to the Cabal.[20]

James Lovell never repented. He saw nothing in his conduct toward Washington but the acts of an honest republican safeguarding the public weal. Thus he saw nothing ironic, as one of General Washington's most astringent critics during the war, in importuning President Washington for a federal job. The president had no fond memories of the Massachusetts delegate—probably quite the contrary. But Lovell had been a staunch patriot and had given up much for the cause. His family had fractured as his father had declared for the King, and James had suffered a parent's anxiety as his son fought through the war, wounded more than once as a Continental officer. After the war his teaching career failed to offer a secure future, nor did the local offices he held. So he turned to Washington: "When I first addressed myself to your Excellency, thirteen years ago," he wrote in the summer of 1789, "my *Life & Liberty* were at Stake, now, the *Comfort of all my latter Days* is at Hazard."[21] This from the republican zealot who had so violently objected to pensions for Continental officers. Yet Lovell had as much right as anyone—and more right than many—to ask something in return from the republic he had helped to found. Washington came through. He appointed Lovell naval officer of the port of Boston and Charlestown, a post he held until his death in 1814.[22] To have refused Lovell in a reasonable request would have been small. George Washington was not small.

THE CABAL WAS a unique chapter in the history of the War for Independence; it was the only time Washington's leadership of the Continental Army was imperiled. It unfolded amid a context of military adversity, ideological divisiveness, fear for the future of the cause, and a poisoned political atmosphere fraught with personal animosities—a toxic mix indeed. Criticisms of Washington, and parallel praise of Horatio Gates, came to a head with the discovery of Thomas Conway's letter to Gates. "The Letter" was not yet the Cabal; neither Conway nor Gates were discussing an effort to remove the commander in chief. But the fallout from "the Letter" was the entré to more serious developments; it was productive of anger and mistrust at a time when the patriot cause most needed unity. These tensions framed the efforts by the Board of War to expand its remit from support functions to direct participation in the army's daily activities and operational affairs. Washington's efforts to fight off the board's challenge to his prerogatives had far-reaching consequences. The humbling of Gates and Mifflin, the fall of Conway, the court-martial of Lee, and the silencing of congressional critics was the stuff of patriot politics at its highest. It was the making of the general as the icon of the Revolution. If this surprised and distressed some of Washington's most astringent critics—and one thinks here of the continued yammering of Samuel Adams—and if the general had proved more durable than his antagonists had anticipated, these developments hardly meant the challenge to his command had been minimal. Much less did it mean that Washington's perception of his critics was the stuff of paranoia or overreaction. The commander in chief and his allies had not been tilting at windmills or fencing with shadows.

In 1941 Bernard Knollenberg, fine scholar and distinguished public servant that he was, was wrong in concluding the Cabal was a myth. So were authors who followed him in denying the existence of the Cabal. They failed to credit the very obvious actions of the Board of War as inimical to Washington's authority as commander in chief. Under the leadership of Horatio Gates and Thomas Mifflin, the board, with congressional acquiescence, *had* acted, if not to force Washington from office, at least to curtail his role as commanding general. They initiated measures aimed very directly at assuming control of key aspects of the American military effort, measures these pages have deemed an "administrative coup." That the Cabal failed does not negate the fact that at a critical stage of the War for Independence a group of dedicated patriots had found Washington lacking and tried, at the very least, to limit his role as commanding general, if not to take leadership of the Continental Army completely out of his hands. Was the Cabal real? It certainly was.

NOTES

ABBREVIATIONS

APS	American Philosophical Society, Philadelphia.
DLAR	David Library of the American Revolution, Washington Crossing, PA.
FAM	Fenimore Art Museum and The Farmers Museum Research Library, Cooperstown, NY.
HSP	Historical Society of Pennsylvania, Philadelphia.
JCC	*Journals of the Continental Congress, 1774-1789*. 34 vols. Edited by Worthington C. Ford et al. Washington, D.C.: U.S. Government Printing Office, 1904-1937.
LC	Library of Congress, Washington, DC.
LDC	Smith, Paul H. and Ronald M. Gephart, eds. *Letters of Delegates to Congress, 1774-1789*. 26 vols.Washington, DC: Library of Congress, 1976-2000.
MHS	Massachusetts Historical Society, Boston.
NYHS	New-York Historical Society, New York City.
NYPL	New York Public Library, New York City.
PAH	Hamilton, Alexander. *The Papers of Alexander Hamilton*. Edited by Harold C. Syrett and Jacob E. Cooke. 27 vols. New York: Columbia University Press, 1961-87.
PCC	Papers of the Continental Congress, National Archives.
PGW	Washington, George. *The Papers of George Washington*. Edited by W. W. Abbot, et al., Charlottesville: University Press of Virginia, 1987–.
PGWde	Washington, George. *The Papers of George Washington Digital Edition*. Edited by Theodore J. Crackel et al. Charlottesville: University of Virginia Press, Rotunda, 2007.
PHL	Laurens, Henry. *The Papers of Henry Laurens*. Edited by David R. Chesnutt and C. James Taylor. 16 vols. Columbia, SC: University of South Carolina Press, 1968–2002.
PMHB	*Pennsylvania Magazine of History and Biography.*
PNG	Greene, Nathanael. *The Papers of Nathanael Green*. 8 vols. Edited by Richard K. Showman et al. Chapel Hill: University of North Carolina Press, for the Rhode Island Historical Society, 1976.

PTJ	Jefferson, Thomas. *The Papers of Thomas Jefferson.* Edited by Julian P. Boyd et al. Princeton: Princeton University Press, 1950–.
PUL	Princeton University, Firestone Library.
PWL	Livingston, William. *The Papers of William Livingston.* Edited by Carl E. Prince and Dennis P. Ryan. 5 vols. Trenton: New Jersey Historical Commission, 1979–1988.
SPJJde	*The Selected Papers of John Jay Digital Edition.* Edited by Elizabeth M. Nuxoll. Charlottesville: University Press of Virginia, Rotunda, 2014–.
VFNHP	Valley Forge National Historical Park Library.
VHS	Virginia Historical Society, Richmond.
WSA	Adams, Samuel. *The Writings of Samuel Adams.* 4 vols. Edited by Harry Alonzo Cushing. New York: G.P. Putnam's Sons, 1907.

PREFACE

1. Jack P. Green, "Landon Carter (1710-1778)," *Dictionary of Virginia Biography*, in *Encyclopedia Virginia* (Virginia Foundation for the Humanities, 15 Aug. 2013), http://www.EncyclopediaVirginia.org/ Carter_Landon_1710-1778; accessed 16 Mar. 2017.

2. George Washington to Landon Carter, 30 May 1778, *The Papers of George Washington* [hereafter *PGW*], Revolutionary War Series [RWS], ed. Edward G. Lengel (Charlottesville: University Press of Virginia, 2006), 15:267.

3. Ibid., 15:268–270.

4. Mercy [Otis] Warren, *History of the Rise, Progress and Termination of the American Revolution. Interspersed with Biographical, Political and Moral Observations,* 3 vols. (Boston: Manning and Loring, 1805), I:394; Carlo Botta, *History of the War of the Independence of the United States of America.* Trans. by George Alexander Otis, 2 vols. (New Haven, CT: Nathan Whiting, 1837 [orig. in Italian, 1809]), I:63–64; John Marshall, *The Life of George Washington, Commander in Chief of the American Forces, during the War Which Established the Independence of His Country, and First President of the United States,* 5 vols. (Philadelphia: C.P. Wayne, 1804-1807), 3:334–39; George Bancroft, *History of the United States,* 10 vols. (Boston: Little, Brown and Co., 1834-74), IX:454–58, 460–64. The views of Marshall and Bancroft remained virtually unchallenged for over a century. For other examples in this regard, see also, Richard Hildreth, *The History of the United States of America,* 6 vols. (New York: Harper & Bros., 1849-52), III:215, 232–37; Hildreth, while echoing Marshall and Bancroft, at least conceded not all of Washington's critics had base motives. Still later, Edward Channing in his *History of the United States,* 6 vols. (New York: Macmillan, 1920-25), 3:276, accepted the fact of an "attempt to appoint Gates to chief command in Washington's place," but cautioned this should not detract from Gates's achievement at Saratoga.

5. *The Writings of George Washington: Being the Correspondence, Addresses, Messages, and Other Papers, Official and Private, Selected and Published from the Original Manuscripts,* ed. by Jared Sparks, 12 vols. (Boston: Russell, Odiorne, and Metcalf, and Hilliard, Gray, and Co., 1833-39). Spark's transcriptions led to some controversy. They drew the criticism principally of British historian Philip Henry Stanhope (Viscount Mahon) who accused him of making additions to and omissions from Washington's original texts. However, Sparks was able to explain most of the points in contention, which largely satisfied Mahon. See Herbert B. Adams, *The Life and Writings of Jared Sparks: Comprising Selections from His Journals and Correspondence,* 2 vols. (Boston: Houghton, Mifflin and Company, 1893), 1:xxvi–xxx, xlvin2.

6. Jared Sparks to Robert Gilmore, 31 Jan. 1832, Historical MSS Collection, MS-5320, Spe-

cial Collections, Fred W. Smith National Library, George Washington's Mount Vernon, Mount Vernon, VA. Gilmore was an autograph collector with a special interest in the American Revolution.

7. *Writings of George Washington*, Sparks, ed., V:483–518.

8. Bernhard Knollenberg, *Washington and the Revolution, a Reappraisal: Gates, Conway, and the Continental Congress* (New York: Macmillan, 1941). For a cautionary note on Knollenberg, see Louis Reichenthal Gottschalk's review of "*Washington and the Revolution: A Reappraisal. Gates, Conway, and the Continental Congress*, by Bernhard Knollenberg," *Journal of Modern History* 13, No. 1 (March 1941):97–98.

9. Samuel White Patterson, *Horatio Gates: Defender of American Liberties* (New York: Columbia University Press, 1941); Paul David Nelson, *General Horatio Gates: A Biography* (Baton Rouge: Louisiana State University Press, 1976); Kenneth R. Rossman, *Thomas Mifflin and the Politics of the American Revolution* (Chapel Hill: University of North Carolina Press, 1952).

10. As Nelson has observed, James T. Flexner's *George Washington: In the American Revolution, 1775-1783*, published in 1968, has the ring of a John Marshall or George Bancroft; Nelson, *Horatio Gates*, xii. While discounting the existence of any major organized conspiracy, Douglas Southall Freeman certainly agreed a number of congressional delegates were hostile to Washington and that Gates, Mifflin, and Conway were interested in seeing Washington depart; see Freeman's *George Washington: A Biography*, 7 vols. (New York: Scribner, 1948-54), 4:587–611.

11. For a concise summary of the modern understanding of the Conway Cabal, see Don Higginbotham, *The War of American Independence: Military Attitudes, Policies, and Practice, 1763-1789* (New York: Macmillan, 1971), 216–22.

12. Thomas Mifflin to Horatio Gates, 28 Nov. 1777, in Bennett Nolan, *George Washington and the Town of Reading in Pennsylvania* (Reading, PA: Chamber of Commerce of Reading, 1931), 72–73; Benjamin Rush, *The Autobiography of Benjamin Rush: His "Travels through Life" Together with His Commonplace Book for 1789-1813*, ed. by George W. Conner (Philadelphia: American Philosophical Society, 1948), 137–38; Benjamin Rush, *The Selected Writings of Benjamin Rush*, ed. by Dagobert Runes (New York: Philosophical Library, 1947), vi–vii.

13. *E.g.*, Dave Richard Palmer, *George Washington and Benedict Arnold: A Tale of Two Patriots* (Washington, DC: Regnery, 2006), 267–71, 273–76, 278; J. Kent McGaughy and Gregory D. Massey, "Conway Cabal: Was There a Secret Plot to Remove George Washington as Commander in Chief in the Winter of 1777-1778?" in *History in Dispute*, Volume 12: *The American Revolution*, ed. Keith Krawczynski (Detroit: Thomson Gale, 2003), unpaginated e-book; Thomas Fleming, *Washington's Secret War: The Hidden History of Valley Forge* (New York: HarperCollins, 2005); Harlow Giles Unger, *Dr. Benjamin Rush: The Founding Father Who Healed a Wounded Nation* (New York: Da Capo Press, 2018), 67–72; and especially Mark Edward Lender and Garry Wheeler Stone, *Fatal Sunday: George Washington, the Monmouth Campaign, and the Politics of Battle* (Norman: University of Oklahoma Press, 1916), 19–44.

14. Higginbotham, *War of American Independence*, 221.

15. John Entick and William Crakelt, *Entick's New Spelling Dictionary: Teaching to Write and Pronounce the English Tongue with Ease and Propriety, in Wich Each Word is Accented According to Its Just and Natural Pronunciation . . . with a List of Proper Names of Men and Women . . ., To wich is Prefixed a Gammatical Introduction to the English Tongue*, rev. ed. (London: Printed for Charles Dilly, 1787), 49. Various printings of Entick's appeared in America after the war. *E.g.*, John Entick and Lindley Murray, *Entick's New Spelling Dictionary:*

Teaching to Write and Pronounce the English Tongue with Ease and Propriety . . . : to Which Are Added, an Alphabetical Account of the Heathen Deities, a . . . Table of Remarkable Events, Discoveries and Inventions, and a List of the Post-Towns in the United States . . . To This Work is Prefixed, An abridgment of the English Grammar (New Haven, CT: Increase Cooke & Co., 1812).

CHAPTER ONE: THE SEASON OF HOPE

1. Samuel Mather to Samuel Adams, 27 January 1777, Samuel Adams Papers, Manuscripts and Archives Division, NYPL.

2. Samuel Mather, *The Dying Legacy of an Aged Minister of the Everlasting Gospel* (Boston: Printed by Benjamin Edes and Sons, 1783), i.

3. E.g., Samuel Adams to James Warren, 18 June 1777, in Paul H. Smith and Ronald M. Gephart, eds. *Letters of Delegates to Congress, 1774-1789* [hereafter *LDC*], 26 vols. (Washington, DC: Library of Congress, 1976-2000), 7:208.

4. Alan Greenspan, "The Challenge of Central Banking in a Democratic Society," Francis Boyer Lecture, American Enterprise Institute for Public Policy, 5 Dec. 1996, Washington, DC; Greenspan's term quickly passed into general usage.

5. Mark Edward Lender, "Small Battles Won: New Jersey and the Patriot Military Revival," *New Jersey Heritage* 1, no. 2 (2002):30–37.

6. "Biographical Sketch of Hannah Winthrop," Massachusetts Historical Society [hereafter MHS], http://www.masshist.org/features/warren-winthrop/sketches#winthrop, accessed 23 Mar. 2017; Hannah Winthrop to Mercy Otis Warren, 14 Jan. 1777, Correspondence of Mercy Otis Warren and Hannah Winthrop, MHS.

7. William Livingston to John Jay, 3 Mar. 1777, *The Papers of William Livingston* [hereafter *PWL*], edited by Carl E. Prince and Dennis P. Ryan, 5 vols. (Trenton: New Jersey Historical Commission, 1979-88), 1:265. On the state of Washington's army, see George Washington [GW] to John Hancock, 8 Sept. 1776, *The Papers of George Washington Digital Edition* [*PGWde*], Revolutionary War Series [RWS], Theodore J. Crackel, ed. (Charlottesville: University Press of Virginia, Rotunda, 2007), 8:9.

8. James Kirby Martin and Mark Edward Lender, *A Respectable Army: The Military Origins of the Republic, 1763-1789*, 3rd ed. (Malden, MA: Wiley Blackwell, 2015), 76–77.

9. Josiah Quincy, *The Journals of Major Samuel Shaw: The First American Council at Canton, with a Life of the Author* (Boston: Wm. Crosby and H. P. Nichols, 1847), 31.

10. GW to William Heath, 3 Feb. 1777, *PGWde*, RWS, 8:230.

11. David C. Munn, *Battles and Skirmishes of the American Revolution in New Jersey* (Trenton, NJ: Bureau of Geology and Topography, Department of Environmental Protection, 1976), 127–28.

12. Jared C. Lobdell, "Six Generals Gather Forage: The Engagement at Quibbletown, 1777," *New Jersey History* 102 (1984): 35–50.

13. David B. Mattern, *Benjamin Lincoln and the American Revolution* (Columbia: University of South Carolina Press), 1995, 37–38; Mark Urban, *Fusiliers: The Saga of a British Redcoat Regiment in the American Revolution* (New York: Walker & Company, 2007), 104–106; Johann Ewald, *Diary of the American War: A Hessian Journal*, trans. and ed. by Joseph P. Tustin (New Haven: Yale University Press, 1979), 56–57.

14. GW to John Hancock, 8 Sept. 1776, *PGWde*, RWS, 6:249.

15. Mark Edward Lender, *The War for American Independence* (Santa Barbara, CA: ABC-CLIO, 2016), 31.

16. Charles H. Lesser, ed., *The Sinews of Independence: Monthly Strength Reports of the Continental Army* (Chicago: University of Chicago Press, 1976), 46.
17. "Orderly Book of Gen. John Peter Muhlenberg, March 26-December 20, 1777," *Pennsylvania Magazine of History and Biography* [*PMHB*] 33, No. 1 (1909):455–456; *Annual Register* (London), 1777, 19–21.
18. Elbridge Gerry to Thomas Gerry, 17 June 1777, *LDC*, 7:201. For a similarly buoyant perspective, see James Wilson to Arthur St. Clair, 3 July 1777, ibid., 7:287.
19. John Adams to John Sullivan, 8 June 1777, *LDC*, 7:176; Francis Lightfoot Lee to Landon Carter, 8 June 1777, ibid., 7:177; Thomas Burke to Richard Caswell, 27 June 1777, ibid., 7:257.
20. New York Delegates to the New York Council of Safety, 19 June 1777, ibid., 7:233.
21. James Lovell to Joseph Trumbull, 24 June 1777, ibid., 7:247.
22. Abraham Clark to James Caldwell, 18 June 1777, ibid., 7:209; William Duer to Philip Schuyler, 19 June 1777, ibid., 7:230. Clark and Duer would later express reservations about Washington's leadership—Duer especially so.
23. Benjamin Rush to Anthony Wayne, 18 June 1777, Anthony Wayne Papers, no. 0699, Historical Society of Pennsylvania, Philadelphia.
24. Adams to Richard Henry Lee, 15 July 1777, *The Writings of Samuel Adams* [hereafter *WSA*], 4 vols., ed. by Harry Alonzo Cushing (New York: G.P. Putnam's Sons, 1907), 3:386–87. See also Adams to Nathanael Greene, 12 May 1777, ibid., 3:370–71
25. Samuel Adams to Elizabeth Adams, 17 June 1777, *LDC*, 7:201; Samuel Adams to James Warren, 18 June 1777, ibid., 7:208.
26. John Adams to Abigail Adams, 14 June 1777, ibid., 7:195; Samuel Adams to James Warren, 18 June 1777, ibid., 7:208.
27. Ira D. Gruber, *The Howe Brothers and the American Revolution* (Chapel Hill: University of North Carolina Press, 1975); Troyer Steele Anderson, *Command of the Howe Brothers during the American Revolution* (New York: Oxford University Press, 1936); Andrew Jackson O'Shaughnessy, *The Men Who Lost America: British Leadership, the American Revolution, and the Fate of the Empire* (New Haven: Yale University Press, 2013).
28. James Lovell to Joseph Trumbull, 24 June 1777, *LDC*, 7:247; Robert Morris to Jonathan Hudson, 24 June 1777, ibid., 7:248; John Penn to Richard Caswell, 25 June 1777, ibid., 7:249; Thomas Burke to Richard Caswell, 11 May 1777, ibid., 7:69.
29. Quincy, ed., *Journals of Samuel Shaw*, 33; *Annual Register* (London), Spring 1777, 20.
30. *E.g.*, "Journal of Major Ennion Williams," in William Henry Egle, ed., *Journals and Diaries of the Revolution, with Lists of Officers and Soldiers, 1775-1783* (Harrisburg, PA: E. K. Myers, 1893), 13. Major Williams found Washington in an irritable mood complaining about the conduct of some of his officers and of civilian contacts with the enemy. It was an uninspiring interview. See also Edward G. Lengel and Mark Edward Lender, "The Middle Theater: The Decisive Front of Independence," in *Theaters of the American Revolution*, James Kirby Martin and David L. Preston, eds. (Yardley, PA: Westholme, 2017), 55–56.
31. Paul David Nelson, *General Horatio Gates: A Biography* (Baton Rouge: Louisiana State University Press, 1976), 53; Douglas Southall Freeman, *George Washington: A Biography*, 7 vols. (New York, Scribner, 1948-54), 4:98–99.
32. Joseph Reed to Charles Lee, 21 Nov. 1776, in William B. Reed, *Life and Correspondence of Joseph Reed* (Philadelphia: Lindsay and Blakiston, 1847), I:255–56; Joseph Reed to Charles Lee, 21 Nov. 1776, in *Collections of the New York Historical Society for the Year 1872. The Lee Papers* (New York: New York Historical Society, 1873), II:293–94 (hereafter cited as *Lee Papers*); GW to Joseph Reed, 30 Nov. 1776, *PGWde*, RWS, 7:237–39; Charles Lee to Horatio Gates, 12–13 Dec. 1776, *Lee Papers*, II:348.

33. *E.g.*, after the war John Jay, then chief justice, learned of rumors New England legislators may have been interested in replacing Washington with Lee, and that Washington was fortunate a British raid had captured Lee in mid-December 1776. John Jay, entry of 21 Apr. 1790, Circuit Court Diary, 16 Apr. 1790-23 Apr. 1792, Papers of John Jay, Rare Book & Manuscript Library, Columbia University.
34. Benjamin Rush's Notes of Debates, 19 Feb. 1777, *LDC*, 6:232–35. After the war (1790) Rush wrote a slightly different version of Adams's comments; Benjamin Rush to John Adams, 13 Apr. 1790, *Founders Online,* National Archives, http://founders.archives.gov/ documents/Adams/99-02-02-0911.
35. Benjamin Rush's Notes of Debates, 8 Apr. 1777, *LDC*, 6:558.
36. Paul David Nelson, *The Life of William Alexander, Lord Stirling* (Birmingham: University of Alabama Press, 1987), 41–60, 61–78, *passim*; older, but still valuable, are Alan Valentine, *Lord Stirling* (New York: Oxford University Press, 1969) and William Alexander Duer, *The Life of William Alexander, Earl of Stirling* (New York: New Jersey Historical Society, 1847).
37. Nelson, *Lord Stirling*, 106–107.
38. Mercy [Otis] Warren, *History of the Rise, Progress and Termination of the American Revolution. Interspersed with Biographical, Political and Moral Observations*, 3 vols. (Boston: Manning and Loring, 1805), I:399; William Heath to GW, 26 Apr. 1777, *PGWde*, RWS, 9:277, n1; Thomas Conway to John Sullivan, 3 Jan. 1778, in John Sullivan, *The Letters and Papers of Major General John Sullivan*, ed. by Otis G. Hammond, 3 vols. (Concord: New Hampshire Historical Society, 1930-39), 2:2.
39. John Adams to James Warren, 27 Apr. 1777, *Papers of John Adams*, ed. by Robert J. Taylor (Cambridge, MA: Harvard University Press, 2006), 5:164.
40. Samuel Adams to Richard Henry Lee, 29 June 1777, *LDC*, 7:263; John Lendrum, *A Concise and Impartial History of the American Revolution. To Which Is Prefixed, a General History of North and South America: Together with an Account of the Discovery and Settlement of North America, and a View of the Progress, Character, and Political State of the Colonies Previous to the Revolution. From the Best Authorities* (Boston: Printed by I. Thomas and E.T. Andrews, 1795), 150; Thomas Conway to Charles Carroll of Carrollton, 14 Nov. 1777, in Kate Mason Rowland, *The Life of Charles Carroll of Carrollton, 1737-1832, with His Correspondence and Public Papers*, 2 vols. (New York: G.P. Putnam's Sons, 1898), 1:229.
41. Intelligence Report, January 1778, Henry Clinton Papers, Clements Library, University of Michigan, Ann Arbor.
42. GW to William Heath, 19 July 1777, *PGWde*, RWS, 16:339.
43. John Adams to Abigail Adams, 1 Aug. 1777, *LDC*, 7:400; John Adams to Abigail Adams, 23 Aug. 1777, ibid., 7:532; John Adams to Abigail Adams, 23 Aug. 1777, 4:00 p.m., ibid., 7:533.
44. Richard Henry Lee to Thomas Jefferson, 25 Aug. 1777, ibid., 7:551; Samuel Chase to Thomas Johnson, 23 Aug. 1777, ibid., 7:534; Thomas Burke to Richard Caswell, 2 Sept. 1777, ibid., 7:590.
45. John Adams to Abigail Adams, 23 Aug. 1777, 4:00 p.m., ibid., 7:533.

CHAPTER TWO: A GENERAL UNDER FIRE

1. Jonathan Dickinson Sergeant to James Lovell, 20 Nov. 1777, *LDC*, 8:296.
2. Richard Peters to GW, 9 Sept. 1777, *PGWde*, RWS, 11:178n1; John Hancock to GW, 10 Sept. 1777, ibid., 11:183.
3. Robert Hanson Harrison to John Hancock, 10 Sept. 1777, Papers of the Continental Congress [hereafter PCC], 1774-89, item 152, Microfilm Edition, National Archives, Washington, DC.

4. Edward G. Lengel, *General George Washington: A Military Life* (New York: Random House, 2005), 224.
5. Charles Carroll of Carrollton to Thomas Johnson, 8 Sept. 1777, *LDC.*, 7:628; Eliphalet Dyer to Samuel Gray, 1 Sept. 1777, ibid., 7:580.
6. John Adams to Abigail Adams, 1 Sept. and 14 Sept. 1777, ibid., 7:579–80, 661.
7. For the most recent account of the battle, see Michael Harris, *Brandywine: A Military History of the Battle that Lost Philadelphia but Saved America, September 11, 1777* (El Dorado Hills, CA: Savas Beatie, 2016).
8. Samuel Chase to Thomas Johnson, 12 Sept. 1777, *LDC*, 7:649.
9. Eliphalet Dyer to Joseph Trumbull, 12 Sept. 1777, ibid., 7:649–51.
10. Margaret Stedman to Mrs. Fergusson, Graeme Park, 11 Sept. 1777, "Excitement in Philadelphia on Hearing of the Defeat at Brandywine," *Pennsylvania Magazine of History and Biography* [*PMHB*] 14 (1890):64–65.
11. Eliphalet Dyer to Joseph Trumbull, 12 Sept. 1777, *LDC.*, 7:649–51; Cornelius Hartnett to William Wilkinson, 13 Sept. 1777, ibid., 7:655; Samuel Adams to Elizabeth Adams, 17 Sept. 1777, ibid., 7:677; Richard Henry Lee to Patrick Henry, 13 Sept. 1777, ibid., 7:656.
12. Thomas J. McGuire, *The Philadelphia Campaign: Brandywine and the Fall of Philadelphia* (Mechanicsburg, PA: Stackpole Books, 2006), 1:269.
13. John Adams's Diary, 16 Sept. 1777, *LDC*, 7:668.
14. John Adams, *Diary and Autobiography of John Adams*, 4 vols., L.H. Butterfield, ed. (New York: Atheneum, 1964), 2: 265 (hereafter Adams [John], *Diary*).
15. Elbridge Gerry to James Warren, 17 Sept. 1777, *LDC*, 7:684; Robert Morris to Abraham Whipple, 17 Sept. 1777, ibid., 7:690.
16. Thomas Burke to Richard Caswell, 17 Sept. 1777, ibid., 7:678–80.
17. James Lovell to William Whipple, 17 Sept. 1777, ibid., 7:687.
18. Johann Kalb to the comte de Broglie, 24 Sept. 1777, in Friedrich Kapp, *The Life of John Kalb: Major-General in the Revolutionary Army* (New York: Henry Holt and Company, 1884), 127.
19. Lengel and Lender, "The Middle Theater," 70.
20. Walter Isaacson, *Benjamin Franklin: An American Life* (New York: Simon & Schuster, 2003), 342.
21. General Orders, 3 Oct. 1777, *PGWde*, RWS, 11:373–74.
22. Christopher Ward, *The War of the Revolution*, 2 vols. (New York: Macmillan, 1952), 1:362–71; North Carolina Delegates to Richard Caswell, 20 Oct. 1777, *LDC*, 8:154; North Callahan, *Henry Knox: George Washington's General* (New York: Rinehart & Co., 1958), 123–24.
23. James Lovell to the Massachusetts Council, 16 Oct. 1777, *LDC*, 8:128; James Lovell to Joseph Whipple, 21 Nov. 78, ibid., 8:303.
24. *Papers of John Adams*, ed. by Robert J. Taylor *et al.*, 18 vols. (Cambridge, MA: Harvard University Press, 1977–), 5:315–16.
25. Benjamin Rush to Anthony Wayne, 18 June 1777, Anthony Wayne Papers, no. 0699, Historical Society of Pennsylvania, Philadelphia.
26. Henry Laurens to John Laurens, 16 Oct. 1777, in *Letters of Members of the Continental Congress,* ed. by Edmund Cody Burnett, 8 vols. (Washington, DC: Carnegie Institution of Washington, 1921-36), 2:521.
27. David Freeman Hawke, *Benjamin Rush: Revolutionary Gadfly* (Indianapolis: Bobbs-Merrill, 1971), 204–207.
28. "Historical Notes of Dr. Benjamin Rush, 1777," ed. S. Weir Mitchell, *PMHB* 27, no. 2 (1903):147.

29. Thomas Nelson to George Weedon, 28 Oct. 1777, p. 4, George Weedon Military Correspondence, American Philosophical Society, Philadelphia.
30. Thomas Balch, ed., *Letters and Papers Relating Chiefly to the Provincial History of Pennsylvania, with Some Notices of the Writers* (Philadelphia: Crissy & Markley, 1855), 259–60. The best account of the defense of the Delaware forts in 1777 is in John W. Jackson, *The Pennsylvania Navy, 1775-1781: The Defense of the Delaware* (New Brunswick, NJ: Rutgers University Press, 1974), 120–281; a more concise version is Mark Edward Lender, *The River War* (Trenton: New Jersey Historical Commission, 1979).
31. 14 Nov. 1777, *Journals of the Continental Congress, 1774-1789* [*JCC*], ed. by Worthington C. Ford et al., 34 vols. (Washington, DC.: U.S. Government Printing Office, 1904-37), 9:905; James Lovell to Horatio Gates, 5 Nov. 1777, *LDC*, 8:237.
32. Council of War, 8 Nov. 1777, *PGWde*, RWS, 12:163
33. Richard Henry Lee to Patrick Henry, 24 Nov. 1777, *LDC*, 8:317.
34. *E.g.*, James Duane to John Jay, 2 Dec. 1777, Papers of John Jay, no. 324, Digital Collections, Rare Books and Manuscripts Library, Columbia University.
35. Elbridge Gerry to James Warren, 12 Dec. 1777, *LDC*, 8:403–405.
36. Robert K. Wright, Jr. and Morris J. MacGregor, Jr., *Soldier-Statesmen of the Constitution* (Washington, DC: U.S. Army Center of Military History, 1987), 109–10; Francis B. Heitman, *Historical Register of Officers of the Continental Army during the War of the Revolution, April 1775, to December 1783* (Washington, DC: Rare Book Shop Publishing, 1914), 391; Kenneth R. Rossman, *Thomas Mifflin and the Politics of the American Revolution* (Chapel Hill: University of North Carolina Press, 1952), 12–68.
37. Alexander Graydon, *Memoirs of a Life, Chiefly Passed in Pennsylvania, within the Last Sixty Years, with Occasional Remarks upon the General Occurrences, Character and Spirit of that Eventful Period* (Harrisburg, PA: Printed by John Wyeth, 1811), 262–63. Mifflin was also annoyed when Congress restored Benedict Arnold's seniority as a major general, thus making Arnold senior to Mifflin; Palmer, *Washington and Arnold*, 263.
38. Rossman, *Thomas Mifflin*, 96–98.
39. Graydon, *Memoirs*, 278–79.
40. Terry Golway, *Washington's General: Nathanael Greene and the Triumph of the American Revolution* (New York: Henry Holt, 2005), 149, 155–58; Rossman, *Thomas Mifflin*, 96–98.
41. Greene quoted in ibid., 96.
42. Joseph Reed to GW, 7 Mar. 1776, *PGWde*, RWS, 3:428, 430; Rossman, *Thomas Mifflin*, 47–51, 76–77, 94–96, 103–104.
43. Thomas Mifflin to Horatio Gates, 17 Nov. 1777, Horatio Gates Papers, Manuscripts and Archives Division, NYPL.
44. If other letters expressed similar sentiments before June 17 they have not come to light. For many years Mifflin's letter had been incorrectly attributed to James Lovell, but Mifflin's authorship is explained in *LDC*, 8:315n5. The editors of *LDC* also have pointed out that Douglas Southall Freeman had searched in vain for Mifflin's letter as he explored the Cabal in his biography of Washington.
45. Alexander Scammell to Timothy Pickering, 6 Feb. 1778, Burnett, *LMCC*, 3:79n3; Timothy Pickering to Alexander Scammell, 17 Feb. 1778, in Octavius Pickering, *The Life of Timothy Pickering* (Boston: Little, Brown, and Company, 1867), I:206–207. See also William Rawle, "Sketch of the Life of Thomas Mifflin," *Register of Pennsylvania* (Philadelphia), 31 July 1830, 69, for a similar disclaimer.
46. Edwin F. Halfield, "Jonathan Dickinson Sergeant," *Pennsylvania Magazine of History and Biography* 2 (1878):338–442.

47. Jonathan Dickinson Sergeant to James Lovell, 20 Nov. 1777, *LDC*, 8:296, 297n1. Sergeant's letter today is in the Samuel Adams Papers, NYPL, so Lovell obviously sent it on to his fellow Massachusetts radical.
48. James Lovell to Joseph Whipple, 21 Nov. 1777, *LDC*, 8:302–303.
49. James Lovell to Horatio Gates, 27 Nov. 1777, ibid., 8:329.
50. James Monroe to John Thornton, 21 Nov. 1777, *The Papers of James Monroe: Selected Correspondence and Papers, 1776-1794*, ed. by Daniel Preston, 5 vols. (Westport, CT: Greenwood Press, 2003-2014), 2:7.
51. Joseph Ward to James Lovell, 4 Dec. 1777, Samuel Adams Papers, NYPL; Joseph Ward to Samuel Adams, 4 Dec. 1777, Joseph Ward Papers, Chicago Historical Society. The key sections of these two letters are virtually identical, and Ward probably knew both of his correspondents; the three men were all from Boston.
52. Kalb quoted in Kapp, *Life of Kalb*, 137, 145.
53. Samuel Hay to William Irvine, 28 Nov. 1777, Draper MSS, Ser. AA, Irvine Papers, State Historical Society of Wisconsin; a similar Hay to Irvine letter is in the Papers of William Irvine, HSP.
54. Thomas Fleming, *Washington's Secret War: The Hidden History of Valley Forge* (New York: HarperCollins, 2005), 102; Hugh F. Rankin, "Anthony Wayne: Military Romanticist," in Billias, *Washington's Generals*, 269; Wayne quoted in Worthington Chauncey Ford, ed., "Defences of Philadelphia in 1777," *PMHB* 20, no. 1 (1896):109–11.
55. Daniel Brodhead to Horatio Gates, 7 Nov. 1777, quoted in J. Bennett Nolan, *George Washington and the Town of Reading in Pennsylvania* (Reading, PA: Chamber of Commerce of Reading, 1931), 67–68.
56. Arthur St. Clair to Horatio Gates, 21 Nov. 1777, in William Henry Smith, ed., *The St. Clair Papers: The Life and Public Services of Arthur St. Clair, Soldier of the Revolutionary War, President of the Continental Congress and Governor of the North-Western Territory, with His Correspondence and Other Papers, Arranged and Annotated*, 2 vols. (Cincinnati: Robert Clarke & Co., 1882), 1:445.
57. Joseph Lee Boyle, Boyle Resource Files, "Cabal File," Typescript, Valley Forge National Historical Park Library, 14.
58. Ford, ed., "Defences of Philadelphia in 1777," 95–111; continued in *PMHB* 21, no. 1 (1897):56–61.
59. "Remonstrance of Council and Assembly [of Pennsylvania] to Congress, 1777, in Samuel Hazard, ed., *Pennsylvania Archives*, Ser. 1, VI (Philadelphia: Printed by Joseph Stevens, 1853), 104–105. The controversy over where the Continental Army would go into winter quarters is detailed in Wayne K. Bodle, "The Vortex of Small Fortune: The Continental Army at Valley Forge, 1777-1778." Valley Forge Historical Research Report, Vol. 1. Valley Forge National Historical Park: U.S. Department of the Interior, National Park Service, 1980, 112–14.
60. Elbridge Gerry to John Adams, 3 Dec. 1777, *LDC*, 8:373; 28 Nov. 1777, *JCC*, 9:972.
61. Committee at Headquarters to Henry Laurens, 6 and 10 Dec. 1778, ibid., 8:380–81, 399; 16 Dec. 1777, *JCC*, 11:1029–31.
62. GW to Henry Laurens, 22 Dec. 1778, *PGWde*, RWS, 12:669.
63. "Whitemarsh, Pennsylvania," in Harold E. Selesky, ed., *Encyclopedia of the American Revolution*, 2nd ed., 2 vols. (Detroit: Thomson Gale, 2006), 2:1267–68.
64. Cornelius Harnett to Thomas Burke, 16 Dec. 1777, *LDC*, 8:425; Elbridge Gerry to John Adams, 8 Dec. 1777, ibid., 8:387; James Lovell to Samuel Adams, 20 Dec. 1777, ibid., 8:451.
65. Hawke, *Benjamin Rush*, 215–17. Hawke fully discusses the Rush letter to Henry and Washington's reaction.

66. Anonymous [Benjamin Rush] to Patrick Henry, 12 Jan. 1778, in Patrick Henry to GW, 20 Feb. 1778, *PGWde*, RWS, 13:609–11n1.
67. Ibid.
68. Patrick Henry to GW, 5 Mar. 1778, ibid., RWS, 14:65–67.
69. Francis Lightfoot Lee to Samuel Adams, 22 Dec. 1777, *LDC*, 8:460; Samuel Adams to Richard Henry Lee, 1 Jan. 1778, *WSA*, 4:1–2.
70. Christopher Marshall, *Extracts from the Diary of Christopher Marshall: Kept in Philadelphia and Lancaster during the American Revolution, 1774-1781*, ed. by William Duane (Albany, NY: Joel Munsell, 1877), 147, 153, 154, 159.
71. A formal inquiry cleared St. Clair of wrongdoing, but he never held another important command during the Revolution. The loss of Fort Ticonderoga brought a dispute between political partisans of Schuyler and Horatio Gates to a head, with Congress replacing Schuyler with Gates. John G. Pell, "Philip Schuyler: General as Aristocrat," in George Athan Billias, *George Washington's Generals* (New York: William Morrow, 1964), 68.
72. John Adams to Abigail Adams, 18 July 1777, *LDC*, 7: 350–51.
73. Adams quoted in Richard M. Ketchum, *Saratoga: Turning Point of America's Revolutionary War* (New York: Henry Holt, 1997), 335; Adams to James Warren, 12 Aug. 1777, *LDC*, 7:460.
74. Henry Laurens to the Rhode Island Expedition Commissioners, 15 Dec. 1777, ibid., 8:415; Henry Marchant to Richard Henry Lee, 15 Dec. 1777, ibid., 8:416.
75. *E.g.*, Thomas Nelson to George Weedon, 19 Dec. 1777, p. 10, George Weedon Military Correspondence, American Philosophical Society, Philadelphia.
76. Nathanael Greene to GW, 24 Nov. 1777, *PGWde*, RWS, 12:376–78.
77. Henry Knox to GW, 26 Nov. 1777, ibid., 12:414–15.
78. Resolution of 10 Dec. 1777, *JCC*, 9:1013–15; GW to Henry Laurens, 14–15 Dec. 1777, *PGWde*, RWS, 12:606.

CHAPTER THREE: IDEOLOGUES AND GENERALS

1. Resolution of 28 Nov. 1777, *JCC*, 9:976.
2. Benjamin Rush to Samuel Adams, 1 Oct. 1777, in L.H. Butterfield, ed., *Letters of Benjamin Rush* (Princeton, NJ: Princeton University Press, 1951), 156–57.
3. James Thomas Flexner, *Washington: The Indispensable Man* (Boston: Little, Brown and Company, 1969).
4. French officers in Continental employ apparently were murmuring; Dave Richard Palmer, *George Washington and Benedict Arnold: A Tale of Two Patriots* (Washington, DC: Regnery, 2006), 267; [Emmanuel de] Pliarne to Charles Carroll of Carrollton, 26 Nov. 1777, in Rowland, ed., *Charles Carroll*, 1:231.
5. The best biography of Duer is Robert F. Jones, *King of the Alley: William Duer, Politician, Entrepreneur, and Speculator, 1768-1799* (Philadelphia: American Philosophical Society, 1992). On Duer's frustration with the state of the army, see Louis Gottschalk and Josephine Fennell, eds., "Duer and the 'Conway Cabal,'" *American Historical Review* 52 (October 1946):87–96.
6. William Duer to Francis Lightfoot Lee, 14 Feb. 1778, *LDC*, 9:95–102; Gouverneur Morris to Robert R. Livingston, 19 Mar. 1778, ibid., 9:264.
7. Benjamin Rush, *The Autobiography of Benjamin Rush: His "Travels through Life" together with His Commonplace Book for 1789-1813*, ed. by George W. Conner (Philadelphia: American Philosophical Society, 1948), 148; Abraham Clark to William Alexander (Lord Stirling), 20 Dec. 1777, *LDC*, 8:444–45; Jonathan Dickinson Sergeant to James Lovell, 20 Nov. 1777, ibid., 8:296.

8. Warren, *American Revolution*, 1:395.
9. Oliver Perry Chitwood, *Richard Henry Lee: Statesman of the Revolution* (Morgantown: West Virginia University Library, 1967), 214–18; J. Kent McGaughy, *Richard Henry Lee of Virginia: A Portrait of an American Revolutionary* (Lanham, MD: Rowman & Littlefield, 2004), 137–38.
10. Francis Wharton and John Bassett Moore, eds., *The Revolutionary Diplomatic Correspondence of the United States*, 6 vols. (Washington, DC: Government Printing Office, 1889), 2:71n, 74, 78; Freeman, *George Washington*, 4:98–99; Nelson, *Horatio Gates*, 53.
11. Francis Lightfoot Lee to Samuel Adams, 22 Dec. 1777, *LDC*, 8:460; Richard Henry Lee to Samuel Adams, 23 Nov. 1777, ibid., 8:313.
12. Samuel Adams to Richard Henry Lee, 1 Jan. 1778, *WSA*, 4:1–2.
13. James Craik to GW, 6 Jan. 1778, *PGWde*, RWS, 13:160–62.
14. Lund Washington to GW, 18 Feb. 1778, ibid., RWS, 13:587–88, Lund Washington to GW, 18 Mar. 1778, ibid., RWS, 14:220–222.
15. Benjamin Harrison to Robert Morris, 18 Dec. 1777, in Chitwood, *Richard Henry Lee*, 215.
16. John Fitzgerald to GW, 17 Mar. 1778, ibid., RWS, 14:209–210.
17. Richard Henry Lee to GW, 2 Jan. 1778, *PGWde*, RWS, 13:120–21; GW to Richard Henry Lee, ibid., RWS, 13:549–50.
18. On the break in Washington-Lee correspondence, see Chitwood, *Richard Henry Lee*, 219–220. Richard Henry Lee to GW, 12 June 1781, *Founders Online,* National Archives, http://founders.archives.gov/documents/Washington/99-01-02-06037.
19. GW to Richard Henry Lee, 15 July 1781, *Founders Online,* National Archives, http://founders.archives.gov/documents/Washington/99-01-02-06419.
20. *E.g.*, Edward Rutledge to John Jay, 25 Dec. 1778, Item 412, Papers of John Jay, Rare Books and Manuscripts Library, Columbia University, New York; Walter Stewart to Nathanael Greene, 4 Jan. 1778 [1779] and 29 Jan. 1779, *The Papers of Nathanael Green,* 8 vols., ed by Richard K. Showman, Robert E. McCarthy, Margaret Cobb, and Dennis M. Conrad (Chapel Hill: University of North Carolina Press, for the Rhode Island Historical Society, 1976–), 3:139, 194.
21. Andrew Jackson O'Shaughnessy, *The Men Who Lost America: British Leadership, the American Revolution, and the Fate of the Empire* (New Haven: Yale University Press, 2013), 6; Gruber, *Howe Brothers*, 45–47; David Hackett Fischer, *Washington's Crossing* (New York: Oxford University Press, 2004), 67.
22. O'Shaughnessy, *The Men Who Lost America*, 5–8, 83. Legally the appointment of senior commanders was the prerogative of the Crown, but realistically the Crown usually acted on the advice of the cabinet; ibid., 84.
23. Joel Tyler Headley, *Washington and the Generals of the American Revolution*, 2 vols. (Philadelphia: Carey and Hart, 1847), 1:165.
24. Fred Anderson, *Crucible of War: The Seven Years' War and the Fate of Empire in British North America, 1754-1766* (London: Faber and Faber, 2001), *passim.*
25. Ibid., 553.
26. Germain quoted in William H. Hallahan, *The Day the American Revolution Began: 19 April 1775* (New York: Perennial, 2001), 278.
27. Daniel A. Baugh, "Byng, John (bap. 1704, d. 1757)," in *Oxford Dictionary of National Biography* (Oxford, England: Oxford University Press, 2004).
28. Andrew Lambert, *Admirals: The Naval Commanders Who Made Britain Great* (London: Faber and Faber, 2008), 144; N.A.M. Rodger, *The Command of the Ocean: A Naval History of Britain, 1649-1815* (London: Allen Lane, 2004), 272.

29. R[ichard] K[idder] Meade to "Bro" [Everard Meade], 14 June 1778, in John Esten Cooke, ed., "Revolutionary Letters," *Southern Literary Magazine* 28, no. 4 (1859):296–302; Robert Troup to John Jay, 16 Aug. 1778, *Selected Papers of John Jay*, ed. by Elizabeth M. Nuxoll (Charlottesville: University Press of Virginia, Rotunda, 2014–), 1:534.
30. John Adams to Abigail Adams, 14 Aug. 1778, *The Adams Papers*, ed. by Lyman Butterfield and Marc Friedlaender (Cambridge, MA: Harvard University Press, 1973), 3:73.
31. John Lendrum, *A Concise and Impartial History of the American Revolution. To Which Is Prefixed, a General History of North and South America: Together with an Account of the Discovery and Settlement of North America, and a View of the Progress, Character, and Political State of the Colonies Previous to the Revolution. From the Best Authorities*, 2 vols. (Boston: Printed by I. Thomas and E.T. Andrews, 1795), 2:546–47; *Annual Register, 1779* (London), 75–105, 129–152; Francis Lewis to George Clinton, 8 Mar. 1779, Jared Sparks Collection of Documents Concerning the American Revolution, 1740-1866, Sparks MS 49.1 (22), Houghton Library, Harvard University.
32. 19–21 Feb. 1777, *JCC*, 7:131–33, 138–39, 141–42; Rush, *Autobiography*, 141; Rush, "Historical Notes of Dr. Benjamin Rush, 1777" ed. by S. Weir Mitchell, *Pennsylvania Magazine of History and Biography* 27, No. 2 (1903):139–40; James Wilson to Arthur St. Clair, 20 Feb.1777, *LDC*, 6:333.
33. Caroline Cox, *A Proper Sense of Honor: Service and Sacrifice in George Washington's Army* (Chapel Hill: University of North Carolina Press, 2007), xvi, 1–36, 37–72; Jonathan Gregory Rossie, *The Politics of Command in the American Revolution* (Syracuse, NY: Syracuse University Press, 1975), 135–53, *passim*.
34. Harry M. Ward, *Duty, Honor or Country: General George Weedon and the American Revolution* (Philadelphia: American Philosophical Society, 1979), 116–37.
35. James Kirby Martin, *Benedict Arnold, Revolutionary Hero: An American Warrior Reconsidered* (New York: New York University Press, 1997), 321–29, 332–41.
36. Kapp, *Life of Kalb*, 121–22; Palmer, *Washington and Arnold*, 267–68.
37. David Smith, *Whispers Across the Atlantic: General William Howe and the American Revolution* (New York: Osprey Publishing, 2017), 178.
38. Nelson, *Horatio Gates*, 58–60, 79–81, 84–87, 101–103, 106–107.
39. Charles Thomson's Notes of Debates, 26 July 1777, *LDC*, 7:382.
40. Resolution of 28 Nov. 1777, *JCC*, 9:976.
41. John Sullivan, *The Letters and Papers of Major General John Sullivan*, ed. by Otis G Hammond, 3 vols. (Concord: New Hampshire Historical Society, 1930-1939), 1:531–32, 555–56; Whittemore, *John Sullivan*, 67–68.
42. Roger Sherman to Samuel Adams, 11 July 1777, Samuel Adams Papers, MssCol 20, Manuscripts and Archives Division, NYPL; Samuel Adams to James Warren, 31 July 1777, *LDC*, 7:397; John Hancock to Philip Schuyler and Arthur St. Clair, 5 Aug. 1777, ibid., 7:416–17; Smith, ed., *St. Clair Papers*,1:70–71.
43. Charles Thomson's Notes of Debates, 26 July 1777, *LDC*, 7:382–83; New England Delegates to GW, 2 Aug.1777, ibid., 7:405; GW to John Hancock, 3 Aug. 1777, *PGWde*, 10:492–93; John Hancock to GW, 4 Aug. 1777, *LDC*, 7:412.
44. Charles Barney Whittelsey, "Historical Sketch of Joseph Spencer: Major-General of the Continental Troops, Member of the Council of Safety, Congressman, Judge, Deputy, Deacon, and Farmer," Connecticut Society of the Sons of the American Revolution, http://www.connecticutsar. org/patriots/spencer.htm, accessed 23 Apr. 2017; *JCC*, 9:1018–20; James Lovell to John Adams, 1 Dec. 1777, *LDC*, 8:363; Benjamin Silliman, "Major-General Joseph Spencer," *PMHB* 3, no. 1 (1879):435–437.

45. Richard Henry Lee to Patrick Henry, 24 Nov. 1777, ibid., 8:318; William Ellery to William Whipple, 20 Oct. 1777, Thomas Addis Emmet Collection, Manuscripts and Archives Division, NYPL.
46. John Hancock to GW, 12 Sept. 1777, *LDC*, 7:654–55; Charles Carroll to GW, 27 Sept. 1777, ibid., 8:21–22.
47. Michael M. Greenburg, *The Court–Martial of Paul Revere: A Son of Liberty and America's Forgotten Military Disaster* (Lebanon, NH: University Press of New England, 2014), 163–68, 187–89.
48. 1 Dec. 1779, *JCC*, 15:1334; J[ames] L[ovell] to Samuel Adams, 21 Dec. 1779, *LDC*, 14:292. The Marine Committee of Congress tried to get a copy of the court-martial proceedings but apparently never received it; John Brown to Commissioners of the Navy Board of the Eastern Department, 10 Dec. 1779, in Charles Oscar Paullin, ed., *Out-Letters of the Continental Marine Committee and Board of Admiralty, August, 1776-September, 1780* (New York: Naval History Society, 1914), II:136–37.
49. Esek Hopkins, *The Letter Book of Esek Hopkins: Commander-in-Chief of the United States Navy, 1775-1777*, ed. by Alverda S. Beck (Providence: Rhode Island Historical Society, 1932), 7; Naval Committee to Esek Hopkins, 5 Jan. 1776, *LDC*, 3:34–36; Thomas Jefferson's Notes on the Inquiry into Esek Hopkins's Conduct, 2 Aug. 1776; ibid., 4:660–64.
50. For the grievances of Hopkins's officers, see Marine Committee Examination of John Grannis, c. 25 Mar. 1777, *LDC*, 6:487–90, 490–91n2. On his suspension and dismissal see Hopkins, *Letter Book*, 143; Henry Laurens to Esek Hopkins, 2 Jan. 1778, *LCD*, 8:519.
51. Martin and Lender, *A Respectable Army*, 70–78.
52. Rush, *Autobiography*, 139. For a full discussion of Washington's views on the matter, see Martin and Lender, *A Respectable Army*, Chapter 3.
53. James Lovell, *An Oration Delivered April 2d, 1771: At the Request of the Inhabitants of the Town of Boston; to Commemorate the Bloody Tragedy of the Fifth of March, 1770* (Boston: Printed by Edes and Gill, 1771), 8.
54. Surprisingly, given his prominence in Congress, Lovell lacks a full biography. This sketch is taken from Helen F. Jones, "James Lovell in the Continental Congress 1777-1782" (Ph.D. dissertation, Columbia University, 1968). See esp. 80–100 for Lovell's antagonism toward Washington. See also "Lovell, James (1737-1814)," *Biographical Directory of the United States Congress*, http://bioguide.congress.gov/ scripts/biodisplay.pl?index=L000463, accessed 1 Apr. 2017; "The American Revolution's One-Man National Security Agency," *Cryptologic Almanac—NSA/CSS*, http://www.nsa.gov/about/ ryptologic_heritage/center_crypt_history/almanac/, accessed 1 Apr. 2017.
55. *E.g.*, James Lovell to Joseph Whipple, 21 Nov. 1777, *LDC*, 8:302–303.
56. Ann Clark Hart, *Abraham Clark: Signer of the Declaration of Independence* (San Francisco: Pioneer Press, 1923), 5.
57. On congressional opposition to half-pay for life and movement toward a compromise allowing half-pay for a limited number of years, see Francis Lewis to the New York Convention, 30 Mar. 1778, ibid., 9:354. On the protracted controversy over officers' pensions, see Martin and Lender, *A Respectable Army*, 110–12, 114, 128–29, 154, 166–67, 197, 202.
58. James Lovell to Samuel Adams, 13 Jan. 1778, *LDC*, 8:580–81.
59. Chevalier de la Luzerne to comte de Vergennes, 18 July 1779, in John Durand, trans. and ed., *New Materials for the History of the American Revolution: Translated from Documents in the French Archives and Edited* (New York: Henry Holt and Company, 1889), 219.
60. James Lovell to Samuel Adams, 20 Jan. 1778, *LDC*, 8:618.
61. Chevalier de la Luzerne to comte de Vergennes, 28 Jan. 1781, in Durand, *New Materials from the French Archives*, 234–35.

62. James Lovell to Samuel Adams, 10 Mar. 1778, *LDC*, 9:262; James Lovell to Samuel Adams, 27 Mar. 1778, Samuel Adams Papers, NYPL; S[amuel] A[dams] to James Lovell, 31 Mar. 1778, Sol Feinstone Collection, item 50, David Library of the American Revolution, Washington Crossing, PA.
63. Samuel Adams to James Warren, 7 Jan. 1776, Samuel Adams, *WSA* 3:250; John Adams is quoted *JCC*, 4:360n.
64. Charles Lee to James Bowdoin, 30 Nov. 1776, in Peter Force and M. St. Clair, eds., *American Archives: Consisting of a Collection of Authentick Records, State Papers, Debates, and Letters and Other Notices of Publick Affairs, the Whole Forming a Documentary History of the Origin and Progress of the North American Colonies*, 9 Vols. (Washington, DC: M. St. Clair Clarke and Peter Force, 1837-53), 5th Ser., 3:933–34 (hereafter Force, *American Archives*).
65. Benjamin Rush to John Adams, 1 Oct. 1777, *Letters of Benjamin Rush*, ed. by L.H. Butterfield (Princeton, NJ: Princeton University Press, 1951), 156–57.
66. For a good general biography of Rush, see Alyn Brodsky, *Benjamin Rush: Patriot and Physician* (New York: Truman Talley Books/St. Martin's Press, 2004).
67. David Freeman Hawke, *Benjamin Rush: Revolutionary Gadfly* (Indianapolis: Bobbs-Merrill, 1971); Thomas Fleming, *Washington's Secret War: The Hidden History of Valley Forge* (New York: HarperCollins, 2005), 93–97, 144–48, *passim.*
68. Benjamin Rush to John Adams, 1 Oct. 1777, *Letters of Benjamin Rush*, 157.
69. Henry Marchant to [Samuel Adams], 22 Dec.1777, Samuel Adams Papers, NYPL.
70. Samuel Adams to Richard Henry Lee, 15 July 1777, Samuel Adams, *Writings*, III:386.
71. Marshall, *Diary Extracts*, 154–55.
72. Fleming, *Washington's Secret War*, 86–87.
73. Elbridge Gerry to James Warren, 12 Dec. 1778, *LDC*, 8:404–405; Lovell to Samuel Adams, 20 Dec. 1777, ibid., 8:451; Committee for Foreign Affairs to the Commissioners at Paris, 2 Dec. 1777, ibid., 8:367. Lovell and Lee wrote the letter to Paris on behalf of the committee.
74. Maxine N. Lurie and Marc Mappen, eds., *Encyclopedia of New Jersey* (New Brunswick, NJ: Rutgers University Press, 2004), 479. De Lisle is correctly identified as Livingston in *The Papers of William Livingston* [*PWL*], ed. by Carl E. Prince and Dennis P. Ryan, 5 vols. (Trenton: New Jersey Historical Commission, 1979-1988), 2:4–5.
75. "De Lisle" [William Livingston], *New Jersey Gazette*, 23 Apr. 1778, *PWL*, 2:300–304.
76. Committee at Camp to Henry Laurens, 5 Feb. 1778, *LDC*, 9:23.
77. "The Thoughts of a Freeman," 17 Jan. 1778, *PGWde*, RWS, 13:364–65n1.
78. Henry Laurens to GW, 27 Jan. 1778, ibid., RWS, 13:364.
79. "The Thoughts of a Freeman," 17 Jan. 1778, ibid., RWS, 13:364–65n1.
80. Ibid. No one ever claimed authorship of the tract, although it was likely a member of Congress. It would be interesting to know the unnamed delegate who just happened to pick up the "Thoughts" "on the stairs." No one else saw it there? Was it dropped a moment before the delegate saw it? To say the least the circumstances are suspicious. The tract has the tone of James Lovell's pen, and Lovell was expressing thoughts similar to the "Freeman" in lengthy letters to Samuel Adams at about the same time. Was Lovell the unnamed delegate? But this is only a guess. Thomas Fleming thinks Rush may have been the author (*Washington's Secret War*, 189), but this is a guess as well. Arguing in favor of Rush is the fact the "Freeman" sent an anonymous letter, which was Rush's wont. Lovell, zealot that he was, was more likely to be aboveboard. We just don't know.
81. Aside from the Library of Congress, there are copies in the collections of the Historical Society of Pennsylvania, Philadelphia, and the South Carolina Historical Society, Charleston;

editor's source note, *PGWde*, RWS, 13:364. See also *The Writings of George Washington: Being the Correspondence, Addresses, Messages, and Other Papers, Official and Private, Selected and Published from the Original Manuscripts*, 12 vols., ed. by Jared Sparks (Boston: Russell, Odiorne, and Metcalf; and Hilliard, Gray, and Co., 1833-39), V:497–99.
82. Warren, *American Revolution*, 1:396; Carlo Botta, *History of the War of the Independence of the United States of America*, trans. by George Alexander Otis, 2 vols. (New Haven, CT: Nathan Whiting, 1837 [orig. in Italian, 1809]), 65; David Ramsay, *The Life of George Washington: Commander in Chief of the Armies of the United States in the War Which Established Their Independence, and First President of the United States* (London: Printed by Luke Hanfard & Sons, 1807), 102.
83. GW to Henry Laurens, 31 Jan. 1778, *PGWde*, RWS, 13:420–21.
84. Amos Blanchard, *American Military Biography: Containing the Lives and Characters of the Officers of the Revolution Who Were Most Distinguished in Achieving Our National Independence. Also, the Life of Gilbert Motier La Fayette, Major-General of the Continental Army* (Cincinnati: E. Walters, 1830), 86.
85. The best biography of Gates is Paul David Nelson, *General Horatio Gates: A Biography* (Baton Rouge: Louisiana State University Press, 1976). Unless otherwise noted, this sketch of Gates is drawn from Nelson. On Gates's move to Virginia see pp. 25–36.
86. *E.g.*, Horatio Gates to GW, 22 June 1775, *PGWde*, RWS, 1:23.
87. Matthias Ogden to Aaron Burr, 26 July 1776, Force, *American Archives*, 5 ser., I:603–604.
88. Nelson, *General Horatio Gates*, 68–72.
89. Adams to Richard Henry Lee, 15 July 1777, in Adams (Samuel), *Writings*, III: 388; Samuel Adams to Horatio Gates, Oct. 1777, ibid., III: 413; James Lovell to Horatio Gates, 27 Nov. 1777, *LDC*, 8:329.
90. Lurie and Mappen, eds., *Encyclopedia of New Jersey*, 732.
91. Lender and Stone, *Fatal Sunday*, 320–21, 356.
92. Francis B. Heitman, *Historical Register of Officers of the Continental Army during the War of the Revolution, April 1775, to December, 1783* (Washington, DC: Rare Book Shop Publishing Company, 1914), 64, 358.
93. Ibid., 158; Stryker, William S., comp., *Official Register of the Officers and Men of New Jersey in the Revolutionary War* (Trenton, NJ: Wm. T. Nicholson, 1872), 385; Shirley Hunter Smith, "Abraham Clark," Society of the Descendants of Signers of the Declaration of Independence, http://www.dsdi1776.com/signers-by-state/abraham-clark/, accessed 29 Apr. 2017; Charles A. Goodrich, *Our Lives, Our Fortunes, and Our Sacred Honour: The Lives of the Signers to the Declaration of Independence* (New York: William Reed and Co., 1829), 232.

CHAPTER FOUR: POISON PENS

1. GW to Thomas Conway, 5 Nov.1777, *PGWde*, RWS, 12:129–30.
2. Henry Laurens to John Laurens, 28 Jan. 1778, *LDC*, 8:678.
3. Eric Robson, *The American Revolution in Its Political and Military Aspects, 1763-1783* (New York: Norton, 1966), 170; Warren, *American Revolution*, 1:395.
4. GW to Landon Carter, 30 May 1778, *PGWde*, 15:268–70.
5. Douglas Southall Freeman, *George Washington: A Biography*, 7 vols. (New York: Scribner, 1948-54), 4:611.
6. GW to Horatio Gates, 30 Oct. 1777, *PGWde*, RWS, 12:59–60. By October 26 Washington had a fairly accurate understanding of events at Saratoga, and he understood that Wilkinson was carrying Gates's official report to Congress; Robert Hanson Harrison to Major

[John?] Clarke, 27 Oct. 1777, Gilder Lehrman Collection, No. GLC04786, Gilder Lehrman Institute, New York.

7. Horatio Gates to GW, 2 Nov. 1777, *PGWde*, RWS, 12:93–94.

8. GW to Alexander Hamilton, 30 Oct. 1777, ibid., RWS, 12:60–61.

9. James Monroe to John Thornton, 21 Nov. 1777, *The Papers of James Monroe: Selected Correspondence and Papers, 1776-1794*, ed. by Daniel Preston, 5 vols. (Westport, CT: Greenwood Press, 2003-14), 22:7; Council of War, 29 Oct. 1777, *PGWde*, RWS, 12:47–48; GW to Alexander Hamilton, 30 Oct. 1777, ibid., RWS, 12:60–61.

10. Alexander Hamilton to GW, 6 Nov. 1777, ibid., RWS, 12:141–42. For a full discussion of Hamilton's northern mission, see Michael E. Newton, *Alexander Hamilton: The Formative Years* (Phoenix, AZ: Eleftheria Publishing, 2015), 219–29. According to historian Dave Palmer, Benedict Arnold, who had fallen out with Gates after Saratoga, thought Gates deliberately withheld the reinforcements Washington wanted, waiting for Congress to relieve Washington and send for him (Gates). Arnold's opinion, of course, was jaundiced. See Palmer, *Washington and Arnold*, 266.

11. Resolution of 5 Nov. 1777, *JCC*, 9:865–68. Absent the restriction on Washington's ability to freely move troops between theaters, the Adamses, Marchant, and Dyer actually voted against the resolution.

12. Harry M. Ward, *Duty, Honor or Country: General George Weedon and the American Revolution* (Philadelphia: American Philosophical Society, 1979), 105, 110; Thomas Conway to Robert Morris, 9 Aug. 1777, Sol Feinstone Collection, APS; Thomas Conway to Robert Morris, 8 Sept. 1777, ibid.; John Sullivan to John Adams, 11 Oct. 1777, *Papers of John Adams*, 18 vols., ed. by Robert J. Taylor *et al.* (Cambridge, MA: Harvard University Press, 1977–), V:325; Dave Richard Palmer, *George Washington and Benedict Arnold: A Tale of Two Patriots* (Washington, DC: Regnery, 2006), 267.

13. Richard Peters to Anthony Wayne, 6 Dec, 1777, Wayne Manuscripts, Vol. 4, HSP.

14. Thomas Conway to Robert Morris, 8 Sept. 1777, Sol Feinstone Collection, APS.

15. Thomas Conway to Charles Carroll of Carrollton, 14 Nov. 1777, in Kate Mason Rowland, *The Life of Charles Carroll of Carrollton, 1737-1832, with His Correspondence and Public Papers*, 2 vols. (New York: G.P. Putnam's Sons, 1898),1:225–30. Why did Conway write Carroll? Apparently Conway believed their shared Catholicism made Carroll something of an ally, especially since Carroll, like most of Congress, originally had seen the Frenchman in a positive light. But when Conway learned Carroll looked askance at his campaign for promotion, he made a clean breast of his feelings to Carroll who had just left Congress for his home in Maryland. While the letter was written some two weeks after Conway had become embroiled with Washington in the Cabal controversy, the case Conway outlined in his letter represented his thinking since at least September 1777.

16. Ibid., 226–27.

17. Ibid., 229–30.

18. Benjamin Rush to John Adams, 13 Oct. 1777, *Adams Papers*, 5:315–16; Rush wrote Adams another letter of similar import on 31 Oct. 1777, ibid., 5:323.

19. Emmanuel de Pliarne to Charles Carroll of Carrollton, 26 Nov. 1777, in Rowland, *Charles Carroll of Carrollton*, 1:231.

20. Dave Richard Palmer, *George Washington and Benedict Arnold*, 268, thinks that by this time Lee was in fact no friend of Washington's and that in writing him Washington was unknowingly playing into the hands of his critics.

21. GW to Richard Henry Lee, 16 Oct. 1777, *PGWde*, RWS, 11:529–30.

22. Ibid., RWS, 11:530.

23. John Fitzgerald to GW, 17 Mar. 1778, *PGWde*, RWS, 14:209–210.
24. Alexander Hamilton to George Clinton, 13 Feb. 1778, *The Papers of Alexander Hamilton* [hereafter *PAH*], ed. by Harold C. Syrett and Jacob E. Cooke, 27 vols. (New York: Columbia University Press, 1961-87), 1:428.
25. Conway later explained he thought he had written the letter on 9 or 10 October 1777; Thomas Conway to GW, *PGWde*, RWS, 12:130.
26. Andro Linklater, *An Artist in Treason: The Extraordinary Double Life of General James Wilkinson* (New York: Walker, 2009), 53.
27. William Alexander (Lord Stirling) to GW, 3 November 1777, *PGWde,* RWS, 12:110–11.
28. Linklater, *An Artist in Treason*, 24–25.
29. Ibid., 47–49.
30. James Wilkinson, *Memoirs of My Own Times*, 3 vols. (Philadelphia: Printed by Abraham Small, 1816), I:330–32; Linklater, *An Artist in Treason*, 48, 53; Paul David Nelson, *The Life of William Alexander, Lord Stirling* (Birmingham: University of Alabama Press, 1987), 120–21.
31. Wilkinson's version of the affair is in his *Memoirs*, I:382–411.
32. From a 1943 German propaganda sheet warning industrial workers not to talk about their work, Art.IWM PST 5658, Imperial War Museum, London, http://www.iwm.org.uk/collections/ item/object/5866, accessed 25 Sept. 2017.
33. Elbridge Gerry to James Warren, 28 Oct. 1777, *LDC*, 8:206; John Adams to Abigail Adams, 24 Oct. 1777, ibid., 8:170.
34. John Adams to Thomas McKean, 26 Nov. 1815, *Founders Online*, National Archives, http://founders.archives.gov/documents/Adams/99-02-02-6545. The story of the "spurs" clearly made an impression and years afterward old patriots happily retold it. *E.g.*, William Ellery to William Stedman, 19 Feb. 1807, No. GLC00298, Gilder Lehrman Collection, Gilder Lehrman Institute, New York; Thomas McKean to John Adams, 20 Nov. 1815, *Founders Online,* National Archives, http://founders.archives.gov/ documents/Adams/99-02-02-6543. McKean, tongue in check, has Samuel Adams making the suggestion "with a grave & solemn face" as a formal motion in Congress. In 1827 Robert Troup, a one-time aide to Gates and close friend of Hamilton, credited the "spurs" anecdote to Roger Sherman of Connecticut; Robert Troup, "Memorandum respecting General Conway's cabal with General Gates against the military character of General Washington," 26 Oct. 1827, Jared Sparks Collection of Documents Concerning the American Revolution, 1740-1866 (Sparks 49.1–49.3), Houghton Library, Harvard University.
35. Harry M. Ward, *George Washington's Enforcers: Policing the Continental Army* (Carbondale: Southern Illinois University Press, 2006).
36. GW to Thomas Conway, 5 Nov.1777, *PGWde*, RWS, 12:129–30.
37. Thomas Conway to GW, 5 Nov.1777, ibid., RWS, 12:130.
38. Benjamin Rush to John Adams, 21 Oct. 1777, *Papers of John Adams*, 17 vols., ed. by Robert J. Taylor *et al.* (Cambridge, MA: Harvard University Press, 1977-2014), 5:316–19.
39. Henry Laurens to Isaac Motte, 26 Jan. 1778, *LDC*, 8:655, 657n5; John Fitzpatrick to GW, 16 Feb. 1778, ibid., 8:657n5.
40. Thomas Conway to GW, *PGWde*, RWS, 12:130-31.
41. Ibid., 12:131.
42. Washington's activities are found in the General Orders and letters of 5 Nov. in ibid., 12:129-40.
43. Thomas Conway to GW, 16 Nov. 1777, ibid., 12:276–77.

44. GW to Horatio Gates, 14 Nov. 1777, *PGWde*, RWS, 12:251–52; GW to Horatio Gates, 2 Dec. 1777, ibid., 12:496–98.
45. Thomas Mifflin to Horatio Gates, 28 Nov. 1777, in J. Bennett Nolan, *George Washington and the Town of Reading in Pennsylvania* (Reading, PA: Chamber of Commerce of Reading, 1931), 72–73.
46. "Gen. Thomas Conway's Statement," 3 Jan. 1778, in John Sullivan, *The Letters and Papers of Major General John Sullivan*, ed. by Otis G Hammond, 3 vols. (Concord: New Hampshire Historical Society, 1930-1939), 2:1–2.
47. Horatio Gates to GW, 8 Dec. 1777, *PGWde*, RWS, 12:576–77.
48. Editor's note, *LDC*, 8:599n5.
49. Friedrich von Muenchhausen, *At General Howe's Side, 1776-1778: The Diary of General William Howe's Aide de Camp, Captain Friedrich von Muenchhausen*, trans. by Ernst Kipping, annot. by Samuel Smith (Monmouth Beach, NJ: Philip Freneau Press, 1974), 45, 51.
50. Charles Grey to unidentified, 28 Nov. 1777, De Coppet Collection, Firestone Library, Princeton University.
51. Horatio Gates to Thomas Conway, 3 Dec. 1777, in Wilkinson, *Memoirs*, I:374–76.
52. James Ripley Jacobs, *Tarnished Warrior: Major-General James Wilkinson* (New York: Macmillan, 1938),148.
53. Wilkinson, *Memoirs*, I:372–73.
54. Troup, "Memorandum respecting Conway's cabal," 26 Oct. 1827, Sparks Collection, 49.1–49.3, Houghton Library, Harvard University.
55. Horatio Gates to GW, 4 Jan. 1778, *PGWde*, RWS, 13:139.
56. Troup, "Memorandum respecting Conway's cabal," 26 Oct. 1827, Sparks Collection, 49.1–49.3, Houghton Library, Harvard University.
57. GW to Horatio Gates, 4 Jan. 1778, *PGWde*, RWS, 13:138–39.
58. Horatio Gates to GW, 23 Jan. 1777, ibid., 13:319–22, n6.
59. Joseph Jones to GW, ibid., 13:310–11.
60. GW to Horatio Gates, 9 Feb. 1778, ibid., 13:484–86.
61. Ibid., 13:486–87.
62. Abraham Clark to William Alexander, 15 Jan. 1778, *LDC*, 8:597. On Clark's earlier criticism of Washington, see Jonathan Gregory Rossie, *The Politics of Command in the American Revolution* (Syracuse, NY: Syracuse University Press, 1975), 183.
63. Horatio Gates, 19 Feb. 1778, *PGWde*, RWS, 13:590.
64. GW to Horatio Gates, 24 Feb. 1778, ibid., 13:654–55.
65. James Wilkinson to Lord Stirling, 6 Jan. 1778, in Wilkinson, *Memoirs*, I:382–83.
66. James Wilkinson to Horatio Gates, 22 Feb. 1778, in Wilkinson, ibid., I:385–86; Horatio Gates to James Wilkinson, 23 Feb. 1778, ibid., I:386–87.
67. The above account of Wilkinson's activities is drawn from the following: 6 Nov. 1777, *JCC*, 9:870; Jacobs, *Tarnished Warrior*, 45–46, 50–56; Selesky, *Encyclopedia*, 2:1272; Linklater, *An Artist in Treason*, 50, 54–58.
68. Jacobs, *Tarnished Warrior*, 53.
69. Ibid., 53–54.
70. James Wilkinson to GW, 28 Mar. 1778, *PGWde*, RWS, 14:344.

CHAPTER FIVE: "BE WARE OF YOUR BOARD OF WAR"

1. Henry Laurens to John Laurens, 8 Jan. 1778, *LDC*, 8:546.
2. Benjamin Harrison to Robert Morris, 19 Feb. 1778, ibid., 8:651n2.
3. Jordan D. Fiore, "Carlo Botta: An Italian Historian of the American Revolution," *Italica*

28, No. 3 (1951):155–171; David Bailie Warden to Thomas Jefferson, 19 Jan. 1810, *Papers of Thomas Jefferson*, Retirement Ser., ed. by J. Jefferson Looney (Princeton, NJ: Princeton University Press, 2005), 2:161–162; Thomas Jefferson to Carlo Botta, 15 July 1810, ibid., Retirement Ser., 2:529–30.

4. Carlo Botta, *History of the War of the Independence of the United States of America*, trans. by George Alexander Otis, 2 vols. (New Haven, CT: Nathan Whiting, 1837 [orig. in Italian, 1809]), I:63–64.

5. 12 June 1776, *JCC*, 5:434–35.

6. Between January and December 1777 ten delegates served on the Board of War; "Standing Committees: War, Board of," *JCC*, 9:1080.

7. Jonathan Gregory Rossie, *The Politics of Command in the American Revolution* (Syracuse, NY: Syracuse University Press, 1975), 137, 148–49; Harry M. Ward, *The Department of War, 1781–1795* (Pittsburgh, PA: University of Pittsburgh Press, 1962), 2; John Adams, *Diary and Autobiography of John Adams*, 4 vols., ed. by L.H. Butterfield (New York: Atheneum, 1964), 3:342.

8. Richard Henry Lee to GW, 20 Oct. 1777, *PGWde*, RWS, 11:562–63.

9. *E.g.*, on July 18 Congress resolved to appoint three new members to the Board of War who were not members of Congress. They would work "under the direction of the present board." But the appointments were deferred and then never made; 18 July 1777, *JCC*, 8:563, and 22 July 1777, ibid., 8:571.

10. 17 Oct. 1777, ibid., 9:818–20. The decision to create a three-man board of non-members must have come after a sudden change of mind among the delegates, as only hours before Congress had named four of its members to the old Board of War; ibid., 9:813.

11. Rossman, *Thomas Mifflin*, 106.

12. Richard Henry Lee to GW, 20 Oct. 1777, *PGWde*, RWS, 11:562–63; General Orders, 16 May 1776, ibid., RWS, 4:310. The following month Reed became adjutant general, although his relationship with Washington soured later in the year when Washington inadvertently discovered correspondence between Major General Charles Lee and Reed critical of his (Washington's) leadership. Thereafter Reed and the commander in chief shared a formal but hardly a close relationship. As far as we know, Washington made no objection when Reed was mentioned as a possible member of the new Board of War. William B. Reed, *Life and Correspondence of Joseph Reed*, 2 vols. (Philadelphia: Lindsay and Blakiston, 1847), 1:189–90.

13. GW to Richard Henry Lee, 28 Oct. 1777, *PGWde*, RWS, 12:40–42.

14. Recall Washington's blistering assessment of Conway in a letter to Lee of 16 October 1777, ibid., 11:529–30.

15. Richard Henry Lee to GW, 20 Oct. 1777, *PGWde*, RWS, 11:562–63.

16. William Williams to Jonathan Trumbull, Sr., 28 Nov. 1777, *LDC*, 8:341.

17. Richard Henry Lee to Thomas Mifflin, 2 Nov. 1777, *LDC*, 8:222–23.

18. Rossman, *Thomas Mifflin*, 106–108.

19. Richard Henry Lee to GW, 20–22 Nov. 1777, *PGWde*, RWS, 12:330–33.

20. Rossman, *Thomas Mifflin*, 109.

21. Richard Henry Lee to Samuel Adams, 23 Nov. 1777, *LDC*, 8:313; Richard Henry Lee to GW, 20–22 Nov. 1777, *PGWde*, RWS, 12:330–33.

22. Ibid., 12:330–33.

23. Wayne K. Bodle, "The Vortex of Small Fortune: The Continental Army at Valley Forge, 1777-1778." Valley Forge Historical Research Report (Valley Forge National Historical Park: U.S. Department of the Interior, National Park Service, 1980), 223–24.

24. 24 Nov. 1777, *JCC*, IX: 959–60, 960n1; 27 Nov. 1777, ibid., IX:971–72. Nelson, *Horatio Gates*, 154–55, and Rossman, *Thomas Mifflin*, 112–13, mention a curious incident regarding Mifflin and the board presidency. They cite a letter by James Duane, delegate from New York, to Philip Schuyler, in which Duane claimed Mifflin wanted both Schuyler and Gates on the Board of War, with Schuyler as president. See Duane to Schuyler, 19 Nov. 1777, *LDC*, 8:282–83. Nelson thinks this precipitated another round in the ongoing fight between the congressional adherents of the two generals before Mifflin threw his full support to Gates. Rossman thinks Mifflin was just "playing politics," whatever that may have meant. Actually, neither the *Journals* of Congress nor any other sources reflect any congressional battle over Gates's appointment as board president, much less a board seat for Schuyler. Duane's is the *only* reference in this regard, and the New Yorker may have reported a mistaken impression of remarks by Mifflin or by someone else talking about Mifflin. We don't know. We do know that the contemporary record shows overwhelming support for Gates and that Mifflin was consistent in his support for the Hero of Saratoga. There was some controversy, however, when Schuyler's partisans suggested he replace Mifflin as quartermaster general; this took place around the time Congress was restructuring the Board of War and may have been the incident Nelson reported. See Jonathan Bayard Smith to Joseph Reed, 25 Feb. 1778, *LDC*, 9:176, 179n1.
25. James Duane to Horatio Gates, 16 Dec. 1777, ibid., 8:421.
26. Thomas Mifflin to Horatio Gates, 17 November 1777, Horatio Gates Papers, NYHS; James Lovell to Horatio Gates, 27 Nov. 1777, *LDC*, 8:329.
27. James Lovell to Joseph Trumbull, 28 Nov. 1777, ibid., 8:339; William Williams to Jonathan Trumbull, Sr., 28 Nov. 1777, ibid., 8:341.
28. James Lovell to Horatio Gates, 27 Nov. 1777, ibid., 8:329.
29. Nelson, *Horatio Gates*, 160–61. Nelson correctly points out that some authors have seen Mifflin's actions in a dark light, arguing that in fact he misled Congress into appointing a Board of War he knew would be inimical to Washington. Not true: Mifflin knew what he was doing—but so did the delegates.
30. Nelson, *Horatio Gates*, 155–56.
31. 13 Dec. 1777, *JCC*, 9:1023–24.
32. Council of War, 29 Oct. 1777, *PGWde*, RWS, 12:48.
33. David A. Clary and Joseph W.A. Whitehorne, *The Inspectors General of the United States Army, 1777-1903* (Washington, DC: Office of the Inspector General and Center of Military History, United States Army, 1987), 24–25.
34. Rossie, *Politics of Command*, 192–93.
35. Thomas Conway to Thomas Mifflin, 11 Nov. 1777, Horatio Gates Papers, NYHS.
36. John Laurens to Henry Laurens, 28 Feb. 1778, in John Laurens, *The Army Correspondence of Colonel John Laurens in the Years 1777-8: Now First Printed from Original Letters to His Father, Henry Laurens, President of Congress; with a Memoir by Wm. Gilmore Simms,* ed. by W.M. Gilmore Simms (New York: Bradford Club, 1867), 132–33.
37. Certain General Officers to GW, 31 Dec. 1777, *PGWde*, RWS, 13:79-81. A day earlier Major General John Sullivan had warned Washington the brigadiers were preparing their letter; Sullivan to GW, 30 Dec. 1777, ibid., 13:76.
38. John Sullivan to GW, 2 Jan. 1778, *PGWde*, RWS, 13: 122n1; The brigadiers were Henry Knox, William Maxwell, Enoch Poor, Lachlan McIntosh, George Weedon, Jedediah Huntington, Charles Scott, J.M. Varnum, and John Peterson. 19 Jan. 1778, JCC, 10:63; Henry Laurens to John Rutledge, 30 Jan. 1778, *LDC*, 8:694. In the same letter Laurens told Rutledge that a petition from colonels protesting Wilkinson's promotion met an identical fate.

Major Generals Nathanael Greene and John Sullivan also contacted Congress expressing grave concerns over the Conway promotion; Nathanael Greene to Congress, 12 Jan. 1778, *PNG*, 2:252–53; John Sullivan to Henry Laurens, 20 Jan. 1778, PCC, roll 178, item 160.

39. Clary and Whitehorne, *The Inspectors General*, 26.

40. 13 December 1777, *JCC*, 9:1023–26.

41. Council of War, 29 Oct. 1777, *PGWde*, RWS, 12:48.

42. Clary and Whitehorne, *The Inspectors General*, 28.

43. 13 December 1777, *JCC*, 9:1023.

44. Recall from chapter 3 Duer's plaintive letter to Francis Lightfoot Lee, 14 Feb. 1778, *LDC*, 9:95–102.

45. Francis Lightfoot Lee to Richard Henry Lee, 15 Dec. 1777, *LDC*, 8:417; Eliphalet Dyer to Joseph Trumbull, 15 Dec. 1777, ibid., 8:414; William Ellery to William Whipple, 21 Dec. 1777, ibid., 8:453.

46. Alexander Hamilton to William Duer, 18 June 1778, *PAH*, 1: 497–501.

47. Thomas Conway to GW, 29 Dec. 1777, *PGWde*, RWS, 13:40–41.

48. GW to Thomas Conway, 30 Dec. 1777, ibid., 13:66–67.

49. Thomas Conway to GW, 31 Dec. 1777, ibid., 13:77–78.

50. GW to Henry Laurens, 2 Jan. 1778, ibid., 13:119.

51. *E.g.*, in January Rhode Island brigadier James Mitchell Varnum instituted a rigorous training program, and he intended to "maneuver the whole division daily" once his officers knew the regimen "perfect[ly]." Richard Platt to Alexander McDougall, 24 Jan. 1778, Manuscript Collection, Philip S. and A.S.W. Rosenbach Foundation, Philadelphia.

52. Remarks Concerning the Office of Inspector General, Jan.–Mar. 1778, *PAH*, 1:422–43; Alexander Hamilton to GW, before 29 Jan. 1778; ibid., 1:414–421.

53. Abraham Clark to William Alexander [Lord Stirling], 15 Jan. 1778, *LDC*, 8:597.

54. Clary and Whitehorne, *The Inspectors General*, 38–43; Selesky, *Encyclopedia of the Revolution*, 2:1110–11.

55. GW to Henry Laurens, 30 Apr. 1778, *PGEde*, RWS, 14:681–82; 5 May 1778, *JCC*, 11:465–66.

56. GW to the Board of War, 2–3 Jan. 1778, ibid., 13:110–12.

57. For historians who have seen no intentional designs on Washington's authority in the December 13 congressional resolution or in the actions of the board in the matter of the inspector generalship, see Knollenberg, *Washington and the Revolution*, 37–49; Rossman, in *Thomas Mifflin*, curiously did not deal with the inspector general controversy but found "nothing sinister" in the board's actions generally, p. 114.

58. John Laurens to Henry Laurens, 3 Jan. 1778, in John Laurens, *Army Correspondence*, 103.

59. Alexander Hamilton to George Clinton, 13 Feb. 1778, *PAH*, 1:428.

60. Henry Laurens to John Laurens, 8 Jan. 1778, *LDC*, 8:547.

61. Ibid., 8:546–47.

62. Ibid., 8:545.

63. *E.g.*, Henry Laurens to William Livingston, 27 Jan. 1778, *LDC*, 8:664; Henry Laurens to John Rutledge, 30 Jun. 1778, ibid., 8:692–93.

64. *E.g.*, Higginbotham, *War of American Independence*, 221; and Nelson, *Horatio Gates*, 159.

65. Ibid., 159.

66. Benjamin Harrison to Robert Morris, 19 Feb. 1778, *LDC*, 8:651n2.

CHAPTER SIX: "DISGUST" UPON "DISGUST"

1. GW to Henry Laurens, 23 Dec. 1777, *PGWde*, RWS, 12:684.
2. GW to James Mitchell Varnum, 4 Nov. 1777, ibid., 12:128–29.
3. Alexander Hamilton to William Duer, 18 June 1778, *PAH*, 1: 497–501.
4. Henry Laurens to John Laurens, 8 Jan. 1778, *LDC*, 8:546; Benjamin Harrison to Robert Morris, 19 Feb. 1778, ibid., 8:651n2.
5. The best study of the broader Valley Forge experience, linking the military and civilian communities, is Wayne K. Bodle's incisive *The Valley Forge Winter: Civilians and Soldiers in War* (University Park: Pennsylvania State University Press, 2002). For emphases on the military aspects of the Valley Forge experience, see Paul Lockhart, *The Drillmaster of Valley Forge: The Baron de Steuben and the Making of the American Army* (New York: Smithsonian Books, 2008); and John B.B. Trussell, *Birthplace of an Army: A Study of the Valley Forge Encampment* (Harrisburg: Pennsylvania Historical and Museum Commission, 1998).
6. GW to Henry Laurens, 23 Dec. 1777, *PGWde*, RWS, 12:683.
7. *Merriam-Webster Dictionary*, https://www.merriam-webster.com/dictionary/logistics; accessed 5 Jan. 2018.
8. Lender, *War for Independence*, 213.
9. Heitman, *Historical Register*, 129; "Stewart, Charles," *Biographical Directory of the United States Congress*, http://bioguide.congress.gov/scripts/biodisplay.pl?index=s000903, accessed 8 Jan. 2018; on the early evolution of the support departments (to 1778), see Erna Risch, *Supplying Washington's Army* (Washington, DC: Center of Military History, United States Army, 1981), 29–42.
10. "Supply of the Continental Army," Selesky, *Encyclopedia*, 2:1131–33; Rossman, *Thomas Mifflin*, 40–54, 65–67, 82.
11. Most studies of logistics have not emphasized combat operations or active campaigning as supply problems in and of themselves. Don Higginbotham, *The War of American Independence: Military Attitudes, Policies, and Practice, 1763-1789* (New York: Macmillan, 1971), 308, and R. Arthur Bowler, *Logistics and the Failure of the British Army in America: 1775-1783* (Princeton, NJ: Princeton University Press, 1975), 1–11, are worthy exceptions.
12. Board of War to GW, 19 June 1777, *LDC*, 7:221; Erna Risch, *Supplying Washington's Army* (Washington, DC: Center of Military History, United States Army, 1981), 436.
13. Ephraim Blaine to Charles Stewart, 26 Dec. 1777, Colonel Charles Stewart Papers [hereafter CSP], Fenimore Art Museum Library, Cooperstown, NY.
14. Thomas Jones to Charles Stewart, 15 Feb. 1778, CSP, Fenimore Art Museum Library, Cooperstown, NY.
15. Risch, *Supplying Washington's Army*, 39–40.
16. 10 Jan. 1778, *JCC*, 10:39–41.
17. James Lovell to Samuel Adams, 13 Jan. 1778, *LDC*, 8:580.
18. James Lovell to Samuel Adams, 20 Jan. 1778, ibid., 8:618.
19. Timothy Pickering to Alexander Scammell, 17 Feb. 1778, in Octavius Pickering, *The life of Timothy Pickering*, 2 vols. (Boston: Little Brown, and Company, 1867), 1:206–207.
20. Gerard H. Clarfield, *Timothy Pickering and the American Republic* (Pittsburgh, PA: University of Pittsburgh Press, 1980), 44–46.
21. William Penn Cresson, *Francis Dana: A Puritan Diplomat at the Court of Catherine the Great* (New York: L. MacVeagh, Dial Press, 1930), 40–47. Dana had been impressed with Gates, but at Valley Forge he saw things through Washington's eyes. He became friends with the commanding general, dined with him on rude army fare, no doubt served to drive home

the plight of the soldiery. Dana family lore tells how Francis, out to get some night air at Valley Forge, came across a brooding Washington who confided: "Congress, sir, does not trust me—I cannot continue thus" (p. 45). The alleged incident supposedly turned Dana fully in Washington's favor.

22. Folsom lacks a significant biography and is known only through brief biographical treatments; *e.g.*, Henry M. Baker, "General Nathaniel Folsom," *Proceedings of the New Hampshire Historical Society*, 4, pt. 1 (1899-1902):153–67; Jacob Chapman, *A Genealogy of the Folsom Family: John Folsom and His Descendants, 1615-1882* (Concord, NH: Republican Press Association, 1882), 252–53; "Nathaniel Folsom," in Mark Grossman, *Encyclopedia of the Continental Congress* [hereafter *ECC*], 2 vols. (Amenia, NY: Grey House Publishing, 2015), 1:398–401.

23. Phillip Papas, *Renegade Revolutionary: The Life of General Charles Lee* (New York: New York University Press, 2014), 199–200; "List of Delegates to Congress," *LDC*, 8:xxii; "John Harvie," *ECC*, 1:588–90; *DAB*, 8:375.

24. James Lovell to Samuel Adams, 20 Jan. 1778, *LDC*, 8:618.

25. Richard Peters to Robert Morris, 21 Jan. 1778, in Burnett, *Letters*, 3:45n6; Jedidiah Huntington to Joseph Trumbull, 31 Jan. 1778, quoted in Bodle, "Vortex of Small Fortunes," 197.

26. Henry Laurens to Lafayette, 22 Jan. 1778, *LDC*, 8:634.

27. 10 Jan. 1778, *JCC*, 10:39–41, 67; Harvie was the added fourth delegate; ibid., 10:65–67.

28. Lewis A. Leonard, *The Life of Charles Carroll of Carrollton* (New York: Moffat, Yard, and Company, 1918), 164–70; Charles Carroll of Carrollton to Charles Carroll of Annapolis, 8–9 November 1777, in Charles Carroll of Carrollton and Charles Carroll of Annapolis, *Dear Papa, Dear Charley: The Peregrinations of a Revolutionary Aristocrat, as Told by Charles Carroll of Carrollton and His Father, Charles Carroll of Annapolis, with Sundry Observations on Bastardy, Child-Rearing, Romance, Matrimony, Commerce, Tobacco, Slavery, and the Politics of Revolutionary America*, ed. by Ronald Hoffman, 3 vols. (Chapel Hill: University of North Carolina Press, 2001), 2:1080.

29. Gouverneur Morris, *The Diary and Letters of Gouverneur Morris*, ed. by Anne Cary Morris, 2 vols. (New York: Charles Scribner's Sons, 1888), 1:7.

30. William Duer to Robert R. Livingston, 10 Mar. 1778, *LDC*, 8:254.

31. Gouverneur Morris to John Jay, 5 Feb. 1778, quoted in William Howard Adams, *Gouverneur Morris: An Independent Life* (New Haven: Yale University Press, 2003), 97.

32. Ellen Hart Smith, *Charles Carroll of Carrollton* (Cambridge, MA: Harvard University Press, 1942), 177–78.

33. Perhaps the most apt modern variant of this political wisdom was the quip by British Labor's Roy Hattersley in 1992: "The party which sets the agenda wins the election"; in Steve Barnett and Ivor Gaber, *Westminster Tales: The Twenty-first Century Crisis in Political Journalism* (London, UK: Continuum, 2001), 97. Margaret Thatcher's Conservatives had just thumped Labor in a general election, and Hattersley conceded that Thatcher had set the agenda.

34. GW to a Continental Congress Camp Committee, 29 Jan. 1778, *PGWde*, RWS, 13:376–409.

35. GW to Henry Laurens, 23 Dec. 1777, ibid., 12:684.

36. GW to a Continental Congress Camp Committee, 29 Jan. 1778, ibid., 13:396–97.

37. Ibid., 13:393–96.

38. On the principles of war, see John I. Alger, *The Quest for Victory: The History of the Principles of War* (Westport, CT: Greenwood Press, 1982); on Washington's readings on the subject, see O. L. Spaulding, "The Military Studies of George Washington," *American Historical Review* 29 (1923-4): 675–80. A more recent and excellent summary of Washington's military reading is in Kevin J. Hayes, *George Washington: A Life in Books* (New York: Oxford University Press, 2017), 175, 179–82, 187.
39. Washington to James Mitchell Varnum, 4 Nov. 1777, *PGWde*, RWS, 12:128–29.
40. Chairman, Joint Chiefs of Staff, *Joint Operations (Joint Publication 3-0)* (Washington, DC: U.S. Joint Chiefs of Staff, 17 January 2017), A-2.
41. *E.g.*, William Livingston to GW, 12 Jan. 1778, *PGWde*, RWS, 13:208; Rhode Island Council of War to GW, 15 Jan. 1778, ibid., 13:253; GW to William Livingston, 20 Jan. 1778, ibid., 13:296; Tench Tilghman to Lord Stirling, 24 Jan. 1778, ibid., 13:336; GW to William Buchanan, 7 Feb. 1778, ibid., 13:465–66; Risch, *Supplying Washington's Army*, 42, 220–21.
42. Tench Tilghman to Charles Stewart, 18 Feb. 1778, William A. Oldridge Collection of George Washington's Headquarters Staff Writings, MMC-1589 Manuscript Division, Library of Congress.
43. Authority to Collect Clothing, c. 1 Nov. 1777, *PGWde*, RWS, 12:76; GW to Henry Laurens, 14–15 Dec. 1777, *PGWde*, RWS, 12:606; Risch, *Supplying Washington's Army*, 21, 214–15; E. Wayne Carp, *To Starve the Army at Pleasure: Continental Army Administration and American Political Culture, 1775-1783* (Chapel Hill: University of North Carolina Press, 1984), 77.
44. 15 Jan. 1778, *JCC*, 10:54–55. In granting the Board of War limited authority to set prices, Congress had in mind an upcoming inter-colonial convention on price controls to convene in New Haven, Connecticut. Congress wanted no conflicts between the board's procurement efforts and any price controls agreed to in New Haven.
45. 15 Jan. 1778, *JCC*, 10:55.
46. Jacqueline Thibaut, "This Fatal Crisis: Logistics and the Continental Army at Valley Forge, 1777-1778," Valley Forge Historical Research Report, Vol. 2 (Valley Forge National Historical Park: U.S. Department of the Interior, National Park Service, 1982), 198.
47. Curiously, the chief biographies of Gates and Mifflin do not dwell at length on this aspect of the board's foray into direct commissary operations. Rossman, *Thomas Mifflin*, devotes no attention to the matter, nor does Knollenberg in *Washington and the Revolution*. Nelson, *Horatio Gates*, 179–81, does reference Gates's efforts to supply the army but not the conflicts between the board's efforts and those of the established commissary department or those of Pennsylvania state procurement agents.
48. The various memoranda and resolutions establishing the Board of War's commissary arrangements are in *Pennsylvania Archives: Selected and Arranged from Original Documents,* 1st Ser., 12 vols., ed. by Samuel Hazard (Philadelphia: Printed by Joseph Severns & Co., 1853–56), 6:303–14; Horatio Gates to Superintendents, 31 Jan. 1778, ibid., 6:307–309.
49. Rossman, *Thomas Mifflin*, 125.
50. 30 Jan. 1778, *JCC*, 10:102.
51. Ibid.
52. Wayne K. Bodle, "The Vortex of Small Fortune: The Continental Army at Valley Forge, 1777-1778." Valley Forge Historical Research Report, Vol. 1 (Valley Forge National Historical Park: U.S. Department of the Interior, National Park Service, 1980), 222.
53. 30 Jan. 1778, *JCC*, 10:103; 31 Jan. 1778, ibid., 104.
54. Committee at Camp Minutes of Proceedings, 28-31 Jan. 1778, *LDC*, 8:673; Bodle, "Vortex of Small Fortunes," 220–21.

55. Committee at Camp to Henry Laurens, 28 Jan. 1778, LDC, 8:676; Martin R. Bush, *Revolutionary Enigma: A Reappraisal of General Philip Schuyler of New York* (Port Washington, NY: Ira J. Friedman, 1969), 135–37.
56. Jonathan Bayard Smith to Joseph Reed, 25 Feb. 1778, *LDC*, 9:176.
57. 5 Feb. 1778, *JCC*, 10:126.
58. Richard Henry Lee to George Washington, 20 Nov. 1777, *LDC*, 8:293.
59. Department of the Army, *Stability Operations and Support Operations* (FM 3-07) (Washington, DC: Department of the Army, 20 February 2003), 1–17.
60. For discussions of "scope creep" and related phenomena, see Cecilia Rossignoli and Francesca Ricciardi, *Towards a Dynamic Model for Understanding Business Network Performance* (Cham, Switzerland: Springer International Publishing, 2015), 31–34; Daniel Katz and Robert Louis Kahn, *The Social Psychology of Organizations* (New York: Wiley, 1966), 18–33; Theodore M. Mills, *The Sociology of Small Groups* (Englewood Cliffs, NJ: Prentice-Hall, 1967), 14–17.
61. Thibaut, "This Fatal Crisis," 254–56.
62. 17 Feb. 1778, *JCC*, 10:176.
63. Horatio Gates to Henry Laurens, 13 Feb. 1778, PCC, Reports of the Board of War, pp. 517–20, http://www.fold3.com/image/1/382783, accessed 12 Mar. 2018; Jonathan Mifflin to GW, 20 Feb. 1778, *PGWde*, RWS, 13:612–13, esp. n1.
64. Thibaut, "This Fatal Crisis," 258–61.
65. Ephraim Blaine to Charles Stewart, 21 Feb. 1778, CSP, Fenimore Art Museum Library, Cooperstown, NY. Blaine's later plan, never adopted, is in: [Outline for a proposed system of supply for the continental troops, submitted by Blaine to Congress], n.p., n.d., Charles Stewart Family Papers, 1768-1877, Houghton Library, Harvard University.
66. Lafayette to GW, 5 Jan. 1777, *PGWde*, RWS, 13:144–46.
67. Ephraim Blaine to Robert Hanson Harrison, 18 Jan. 1778, Ephraim Blaine Letter Book, Peter Force Collection, MS 17137, Ser. 8D, no.12, Library of Congress; Ephraim Blaine to Robert Hanson Harrison, 18 Jan. 1778, George Washington Papers, Roll 46, Library of Congress, copy in Joseph Lee Boyle Resource Files, Valley Forge National Historical Park Library.
68. "Memorandum," Robert H. Harrison, 18 Jan. 1778, Oldridge Collection, Library of Congress.
69. Pennsylvania Council to the Board of War, 16 Feb. 1778, *Pa. Archives*, 1st Ser., 6:268–69.
70. John Harvie and Gouverneur Morris to the Pennsylvania Council, 24 Jan. 1778, *LDC*, 8:640.
71. Heitman, *Historical Register*, 374. Lee's regiment was one of sixteen "additional regiments" raised under congressional authority and not part of any state line; Fred Anderson Berg, *Encyclopedia of Continental Army Units: Battalions, Regiments and Independent Corps* (Harrisburg, PA: Stackpole Books, 1972), 61–62.
72. William Stephens Smith to GW, 25 Jan. 1778, *PGWde*, RWS, 13:345–47; GW to Horatio Gates, 26 Jan. 1778, ibid., 13:350–51.
73. On discovery of counterfeit currency, see Pennsylvania Supreme Executive Council to GW, 22 Jan. 1778, ibid., 13:315–16; Horatio Gates to Thomas Wharton, 31 Jan. 1778, *Pa. Archives*, 1st Ser., 6:216; Deposition of James Christy, 3 Feb. 1778, ibid., 1st Ser., 6:233.
74. 30 Jan. 1778, *JCC*, 10:101. There are editorial summaries of the passport incident, including related correspondence from the involved parties, in *LDC*, 8:641-42n1 and in *PGWde*, RWS, 13:245–47n1–2.

75. GW to Horatio Gates, 27 Jan. 1778, ibid., 13:361–62.
76. Report of the Board of War, 28 Jan. 1778, PCC, pp. 461–62, http://www.fold3.com image/246/382605; accessed 3 Mar. 2018.
77. GW to Horatio Gates, 21 Feb. 1778, *PGWde*, RWS, 13:617–18.
78. Henry Knox to GW, 21 Jan. 1778, ibid., 13:304–305; Henry Knox to GW, 4 Feb. 1778, ibid., 13:449–50.
79. Henry Knox to GW, 16 Feb. 1778, ibid., 13:560–61. Knox's letter is unclear as to what he thought Gates had in mind in moving the artillery to Farmington; but Knox did note Gates's intention to use other stores and munitions then in the armory at Springfield, Massachusetts, for the Canadian venture.
80. James Duane to Horatio Gates, 16 Dec. 1777, *LDC*, 8:421; Rossie, *Politics of Command*, 204.
81. 22 Jan. 1778, *JCC*, 10:84–85. "Apparently" because the *Journals* did not record the vote, although no other sources indicate any congressional opposition to the "irruption."
82. 23 Jan. 1778, ibid., 10:87. Curiously, the appointments did not receive unanimous approval. Charles Thomson, secretary to Congress, jotted down the vote on the back of a treasury report: "Fayette, 6; Conway, 6; Stark, 8; [New York major general Alexander] McDougall, 1; [Massachusetts brigadier general John] Glover, 1." Thomson did not note how individual states voted or for what positions in the command hierarchy; ibid., 10:87n1. On planning for the Canadian operation and its ultimate fate, see Justin Smith, *Our Struggle for the Fourteenth Colony: Canada and the American Revolution*, 2 vols. (New York: G.P. Putnam's Sons, 1907), 2:471–513.
83. Horatio Gates to GW, 24 Jan. 1778, *PGWde*, RWS, 13:329.
84. Horatio Gates to GW, 24 Jan. 1778, ibid., 13:329–30.
85. Horatio Gates to Lafayette, 24 Jan. 1778, Horatio Gates Papers, NYHS; Horatio Gates to Thomas Conway, 24 Jan. 1778, ibid.; Horatio Gates to John Stark, 24 Jan. 1778, ibid.; Berg, *Continental Army Units*, 16–17.
86. Lengel and Lender, "The Middle Theater," 72, 87; GW to Horatio Gates, 30 Oct. 1777, *PGWde*, RWS, 12:59–60.
87. Nelson, *Horatio Gates*, 172–76; editor's note, *LDC*, 8:635-636n2. It should be noted that Henry Laurens did not agree with the plan; he was explaining the neglect to notify Washington, as the South Carolinian understood it, to a bemused Lafayette.
88. Nelson, *Horatio Gates*, 172.
89. Louis Gottschalk, *Lafayette Joins the American Army* (Chicago: University of Chicago Press, 1937), 110–11, 124.
90. Gérard to Vergennes, 12 Aug. 1778, in *New Materials for the History of the American Revolution: Translated from Documents in the French Archives and Edited*, ed. and trans. by John Durand (New York: Henry Holt and Company, 1889), 173–74; Gérard to Vergennes, 14 May 1779, ibid., 195.
91. Joseph Reed to Jonathan Bayard Smith, 8 Feb. 1778, *LDC*, 9:57–58.
92. Ibid., 9:59–61.
93. Jonathan Bayard Smith to Joseph Reed, 21 Feb. 1778, *LDC*, 9:158; Joseph Reed to Jonathan Bayard Smith, 19 Feb. 1778, ibid., 9:141. In a follow-up letter to Smith (24 Feb. 1777, ibid., 9:168), Reed indicted an "odd Experience of Cullibility [gullibility] in Congress" in making disastrous logistics appointments—certainly a reference to the delegates following the advice of the Board of War. Reed specifically denigrated the Mifflin plan for dividing the quartermaster department.

CHAPTER SEVEN: COUNTERATTACK

1. GW to William Gordon, 15 Feb. 1778, *PGWde*, RWS, 13:545–46.
2. Hortentius [William Livingston], "To His Excellency General Washington," 1 Apr. 1778, *PWL*, 2:278.
3. Henry Laurens to John Laurens, 8 Jan. 1778, *LDC*, 8:547.
4. William Gordon to GW, 8 Jan. 1778, *PGWde*, RWS, 13:173–76; GW to William Gordon, 23 Jan. 1778, ibid., 13:322–23; GW to William Gordon, 15 Feb. 1778, ibid., 13:545–46.
5. John Clark, "Memoir of Major John Clark, of York County, Pennsylvania," *PMHB* 20, No. 1 (1896):77–86.
6. Lender and Stone, *Fatal Sunday*, 195; Clark, "Memoir," 77–86; John A. Nagy, *George Washington's Secret Spy War: The Makings of America's First Spymaster* (New York: St. Martin's Press, 2016), 110–16. Clark ended the war as an army auditor. Washington wrote personally to Henry Laurens endorsing an appointment for Clark. It was clearly a reward for services rendered, and Washington eluded to, but never completely spelled out, the essential services Clark had performed. See GW to Henry Laurens, 2 Jan. 1778, *PGWde*, RWS, 13:118.
7. Elbridge Gerry to James Warren, 12 Dec. 1777, *LDC*, 8:403–405.
8. Henry Knox to Elbridge Gerry, 4 Jan. 1778, in James T. Austin, *The Life of Elbridge Gerry: With Contemporary Letters*, 2 vols. (Boston: Wells and Lilly, 1828-29), 1:238–39.
9. Elbridge Gerry to Henry Knox, 7 Feb. 1778, *LDC*, 9:45.
10. Ibid., 9:45–46.
11. The committee was to meet with GW to discuss a winter campaign. "Jones, Joseph," *Biographical Directory of the United States Congress*, http://bioguide.congress.gov/scripts/biodisplay.pl?index=J000241. The other committee members were Gerry and Robert Morris. 16 Dec. 1777, *JCC*, 9:972, 1029–31; Committee at Headquarters to GW, 10 Dec. 1777, *LDC*, 8:399–400.
12. Joseph Jones to GW, 22 Jan. 1778, *PGWde*, RWS, 13:310. Rossman, *Thomas Mifflin*, 115, reads this letter very differently, citing it as proof that the new War Office members were not antagonistic to Washington—but this reading ignores the fact that Jones specifically cited Mifflin and Gates as acting suspiciously.
13. James Craik to GW, 6 Jan. 1778, *PGWde*, RWS, 13:160–62.
14. Robert Lewis Hooper, Jr., Nathaniel Falconer, Jonathan Mifflin, Jr., to Horatio Gates, 11 Feb. 1778, *Pennsylvania Archives*, 1st Ser., 6:310.
15. John Laurens to Henry Laurens, 8 Jan. 1778, in John Laurens, *Army Correspondence*, 103; John Laurens to Henry Laurens, 9 Feb. 1778, ibid., 121.
16. Arthur S. Lefkowitz, *George Washington's Indispensable Men: The 32 Aides-de-Camp Who Helped Win American Independence* (Mechanicsville, PA: Stackpole Books, 2003), 64–66.
17. GW to William Livingston, 16 Feb. 1778, *PGWde*, RWS, 13:562; Tench Tilghman to Lord Stirling, 24 Jan. 1778, ibid., 13:336; Tench Tilghman to John Clark, 31 Dec. 1777, Oldridge Collection, LC.
18. Tench Tilghman to Robert Morris, 2 Feb. 1778, John Reed Collection, Valley Forge National Historical Park Library.
19. Heitman, *Historical Register*, 112; John W. Jordan, *et al.*, eds., *Encyclopedia of Pennsylvania Biography* (New York, Lewis Historical Publishing Co., 1914), 3:720–23; Lender and Stone, *Fatal Sunday*, 95, 101–102.
20. Tench Tilghman to John Cadwalader, 18 Jan. 1778, Cadwalader Family Papers, General John Cadwalader, Ser. 1, Box 3, Folder 2, HSP.

21. Draft of John Cadwalader to [George Clinton], [?] Jan. 1778, ibid.; this was a virtual duplicate of Tilghman's letter to Cadwalader, just readdressed to Clinton. John Cadwalader to Benjamin Franklin, [?] Jan.1778, *Papers of Benjamin Franklin*, ed. by Leonard Woods Labaree, *et al.*, 42 vols. (New Haven: Yale University Press, 1959-2017), 25:555–56.
22. Benjamin Harrison to Joseph Hewes, 3 Mar. 1778, in *The State Records of North Carolina*, ed. by William L. Saunder *et al.*, 30 vols. (Winston, NC: M.I. & J.C., printers, 1896-1914), 13:61–62.
23. Robert Morris to Richard Peters, 25 Jan. 1778, *LDC*, 8:649–50.
24. Gouverneur Morris to Robert R. Livingston, 10 Mar. 1778, ibid., 9:264.
25. William Duer to Robert R. Livingston, 10 Mar. 1778, ibid., 9:254.
26. Kapp, *Life of Kalb*, 155–56.
27. Timothy Pickering to Alexander Scammel, 17 Feb. 1778, in Octavius Pickering and Charles Wentworth Upham, *The Life of Timothy Pickering*, 4 vols. (Boston, Little, Brown, and Company, 1867-73), 1:206–207; Reports of the Board of War, 11 Apr. 1778, PCC, https://www.fold3.com/image /382963.
28. Richard Peters to Robert Morris, 21 Jan.1778, *LDC*, 8:651n1.
29. John Clark to Nathanael Greene, 10 Jan. 1778, *PNG*, 2:250.
30. On the request for writing paper, see GW to Horatio Gates, 27 Feb. 1778, *PGWde*, RWS, 13:681–82; GW to Horatio Gates, 20 Mar. 1778, ibid., 14:236. The surviving correspondence from January through March 1778 follows: January: GW to Gates (3), Gates to GW (6). February: GW to Gates (9), Gates to GW (9). March: GW to Gates (4), Gates to GW (7). Totals: GW to Gates (16), Gates to GW (18). The letters are found in *PGWde*, RWS, vols. 13 and 14.
31. The largest single collection of staff writings is the William A. Oldridge Collection of George Washington's Headquarters Staff Writings in the Manuscript Division of the Library of Congress, MMC-1589. Of the hundreds of letters by staff members over 1777 and 1778, none are addressed directly to the Board of War. Other communications may exist elsewhere, but the dearth of such letters in the Oldridge Collection is indicative of how little communication existed between the army's senior command and the board.
32. Henry Laurens to the Committee at Camp, 20 Feb. 1778, *LDC*, 9:146.
33. Committee at Camp to Henry Laurens, 20 Feb. 1778, ibid., 9:143–44.
34. Joseph Reed to Jonathan Bayard Smith, 19 Feb. 1778, ibid., 9:141.
35. Committee at Camp Minutes of Proceedings, 22–28 Feb. 1778, ibid., 9:158.
36. Committee at Camp to Henry Laurens, 25 Feb. 1778, ibid., 9:169.
37. Ibid., 9:171–72.
38. Timothy Pickering to Alexander Scammel, 17 Feb. 1778, in Pickering and Upham, *Life of Pickering*, 1:207.
39. Henry Laurens to the Committee at Camp, 21 Feb. 1778, ibid., 9:154; 2 Mar. 1778, *JCC*, 10:210; Risch, *Supplying Washington's Army*, 42; Heitman, *Historical Register*, 137, 326.
40. 2 Mar. 1778, *JCC*, 10:210.
41. 9 Mar. 1778, ibid., 10:235–37; 13 Mar. 1778, ibid., 10:248–52.
42. 13 Mar. 1778, ibid., 10:248–52.
43. 20 Mar. 1778, ibid., 10:272–73.
44. Boyle, "Vortex of Small Fortunes," 297–98.
45. Gottschalk, *Lafayette Joins the American Army*, 112–19, 124–25.
46. Lafayette to Henry Laurens, 26 Jan. 1778, "Letters from the Marquis de Lafayette to Hon. Henry Laurens, 1777-1780," *South Carolina Historical Magazine* [hereafter *SCHM*] VII, No. 3 (1906):126–28.

47. Henry Laurens to John Rutledge, 3 Feb. 1778, *LDC*, 9:19.
48. Lafayette, *Memoirs*, 1:39.
49. Lafayette to Henry Laurens, 31 Jan. 1778, "Letters from Lafayette to Henry Laurens," *SCHM* VII, No. 4 (1906):183–84. In fact Lafayette did not like Duer. Duer actually had wanted to accompany the "irruption" and had planned on traveling to Albany with the Frenchman, but the major general would not have it. He considered Duer one of the most severe of Washington's critics (this was correct) and refused to have anything to do with him. Learning of Lafayette's animosity, Duer withdrew his request to go north although he was anything but happy about it. William Duer to Francis Lightfoot Lee, 14 Feb. 1778, *LDC*, 9:96, 102n3.
50. Horatio Gates to Henry Laurens, c. 31 Jan. 1778, quoted in Gottschalk, *Lafayette Joins the American Army*, 123.
51. Henry Laurens to John Rutledge, 3 Feb. 1778, *LDC*, 9:19.
52. Gottschalk, *Lafayette Joins the American Army*, 113–14; Gouverneur Morris to Henry Laurens, 26 Jan. 1778, *LDC*, 8:658, 658–59n1; John Laurens to Henry Laurens, 28 Jan. 1778, John Laurens, *Military Correspondence*, 112–14.
53. Gottschalk, *Lafayette Joins the American Army*, 114, 117.
54. Benedict Arnold to Thomas Conway, 16 Feb. 1778, PCC, Roll 183, https://www.fold3.com/image/369035.
55. Nelson, *Horatio Gates*, 175; Henry Laurens to Lafayette, 4 Mar. 1778, *LDC*, 9:213–14.
56. Committee at Camp to Henry Laurens, 11 Feb. 1778, ibid., 9:72–73.
57. Ibid., 9:73–75.
58. Ibid., 9:75n2.
59. 16 Feb. 1778, *JCC*, 10:172; 23 Feb. 1778, ibid., 10:190–92; the committee members were Oliver Wolcott, Francis Lightfoot Lee, William Ellery, and Thomas McKean.
60. 24 Feb. 1778, ibid., 10:193; 26 Feb. 1778, ibid., 10:196; 2 Mar. 1778, ibid., 10:216–17.
61. 13 Mar. 1778, ibid., 10:253.
62. Gérard to Vergennes, 14 May 1779, in Durand, ed., *Documents in the French Archives*, 195.
63. Henry Laurens to Lafayette, 12 Jan. 1778, *LDC*, 8:571–72. Two weeks later Laurens wrote much the same thing to his friend Isaac Motte, 26 Jan. 1778, ibid., 8:655.
64. Henry Laurens to John Rutledge, 11 Mar. 1778, ibid., 9:269–70.
65. Wright, *Continental Army*, 123.
66. Henry Laurens to Lafayette, 4 Mar. 1778, *LDC*, 9:214; Committee at Camp to GW, 6 Mar. 1778, ibid., 9:225.
67. Timothy Pickering to John Laurens, 13 Mar. 1778, Reports of the Board of War and Ordnance, 1776-81, PCC, 1:551; https://www.fold3.com/image/382877. Mullens eventually received a brevet promotion to lieutenant colonel in June 1778, upon which he returned to France; Heitman, *Historical Register*, 304. On the promotion of Lafayette's aides, see 2 Feb. 1778, *JCC*, 10:107.
68. GW to John Fitzgerald, 28 Feb. 1778, *PGWde*, RWS, 13:694.
69. Hortentius [William Livingston], "To His Excellency General Washington," *New Jersey Gazette* (Trenton), 1 Apr. 1778, in *PWL*, 2:278; William Livingston to GW, 2 Mar. 1778, ibid., 2:242.
70. John Fitzgerald to GW, 17 Mar. 1778, *PGWde*, RWS, 14:209; Lund Washington to GW, 18 Mar. 1778, ibid., RWS, 14:221–22.
71. John Henry to Thomas Johnson, 10 Mar. 1778, *LDC*, 9:258.

72. Eliphalet Dyer to William Williams, 10 Mar. 1778, ibid., 9:257.
73. Other historians have taken Dyer's note to Williams at face value, citing it as evidence that the Cabal simply did not exist as any real threat to Washington's command. *E.g.*, Knollenberg, *Washington and the Revolution,* 72; and Nelson, *Horatio Gates*, 176. In light of events between December 1777 and March 1778 this perspective on Dyer's comment is untenable.

CHAPTER EIGHT: PAYBACK

1. Elias Boudinot to Alexander Hamilton, 8 July 1778, *LDC*, 10:238.
2. GW to Landon Carter, 30 May 1778, *PGWde*, RWS, 15:268.
3. Henry Laurens to Lafayette, 24 Mar. 1778, *PHL*, 13:29.
4. Lafayette, however, told Laurens he thought New York patriots would be "more exesperated against gal [general] gates than you could ever believe." It seems the marquis was projecting his personal feelings toward Gates on New Yorkers. Lafayette to Henry Laurens, 20 Mar. 1778, *PHL*, 13:18.
5. GW to Horatio Gates, 24 Apr. 1778, *PGWde*, RWS, 14:612; GW to George Clinton, 30 Apr. 1778, ibid., 14:678; GW to Horatio Gates, 17 May 1778, ibid., 15:139–40.
6. Horatio Gates to GW, 21 May 1778, ibid., 15:177–78; 14 May 1778, *JCC*, 11:498–99; Friedrich Steuben to GW, *PGWde*, RWS, 16:157–58; GW to Henry Laurens, 24 July 1778, ibid., 16:152.
7. GW to Lord Stirling, 21 Mar. 1778, ibid., 14:262; James Wilkinson to GW, 28 Mar. 1778, ibid., 14:344.
8. James Wilkinson to Henry Laurens, 25 Mar. 1778, as copied by Laurens from the original letter, *LDC*, 9:359n2. Wilkinson later claimed to have sent a sharper note (dated 25 Mar.) as follows: "am sorry I should be constrained to resign that office; but after the act of *treachery* and *falsehood* in which I have detected Major-General Gates, the president of that board, it is impossible for me to reconcile it to my honor to serve with him." Wilkinson, *Memoirs*, I:409–10. There is no reason to doubt Laurens's version.
9. Henry Laurens to James Wilkinson, 21 Mar. 1778, *LDC*, 9:359.
10. Nelson, *Horatio Gates*, 195–97.
11. Edmund Pendleton, *The Letters and Papers of Edmund Pendleton*, ed. by David John Mays, 2 vols. (Charlottesvile: University Press of Virginia, 1967), 1:271–72.
12. William Palfrey to Nathanael Greene,14 Jan. 1779, *PNG*, 3:165; Nathanael Greene to Alexander McDougall, 8 Nov. 1778, ibid., 3:49.
13. Joseph Reed to Nathanael Greene, 5 Nov. 1778, ibid., 3:41; George Lux to Nathanael Greene, 24 Oct. 1778, ibid., 3:14–15.
14. Gouverneur Morris to GW, 21 May 1778, *LDC*, 9:728–29; GW to Thomas Mifflin, 24 Apr. 1778, *PGWde*, RWS, 14:617; Lender and Stone, *Fatal Sunday*, 80.
15. Rossman, *Thomas Mifflin*, 157–60, 165–91.
16. Kapp, *Life of Kalb*, 154–57.
17. 23 Mar. 1778, *JCC*, 10:280; Henry Laurens to Lafayette, 24 Mar. 1778, *PHL*, 13:27.
18. Thomas Conway to Henry Laurens, 22 Apr. 1778, ibid., 13:169; William McKendry, "Copy of the Journal of William McKendry," *Proceedings of the Massachusetts Historical Society* 2, 2nd Ser. (May 1886):444.
19. Henry Laurens to Lafayette, 4 Mar. 1778, *PHL*, 13:27; Nelson, *Horatio Gates*, 176. John Jay was convinced Gates was trying to distance himself from Conway but that Conway didn't seem to realize it; John Jay to Gouverneur Morris, 29 Apr. 1778, *The Selected Papers of John Jay*, ed. by Elizabeth M. Nuxoll, 7 vols. (Charlottesville: University Press of Virginia, Rotunda, 2014–), 1:514.

20. Thomas Conway to Henry Laurens, 22 Apr. 1778, *PHL*, 13:169; 28 Apr. 1778, *JCC*, 10:399.
21. Henry Laurens to the chevalier de Neuville, 30 Apr. 1778, *PHL*, 13:219–20.
22. John Shy, "Charles Lee: The Soldier as Radical," in George Athan Billias, ed., *George Washington's Generals* (New York: William Morrow, 1964), 22–53.
23. This sketch of Lee is based on John R. Alden, *General Charles Lee: Traitor or Patriot?* (Baton Rouge: Louisiana State University Press, 1951); Shy, "Charles Lee," 22–53; and Phillip Papas, *Renegade Revolutionary: The Life of General Charles Lee* (New York: New York University Press, 2014).
24. Alden, *General Charles Lee*, 14.
25. Charles W. Snell, "General Charles Lee House. 'Prato Rio,'" National Register of Historic Places Inventory—Nomination Form, National Park Service, 27 July 1972; Papas, *Renegade Revolutionary*, 4.
26. Papas, *Renegade Revolutionary*, 93–113.
27. Joseph Reed to Charles Lee, 21 Nov. 1776, in William B. Reed, *Life and Correspondence of Joseph Reed* (Philadelphia: Lindsay and Blakiston, 1847), I: 255–56; Reed to Lee, 21 Nov. 1776, in *Collections of the New York Historical Society for the Year 1872. The Lee Papers* (New York: New York Historical Society, 1873), II: 293–94 (hereafter cited as *Lee Papers*); Lee to Horatio Gates, 12–13 Dec. 1776, ibid., 348.
28. GW to Charles Lee, 3 Dec. 1776. Lee's dilatory march is detailed in Arthur S. Lefkowitz, *The Long Retreat: The Calamitous American Defense of New Jersey, 1776* (Metuchen, NJ: Upland Press, 1998), 107–11; Shy, "Charles Lee," 39; Lee to GW, 4 Dec. 1776, *PGWde*, RWS:7:259
29. Parole, 5 Apr. 1778, *Lee Papers*, II: 382.
30. Scheme for Putting an End to the War, Submitted to the Royal Commissioners, 29th March, 1777, *Lee Papers*, II: 361–66; George H. Moore, "The Treason of Charles Lee, Major General," *Lee Papers*, IV:339–427; also published separately, George H. Moore, *The Treason of Charles Lee, Major General* (New York: Charles Scribner, 1860).
31. Alden, *General Charles Lee*, 175–79; Shy, "Charles Lee," 40–41.
32. Paul Lockhart, *The Drillmaster of Valley Forge: The Baron de Steuben and the Making of the American Army* (New York: Smithsonian Books, 2008), 132–33; James Varnum to GW, 5 May 1778, *PGWde*, RWS:15:54–56; Alexander Hamilton to Elias Boudinot, 26 July 1778, *PAH*, 1:528–29.
33. Lee, "Plan of an Army," *Lee Papers*, II:384, 388.
34. Warren, *History of the American Revolution*, II:95; Shy, "Charles Lee," 42.
35. Ibid., 79.
36. That Charles Lee met with Richard Henry Lee on his initial visit to York is a surmise but a logical one; we know that he met with R.H. Lee in York on his way back from a visit to his home in Virginia, before his return to Valley Forge. Richard Henry Lee to John Page, 4 May [1778], *LDC*, 9:599. Lee also met with delegates John Banister of Virginia and Charles Carroll of Carrollton (whom Lee considered friends); John Banister to St. George Tucker, 15 Apr. 1778, ibid., 9:416; Charles Carroll of Carrollton to Charles Carroll, Sr., 20 Apr. 1778, ibid., 9:448. He probably met with other delegates as well. Gates also wanted to meet with Lee at York, although Lee evidently missed him; Henry Laurens to GW, 24–25 Apr. *PGWde*, RWS, 14:613–14.
37. Thomas Burke to Richard Caswell, 9 Apr. 1778, *LDC*, 9:393.
38. Henry Laurens to John Laurens, 6 July 1778, *LDC*, 10:230, 323n3; Alden, *General Charles Lee*, 191; Lee to Henry Laurens, 17 Apr. 1778, *Lee Papers*, II:390.

39. Henry Laurens to John Laurens, 17 June 1778, *LDC*, 10:126.
40. Lee to Benjamin Rush, 4 June 1778, *Lee Papers*, II:397.
41. Nathanael Greene to Griffin Greene, 25 May 1778, ibid., II:406, 408.
42. Boudinot, *Journal*, 78; Lee to Gates, 4 Apr. 1778, *Lee Papers*, III:321.
43. Alexander Hamilton to Anthony Wayne, 18 June 1778, Anthony Wayne Papers, No. 0699, Vol. 5, HSP.
44. Nathanael Greene to GW, 24 June 1778, *PGWde*, RWS, 15:526.
45. Walter Stewart to Nathanael Greene, 4 Jan. 1778 [1779], *PNG*, 3:139; Walter Stewart to Nathanael Greene, 29 Jan. 1778, ibid., 3:194.
46. Evan Edwards to Charles Lee, 30 Aug. 1778, *Lee Papers*, III:229.
47. Elias Boudinot to Alexander Hamilton, 8 July 1778, *LDC*, 10:238.
48. Gérard to Vergennes, 12 Aug. 1778, in Durand, ed., *Documents in the French Archives*, 173–74.
49. Rossman, *Thomas Mifflin*, 134–38, 152–55; Horatio Gates to GW, 6 July 1778, *PGWde*, RWS, 16:32.
50. Alexander Hamilton to Elias Boudinot, 5 July 1778, *PAH*, 1:512.
51. Charles Lee to Horatio Gates, 18 Dec. 1778, *Lee Papers*, 3:278.
52. Lender and Stone, *Fatal Sunday*, 400; [Edmund Burke], *An Impartial History of the War in America between Great Britain and Her Colonies, from Its Commencement to the End of the Year 1779* (London: Printed for R. Faulder, 1780), 565.
53. Lender and Stone, *Fatal Sunday*, 400–403.
54. Brigadier General Samuel Patterson of Delaware thought Conway responded to Cadwalader questioning his (Conway's) conduct at the Battle of Germantown; Samuel Patterson to Caesar Rodney, 6 July 1778, in *Washington-Madison Papers Collected and Preserved by James Madison, Estate of J.C. McGuire.* Auction Catalogue (Philadelphia: Thomas Birch's Sons, 1892), 238. David Salisbury Franks to GW, 4 July 1778, *PGWde*, RWS, 16:21. A quite fanciful account of the duel is in Amos Blanchard, *American Military Biography: Containing the Lives, Characters, and Anecdotes of the Officers of the Revolution, Who Were Most Distinguished in Achieving Our National Independence* ([Cincinnati]: n.p., 1825), 37.
55. Gérard to Vergennes, 17 Jan. 1779, in Durand, ed., *Documents in the French Archives*, 187.
56. Committee of Arrangement to Henry Laurens, 7 Sept. 1778, *LDC*, 10:593; John Cadwalader to Henry Laurens, 19 Sept. 1778, Cadwalader Family Papers, Relating to the Revolution, Ser.1, Box 3, Folder 2, HSP; 10 Sept. 1778, *JCC*, 12:897, 941.
57. Greene quoted in Mark Abbott Stern, *David Franks: Colonial Merchant* (University Park: Pennsylvania State University Press, 2010), 3.
58. Thomas McKean to William Atlee, 7 July 1778, *LDC*, 13:237.
59. Unknown French Officer, "Characteristics of the States and Sentiments of the People," n.d., in Durand, ed., *Documents in the French Archives*, 17, 21–22. The officer returned to France for health reasons in 1779; his letter almost certainly dates from late 1778.
60. Gérard to Vergennes, 12 Aug.1778, in Durand, ed., *Documents in the French Archives*, 174.
61. Horatio Gates to John Jay, 15 Jan. 1779, PCC, Item 171, Roll 190:195–96, http://www.fold3.com/image/251969.
62. GW to Henry Laurens, 11 Nov. 1778, *PGWde*, RWS, 18:94–112; 1 Jan. 1779, *JCC*, 13:11–14.
63. Nelson, *Horatio Gates*, 197–201.
64. Horatio Gates to John Jay, 15 Mar. 1779, *SPJJde*, 1:610–11. With this letter to Jay, Gates included a copy of his letter to GW of 4 Mar. 1779, *PGWde*, RWS, 19:357–58.

65. When Jay received Gates's packet on April 4, including the Gates-Washington letters, he replied only that he would have Congress read them the following day. Congress did so and referred them to the Board of War, from which they apparently never emerged. John Jay to Horatio Gates, 4 Apr. 1779, *LDC*, 12:286–87; 5 Apr. 1779, *JCC*, 13:419–20.
66. GW to John Jay, 14 Apr.1779, *PGWde*, RWS, 20:57–64.
67. Ibid.
68. Credit this observation to the editors of *LDC*, 13:287n1, citing Freeman, *Washington*, 5:103.
69. John Jay to GW, 21 Apr. 1779, *PGWde*, RWS, 20:150–51.
70. John Jay to GW, 10 May 1779, *LDC*, 12:454.
71. John Jay to GW, 11 May 1779, ibid., 12:455.
72. Lender and Stoner, *Fatal Sunday*, 401–402; Selesky, ed., *Encyclopedia*, 2:862; George Weedon to Nathanael Greene, 10 Mar. 1779, *PNG*, 3:340.
73. Edward Rutledge to John Jay, 25 Dec. 1778, *SPJJde*, 1:559. A week earlier Rutledge had sent a similar warning to GW, 18 Dec. 1778, *PGWde*, RWS, 18:454–56.
74. Nathanael Greene to GW, 22 Mar. 1780, *Founders Online*, National Archives, http://founders.archives.gov/documents/Washington/99-01-02-01195.
75. John Sullivan to GW, 1 Dec. 1779. *PGWde*, RWS, 23:503–506.
76. Luzerne to Vergennes, 28 Jan. 1778, in Durand, ed., *Documents in the French Archives*, 234–35.
77. Alexander Hamilton to John Laurens, 11 Sept. 1779, *PAH*, 2:165–69.

EPILOGUE

1. Elbridge Gerry to Henry Knox, 7 Feb. 1778, *LDC*, 9:45–46.
2. Abraham Clark to William Alexander [Lord Stirling], 15 Jan. 1778, ibid., 8:597.
3. In a previous book I used the "cacophony" analogy regarding the Cabal, which is accurate, but without realizing that Dave R. Palmer had used it first in his *Washington and Arnold*, 264. So credit where due.
4. John Ferling, *The Ascent of George Washington: The Hidden Political Genius of an American Icon* (New York: Bloomsbury Press, 2009).
5. GW to Joseph Reed, *PGWde*, RWS, 18:397.
6. For a similar view of GW's qualities as a diplomat-commander, see Higginbotham, *War of American Independence*, 85–88.
7. *E.g.*, Nelson, *Horatio Gates*, 176; Higginbotham, *War of American Independence*, 220–21.
8. James Madison to Thomas Jefferson, 17 Oct. 1788, *PTJ*, 14:17–18.
9. As we know, use of the term "cabal" was common enough during the Revolution, although the earliest historians of the Revolution, while seeing Conway as linked to anti-Washington animus, did not adopt the use of "Conway Cabal." In the 1830s, while collecting materials for his Washington biography and edition of Washington's papers, Jared Sparks published a compendium of documents related to the Cabal which he labeled "Conway's Cabal." See *The Writings of George Washington: Being the Correspondence, Addresses, Messages, and Other Papers, Official and Private, Selected and Published from the Original Manuscripts*, ed. by Jared Sparks, 12 vols. (Boston: Russell, Odiorne, and Metcalf, and Hilliard, Gray, and Co., 1833-39), 5:483–518. He also had a research file, now at Harvard, docketed as the "Conway Cabal": Jared Sparks Collection of Documents Concerning the American Revolution, 1740-1866, Conway Cabal file, Houghton Library, Harvard University
10. Madame Conway [Françoise Antoinette Jeane Langlois de Bouchet] to William Templeton Franklin, 25 Sept. 1778, William Templeton Franklin Papers, CI:63, American Philosophical Society, Philadclphia.

11. André Lasseray, *Les Français sous les Treize Étoiles*, 2 vols. (Mâcon, France: Protat Frères, 1935), 1:160–66; Thomas Conway to Richard Henry Lee, 23 May 1778, Richard Henry Lee Papers, 2:59, American Philosophical Society, Philadelphia. On reports of Conway's service in India, see Thomas Barclay to Thomas Jefferson, *PTJ*, 11:536; Thomas Jefferson to John Jay, 3 Aug. 1788, ibid., 13:465; Paul Jodrell to Thomas Jefferson, 25 Sept. 1789, ibid., 15:478.

12. Lafayette to GW, 9 Mar. 1784, *PGW*, Confederation Ser., 1:184–89; Lasseray, *Les Français sous les Treize Étoiles*, 1:165–66; Paul David Nelson, "Conway, Thomas," *ANB*, 5:364–65.

13. Nelson, *Horatio Gates*, 240–65.

14. Nelson has depicted Gates's role as essentially meddlesome but naïve at Newburgh, not realizing his actions would set off a chain of disturbing events. Richard H. Kohn, however, has traced a darker narrative, seeing Gates as fully cognizant of what he was about. See Nelson, *Horatio Gates*, 270–81; and; Richard H. Kohn, "The Inside Story of the Newburgh Conspiracy: America and the Coup d'Etat," *William and Mary Quarterly* 3rd Ser., XXVII (1970):199–200.

15. John Armstrong, Jr., to Horatio Gates, 29 May 1783, Horatio Gates Papers, NYPL; John Armstrong, Jr., to Horatio Gates, 4 Feb. 1796, Historical MSS Collection, Special Collections, MS-5464, Fred W. Smith Library, George Washington's Mount Vernon, Mount Vernon, VA.

16. Rossman, *Thomas Mifflin*, 165–201, 298–311.

17. Mary Stockwell, *Unlikely General: "Mad" Anthony Wayne and the Battle for America* (New Haven: Yale University Press, 2018), 166–69, 189–90, 244–46, 275–76.

18. Wilkinson has generated a literature all his own, little of it complimentary other than his own self-serving memoir (James Wilkinson, *Memoirs of My Own Times*, 3 vols. [Philadelphia: Printed by Abraham Small, 1816]). A helpful biographical sketch is in Selesky, *Encyclopedia*, 2:1272–73. A good modern biography is Andro Linklater, *An Artist in Treason: The Extraordinary Double Life of General James Wilkinson* (New York: Walker, 2010).

19. Dominick Mazzagetti, *Charles Lee: Self before Country* (New Brunswick, NJ: Rutgers University Press, 2013), 205–207.

20. Rush, *Autobiography*, 137–38; Rush, *Selected Writings*, vi–vii.

21. James Lovell to GW, June-July 1789, *PGW*, Presidential Ser., 3:94.

22. Helen F. Jones, "James Lovell in the Continental Congress 1777-1782" (PhD dissertation, Columbia University, 1968), 571–80.

BIBLIOGRAPHY

MANUSCRIPT SOURCES

Samuel Adams Papers, Chicago Historical Society.

Samuel Adams Papers, Manuscripts and Archives Division, The New York Public Library.

George Bancroft Collection, The New York Public Library.

Joseph Lee Boyle Resource Files, Valley Forge National Historical Park Library.

Thomas Burke Papers, Southern Historical Collection, The Wilson Library, University of North Carolina, Chapel Hill.

Cadwalader Family Papers, Historical Society of Pennsylvania, Philadelphia.

Henry Clinton Papers, Clements Library, University of Michigan, Ann Arbor.

Papers of the Continental Congress, 1774-1789, Microfilm Edition, National Archives, Washington, DC.

Andre De Coppet Collection, 1566-1942, Firestone Library, Princeton University.

Draper Manuscripts, Historical Society of Wisconsin, Madison.

Dreer Collection, Generals of the American Revolution, Historical Society of Pennsylvania, Philadelphia.

Thomas Addis Emmet Collection, Manuscripts and Archives Division, The New York Public Library.

Sol Feinstone Collection, American Philosophical Society, Philadelphia.

William Temple Franklin Papers, American Philosophical Society, Philadelphia.

Horatio Gates Papers, New-York Historical Society, New York.

Horatio Gates Papers, Manuscripts and Archives Division, The New York Public Library.

Gratz Collection, Historical Society of Pennsylvania, Philadelphia.

Nathanael Greene Papers, American Philosophical Society, Philadelphia.

Jacob Hiltzheimer Diaries, American Philosophical Society, Philadelphia.

The Papers of John Jay, Digital Collections, Rare Books and Manuscripts Library, Columbia University.

Henry Knox Papers, Massachusetts Historical Society, Boston.

John Lamb Papers, 1762-1887, New-York Historical Society.

Richard Henry Lee Papers, American Philosophical Society, Philadelphia.

Gilder Lehrman Collection, Gilder Lehrman Institute, New York.

Papers of General Daniel Morgan, Series V, Theodorus Bailey Myers Collection, Manuscripts and Archives Division, The New York Public Library.

William A. Oldridge Collection of George Washington's Headquarters Staff Writings, Library of Congress.

Park Collection, Morristown National Historical Park, Morristown, NJ.

Joseph Reed Papers, The New-York Historical Society, New York.

Rush Family Papers, 1748-1876, Series 1, Library Company of Philadelphia.

Rush Family Papers, Series 11: Papers of Benjamin Rush, Firestone Library, Princeton University.

Lloyd W. Smith Collection, Morristown National Historical Park, Morristown, NJ.

Society Collection, Historical Society of Pennsylvania, Philadelphia.

Jared Sparks Collection of Documents Concerning the American Revolution, 1740-1866, Houghton Library, Harvard University.

Charles Stewart Family Papers, 1768-1877 (MS Am 1243). Houghton Library, Harvard University.

Colonel Charles Stewart Papers, 1752-1818, Fenimore Art Museum & The Farmers' Museum Research Library, Cooperstown, NY.

Joseph Ward Papers, Chicago Historical Society.

Mercy Otis Warren and Hannah Winthrop Correspondence, Massachusetts Historical Society.

Anthony Wayne Letters, Special Collections and Archives, West Chester University of Pennsylvania.

Anthony Wayne Papers, Historical Society of Pennsylvania, Philadelphia.

George Weedon Military Correspondence, American Philosophical Society, Philadelphia.

MEMOIRS, PUBLISHED PAPERS, AND RELATED

Adams, John. *Diary and Autobiography of John Adams*, 4 vols. Edited by L.H. Butterfield *et al.* New York: Atheneum, 1964.

————. *Papers of John Adams.* 17 vols. Edited by Robert J. Taylor *et al.* Cambridge, MA: Harvard University Press, 1977-2014.

Adams, Samuel. *The Writings of Samuel Adams*, 4 vols. Edited by Harry Alonzo Cushing. New York: G.P. Putnam's Sons, 1907.

Ames, Fisher. *Works of Fisher Ames*. Boston: T.B. Wait & Co., 1809.

Archives of the State of New Jersey [*New Jersey Archives*]. First Series. *Documents Relating to the Colonial History of the State of New Jersey.* 33 vols. Newark, NJ: 1880-1928.

Archives of the State of New Jersey [*New Jersey Archives*]. Second Series. *Documents Relating to the Revolutionary History of the State of New Jersey.* 5 vols. Trenton, NJ: 1901-1907.

[Balch, Thomas, ed.] *Letters and Papers Relating Chiefly to the Provincial History of Pennsylvania, with Some Notices of the Writers.* Philadelphia: Crissy & Markley, 1855.

Blaine, Ephraim. *"My last Shift Betwixt Us & death": The Ephraim Blaine Letterbook, 1777-1778.* Edited by Joseph Lee Boyle. Bowie, MD: Heritage Books, 2001.

Bloomfield, Joseph. *Citizen Soldier: The Revolutionary War Journal of Joseph Bloomfield.* Edited by Mark E. Lender and James Kirby Martin. Newark: New Jersey Historical Society, 1982.

Boudinot, Elias. *Journal of Historical Recollections of American Events during the Revolutionary War.* Philadelphia: F. Bourquin, 1894.

Boyle, Joseph Lee. *Writings from the Valley Forge Encampment of the Continental Army, December 19, 1777 to June 19, 1778.* Bowie, MD: Heritage Books, 2003.

Burr, Aaron. *Political Correspondence and Public Papers of Aaron Burr.* 2 vols. Edited by Mary-Jo Kline. Princeton, NJ: Princeton University Press, 1993.

Cadwalader, John. "Selections from the Military Papers of General John Cadwalader." *Pennsylvania Magazine of History and Biography* 32, No. 2 (1908):149–74.

Chase, Eugene Parker, ed. *Our Revolutionary Forefathers: The Letters of Fancois, Marquis de Barbe-Marbois.* New York: Duffield, 1929.

Clark, John. "Memoir of Major John Clark, of York County, Pennsylvania." *Pennsylvania Magazine of History and Biography* 20, No. 1 (1896):77–86.

Clinton, Henry. *The American Rebellion: Sir Henry Clinton's Narrative of His Campaigns, 1775-1782, with an Appendix of Original Documents.* Edited by William B. Willcox. New Haven: Yale University Press, 1954.

Commager, Henry Steele and Richard B. Morris, eds. *The Spirit of Seventy Six: The Story of the American Revolution as Told by Participants.* New York: Harper & Row, 1967.

Continental Congress. *Journals of the Continental Congress, 1774-1789.* 34 vols. Edited by Worthington C. Ford *et al.* Washington, D.C.: U.S. Government Printing Office, 1904-1937.

Continental Congress. *Papers of the Continental Congress, 1774-1789.* Washington, DC: National Archives, National Archives and Records Service, General Services Administration, 1958-1959. Microfilm publication # 274.

Cooke, John Esten, ed. "Revolutionary Letters." *Southern Literary Messenger* 28, No. 4 (1859):295–302.

Cresswell, Nicholas. *The Journal of Nicholas Cresswell, 1774-1777.* New York: Dial Press, 1924.

Dann, John C., ed. *The Revolution Remembered: Eyewitness Accounts of the War for Independence.* Chicago: University of Chicago Press, 1980.

Davies, Kenneth Gordon, ed. *Documents of the American Revolution, 1770-1783.* 21 vols. Dublin: Irish University Press, 1972–81.

Dearborn, Henry. *Revolutionary War Journals of Henry Dearborn, 1775-1783.* Edited by Lloyd A. Brown and Howard H. Peckham. Chicago: Caxton Club, 1939.

Denny, Ebenezer. *Military Journal of Major Ebenezer Denny, an Officer in the Revolutionary and Indian Wars, with an Introductory Memoir.* Philadelphia: J.B. Lippincott, 1859.

Duponceau, Peter S. "Autobiographical Letters of Peter S. Duponceau." *Pennsylvania Magazine of History and Biography* 50, No. 1 (1916):172–86.

Durand, John, trans and ed. *New Materials for the History of the American Revolution: Translated from Documents in the French Archives and Edited.* New York: Henry Holt and Company, 1889.

Egle, William Henry, ed. *Journals and Diaries of the Revolution, with Lists of Officers and Soldiers, 1775-1783*. Harrisburg, PA: E. K. Myers, 1893.

Ewald, Johann. *Diary of the American War: A Hessian Journal*. Translated and edited by Joseph P. Tustin. New Haven: Yale University Press, 1979.

"Excitement in Philadelphia on Hearing of the Defeat at Brandywine." *Pennsylvania Magazine of History and Biography* 14 (1890):64–67.

Force, Peter and M. St. Clair, eds., *American Archives: Consisting of a Collection of Authentick Records, State Papers, Debates, and Letters and Other Notices of Publick Affairs, the Whole Forming a Documentary History of the Origin and Progress of the North American Colonies*. 9 vols. Washington, DC: M. St. Clair Clarke and Peter Force, 1837-1853.

Ford, Paul Leicester, ed. "Dr. Rush and General Washington." *Atlantic Monthly* 75, No. 451 (May 1895):633–40.

Ford, Worthington Chauncey, ed. "Defences of Philadelphia in 1777." *Pennsylvania Magazine of History and Biography* 20, No. 1 (1896):87–115, 213–47, 391–404, 520–51; continued in 21, No. 1 (1897):51–71.

Gibbes, R.W., ed. *Documentary History of the American Revolution: Consisting of Letters and Papers Relating to the Contest for Liberty, Chiefly in South Carolina, from the Originals in the Possession of the Editor, and Other Sources*. 3 vols. New York: D. Appleton, 1853-1857.

Gordon, William. "Letters of the Reverend William Gordon, Historian of the American Revolution, 1770-1799." *Proceedings of the Massachusetts Historical Society* 63, Third Series (June 1929-1930):303–613.

Graydon, Alexander. *Memoirs of a Life, Chiefly Passed in Pennsylvania, within the Last Sixty Years, with Occasional Remarks upon the General Occurrences, Character and Spirit of that Eventful Period*. Harrisburg, PA: Printed by John Wyeth, 1811.

Greene, Nathanael. *The Papers of Nathanael Greene*. 8 vols. Edited by Richard K. Showman, Robert E. McCarthy, Margaret Cobb, and Dennis M. Conrad. Chapel Hill: University of North Carolina Press, for the Rhode Island Historical Society, 1976–.

Hamilton, Alexander. *The Papers of Alexander Hamilton*. Edited by Harold C. Syrett and Jacob E. Cooke. 27 vols. New York: Columbia University Press, 1961-87.

Hazard, Samuel, ed. *Pennsylvania Archives*. Ser. 1, Vol. VI. Philadelphia: Printed by Joseph Stevens, 1853.

Heath, William. *Memoirs of Major-General Heath*. Boston: I. Thomas and E.T. Andrews, 1798.

Hopkins, Esek. *The Letter Book of Esek Hopkins: Commander-in-Chief of the United States Navy, 1775-1777*. Edited by Alverda S. Beck. Providence: Rhode Island Historical Society, 1932.

Humphreys, David. *The Miscellaneous Works of David Humphreys: Late Minister Plenipotentiary from the United States of America to the Court of Madrid*. New York: T. and J. Swords, 1804.

Jay, John. *The Correspondence and Public Papers of John Jay*. 4 vols. Edited by Henry P. Johnston. New York: G.P. Putnam's Sons, 189-93.

————. *The Selected Papers of John Jay Digital Edition*. Edited by Elizabeth M. Nuxoll. Charlottesville: University Press of Virginia, Rotunda, 2014–.

Lafayette, Marie Joseph Paul, Marquis de. *Lafayette in the Age of the American Revolution: Selected Letters and Papers, 1776-1790.* Vol. 2, *April 10, 1778-March 20, 1780.* Edited by Stanley J. Idzerda, Roger E. Smith, Linda J. Pike, and Mary Ann Quinn. Ithaca, NY: Cornell University Press, 1979.

———. "Letters from the Marquis de Lafayette to Hon. Henry Laurens, 1777-1780," *South Carolina Historical Magazine* VII, No. 3 (1906):115–29.

———. *Memoirs: Correspondence and Manuscripts of General Lafayette, Published by His Family.* London: Saunders and Otley, 1837.

Lamb, R[oger]. *Memoir of His Own Life.* Dublin: Printed by J. Jones, 1811.

Laurens, Henry. *The Papers of Henry Laurens.* Edited by David R. Chesnutt and C. James Taylor. 16 vols. Columbia: University of South Carolina Press, 1968–2002.

Laurens, John. *The Army Correspondence of Colonel John Laurens in the Years 1777-8: Now First Printed from Original Letters to His Father, Henry Laurens, President of Congress; with a Memoir by Wm. Gilmore Simms.* Edited by W.M. Gilmore Simms. New York: Bradford Club, 1867.

Lee, Charles. *Anecdotes of the late Charles Lee, Esq . . . Second in Command in the Service of the United States of America, during the Revolution.* 2nd Edition. Edited by Edward Langworthy. London: Printed for S. Jordan, 1797 [orig. 1792].

———. *Collections of the New York Historical Society. The Lee Papers, 1754-1811.* 4 Vols. New York: New-York Historical Society, 1871-1874.

———, defendant. *Proceedings of a General Court Martial, held at Brunswick, in the State of New Jersey, by order of his excellency General Washington...for the trial of Major General Lee, July 4th, 1778. Major General Lord Stirling, President.* Philadelphia: Printed by John Dunlap, 1778.

Lee, Francis, ed. *Documents Relating to the Revolutionary History of the State of New Jersey, Vol. II, 1778.* Trenton, NJ: John L. Murphy Publishing, 1903.

Lee, Henry. *Memoirs of the War in the Southern Department of the United States.* 2 vols. Philadelphia: Bradford and Inskeep, 1812.

Lee, Richard Henry. *The Letters of Richard Henry Lee, 1762–1794.* 2 vols. Edited by James Curtis Ballagh. New York: Macmillan, 1911-1914.

Lesser, Charles H., ed. *The Sinews of Independence: Monthly Strength Reports of the Continental Army.* Chicago: University of Chicago Press, 1976.

Livingston, William. *The Papers of William Livingston.* Edited by Carl E. Prince and Dennis P. Ryan. 5 vols. Trenton: New Jersey Historical Commission, 1979-1988.

Lovell, James. *An Oration Delivered April 2d, 1771: At the Request of the Inhabitants of the Town of Boston; to Commemorate the Bloody Tragedy of the Fifth of March, 1770.* Boston: Printed by Edes and Gill, 1771.

Marshall, Christopher. *Extracts from the Diary of Christopher Marshall: Kept in Philadelphia and Lancaster during the American Revolution, 1774-1781.* Edited by William Duane. Albany, NY: Joel Munsell, 1877.

Mather, Samuel. *The Dying Legacy of an Aged Minister of the Everlasting Gospel.* Boston: Printed by Benjamin Edes and Sons, 1783.

McHenry, James. *Journal of a March, a Battle, and a Waterfall: Being the Version Elaborated by James McHenry from His Diary of the Year 1778, Begun at Valley Forge & Containing Accounts of the British, the Indians, and the Battle of Monmouth.* Greenwich, CT: Privately printed, 1945.

McKendry, William. "Copy of the Journal of William McKendry." *Proceedings of the Massachusetts Historical Society*. 2, 2nd Series (May 1886):436–78.

McMichael, James. "Diary of Lieutenant James McMichael, of the Pennsylvania Line, 1776-1778." *Pennsylvania Magazine of History and Biography* 16, No. 2 (1892):129–159.

Meng, John J., ed. *Despatches and Instructions of Conrad Alexandre Gérard, 1778-1780*. Baltimore, MD: Johns Hopkins University Press, 1939.

Monroe, James. *The Writings of James Monroe: Including a Collection of His Public and Private Papers and Correspondence Now for the First Time Printed*. Edited by Stanislaus Murray Hamilton. Vol. 1. New York: G.P. Putnam's Sons, 1898.

Moore, Frank, ed. *Diary of the American Revolution: From Newspapers and Original Documents*. 2 vols. New York: Charles Scribner, 1860.

Morris, Gouverneur. *The Diary and Letters of Gouverneur Morris*. Edited by Anne Cary Morris. 2 vols. New York: Charles Scribner's Sons, 1888.

Muenchhausen, Friedrich von. *At General Howe's Side, 1776-1778: The Diary of General William Howe's Aide de Camp, Captain Friedrich von Muenchhausen*. Trans. by Ernst Kipping, annot. by Samuel Smith. Monmouth Beach, NJ: Philip Freneau Press, 1974.

Muhlenberg, John Peter Gabriel. "Orderly Book of Gen. John Peter Gabriel Muhlenberg, March 26-December 20, 1777." *Pennsylvania Magazine of History and Biography* 33, No. 1 (1909):454–74.

North Carolina. The State Records of North Carolina. Edited by William L. Saunder *et al.* 30 vols. Winston, NC: M.I. & J.C., printers, 1896-1914.

Ogden, Aaron. *Autobiography of Col. Aaron Ogden, of Elizabethtown*. Paterson, NJ: Press Printing and Publishing Company, 1893.

Paullin, Charles Oscar, ed. *Out-Letters of the Continental Marine Committee and Board of Admiralty, August, 1776-September, 1780*. 2 vols. New York: Naval History Society, 1914.

Pendleton, Edmund. *The Letters and Papers of Edmund Pendleton*. Edited by David John Mays. 2 vols. Charlottesvile: University Press of Virginia, 1967.

Quincy, Josiah. *The Journals of Major Samuel Shaw: The First American Council at Canton, with a Life of the Author*. Boston: Wm. Crosby and H.P. Nichols, 1847.

Rankin, Hugh F., ed. *Narratives of the American Revolution as Told by a Young Sailor, a Home-Sick Surgeon, a French Volunteer, and a German General's Wife*. Chicago: Lakeside Press, 1976.

Reed, William B., ed. *Life and Correspondence of Joseph Reed*. 2 vols. Philadelphia: Lindsay and Blakiston, 1847.

Rush, Benjamin. *The Autobiography of Benjamin Rush: His "Travels through Life" together with His Commonplace Book for 1789-1813*. Edited by George W. Conner. Philadelphia: American Philosophical Society, 1948.

———. "Historical Notes of Dr. Benjamin Rush, 1777." Edited by S. Weir Mitchell. *Pennsylvania Magazine of History and Biography* 27, No. 2 (1903):129–50.

———. *Letters of Benjamin Rush*. Ed by Lyman H. Butterfield. 2 vols. Princeton, NJ: Princeton University Press, 1951.

———. *The Selected Writings of Benjamin Rush*. Edited by Dagobert Runes. New York: Philosophical Library, 1947.

St. Clair, Arthur. "The Trial of Major General St. Clair, August, 1778." New-York Historical Society Collections. Vol. 13. New York, 1881.
Schuyler, Philip. "The Trial of Major General Schuyler, October, 1778." New-York Historical Society Collections. Vol. 12. New York, 1880.
Smith, Paul H. and Ronald M. Gephart, eds. *Letters of Delegates to Congress, 1774-1789.* 26 vols. Washington, DC: Library of Congress, 1976-2000.
Smith, William. *Historical Memoirs of William Smith, 1778-1783.* Edited by William Henry Waldo Sabine. New York: New York Times, 1971.
Stedman, Charles. *The History of the Origin, Progress, and Termination of the American War.* London: Printed for the author, 1794.
Steiner, Bernard C. *The Life and Correspondence of James McHenry, Secretary of War under Washington and Adams.* Cleveland: Burrows Brothers Company, 1907.
Stevens, Benjamin Franklin, ed. *Facsimilies of Manuscripts in European Archives Relative to America, 1773-1783.* London: Charles Whittingham and Co., 1898.
Stillé, Charles J. *Major-General Anthony Wayne and the Pennsylvania Line in the Continental Army.* Philadelphia: J.B. Lippincott, 1893.
Stryker, William S., ed. *Documents Relating to the Revolutionary History of the State of New Jersey, Vol. I, 1776-1777.* Trenton, NJ: John L. Murphy Publishing, 1901.
Sullivan, John. *The Letters and Papers of Major General John Sullivan.* Edited by Otis G Hammond. 3 vols. Concord: New Hampshire Historical Society, 1930–1939.
Thacher, James. *Military Journal of the American Revolution.* Boston: Richardson and Lord, 1823.
Trumbull, John and James Lovell. "Revolutionary Letters: John Trumbull and James Lovell, 1771 [1777]." *Historical Magazine* I (October 1857):289–92.
Waldo, Albigence. "Valley Forge, 1777-1778. Diary of Surgeon Albigence Waldo, of the Connecticut Line." *Pennsylvania Magazine of History and Biography* 21, No. 1 (1897):299–323.
Washington, George. *The Papers of George Washington.* Edited by W. W. Abbot, *et al.* Charlottesville: University Press of Virginia, 1987–.
———. *The Papers of George Washington Digital Edition.* Edited by Theodore J. Crackel, *et al.*, Charlottesville: University Press of Virginia, Rotunda, 2007.
———. *The Writings of George Washington from the Original Manuscript Sources, 1745-1799.* 39 vols. Edited by John. C. Fitzpatrick. Washington, DC: U.S. Government Printing Office, 1931-1944.
———. *The Writings of George Washington: Being the Correspondence, Addresses, Messages, and Other Papers, Official and Private, Selected and Published from the Original Manuscripts.* 12 vols. Edited by Jared Sparks. Boston: Russell, Odiorne, and Metcalf, and Hilliard, Gray, and Co., 1833-1839.
Webb, Samuel Blachley. *Correspondence and Journals of Samuel Blachley Webb.* 3 Vols. Edited by Worthington Chauncey Ford. New York: Wickersham, 1893.
Wilkinson, James. *Memoirs of My Own Times.* 3 vols. Philadelphia: Printed by Abraham Small, 1816.

SECONDARY SOURCES

Alden, John Richard. *General Charles Lee, Traitor or Patriot?* Baton Rouge: Louisiana State University Press, 1951.

Alexander, Edward P. *A Revolutionary Conservative: James Duane of New York.* New York: Columbia University Press, 1938.

Allen, Paul. *A History of the American Revolution: Comprehending All the Principal Events both in the Field and in the Cabinet.* 2 vols. Baltimore: Printed for Franklin Betts, 1822.

Anderson, Fred. *Crucible of War: The Seven Years' War and the Fate of Empire in British North America, 1754-1766.* New York: Vintage, 2000.

Anderson, Troyer Steele. *The Command of the Howe Brothers during the American Revolution.* New York: Octagon, 1972 [orig. 1936].

Austin, James T. *The Life of Elbridge Gerry: With Contemporary Letters.* 2 vols. Boston: Wells and Lilly, 1828–29.

Baker, William S., ed. *Itinerary of General Washington from June 15, 1775 to December 23, 1783.* Philadelphia: J.B. Lippincott, 1892.

Bancroft, George. *History of the United States.* 10 vols. Boston: Little, Brown and Co., 1834-74.

Berg, Fred Anderson. *Encyclopedia of Continental Army Units: Battalions, Regiments and Independent Corps.* Harrisburg, PA: Stackpole Books, 1972.

Billias, George Athan. *Elbridge Gerry: Founding Father and Republican Statesman.* New York: McGraw-Hill, 1976.

———, ed. *George Washington's Generals.* New York: William Morrow, 1964.

Birzer, Bradley J. *American Cicero: The Life of Charles Carroll.* Wilmington, DE: ISI Books, 2010.

Blanchard, Amos. *American Military Biography: Containing the Lives and Characters of the Officers of the Revolution Who Were Most Distinguished in Achieving Our National Independence. Also, the Life of Gilbert Motier La Fayette, Major-General of the Continental Army.* Cincinnati: E. Walters, 1830.

Boatner, Mark Mayo III, ed. *Encyclopedia of the American Revolution.* New York: David McKay, 1974.

Bodle, Wayne K. *The Valley Forge Winter: Civilians and Soldiers in War.* University Park: Pennsylvania State University Press, 2002.

Bogin, Ruth. *Abraham Clark and the Quest for Equality in the Revolutionary Era, 1774-1794.* Rutherford, NJ: Fairleigh Dickinson University Press, 1982.

Botta, Carlo. *History of the War of the Independence of the United States of America.* Trans. by George Alexander Otis. 2 vols. New Haven, CT: Nathan Whiting, 1837 [orig. in Italian, 1809].

Boudinot, J. J. *The Life, Public Services, Addresses, and Letters of Elias Boudinot.* Boston: Houghton, Mifflin and Company, 1896.

Boyd, George Adams. *Elias Boudinot: Patriot and Statesman, 1740-1821.* Princeton, NJ: Princeton University Press, 1952.

Brenneman, Gloria E. "The Conway Cabal: Myth or Reality." *Pennsylvania History* 40, No. 2 (April 1973):168–177.

Brodsky, Alyn. *Benjamin Rush: Patriot and Physician.* New York: Truman Talley Books/St. Martin's Press, 2004.

Burnett, Edmund C. *The Continental Congress*. New York: Macmillan, 1941.
Bush, Martin R. *Revolutionary Enigma: A Reappraisal of General Philip Schuyler of New York*. Empire State Historical Publications Series, No. 80. Port Washington, NY: Ira J. Friedman, 1969.
Cadwalader, Sandra L. *The Cadwaladers, 1677-1879: Five Generations of a Philadelphia Family*. Wawa, PA: S.L. Cadwalader, 1996.
Caldwell, Charles. *Memoirs of the Life and Campaigns of the Hon. Nathaniel Greene*. Philadelphia: Robert Desilver, 1819.
Callahan, North. *Henry Knox: George Washington's General.* New York: Rinehart & Co., 1958.
Channing , Edward. *History of the United States*. 6 vols. New York: Macmillan, 1920-25.
Chernow, Ron. *Washington: A Life*. New York: Penguin Press, 2010.
Chitwood, Oliver Perry. *Richard Henry Lee: Statesman of the Revolution*. Morgantown: West Virginia University Library, 1967.
Cifelli, Edward M. *David Humphreys*. Boston: Twayne, 1982.
Clary, David A. and Joseph W.A. Whitehorne. *The Inspectors General of the United States Army, 1777-1903*. Washington, DC: Office of the Inspector General and Center of Military History, United States Army, 1987.
Coleman, John M. *Thomas McKean: Forgotten Leader of the Revolution*. Rockaway, NJ: American Faculty Press, 1975.
Cox, Caroline. *A Proper Sense of Honor: Service and Sacrifice in George Washington's Army*. Chapel Hill: University of North Carolina Press, 2007.
Cresson, William. *Frances Dana: A Puritan Diplomat at the Court of Catherine the Great*. New York: Dial Press, 1930.
Custis, George Washington Parke. *Recollections and Private Memoirs of Washington*. Philadelphia: J.W. Bradley, 1861.
Davis, Matthew L. *Memoirs of Aaron Burr: With Miscellaneous Selections from His Correspondence*. 2 vols. New York: Harper & Brothers, 1837.
Duer, William Alexander. *The Life of William Alexander, Earl of Stirling*. New York: New Jersey Historical Society, 1847.
Ellis, John. *Armies in Revolution*. New York: Oxford University Press, 1974.
Everest, Alan S. *Moses Hazen and the Canadian Refugees in the American Revolution*. Syracuse, NY: Syracuse University Press, 1976.
Ferling, John E. *The Ascent of George Washington: The Hidden Political Genius of an American Icon*. New York: Bloomsbury Press, 2009.
———. *The First of Men: A Life of George Washington*. Knoxville: University of Tennessee Press, 1988.
———, ed. *The World Turned Upside Down: The American Victory in the War of Independence*. New York: Greenwood Press, 1988.
Fiore, Jordan D. "Carlo Botta: An Italian Historian of the American Revolution." *Italica* 28, No. 3 (1951):155-171.
Fischer, David Hackett. *Washington's Crossing*. New York, Oxford University Press, 2004.
Fisher, Sarah Logan. "A Diary of Trifling Occurrences: Philadelphia, 1776-1778." Edited by Nicholas B. Wainwright. *Pennsylvania Magazine of History and Biography* 82, No.4 (October 1958):411–465.
Fiske, John. *Essays Literary and Historical*. Vol. 1. New York: Macmillan, 1902.

Fleming, Thomas. *Washington's Secret War: The Hidden History of Valley Forge*. New York: HarperCollins, 2005.

Flexner, James Thomas. *George Washington in the American Revolution, 1775-1783*. Boston: Little, Brown, 1968.

———. *Washington: The Indispensable Man*. Boston: Little, Brown, 1969.

Freeman. Douglas Southall. *George Washington: A Biography*. 7 vols. New York: Scribner, 1948-54.

Fried, Stephen. *Rush: Revolution, Madness, and the Revolutionary Doctor Who Became a Founding Father*. New York: Crown, 2018.

Garden, Alexander. *Anecdotes of the Revolutionary War in America: with Sketches of Character of Persons the Most Distinguished, in the Southern States, for Civil and Military Services*. Charleston: A.E. Miller, 1822.

Gerlach, Don R. *Proud Patriot: Philip Schuyler and the War of Independence, 1775-1783*. Syracuse, NY: Syracuse University Press, 1964.

Golway, Terry. *Washington's General: Nathanael Greene and the Triumph of the American Revolution*. New York: Henry Holt, 2005.

Goodrich, Charles A. *Our Lives, Our Fortunes, and Our Sacred Honour: The Lives of the Signers to the Declaration of Independence*. New York: William Reed and Co., 1829.

Gordon, William. *The History of the Rise, Progress, and Establishment of the Independence of the United States of America; Including an Account of the late War; and of the Thirteen Colonies, from their Origin to that Period*. 4 vols. London: Printed for the Author, 1788.

Gottschalk, Louis Reichenthal. *Lafayette Joins the American Army*. Chicago: University of Chicago Press, 1937.

———. "*Washington and the Revolution: A Reappraisal. Gates, Conway, and the Continental Congress*. Bernhard Knollenberg," *Journal of Modern History* 13, No. 1 (March 1941):97–98.

Gottschalk, Louis and Josephine Fennell, eds. "Duer and the 'Conway Cabal,'" *American Historical Review* 52 (October 1946):87–96.

Greenburg, Michael M. *The Court-Martial of Paul Revere: A Son of Liberty and America's Forgotten Military Disaster*. Lebanon, NH: University Press of New England, 2014.

Grizzard, Frank E. *George Washington: A Biographical Companion*, Santa Barbara, CA: ABC-CLIO, 2002.

Gruber, Ira D. *The Howe Brothers and the American Revolution*. New York: Norton, 1972.

Halfield, Edwin F. "Jonathan Dickinson Sergeant." *Pennsylvania Magazine of History and Biography* 2 (1878):338–442.

Harrison, S.A. *Memoir of Lieut. Col. Tench Tilghman*. Albany, NY: J. Munsell, 1876.

Hart, Ann Clark. *Abraham Clark: Signer of the Declaration of Independence*. San Francisco: Pioneer Press, 1923.

Hawke, David Freeman. *Benjamin Rush: Revolutionary Gadfly*. Indianapolis: Bobbs-Merrill, 1971.

———. *Honorable Treason: The Declaration of Independence and the Men Who Signed It*. New York: Viking Press, 1976.

Headley, J.T. *Washington and the Generals.* 2 vols. New York: Baker and Scribner, 1847.

Heitman, Francis B. *Historical Register of Officers of the Continental Army during the War of the Revolution, April 1775, to December, 1783.* Washington, DC: Rare Book Shop Publishing Company, 1914.

Henderson, James H. *Party Politics in the Continental Congress.* New York: McGraw-Hill, 1974.

Higginbotham, Don. *Daniel Morgan: Revolutionary Rifleman.* Chapel Hill: University of North Carolina Press, 1961.

———. *The War of American Independence: Military Attitudes, Policies, and Practice, 1763-1789.* New York: Macmillan, 1971.

Hildreth, Richard. *The History of the United States of America.* 6 vols. New York: Harper & Bros., 1849-52.

Holmes, Charles Nevers. "The Conway Cabal." *Magazine of History* XVI, No. 4 (1913):148–60.

Humphreys, Frank Landon. *The Life and Times of David Humphreys.* New York: G.P. Putnam's Sons, 1917.

Irving, Washington. *The Works of Washington Irving. Life of George Washington.* New York: Co-operative Publication Society, 19– [orig. 1855-59].

Isenberg, Nancy. *Fallen Founder: The Life of Aaron Burr.* New York: Viking Press, 2007.

Jacobs, James Ripley. *Tarnished Warrior: Major-General James Wilkinson.* New York: Macmillan, 1938.

Johnson, Allen and Dumas Malone, eds. *Dictionary of American Biography.* 22 vols. New York: Charles Scribner's Sons, 1928-1958.

Johnson, Victor Leroy. *The Administration of the American Commissariat during the Revolutionary War.* Philadelphia: University of Pennsylvania Press, 1941.

Jones, Robert F. *King of the Alley: William Duer, Politician, Entrepreneur, and Speculator, 1768-1799.* Philadelphia: American Philosophical Society, 1992.

Jordan, John C. "York, Penna., in the Revolution." *Pennsylvania Magazine of History and Biography* 32 (1908):487–97.

Jordan, John W. *Encyclopedia of Pennsylvania Biography.* New York: Lewis Historical Publishing Co., 1914.

Kaminski, John P. *George Clinton: Yeoman Politician of the New Republic.* Madison, WI: Madison House Publishers, 1993.

Kapp, Friedrich. *The Life of Frederick William Von Steuben.* New York: Mason Brothers, 1859.

———. *The Life of John Kalb: Major-General in the Revolutionary Army.* New York: Henry Holt and Company, 1884.

Katcher, Philip R.N. *Encyclopedia of British, Provincial, and German Army Units, 1775-1783.* Harrisburg, PA: Stackpole Books, 1973.

Katz, Daniel and Robert Louis Kahn. *The Social Psychology of Organizations.* New York: Wiley, 1966.

Ketchum, Richard M. *Saratoga: Turning Point of America's Revolutionary War.* New York: Henry Holt, 1997.

Knollenberg, Bernhard. *Washington and the Revolution, a Reappraisal: Gates, Conway, and the Continental Congress.* New York: Macmillan, 1940.

Kohn, Richard H. "The Inside Story of the Newburgh Conspiracy: America and the Coup d'Etat." *William and Mary Quarterly* 3rd Ser., 27 (1970):199–200.

Lambert, Andrew. *Admirals: The Naval Commanders Who Made Britain Great.* London: Faber and Faber, 2008.

Leake, Isaac Q. *Memoir of the Life and Times of General John Lamb: An Officer of the Revolution, Who Commanded the Post at West Point at the Time of Arnold's Defection, and His Correspondence with Washington, Clinton, Patrick Henry, and Other Distinguished Men of His Time.* Albany, NY: Joel Munsell, 1857.

Lefkowitz, Arthur S. *George Washington's Indispensable Men: The 32 Aides-de-Camp Who Helped Win American Independence.* Mechanicsville, PA: Stackpole Books, 2003.

Lender, Mark Edward. *The War for American Independence.* Santa Barbara, CA: ABC-CLIO, 2016.

Lender, Mark Edward and Garry Wheeler Stone. *Fatal Sunday: George Washington, the Monmouth Campaign, and the Politics of Battle.* Norman: University of Oklahoma Press, 2016.

Lendrum, John. *A Concise and Impartial History of the American Revolution. To Which Is Prefixed, a General History of North and South America: Together with an Account of the Discovery and Settlement of North America, and a View of the Progress, Character, and Political State of the Colonies Previous to the Revolution. From the Best Authorities.* Boston: Printed by I. Thomas and E.T. Andrews, 1795.

Lengel, Edward G. *General George Washington: A Military Life.* New York: Random House, 2005.

Lewis, Leonard. *The Life of Charles Carroll of Carrollton.* New York: Moffat, Yard, and Company, 1918.

Linklater, Andro. *An Artist in Treason: The Extraordinary Double Life of General James Wilkinson.* New York: Walker, 2010.

Lobdell, Jared C. "Six Generals Gather Forage: The Engagement at Quibbletown, 1777." *New Jersey History* 102 (1984): 35–50.

Lockhart, Paul. *The Drillmaster of Valley Forge: The Baron de Steuben and the Making of the American Army.* New York: Smithsonian Books, 2008.

Lossing, Benson John, ed. *The American Historical Record, and Repository of Notes and Queries.* Philadelphia: John E. Potter and Company, 1874.

———. *The Pictorial Field-Book of the American Revolution: Or, Illustrations, by Pen and Pencil, of the History, Biography, Scenery, Relics, and Traditions of the War for Independence.* 2 vols. New York: Harper & Brothers, 1852.

Marshall, John. *The Life of George Washington, Commander in Chief of the American Forces during the War Which Established the Independence of His Country, and First President of the United States.* 5 vols. Philadelphia: C.P. Wayne, 1804-1807.

Martin, James Kirby. *Benedict Arnold, Revolutionary Hero: An American Warrior Reconsidered.* New York: New York University Press, 1997.

Martin, James Kirby and Mark Edward Lender. *A Respectable Army: The Military Origins of the Republic, 1763-1789.* 3rd ed. Malden, MA: Wiley-Blackwell, 2015.

Massey, Gregory D. *John Laurens and the American Revolution.* Columbia: University of South Carolina Press, 2000.

Mattern, David B. *Benjamin Lincoln and the American Revolution*. Columbia: University of South Carolina Press, 1995.
Mazzagetti, Dominick. *Charles Lee: Self before Country*. New Brunswick, NJ: Rutgers University Press, 2013.
McDermott, Scott. *Charles Carroll of Carrollton: Faithful Revolutionary*. New York: Scepter, 2002.
McDonald, Robert M.S., ed. *Sons of the Father: George Washington and His Protégés*. Charlottesville: University Press of Virginia, 2013.
McGaughy, J. Kent. *Richard Henry Lee of Virginia: A Portrait of an American Revolutionary*. Lanham, MD: Rowman & Littlefield, 2004.
McGaughy, J. Kent and Gregory D. Massey. "Conway Cabal: Was There a Secret Plot to Remove George Washington as Commander in Chief in the Winter of 1777-1778?" In *History in Dispute, Volume 12: The American Revolution*. Edited by Keith Krawczynski. Detroit: Thomson Gale, 2003.
McGuire, Thomas J. *Battle of Paoli*. Mechanicsburg, PA: Stackpole Books, 2000.
Miller, John C. *Sam Adams: Pioneer in Propaganda*. Boston: Little Brown, 1936.
Mintz, Max M. *Gouverneur Morris and the American Revolution*. Norman: University of Oklahoma Press, 1970.
Moore, George H. *The Treason of Charles Lee, Major General*. New York: Charles Scribner, 1860.
Morse, Jedidiah. *The History of America, in Two Books: Containing, 1. A General History of America, 2. A Concise History of the Late Revolution*. Philadelphia: Printed for J. Webster, 1819 [orig. 1790].
Neagles, James C. *Summer Soldiers: A Survey & Index of Revolutionary War Courts-Martial*. Salt Lake City, UT: Ancestry Incorporated, 1986.
Neimeyer, Charles Patrick. *America Goes to War: A Social History of the Continental Army*. New York: New York University Press, 1996.
Nelson, Paul David. *General Horatio Gates: A Biography*. Baton Rouge: Louisiana State University Press, 1976.
———. *The Life of William Alexander, Lord Stirling*. Birmingham: University of Alabama Press, 1987.
Newton, Michael E. *Alexander Hamilton: The Formative Years*. Phoenix, AZ: Eleftheria Publishing, 2015.
Nolan, J. Bennett. *George Washington and the Town of Reading in Pennsylvania*. Reading, PA: Chamber of Commerce of Reading, 1931.
O'Shaughnessy, Andrew Jackson. *The Men Who Lost America: British Leadership, the American Revolution, and the Fate of the Empire*. New Haven: Yale University Press, 2013.
Palmer, Dave Richard. *George Washington and Benedict Arnold: A Tale of Two Patriots*. Washington, DC: Regnery, 2006.
———. *The Way of the Fox: American Strategy in the War for America, 1775-1783*. Westport: Greenwood Press, 1975.
Palmer, John McAuley. *General von Steuben*. New Haven: Yale University Press, 1937.
Pappas, Phillip. *Renegade Revolutionary: The Life of General Charles Lee*. New York: New York University Press, 2014.
Patterson, Samuel White. *Horatio Gates: Defender of American Liberties*. New York: Columbia University Press, 1941.

Peckham, Howard K., ed., *The Toll of Independence: Engagements and Battle Casualties of the American Revolution.* Chicago: University of Chicago Press, 1974.

Pickering, Octavius and Charles Wentworth Upham [vols. 3 and 4]. *The Life of Timothy Pickering.* 4 vols. Boston, Little, Brown, and Company, 1867-73.

Ramsay, David. *The History of the American Revolution.* Philadelphia: Printed by R. Aitken & son, 1789.

———. *The Life of George Washington: Commander in Chief of the Armies of the United States in the War Which Established Their Independence, and First President of the United States.* London: Printed by Luke Hanfard & Sons, 1807.

Rappleye, Charles. *Robert Morris: Financier of the American Revolution.* New York: Simon & Schuster, 2010.

Rawle, William. "Sketch of the Life of Thomas Mifflin." *Register of Pennsylvania* (Philadelphia), July 31, 1830, 65–69.

Reed, William B. *Life and Correspondence of Joseph Reed.* 2 vols. Philadelphia: Lindsay and Blakiston, 1847.

Robson, Eric. *The American Revolution in Its Political and Military Aspects, 1763-1783.* New York: Norton, 1966.

Roche, John F. *Joseph Reed: A Moderate in the American Revolution.* New York: Columbia University Press, 1957.

Rodger, N.A.M. *The Command of the Ocean: A Naval History of Britain, 1649-1815.* London: Allen Lane, 2004.

Rossie, Jonathan Gregory. *The Politics of Command in the American Revolution.* Syracuse, NY: Syracuse University Press, 1975.

Rossignoli, Cecilia and Francesca Ricciardi. *Towards a Dynamic Model for Understanding Business Network Performance.* Cham, Switzerland: Springer International Publishing, 2015.

Rossman, Kenneth R. "Conway and the Conway Cabal." *South Atlantic Quarterly* 41 (1942):32–38.

———. *Thomas Mifflin and the Politics of the American Revolution.* Chapel Hill: University of North Carolina Press, 1952.

Rowland, Kate Mason. *The Life of Charles Carroll of Carrollton, 1737-1832, with His Correspondence and Public Papers.* 2 vols. New York: G.P. Putnam's Sons, 1898.

Saffell, W.T.R. *Records of the Revolutionary War: Containing the Military and Financial Correspondence of Distinguished Officers.* New York: Pudney & Russell, 1858.

Saunders, Jennings B. *Evolution of Executive Department of the Continental Congress 1774-1789.* Gloucester, MA: Peter Smith, 1971 [orig. 1935].

Selesky, Harold E., ed. *Encyclopedia of the American Revolution.* 2nd ed., 2 vols. Detroit: Thomson Gale, 2006.

Shreve, L.G. *Tench Tilghman: The Life and Times of Washington's Aide-de-Camp.* Centerville, MD: Tidewater Publishers, 1982.

Shy, John. *Toward Lexington: The Role of the British Army in the Coming of the American Revolution.* Princeton, NJ: Princeton University Press, 1965.

Silliman, Benjamin. "Major-General Joseph Spencer." *Pennsylvania Magazine of History and Biography* 3, No. 1 (1879):435–37.

Smith, David. *Whispers Across the Atlantic: General William Howe and the American Revolution*. New York: Osprey Publishing, 2017.
Smith, Justin. *Our Struggle for the Fourteenth Colony: Canada and the American Revolution*. 2 vols. New York: G.P. Putnam's Sons, 1907.
Smith, William Henry. *The St. Clair Papers: The Life and Public Services of Arthur St. Clair, Soldier of the Revolutionary War, President of the Continental Congress and Governor of the North-Western Territory, with His Correspondence and Other Papers, Arranged and Annotated*. 2 vols. Cincinnati: Robert Clarke & Co., 1882.
Snowden, Richard. *The History of North and South America: From Its Discovery to the Death of General Washington*. Philadelphia: Jacob Johnson, 1805.
Steiner, Bernard C. *The Life and Correspondence of James McHenry*. Cleveland: Burrows Brothers, 1907.
Stille, Charles J. *Major-General Anthony Wayne and the Pennsylvania Line in the Continental Army*. Philadelphia: J.B. Lipincott, 1893.
Stockwell, Mary. *Unlikely General: "Mad" Anthony Wayne and the Battle for America*. New Haven: Yale University Press, 2018.
Stryker, William S., comp. *Official Register of the Officers and Men of New Jersey in the Revolutionary War*. Trenton, NJ: Wm. T. Nicholson, 1872.
Swiggett, Howard. *The Great Man: George Washington as a Human Being*. Garden City, NY: Doubleday, 1953.
Tilghman, Oswald. *Memoir of Lieut. Col. Tench Tilghman*. Albany: Joel Munsell, 1876.
Tripp, Wendell Edward. *Robert Troup: A Quest for Security in a Turbulent New Nation, 1775-1832*. New York: Arno Press, 1982.
Trussell, John B. *Birthplace of an Army: A Study of the Valley Forge Encampment*. Harrisburg, PA: Pennsylvania Historical and Museum Commission, 1998.
Tucker, Glenn. *Mad Anthony Wayne and the New Nation*. Harrisburg: Stackpole Books, 1973.
Unger, Harlow Giles. *Dr. Benjamin Rush: The Founding Father Who Healed a Wounded Nation*. New York: Da Capo Press, 2018.
U.S. Congress, *Biographical Directory of the American Congress*. Washington, DC: U.S. Government Printing Office, 1971.
U.S. Department of the Army. *Stability Operations and Support Operations* (FM 3-07). Washington, DC: Department of the Army, 20 February 2003.
Upham, Charles W. *The Life of Timothy Pickering*. 3 vols. Boston: Little, Brown, & Company, 1873.
Valentine, Alan. *Lord Stirling*. New York: Oxford University Press, 1969.
Wallace, Willard M. *Appeal to Arms: A Military History of the American Revolution*. Chicago: Quadrangle Books, 1964.
Ward, Christopher. *The War of the Revolution*. 2 vols. New York: Macmillan, 1952.
Ward, Harry M. *Duty, Honor or Country: General George Weedon and the American Revolution*. Philadelphia: The American Philosophical Society, 1979.
———. *George Washington's Enforcers: Policing the Continental Army*. Carbondale, IL: Southern Illinois University Press, 2006.
Warren, Mercy [Otis]. *History of the Rise, Progress and Termination of the American Revolution. Interspersed with Biographical, Political and Moral Observations*. 3 vols. Boston: Manning and Loring, 1805.

Watson, John F. *Annals of Philadelphia and Pennsylvania, in the Olden Time: Being a Collection of Memoirs, Anecdotes, and Incidents of the City and Its Inhabitants, and of the Settlements of the Inland Part of Pennsylvania, from the Days of the Founders*. 2 vols. Philadelphia: Printed by King & Baird, 1850.

Weber, Ralph E. *Masked Dispatches: Cryptograms and Cryptology in American History, 1775-1900*. Fort George G. Meade, MD: National Security Agency, 1993.

Whittemore, Charles P. *A General of the Revolution: John Sullivan of New Hampshire*. New York: Columbia University Press, 1961.

Willcox, William B. *Portrait of a General: Sir Henry Clinton in the War of Independence*. New York: Knopf, 1964.

Williams, C.R. *Biography of Revolutionary Heroes: Containing the Life of Brigadier Gen. William Barton, and Also, of Captain Stephen Olney*. Providence, RI: published by the author, 1839.

Williams, Samuel. *A History of the American Revolution: Intended as a Reading Book for Schools*. New Haven, CT: William Storer, Jun., 1831 [orig. 1795].

Wilson, James Grant and John Fiske, eds. *Appleton's Cyclopedia of American Biography*. New York: D. Appleton and Company, 1888.

Wright, Robert K., Jr. *The Continental Army*. Washington, DC: Center of Military History, U.S. Army, 1983.

Zambone, Albert Louis. *Daniel Morgan: A Revolutionary Life*. Yardley, PA: Westholme, 2018.

Zucker, Adolf Eduard. *General de Kalb: Lafayette's Mentor*. Chapel Hill: University of North Carolina Press, 1966.

NEWSPAPERS

Annual Register, or a Review of the History, Politics, and Literature, for the Year[s] 1777-1779, 1787 (London, J. Dodsley)

Boston Gazette

Dunlap's Pennsylvania Packet, or, the General Advertiser (Philadelphia)

Gentleman's Magazine and Historical Chronicle (London)

London Gazette

Maryland Journal and Baltimore Advertiser (Baltimore)

New Jersey Gazette (Trenton)

Pennsylvania Evening Post

The Public Ledger (London)

Register of Pennsylvania (Philadelphia, Samuel Hazard)

The Remembrancer; or, Impartial Repository of Public Events (London)

Rivington's Royal Gazette (New York)

THESES AND UNPUBLISHED STUDIES

Bodle, Wayne K. "The Vortex of Small Fortune: The Continental Army at Valley Forge, 1777-1778." Valley Forge Historical Research Report, Vol. 1. Valley Forge National Historical Park: U.S. Department of the Interior, National Park Service, 1980.

Jones, Helen F. "James Lovell in the Continental Congress 1777-1782." Ph.D. Diss., Columbia University, 1968.

Kahler, Gerald Edward. "Gentlemen of the Family: General George Washington's Aides-de-Camp and Military Secretaries." MA Thesis, University of Richmond, 1997.

Royer, Helen E. "The Role of the Continental Congress in the Prosecution of the American Revolution in Pennsylvania." Ph.D. Diss., Pennsylvania State University, 1960.

Thibaut, Jacqueline. "This Fatal Crisis: Logistics and the Continental Army at Valley Forge, 1777-1778." Valley Forge Historical Research Report, Vol. 2. Valley Forge National Historical Park: U.S. Department of the Interior, National Park Service, 1982.

INTERNET SOURCES

American Revolution.org. http://www.americanrevolution.org.

Biographical Directory of the United States Congress. http://bioguide.congress.gov/scripts/biodisplay.pl?index=L000463.

"Biographical Sketch of Hannah Winthrop," Massachusetts Historical Society. http://www.masshist.org/features/warren-winthrop/sketches#winthrop.

Cryptologic Almanac—NSA/CSS. "The American Revolution's One-Man National Security Agency." http://www.nsa.gov/about/cryptologic_heritage/center_crypt_history/almanac/.

Founders Online. https://founders.archives.gov/.

"Alexander Graydon." *Penn Biographies.* http://www.archives.upenn.edu/people/1700s/graydon_alexdr.html.

Green, Jack P. "Landon Carter (1710-1778)," Dictionary of Virginia Biography, in *Encyclopedia Virginia* (Virginia Foundation for the Humanities, 15 Aug. 2013), http://www.EncyclopediaVirginia.org/ Carter_Landon_1710-1778.

McGaughy, J. Kent. "Francis Lightfoot Lee (1734-1797)," *Encyclopedia Virginia.* http://www.encyclopediavirginia.org/Francis_Lightfoot_Lee_1734-1797#start_entry.

Preston, Russell. "The Conway Cabal." *American Heritage* 46, No. 1 (1995). http://www.americanheritage.com/content/conway-cabal?page=show.

Ezra Selden to Samuel Mather, May 15, 1778. "Letters from Valley Forge." Americanrevolution.org. http://www.americanrevolution.org/vlyfrgeltrs.html.

Whittelsey, Charles Barney. "Historical Sketch of Joseph Spencer: Major-General of the Continental Troops, Member of the Council of Safety, Congressman, Judge, Deputy, Deacon, and Farmer." Connecticut Society of the Sons of the American Revolution. http://www.connecticutsar.org/patriots/spencer.htm.

ACKNOWLEDGMENTS

IT IS A GENUINE PLEASURE to acknowledge individuals and institutions that assisted in the research and writing of this volume. I especially want to thank Frank J. Esposito, James Kirby Martin, Randall Miller, Christian McBurney, Bill Welsch, and Bruce Venter who read drafts of various chapters. Their comments saved me from many a slip and certainly helped me improve the manuscript. The professional staffs of the Virginia Historical Society, the Library of Virginia, the Historical Society of Pennsylvania, the American Philosophical Society, Morristown National Historical Park, the New York Public Library, the Papers of John Jay, the Fenimore Art Museum, and the New-York Historical Society offered invaluable guidance and research assistance for which I am grateful. At Valley Forge National Historical Park, archivist Dona McDermott unlocked the marvelous collections in her care, which proved a genuine "Mother Load" of source material for this study. At the Firestone Library at Princeton University, my old friend Dr. Don C. Skemer made it a pleasure to go through the manuscripts there.

In 2018 I was honored with a fellowship at the Fred W. Smith National Library for the Study of George Washington at Mount Vernon, which provided crucial financial and research assistance. Special collections librarian Katherine Hoarn was extremely accommodating in digging out some revealing manuscripts from the library's rich collections; and Samantha Snyder was equally helpful in accessing the library's unparalleled collection of secondary literature on Washington. The fellowship immeasurably speeded the completion of this work. My thanks go as well to Stephen McLeod and Anthony King for their administrative support. In Richmond, Sugar & Twine served as my "branch office" and my chief source of excellent coffee and unrivaled cinnamon rolls. Nate Best provided superb copyediting for which I am indeed thankful. Special thanks go as well to Bruce H. Franklin, publisher of Westholme Publishing, whose enthusiasm for the *Cabal!* project was instrumental in bringing it to completion.

As I have in the past, I want to thank my wife Penny Booth Page, whose patience, support, editorial skills, and eye for phrasing—thank God for English majors—were unmatched as *Cabal!* came together. (Advice to younger historians: Always marry the best editor you can find.) Without the aid and encouragement of all of the above this volume never would have seen print.

INDEX